SWORD AND OLIVE BRANCH

General Oliver Otis Howard
1830-1909
Distinguished service to his country in war and peace

SWORD AND OLIVE BRANCH

OLIVER OTIS HOWARD

by JOHN A. CARPENTER
with an Introduction by PAUL A. CIMBALA

FORDHAM UNIVERSITY PRESS
New York
1999

Copyright © 1999 by Fordham University Press

All rights reserved. No part of this publication may be reproduced, stored in a retrieval system, or transmitted in any form or by any means—electronic, mechanical, photocopy, recording, or any other—except for brief quotations in printed reviews, without the prior permission of the publisher.

The North's Civil War, no. 10

Library of Congress Cataloging-in-Publication Data

Carpenter, John A. (John Alcott), 1921–
    Sword and olive branch : Oliver Otis Howard / John A. Carpenter; introduction by Paul A. Cimbala.
    p. cm. — (The North's Civil War ; no. 10)
    Originally published: Pittsburgh : University of Pittsburgh Press, [1964]. With new introd.
    Includes bibliographical references and index.

    1. Howard, O. O. (Oliver Otis), 1830–1909. 2. Generals—United States Biography. 3. United States. Army Biography. 4. United States. Bureau of Refugees, Freedmen, and Abandoned Lands—Officials and employees Biography. 5. Afro-Americans—History—1863–1877. 6. United States—History—Civil War, 1861–1865—Campaigns. 7. Indians of North America—Wars—1866–1895. 8. Howard University Biography. I. Title. II. Series.
E467.1.H8C3   1999
973.7'092—dc21
[B]   99-33067
                                                                                                                             CIP

03 02 01 00 99   5 4 3 2 1
Printed in the United States of America

To the Memory of My Father
CHARLES FRANCIS CARPENTER
and to
TOM, JOHN, *and* JAMES

Contents

	PAGE
Illustrations	viii
Introduction to the 1999 Edition	ix
Preface	xvii
Early Life	1
Prewar Service in the Regular Army	12
Brigade Command	23
Division and Corps Command	36
Chancellorsville and Gettysburg	44
Western Victories	59
The End of the War	73
Early Months of the Freedmen's Bureau	87
Relief Work and Land Policy	103
Labor and Legal Matters	122
The Controversial Bureau	136
Education	157
Howard University	169
Bureau-related Activities: The Barry Farm and the Freedmen's Bank	185
Church Dispute and House Investigation	191
Peace with the Apaches	209
Bounty Paying, Court of Inquiry	220
Washington, D. C.	236
Service in the Northwest	244
Final Army Assignments	270
The Closing Years	290
Notes	300
Bibliography	350
Index	363

Illustrations

General Oliver Otis Howard, 1830–1909	Frontispiece
Mrs. Oliver Otis Howard	Opposite p. 182
Bowdoin College in the 1840s	Opposite p. 183
West Point in 1850	Opposite p. 183
Founders Library, Sixth St. gate,	
* Howard University*	Opposite p. 190
Grant-Lee Hall, Lincoln Memorial	
* University, in the 1890s*	Opposite p. 191

Introduction to the 1999 Edition

The late John A. Carpenter's biography of Oliver Otis Howard, first published in 1964, remains the best full-scale treatment of an individual who was a part of so much of nineteenth-century American history. Howard's work after the Civil War as the one and only commissioner of the Bureau of Refugees, Freedmen, and Abandoned Lands is sufficient for attracting a biographer's attention. Carpenter's subject, however, was much more than Reconstruction's chief bureaucrat; Howard was a participant in some of the most critical events that shaped nineteenth-century American life. Indeed, he may be considered a metaphor of much of nineteenth-century American history.

Howard's biographer was the son of an avid Civil War buff and was fortunate to be able to make a childhood interest his life's work. John Carpenter completed his undergraduate studies in 1942 at Harvard University, where he first became acquainted with O. O. Howard while writing a paper on the general's military career. Setting aside his studies, he served in the U.S. Navy during the Second World War. He renewed his connection with the general as a dissertation subject at Columbia University, where he earned his doctorate in 1954. After leaving Columbia, Carpenter taught at Washington and Jefferson College in Washington, Pennsylvania, until 1965, when he joined the faculty at Fordham University in the Bronx, New York. He remained a professor of history there until his untimely death in 1978.[1]

While at Fordham, Professor Carpenter published a succinct biography of Ulysses S. Grant, but he continued to be fascinated with Howard's Bureau.[2] At the time of his death, he was working on a major study of the personnel of the agency, a collective biography of the 2,441 agents and officers who had served with the Bureau in the Southern states after the Civil War. The draft of "Agents of the Freedmen's Bureau," along with extensive biographical notes on those men of the Bureau, remains available at the Schomberg Center for Research in Black Culture of the New York Public Library. It is well worth reading even in its unfinished state. Writing in the 1970s, Carpenter challenged the old, shallow views of the Bureau and its personnel popularized by such early-twentieth-century historians as J. G. De Roulhac Hamilton, Walter Lynwood Fleming, and E. Merton Coulter.[3] Even more interesting, however, is that Carpenter presented a much more balanced interpretation of the activities of the Bureau's personnel than did the then-prevailing Revisionist view that criticized the agency for significantly and purposely contributing to Reconstruction's failure to advance the freedpeople's cause. Carpenter's research foreshadowed the newer, recently published studies of the Bureau by authors who try to understand the men of the agency without acting as apologists or prosecutors. It is that kind of empathy that makes Carpenter's study of Howard an enduring work of biography.[4]

Born in 1830 in Leeds, Maine, Oliver Otis Howard graduated from Bowdoin College in 1850 and went on to the U.S. Military Academy at West Point. In 1854 he embarked on a fairly ordinary career in America's peacetime army. He experienced conversion to evangelical Christianity, a path that many other searching souls found in antebellum America in the years after the Second Great Awakening. If religion saved him from damnation, war saved him from obscurity. The South's secession from the Union and Lincoln's determination to prevent it rescued Howard from the dull routine and slow promotions typical of the peacetime army. Thousands of men flocked to the colors of the volunteer regiments, providing opportunities for advancement for Howard and his regular army colleagues. Self-interest and higher ideals, however, were not mutually exclusive, as Howard's life illustrates.

O. O. Howard's rapid advance in rank during the Civil War, again something that was not unusual for the talented or the well-connected soldier, placed him at some of the most significant engagements of that conflict. As a brigade commander at Fair Oaks, he suffered wounds that cost him his right arm, an all-too-common occurrence at the front. It was a sacrifice that became a constant reminder of the war, its meaning, and its purpose for him as well as for a number of his comrades who followed him into the Freedmen's Bureau. As a corps commander at Chancellorsville and Gettysburg, Howard played critical roles at Robert E. Lee's tactical masterpiece and at one of his great failures. As commander of the Army of the Tennessee, he accompanied William Tecumseh Sherman on his famous march through Georgia and the Carolinas. He was also present at Sherman's and Confederate Gen. Joseph Johnston's last battle at Bentonville, North Carolina, in March of 1865.

Shortly thereafter, as the nation embarked on Reconstruction, Howard found himself at the center of the great issues of the day. As head of the Freedmen's Bureau, Howard, a mild antislavery man before the war, attempted to implement relatively progressive policies that reflected widely held beliefs about race, charity, and education. Indeed, the faith that postwar reformers had in the power of education was at the heart of Howard's Bureau's activities. Howard's typical nineteenth-century belief in the importance of education for Black uplift made him instrumental in the founding of the university in Washington, D.C., that continues to bear his name.

Howard and his Freedmen's Bureau faced a tough, intransigent opponent in the White South, something the North came to realize not long after the battle flags had been furled. Frustrated, the nation soon turned from the herculean task it had set for itself in Reconstruction and took on other endeavors, including renewed westward expansion. Howard also added a Western dimension to his career. In 1872 he negotiated peace with the Apaches in the Southwest, and in 1878 he ran down Chief Joseph and the Nez Perce in the Northwest. Howard's service prior to his retirement in 1894 included a stint as superintendent of West Point and a promotion to major general in the regular army. Before his death in 1909, he continued to lecture and write about the Civil War, as did many of his former colleagues, while devoting some time to the establishment of Lincoln Memorial University, a monument to the martyred president and a reward for the loyal people of east Tennessee.

Many soldiers and citizens shared in the great trends and events that helped shape Howard's life, but few achieved his prominence. Even fewer shared in the kind of controversy that surrounded Howard's place in the history of what was arguably the United States's most critical era. Given his flaws and his strengths, his failures and his accomplishments, Howard could not help being a lightning rod for contemporary and scholarly criticism. As early as 1864, for example, Howard had to defend his actions at Gettysburg in the face of criticism that attempted to diminish the role he played in that Union victory.[5]

Even Howard's critics concede that he was a courageous man. At Fair Oaks he was twice wounded and had a horse shot out from under him before he went to the rear to have his right arm amputated. At Chancellorsville he grabbed a flag with what was left of that arm and tried to rally his troops in the thick of the fight. At Gettysburg he personally guided men to their positions. At councils of war, even after his corps had been badly handled by Thomas J. "Stonewall" Jackson's Confederates at Chancellorsville, he never shied away from urging on an engagement with the enemy. Indeed, at Bentonville Howard appeared to be more aggressive than Sherman, his commander.

Courage alone, however, does not make a good general, nor can it account for how Howard achieved and maintained high command. Howard attracted the attention and protection of politicians, as did other officers in the volunteer service. He also earned the confidence of Sherman, a man who did not suffer fools lightly. All things considered, Carpenter argues, Howard was a capable, conscientious officer. Yet there are some legitimate questions about Howard's abilities, especially as they relate to his performances at Chancellorsville and Gettysburg.

In his 1964 *Generals in Blue,* a widely used, best-selling reference book, Ezra J. Warner depicts Howard as a negligent and incompetent commander. At Chancellorsville, according to Warner, Howard disobeyed his commander Gen. Joseph Hooker's orders. At Gettysburg, he showed little in the way of decisive action, being pushed back to Cemetery Ridge and Cemetery Hill, a maneuver for which he undeservedly received the thanks of Congress.[6] Warner's assessment of Howard would have pleased Hooker, who continued to hold a grudge against Howard for his failures at Chancellorsville. Gen. Winfield Scott Hancock, who shared the field with Howard on the first day of Gettysburg, would have concurred; he later wrote to Hooker that Howard claimed too much credit and received too much honor for that battle's outcome.[7]

Stephen W. Sears's 1996 study of Chancellorsville—a book worthy of its wide acclaim—also takes Howard to task for being so unprepared for Jackson's attack on May 2, 1863. In no uncertain terms, Sears judges Howard to have been a poor general, one who relied too heavily on headquarters for direction and one who must accept a major portion of the blame for the collapse of the Union Army's right flank.[8] But as James I. Robertson Jr.'s recent biography of Stonewall Jackson shows, things are always more complicated than one would like them to be; despite his unpreparedness, Howard and his corps's

INTRODUCTION TO THE 1999 EDITION   xiii

later actions in the fight deserve some credit for stopping Jackson.[9] And Harry W. Pfanz in his book *Gettysburg: Culp's Hill and Cemetery Hill* acknowledges that from the outset Howard understood the significance of Cemetery Hill and made sure that his subordinates understood, too.[10] In other words, Carpenter's generally positive assessment of Howard's military contributions to the Union cause still has value.

Carpenter's biography of O. O. Howard remains a calm, balanced treatment shaped by solid research and sensible interpretation. He recognizes that individuals grow, and that Howard's military capabilities, like those of many other good officers and soldiers, developed with experience. Carpenter gives Howard good marks for generalship, even as he acknowledges Howard's failings at Chancellorsville. Howard was never surprised by the enemy after that fiasco, Carpenter notes, and it was Howard, not Sherman, who at Ezra Church during the Atlanta Campaign was prepared for a Confederate attack. Carpenter sees in Howard an aggressive, intelligent general who, "once authorized to act on his own initiative . . . rose to the occasion."[11]

Howard's military career, however, did not provoke the controversy that his postwar career as the Freedmen's Bureau's commissioner stirred up. It was almost an impossible situation for him, with vocal Northern radicals criticizing him for doing too little and most White Southerners criticizing him for doing too much for the exslaves. It did not help matters that his commander-in-chief, President Andrew Johnson, was so unfavorably disposed toward an agency that grated on his constitutional sensibilities.[12] Carpenter's treatment of Howard is more sympathetic than the treatments of most other scholars writing around the same time. William McFeely's 1968 study *Yankee Stepfather: General O. O. Howard and the Freedmen,* for example, is a very critical assessment of the general's Reconstruction career. McFeely argues that Howard betrayed the freedpeople, even when he might have helped them, because he was selfishly concerned about his own career and afraid to stand up to Andrew Johnson. It is a provocative study—and in some ways a powerful argument—with which anyone dealing with the Freedmen's Bureau must contend. Nevertheless, it falls short of understanding the Bureau or its commissioner and fails to hold the president and White Southerners accountable for their major contributions to the failure of Reconstruction. It is also a good example of how past and present critics tend to ignore what was possible at the time, or at least what individuals believed was possible.[13]

Even as Howard's work with the Freedmen's Bureau wound down, he found himself engaged in new controversial endeavors in Indian affairs. Today, Chief Joseph of the Nez Perce commands more sympathy than do the soldiers who forced him and his people to give up their homelands in the Wallowa Valley of Oregon for reservation land in Indian Territory.[14] But Howard deserves more than a cardboard representation as the Great White Oppressor. He was too complex for such caricatures, and Carpenter's account, perhaps unfashionable in some circles, still commands our attention.

Many scholars have contributed to our understanding of pieces of Howard's career, either challenging or supporting Carpenter along the way. But the pieces of Howard's career still require the context of his whole life if we are to understand him. In the end, John Carpenter's biography remains the best way to come to know the whole man.

PAUL A. CIMBALA

NOTES

1. Personal correspondence of Frances T. Carpenter to Paul A. Cimbala, Aug. 21, 1997; obituary of John A. Carpenter, *New York Times*, May 17, 1978.

2. John A. Carpenter, *Ulysses S. Grant* (New York: Twayne Publishers, 1970).

3. J. G. de Roulhac Hamilton, *Reconstruction in North Carolina* (New York: Columbia University Press, 1914); Walter L. Fleming, *Civil War and Reconstruction in Alabama* (New York: Columbia University Press, 1905); and E. Merton Coulter, *The Civil War and Reconstruction in Kentucky* (Chapel Hill: University of North Carolina Press, 1929). It is interesting to note that William A. Dunning, who gave his name to a school of Reconstruction scholars who were sympathetic to the Southern interpretation of the era, had a more complex view of the Bureau than did most others of his generation. *Reconstruction, Political and Economic, 1865–1877* (New York: Harper & Brothers, 1907; reprint ed., New York: Harper & Brothers, 1962), 31–34, 46, 68.

4. John A. Carpenter, "Agents of the Freedmen's Bureau," unpublished book manuscript, Manuscripts, Archives, and Rare Books Division, Schomberg Center for Research in Black Culture, The New York Public Library. For examples of newer works on the Bureau that challenge the negative view of the agency without absolving it of its failures, see Donald G. Nieman, *To Set the Law in Motion: The Freedmen's Bureau and the Legal Rights of Blacks, 1865–1868* (Millwood, N.Y.: KTO Press, 1979); Richard Lowe, "The Freedmen's Bureau and Local Black Leadership," *Journal of American History*, 80 (December 1993): 989–98; Barry A. Crouch, *The Freedmen's Bureau and Black Texans* (Austin: University of Texas Press, 1992); and Paul A. Cimbala, *Under the Guardianship of the Nation: The Freedmen's Bureau and the Reconstruction of Georgia, 1865–1870* (Ath-

ens: University of Georgia Press, 1997). For a concise, balanced view of the agency, see Eric Foner, *Reconstruction: America's Unfinished Revolution, 1863–1877* (New York: Harper and Row, 1988), 142–52. For the historiographical context in which Carpenter wrote about Reconstruction while completing his Howard biography and his draft of his book on Bureau agents, see Vernon L. Wharton, "Reconstruction," in *Writing Southern History: Essays in Historiography in Honor of Fletcher M. Green*, edited by Arthur S. Link and Rembert W. Patrick (Baton Rouge: Louisiana State University Press, 1965), 295–315, and LaWanda Cox, "From Emancipation to Segregation: National Policy and Southern Blacks," in *Interpreting Southern History: Historiographical Essays in Honor of Sanford W. Higginbotham*, edited by John B. Boles and Evelyn Thomas Nolan (Baton Rouge: Louisiana State University Press, 1987), 199–253. The historiographical material in the first chapter of Barry Crouch's book should supplement Cox's essay. For a collection of new essays that presents the most recent writings on the Bureau, see Paul A. Cimbala and Randall M. Miller, eds., *The Freedmen's Bureau and Reconstruction: Reconsiderations* (New York: Fordham University Press, 1999).

5. Howard had to defend himself again in 1875. Edwin B. Coddington, *The Gettysburg Campaign: A Study in Command* (New York: Charles Scribner's Sons, 1968), 701n, 702n.

6. Ezra J. Warner, *Generals in Blue: Lives of the Union Commanders* (Baton Rouge and London: Louisiana State University Press, 1964), 237–9.

7. Coddington, *Gettysburg Campaign*, 701n. For a brief look at the feud between Howard and Gen. Winfield Scott Hancock and Howard's efforts to defend his Gettysburg reputation, see Harry W. Pfanz, *Gettysburg: Culp's Hill and Cemetery Hill* (Chapel Hill: University of North Carolina Press, 1993), 379–81.

8. Stephen W. Sears, *Chancellorsville* (Boston: Houghton Mifflin, 1996), 263–87, passim.

9. James I. Robertson, Jr., *Stonewall Jackson: The Man, the Soldier, the Legend* (New York: Macmillan Publishing USA, 1997), 716–724.

10. Pfanz, *Culp's Hill and Cemetery Hill*, 25–30.

11. Carpenter, *Sword and Olive Branch*, 73. For a newer look at Howard's aggressiveness at Bentonville and a favorable assessment of his performance, see Nathaniel Cheairs Hughes, Jr., *Bentonville: The Final Battle of Sherman and Johnston* (Chapel Hill: University of North Carolina Press, 1996).

12. The best complete treatment of Johnson is Hans L. Trefousse, *Andrew Johnson: A Biography* (New York: W. W. Norton, 1989), but also see David Warren Bowen, *Andrew Johnson and the Negro* (Knoxville: University of Tennessee Press, 1989).

13. William S. McFeely, *Yankee Stepfather: General O. O. Howard and the Freedmen* (New Haven: Yale University Press, 1968). An important difference between McFeely's interpretation and Carpenter's is that Carpenter places more responsibility on Andrew Johnson for the unhappy consequences of the nation's policies toward the freedpeople. It is important to read what historian LaWanda Cox has to say about the possibilities of Reconstruction in the last chapter of her book *Lincoln and Black Freedom: A Study in Presidential Leadership* (Columbia: University of South Carolina Press, 1981), 142–84. Cox also notes that too often scholars tend to place the blame for the failure of Reconstruction squarely in the lap of the Yankees, ignoring that the White South had something to do with it. The

latter point—the successful aggressive resistance to Reconstruction on the part of the White South—is something that I discuss in *Under the Guardianship of the Nation*.

14. For a very sympathetic account of the Nez Perce, see David Lavender, *Let Me Be Free: The Nez Perce Tragedy* (New York: Harper Collins, 1992), which enjoyed some popularity as a History Book Club selection.

Preface

Not often in one lifetime does a man have the opportunity Oliver Otis Howard had for such diversified service to his country. Perhaps this is why he is not more generally known today.

Some students of the Civil War will remember his part in the battles of Chancellorsville and Gettysburg, and historians of Reconstruction will mention him as commissioner of the Freedmen's Bureau. Those interested in the Indian wars of the West are probably familiar with Howard's part in the pacification of the Apaches or with his pursuit of Chief Joseph and the Nez Perces in the epic campaign of 1877. Many American Negroes know of Howard's part in the founding of Howard University and of his role in the general field of Negro education. But probably only a few graduates of West Point are aware that he was at one time superintendent of the Military Academy. And Howard has earned some, but comparatively little, recognition in the field of American education as the principal founder of Lincoln Memorial University in Tennessee.

Never before have all the varied contributions of Howard been brought together. That this is so is something of a mystery since the original material available to the biographer is so rich as to be almost overwhelming, and since there can be no doubt about the position Howard must hold as a significant figure in American military, political, and cultural history.

It is my hope that through this biography more people will come to appreciate, as I have, the important contribution of this man who devoted a lifetime to the service of his country and who was ever mindful of his reliance on his avowed master, Jesus Christ.

* * * *

I thank the publishers of *Civil War History, Journal of Negro History, Pacific Northwest Quarterly,* and *Lincoln Herald* for permission to include articles which in altered form make up portions of this work.

Over the years the number of persons to whom I am indebted for help in the preparation of this work has grown tremendously. I would single out particularly the late Mr. Harry S. Howard (son of General Howard) and his daughters, Miss Harriet Howard and Mrs. Kenneth B. Webb. I am grateful to the staff of the Bowdoin College Library and especially Kenneth C. Boyer, former Librarian and now College Editor; the staff of the Howard University Library, and in particular Mrs. Dorothy Porter, Librarian of the Moorland Collection in that library; the personnel of the Library of Congress (especially the helpful staff members of the Manuscripts Division), and of the National Archives, particularly Mrs. Sarah D. Jackson of the Army Section. Various persons in the Library of Washington and Jefferson College have performed many favors for me.

For putting at my disposal the records of their respective institutions I acknowledge here my indebtedness to Sidney Forman, onetime Librarian of the United States Military Academy (now Librarian at Teachers College, Columbia University); to the President and Board of Trustees of Howard University; to the Reverend Carl Kopf, former minister of the First Congregational Church, Washington, D. C.; and to former President Robert L. Kincaid of Lincoln Memorial University.

Dr. Forman also read parts of the manuscript and assisted me with his deep knowledge of the Military Academy. Professor David Donald and the editors of the *Pacific Northwest Quarterly* have given me many useful suggestions for the Civil War and Nez Perce sections, respectively. Professor Allan Nevins and Miss Agnes Delano gave me much valuable advice in the writing of the section on the Civil War. Professor Hal Bridges of the University of Colorado read portions of the manuscript and gave me the benefit of his extensive knowledge of the history of nineteenth century America. Mr. Frederick A. Hetzel and Mrs. Agnes Starrett of the University of Pittsburgh Press have been of great assistance in the editing of the manuscript and doing the many things which editors are called upon to do. Finally, I should like to recognize the part played in the preparation of this work by my wife, Frances T. Carpenter: with infinite patience she typed and retyped the manuscript, prepared the index, and gave me numerous helpful, and often, I am glad to say, critical comments. To her I am most deeply indebted.

J. A. C.

SWORD AND OLIVE BRANCH

Early Life

Leeds is a small Maine village not so very different today from what it was during the second quarter of the nineteenth century. It lies northwest of Augusta on the Androscoggin River in the midst of a farming region. If environment can have an effect on a growing boy then a boy born and raised in the inland farming region of nineteenth-century Maine could be expected to have a healthy body, a familiarity with hard work, and a respect for learning and piety. He would also have respect for the powers of nature, for the winter storms could be severe; but he would know and love the long-awaited spring, the warmth of summer sunshine, and the excitement of autumn with its sparkling red and gold days and its star-filled nights.

Into such an environment, on November 8, 1830, a son was born to Eliza Howard and her husband Rowland Bailey Howard. They named him Oliver Otis for her father, but throughout his life he was usually called Otis. Both parents had a similar Anglo-Saxon ancestry. Rowland Howard was descended from John Howard, or Haward, who had come to America with his brother in 1643 to Duxbury and later settled in Bridgewater, Massachusetts.[1] The Howard family continued for several generations to live in Bridgewater and to produce large families.[2] Seth Howard of the fifth generation and father of Rowland Bailey took his family to Leeds in the year 1802. At that time Rowland Bailey Howard was seven years old. Later he went into business in Peekskill, New York, with an older brother, Ward, but returned to Leeds when his father became embroiled in debts.[3] In 1828 he married Eliza Otis, daughter of Oliver Otis of Leeds. Eliza's mother was Betsey Stinchfield, a native of Maine, whose father Roger had originally come from Gloucester, Massachusetts. Oliver Otis' birthplace was Scituate, Massachusetts, and he was descended from John Otis who had come to Massachusetts from England.[4]

Otis Howard passed nine years on his father's and grandfather's farm, and during that time two brothers were born, the first, Rowland Bailey, when Otis was four. Four years after Rowland came Charles, a sweet, affectionate boy to whom Otis always felt very close. When Otis was about five his father brought back from a visit to relatives in the Hudson River Valley a small Negro boy who stayed in the family for the next four years. The two youngsters worked and played together—an association that may have had a marked influence on Howard's later racial attitudes.[5]

Otis attended the local school during the short winter sessions and seems to have done well in his studies. He was a stocky boy who could take care of himself and he demonstrated his aggressiveness and quick temper in the usual schoolboy scraps.[6] The home environment seemed to be not unlike that of many another nineteenth-century American home. There were chores, school, church and quiet Sabbaths, brotherly quarrels, parental discipline, the steadying influence of a grandfather, and the deep affection of loving parents. Grandfather Otis would tell stories of the Revolution and the father would play the flute on winter evenings.

Otis' father died in 1840, and the normal course of life changed. With three boys to raise, it was not unnatural that Eliza Howard should marry again. In June 1841 she married Colonel John Gilmore, a widower who owned a farm about six miles on the other side of the village. Grandfather Otis had already left to live with another son, and now mother and three sons moved out of the family home and joined their new husband and father.[7]

John Gilmore was a good father to his stepchildren and a good husband to Eliza. Otis was fond of him and later spoke of his mother's second marriage as "a blessing to us all."[8] Howard lived at his new home for only a short time. That first autumn he attended school for two months in Wayne, a nearby village; then at the age of twelve he left home to stay with his mother's older brother, John Otis. Uncle John with his wife and several children lived in Hallowell, a town south of Augusta on the Kennebec River. He was a man of some means who later served as a representative in the Thirty-First Congress. Otis remained with his uncle about two years, attending school during the fall and winter and working on his uncle's farm in the summer months. His next step on the educational ladder was Monmouth Academy, a school for boys and girls not far from Leeds. Howard went there specifically to prepare, or "fit" as it was called, for college.

In the winter of 1846 as a final preparation for college he went forty miles away to the North Yarmouth Academy, a few miles north of Portland. The six months he spent at the academy were a time of concentrated study. His preparation had not been the best, and he found himself behind the other boys in his class. The program was stiff and might well have taken a year or more had he not been determined to enter Bowdoin College in September. For the last five or six weeks of the summer term he got up at four each morning, worked at a standup desk, and allowed himself practically no recreation except an occasional walk.[9] The perseverance paid off, for he passed the entrance examinations and was admitted to the freshman class of Bowdoin College in September 1846.

Otis took readily to his college studies, worked hard, and finished near the top of his small class. He had a genuine interest in learning, though he found it necessary to convince himself that an education was desirable. If after having finished his college course, he mused, he proved to have little talent in a profession, he might regret that he had not become a farmer. ". . . but my ambition is of higher & more extended nature," he told his mother while he was still a freshman. "Education is my first aim. . . . I seek not mere money, but a cultivated and enlightened mind, becoming & corresponding with the age in which we live."[10] And when some of the students quit college because they saw no practical benefit from that type of study, Howard had the mature outlook, at the age of sixteen, to see that "a general education fits a man for any work."[11] His decision was good; Bowdoin gave him the opportunity to learn, and Otis Howard, an ambitious youth, did not let the opportunity pass.

These were years of maturing growth, of adolescent introspection. Otis had the normal youthful aspirations; he wanted desperately to succeed and have the respect of his peers. He frequently chided himself for this and dwelt, in letters and diary, on his own shortcomings and failures or simply philosophized on life in general. The language is flowery to an extreme—Howard fancied himself quite a stylist.[12] "Another day has gone, gone forever," he pondered in his diary, "which gives one less day for me to live & one less for the world to stand. We know yet we consider not how fast time passes, we are too apt to think tomorrow will be like today & to forget our time on earth is limited . . . still we pursue the same careless if not sinful course day after day heedless of all except present gratification. . . . Ought we not exert ourselves on the side of justice and uprightness & do good that we may receive good?"[13] Beneath the hyperbole is an awareness of basic moral problems which would occupy Howard's attention deeply in years to come. With the self-analysis and contradiction of adolescence, however, he confessed to his mother: "I am ambitious, strongly ambitious. . . ."[14] There is an element of truth in this oft-repeated admission. Throughout his life ambition, a normal and conventional characteristic of those who achieve the role of leader in life, would be regarded as a problem to this introspective man.

Howard seems to have led an exemplary life while a student. He was fairly regular in his attendance at church, and he once referred to himself as "very *pious*."[15] Although drinking appears to have been common at Bowdoin, Howard did not indulge.[16] He smoked but tried twice to break the habit. Once in the summer of 1848 he announced to his mother that he had "accomplished quite a reformation" in himself. He had not only stopped using tobacco but had actually overcome the desire for it. The next reference to the subject was in the following March when he proudly announced that he had "locked up" his pipes for the remainder of the term if not for good. His mother replied that she was glad he had done this but not nearly so glad as last summer "when you had *entirely over come the habit*."[17]

The letters and diary of his college years show curiously little concern over national affairs. This was a crucial period of American history. When Howard entered Bowdoin as a freshman, the Mexican War had just begun. Before he was graduated the war had ended and the nation had passed through the crisis which culminated in the Compromise of 1850. His mother referred briefly to the Mexican War on two occasions in the letters she addressed to him,[18] but Howard himself made no mention of it. In the summer of 1848 he said that the forthcoming election between Zachary Taylor, Lewis Cass, and Martin Van Buren, the Whig, Democratic, and Free-Soil candidates, had excited some discussion as had the Wilmot Proviso and the Mexican War. Yet his reference to "the youthful politicians" who were indulging in such discussions hints that he was not a participant.[19] At election time he attended a Whig rally and wrote home that he had opposed three Free-Soilers in a discussion which touched on slavery, "Van Buren's claims on the Texas question—Taylor's principles and in short everything that would claim the attention of politicians occupying a higher & more effective position than ourselves." [20] Although Howard probably took a greater interest in national affairs than is indicated in his letters, there is no evidence that at this time he was thinking deeply on constitutional subjects or on the most pressing national issue, slavery.

He was far more interested in a girl he had met during his first vacation as a freshman. Howard's roommate, who had the intriguing name of Peleg Perley, lived in the town of Livermore, not far from Leeds. Perley's young cousin Elizabeth Ann Waite was visiting relatives in the vicinity. At a party Perley's mother gave for the young people, Otis, aged sixteen, met Lizzie, aged fifteen, and started a relationship which resulted eventually in marriage.[21]

At first he did not let his mother know that he had fallen in love, but it was not long before she noticed a change in him. In the second half of Howard's sophomore year she complained of her son's "abstractedness which I never saw in you before, and disinclination for study. . . ." [22] Otis' classmates, too, noticed the change, and he himself ascribed to Lizzie his abandonment of tobacco. The time finally came when he had to bring his mother in on what was no longer a secret. She had obviously suspected something, or perhaps had heard rumors. She had written him a warning in guarded tones, mentioning possible "shipwreck," and a "well known *evil in the world*." [23] Howard's reply to this is a fine example of filial consideration. He wanted his mother to know that the girl "who possesses a strong influence" over him was not giddy and empty-headed, but "good, sincere and intelligent. . . . There is no engagement," he assured her, "excepting the mutual pledges of devotion, [and] sympathy. . . ." [24]

There occurred the inevitable misunderstanding, separation, and reconciliation. It seems that some time before the end of Howard's junior year Orville Jennings, a classmate, got himself "pretty sadly intoxicated" and while riding in a buggy with Perley, "drove his horse through mud & water as if he would tear everything in pieces." An uncle of Lizzie happened to see this and assuming that the young man with Perley was Otis Howard passed on to the Waite family the news that Otis was intoxicated. The Waites forbade their daughter to see the young man whom they thought was an irresponsible rake, and consequently Otis was, for a time, neglected. Perley at last set things straight and the lovers were reunited.[25] From the time of his junior year on, it was generally conceded that Otis and Lizzie were engaged and they saw each other as often as possible. She was a pretty girl, small, with brown eyes and brown hair, and her demeanor was even more serious than Otis'.

Except for his freshman year, Howard each winter taught school in successive years at Leeds, East Livermore, and Wayne. This was customary for college students, who thus earned a little money to help pay for their education.[26] But it was not until his senior year that Howard began to think seriously of a profession. Apparently, in almost four years of college he had not formed any definite plan. Then, toward the end of June, Uncle John Otis, now a member of Congress, came up with an unexpected solution. He wrote from Washington that his son William would probably not pass the physical examination for West Point and if this should prove true, would Otis be interested? [27]

Later that same year Otis explained to his mother that on hearing of the offer to go to West Point he sat down to think it over. He could, "by industry and frugality," achieve some wealth and ease. Yet this would not satisfy his lofty ideas, so "coming to the quick conclusion to be 'something or nothing,' to sacrifice ease to ambition I decided to accept the appointment." [28] The decision must have come, then, while he was still at Bowdoin. After he had completed his college examinations he returned home to Leeds and laid the matter before his mother. Sensing that her son had already made up his mind, she gave her somewhat reluctant consent.[29] Otis would go to West Point, and he and Lizzie would now have to wait at least four more years for marriage.

Howard's new adventure began pleasantly enough. Lizzie took the boat with him from Portland to Boston, but after two days spent with relatives there he had to move on to New York. He left Lizzie "with rather a heavy heart"; he would not see her again until the following summer. After "a most beautiful sail up the river" from New York, he arrived at West Point a few days before having to report. This gave him the chance to observe a little of what the summer encampment was like, where the great majority of the new class had been since early in the summer.[30] He had to take some examinations, but he got by these successfully and, on the last day of August 1850, Post Orders announced that Oliver O. Howard of Maine had been conditionally admitted as cadet "to rank as such from the 1st proximo." [31]

Life at West Point in 1850 was similar in most respects to what

EARLY LIFE

it is more than a century later. Though the curriculum is different, the discipline and Spartan regime are little changed. Howard readily admitted that the first days were none too pleasant: "My health is good, my face long," he told his mother.[32] Once in uniform his spirits began to revive though he complained frequently during the first month or so of the fatiguing drills with fifteen pound muskets.[33] By the second week in October he apparently found himself and was ready to confess that in the early days he had been homesick, "a little sore from sharp drilling, and a little angry, from having my pride so often touched." Now, however, "every one treats me like a gentleman. I stand in the first section in everything [academically], and with the good will of my new classmates, enjoy myself as much as I ever have in any situation." Study was now a pleasure and prospects brightened.[34]

Of course he had the advantage of four years of college. Yet he was not alone in this and furthermore the curriculum at West Point which stressed mathematical science differed markedly from the classical course at Bowdoin. Although Howard did extremely well in academic matters, the "good will of . . . [his] new classmates" was not to continue. In the spring of 1851 he began to notice that some of the cadets were not speaking to him. In the months to follow what began as the action of a small group spread to an overwhelmingly large percentage of the corps. This ostracism lasted until the end of the summer encampment; the hostility of two or three cadets persisted for over a year.

There were several reasons for this action, the foremost being Howard's association with an enlisted man on the post, the son of a close friend of his own father. This soldier, Warren Lothrop, had fought in the Mexican War and was the orderly sergeant for a company stationed at West Point. Almost the first thing Howard did when he arrived at the Academy was to look up his friend, and all during that fall and winter he continued to see him, visiting at the soldiers' barracks most every Saturday afternoon.[35] At first he was unaware of doing anything unusual, but by December he knew that some of the cadets considered association with enlisted men degrading. Finally, the Commandant of Cadets told Howard that he would have to stop seeing his friend since his failure to observe the rank structure was a breach of the training program of the Academy.[36] This he did, except for infrequent secret visits; but the damage had already been done.

Another reason for some to cut Howard might have been his feelings toward the abolition of slavery. Twice while at West Point he referred to himself in his letters as an abolitionist.[37] There is little evidence that Howard thought deeply on this or any other current topic, but even slight leanings in this direction would automatically damage his reputation in the eyes of many of the cadets.

Nor was Howard's affiliation with the Bible class soon after his arrival at West Point likely to help his position. Just a year later he explained to his mother that he still was a member despite the ridicule of his classmates. Having joined the Bible class he had no intention of giving it up.[38] Probably all these things plus jealousy because of Howard's high standing in the class contributed to the unpleasant situation.

Howard first mentioned the matter to his brother Rowland in May 1851. He wrote of the "feeling of delicacy" which had lately appeared among some of his "more aristocratic & rival classmates." He believed that the refusal to speak stemmed from jealousy and "subtle slander." Those who took the lead were the two who were vying for top honors in the class: Henry L. Abbot, of Boston, and G. W. C. (Custis) Lee, the son of Robert E. Lee. Howard acknowledged that Lee was "one of the finest young men" he had ever met; but for an unaccountable reason he (Lee) had turned against him. When Howard went to his room on an errand, Lee politely told him that he did not want him to come again unless invited. As for Abbot, he told Howard during a private conversation that he wanted no more association with him. Abbot and Howard had previously been close friends.[39]

This was the harder to bear because it came so unexpectedly. As Howard admitted later, he had thought that he was generally liked and was unable to understand what was going on. That summer, in camp, the situation became progressively worse. Life at West Point had become miserable for the proud New Englander. A visit from his mother and Lizzie must have helped some but not enough to prevent Howard, after they had left, from falling into such a state of despondency that he seriously considered resigning.[40] By the end of August, however, the worst seemed to be over.[41]

Even so, there remained a group with whom Howard had no association for at least another year. After classes had resumed in the fall of 1851 he related how he and Lee sat next to each other in mathematics and drawing class day after day, neither one speaking to

EARLY LIFE 9

the other. "It seems queer, non-sensical perhaps," he wrote his mother, "but so it is. I never injured him in the world nor he me but once." [42]

Howard relates in his autobiography the story, which does not appear in his correspondence, how at the height of this difficulty, Captain B. R. Alden, the commandant, advised him informally to "knock some man down." [43] Evidently, Howard took the advice and soon his standing among the cadets improved. By the time he had returned from a brief summer's vacation in August 1852 he could report: "I am now on speaking terms with all but three in my class." [44] Halfway through his final year, Howard reported to his mother that he and Abbot had made up and that he now had the good will of all his classmates. [45]

In October 1852 Howard joined the Dialectic Society, a cadet literary and debating society, and during the latter part of the month engaged in public debate before the cadets, the Academy officers and their wives. The new superintendent, Colonel Robert E. Lee, was present, and according to Howard, "took a great deal of interest in the debate." Howard agreed that this extra-curricular activity had done him much good. [46]

Howard's period of ostracism could not have had a lasting effect on his classmates, for it is very evident that he had a large number of friends, especially in the last two years. One of these was the future Confederate cavalry leader, Jeb Stuart, who seven years later reminded him of "those rambles we once took around Flirtation [Walk]." [47] Two of Howard's closest friends were John T. Greble of Philadelphia and Henry W. Closson of Vermont. He had as a roommate his last year a cadet from Alabama by the name of Chapman. Howard liked him and once referred to him as a gentleman, kindly and unselfish. [48] Yet of the Southerners in the Dialectic Society, he made the general observation that they are "full of gas, seldom ever speak to the point, but have a great flow of language." [49] Even so, there is no indication that sectional origin had anything to do with Howard's choice of associates.

Howard's circle of friends, drawn from the ranks of Northerners and Southerners alike, is an indication that he was not an ardent antislavery man, despite his own admission on two occasions that he was an abolitionist. There is even some evidence that Howard held conservative views on national political questions. He supported Stephen A. Douglas' Kansas-Nebraska Bill which called for the repeal of the Missouri Compromise on the grounds that the Compromise had limited the powers of the states. He also advanced the argument that the Constitution sanctioned slavery.[50] Here was no uncompromising abolitionist!

Howard entered more fully into the social life of the Academy as his standing with his classmates improved. He also achieved recognition from his superiors by being given positions of responsibility. Early in 1853 he was jumped from being a private in the ranks over about fifteen other cadets to the post of quartermaster sergeant.[51] At the start of the summer encampment in 1853 Howard, now a member of the First Class, became a cadet lieutenant, leading him to remark that he was starting this camp "with a lighter heart & & [sic] more agreeable prospects than I did two years ago. . . ."[52] In the last months of his stay at West Point Howard had the distinction of being named cadet quartermaster, in part as recognition of his consistent high academic standing.[53] He was graduated fourth in a class of forty-six, with Custis Lee taking first place in everything.[54]

For all of Howard's feeling of self-importance in his last two years at West Point, for all of his outward display of assurance, he still remained an insecure young man, worried about how his actions would appear to others, eager to make a favorable impression, and torn as usual between pride and a humility which he believed was becoming a Christian. If all this was not enough to cause the young man anxiety, he ran into romantic difficulties in the fall of his final year at the Academy. Soon after Lizzie had paid him a visit in September 1853 he became suspicious that she had transferred her affections to his old Bowdoin roommate, Peleg Perley. He knew that Perley taught school in Portland, Maine and boarded with Lizzie and her mother. Isolated at West Point, Howard brooded over what he believed a friend's betrayal and his betrothed's fickleness. Rowland Howard was his brother's confidant and Rowland, too, thought that there were grounds for suspicion. Both knew, however, that Lizzie had been sick, but even so, since Lizzie was silent, the suspicion persisted until late in the fall. On January 1, 1854 Rowland wrote that Lizzie was sick again, but he also mentioned a reconciliation and so the difficulty which existed only in Howard's mind evaporated.[55]

In the spring of his final year at the Academy Howard again began to think about his future career. A medical doctor advised him to leave the army and become a civil engineer in the West, but this had no appeal for Howard who told his mother: "business matters are ten

Early Life

times more enigmatical to me than difficult mathematical theorems. I am not going to leave a good nest, for the probable or the contingent, but if a good offer comes I will bid Uncle Sam adieu with few regrets." [56]

The prospect of leaving the army, so attractive three years earlier, seemed much less so in 1854. By that time the members of the class had grown warmly attached to one another [57] and Howard wrote enthusiastically to his mother of the gay social life in which he was an active participant: "this has been as happy a year thus far as I have spent at West Point I have been received into the first society of this little place. Mrs Lee has more than compensated all the difficulties that I have had with her son in years gone by from her kind attentions." [58]

Just a few days before leaving for home he admitted that he now loved West Point "almost as much as I used to hate it. . . . The Professors are without exception my fast friends, and I wish I was half as good a man as I have the reputation of being here." [59] Almost in spite of himself, Otis Howard had become a professional soldier. In the years to come he would question his aptitude and fitness for the life of a soldier, but this was to be the only profession he would ever know. Four years at West Point are hard to forget and these years, cruel and wretched though they seemed in part, left an indelible impression on young Howard, who was proud of his accomplishments and touched by the powerful *esprit* of the Academy. In any case, when he returned to Maine in the latter part of June 1854 he would have had almost no choice about the future; the surest way of gaining a steady income was to remain in the army and the steady income was essential because what Otis Howard wanted most was to marry Lizzie Waite.

Prewar Service in the Regular Army

Following a summer's vacation in Maine, spent mostly in the company of Lizzie, Howard reported for duty on September 30, 1854 to Watervliet Arsenal near Troy, New York.[1] Attractively located on the west bank of the Hudson River, the arsenal manufactured gun carriages and small arms, an agreeably relaxed mission in these peacetime years.[2] This assignment was acknowledgement of Howard's high academic standing at West Point, for duty in one of the technical services went only to the top men of any graduating class. Soon Howard was engaged in making inspections, serving as officer of the day, and performing the other routine duties of a brevet second lieutenant. The assignment was in every respect a pleasant one, with one exception. Lizzie was in Portland. Howard visited her during the latter part of December and made arrangements for their marriage, but he was back on duty by January 5.[3] He applied for a leave to begin on February 5, and Otis and Lizzie were married at her home in Portland the evening of February 14.[4] Early in March the young couple arrived at their new home on the arsenal grounds.

They settled quickly into the cheerful routine of keeping house.[5] The Howard household grew within the limitations of a modest salary. They employed a cook toward the end of the summer and Otis bought a cow at an auction.[6] At about the same time they became the proud owners of a horse and carriage.[7]

While Howard was living alone he had attended regularly the Episcopal church in Troy. Lizzie now joined him and in June they rented a pew.[8] In April Otis had been promoted from a brevet to a full-fledged second lieutenant,[9] and the happiness of the family seemed complete when they could look forward to the birth of their first child in December. Just a few weeks before the baby was born, Howard received orders to take temporary command of the Kennebec

Arsenal, Augusta, Maine. Although this would put them near friends and families, it also meant a move at a critical time. But Lizzie stood the trip well and gave birth, on December 16, to a healthy boy whom they named Guy.[10] Otherwise, the six months' temporary duty was uneventful. During the time that he was at Augusta, Howard came to know the editor of the Kennebec *Journal,* James G. Blaine, who had only recently come to Maine. This was the start of a long friendship which lasted down to the Republican leader's death in 1892.[11]

In May Howard received orders to return to Watervliet as soon as a new commanding officer arrived in Augusta.[12] The replacement did not appear until July 30[13] and Howard left Lizzie and Guy to finish out the summer in Maine while he returned to Troy.[14] For the rest of the summer Howard was by himself. Part of the time he took his meals with Lieutenant and Mrs. W. R. Boggs, both Southerners. This was the year of the Frémont-Buchanan campaign and to most Southerners Frémont, the Republican party's first presidential candidate, was the equivalent of an abolitionist. Howard wrote to his wife of an incident that occurred at the Boggs's table which indicates his position on the subject of slavery and national politics. During the course of a discussion on politics, Boggs's sister asked Howard if he were not for Frémont. Howard had been taking little part in the conversation, but when confronted with a direct question he answered that he was. "Immediately I found a cold feeling run around the table," he told Lizzie. "I took my meals in my own house as soon as possible. I haven't taken any notice of their prejudice and I reckon they begin to see that a Frémont man neednt be so much of a scamp after all. . . . I have had quite a number of sectional speeches to put up with. I think it best to keep clear of all quarrels, as my position will not admit of my entering the canvass."[15]

That summer, before Lizzie and Guy arrived, Howard had the chance to do some fishing along the Mohawk River and to travel down the Hudson to see friends at West Point. He also admitted to smoking a cigar every day after lunch.[16] In December he and Lizzie spent a week in New York. They attended the theatre, visited Governors Island, and heard Henry Ward Beecher talk.[17] The second lieutenant and his wife lived as well as possible, with their two servants,[18] carriage, and occasional trips. Howard was proud of his new position in life and wanted to be a credit to his profession. He attended the socially respectable Episcopal church, smoked cigars after lunch, and avoided political controversy.

Just before Christmas orders came to report to the commanding general in Florida for temporary duty as ordnance officer in the field.[15] Howard had never before been in any of the Southern states, and when he landed at Savannah on December 30, 1856, he saw for the first time what the institution of slavery was like. His first impression was not unfavorable and he wrote to his mother that the Negroes seemed happy. "I haven't heard a white man speak an unkind word to a negro since I came from N. York," he told her, "but Irishmen get plenty of abuse from whites & negroes." While he did see one incident on the seamier side of slavery, the separation of a slave woman from her little daughter, it seemed that owners treated their slaves as small children, with a considerable amount of indulgence. "I am glad," he wrote "to observe these things—glad to see that this relation is generally so amicable between the master & his slaves, for having so deep a root it will not speedily be possible to enfranchise them, and their capacity for self government & independence is evidently not yet. They had better be cared for as they are now in this place than turned loose on the world, with all their simplicity & improvident habits, without a proper education." He believed that to say that the slave owners were not Christians was doing them an injustice and had he been brought up where slavery existed he would have held the same convictions as everyone else.[20] A few months later from Fort Brooke he wrote Lizzie that slavery there was "in a very mild form. You wouldn't know the negroes were slaves unless you were told." [21] Lieutenant Howard was a long way from being a fanatic on the slavery question.

From Savannah he continued his journey across the state to Fort Brooke, near Tampa, headquarters of the commander of the Department of Florida, General William S. Harney. Harney was conducting a futile campaign against bands of elusive Seminoles. Howard saw no action. His duties as ordnance officer for the department were not onerous, except at isolated intervals when he had to issue arms to volunteer companies or to collect the weapons when a company was being mustered out.[22]

In Florida Howard lived for a time with a fellow officer and boarded at a hotel in Tampa. Later he established quarters for himself in his office which was on a remote part of the post, continuing to take his meals at the hotel.[23] He made an effort to enter into the social life of the community, and according to what he told Lizzie, once attended a ball so as to create good feeling with the townspeople.²⁴ In other leisure moments he worked in his own garden, read, or enjoyed a smoke with an occasional visitor.²⁵ His mind seemed to be upon worldly more than spiritual things. In a letter to Lizzie in which he enclosed a hundred dollars he expressed satisfaction that they were independent financially and thus in a position "to give the practical denial to those especial friends who have worried you & me on account of our extravagance." ²⁶ A little later he remarked that they were doing quite well financially, having already saved seven hundred and sixty dollars.²⁷

Howard also seemed to enjoy his military contacts and believed that he was advancing his career. Commenting on the trick of fate which separated him from his family, he wrote to Lizzie that the Florida assignment had given him the chance to gain experience, to be known in the army, and "to make valuable accessions to my acquaintance & friendships and gain the confidence of my Colonel & other old & influential officers, by doing an important duty faithfully." ²⁸ He seemed happy in what he called a West Point atmosphere where the conversation concerned old times, the present-day service, and prospects for the future.²⁹ What interested him was how he stood with his fellow officers and he believed his standing was pretty high. He was making an effort, he told Lizzie, not to appear to feel important.³⁰

Yet during the months that Howard was away from his wife and child he seemed to be searching and struggling for a personally satisfying religion. For years his failure to be the kind of Christian his mother wanted him to be was a source of some concern. His church attendance had been regular in Troy, but all was not well in his mind on the question of religion. Shortly before his marriage he confided to his mother, who always had hopes that her son would become a professing Christian, that his heart was "not without religious feeling. I try to do right," he wrote, "though I am always failing." ³¹ Two years later he still was looking critically at his religious attitudes. Again it was to his mother that he poured out his feelings: "Say to me, 'love the Lord thy God with all thy heart' and thy neighbor as thyself—I cannot do it and probably shall not till some terrible stroke has awakened my sensibilities and prostrated my soul with its pride and yearnings earthward in the dust. . . . I am in that state of mind where every man is, who feels that God has made him for a purpose, and he doubts whether or not he is fulfilling it. There would be no use in any outward demonstration. I will not join a church or make any open profession of faith, till I am sure I possess that faith, and am prepared to devote myself to the service of my maker without reserve." [32]

Now in far-off Florida during his frequent hours of solitude religious thoughts were more and more crowding in upon him. His selection of reading material indicated the change which was taking place. In February he was reading, besides Bacon and Shakespeare, the epistles of St. Paul and the life of Captain Hedley Vicars of the British Army.[33] Vicars had been a practicing Christian and appeared to have had a marked influence on his army associates. He served in the Crimean War and was killed in the fighting before Sevastopol. In March Howard was reading the Bible every night.[34]

At about this time word came that several members of his family had found Christ. His brother Charlie had been converted almost four years before,[35] but until the spring of 1857 no other member of the family had followed his example. Then a letter arrived from his brother, Rowland, announcing that he and his fiancée had undergone a conversion. Soon after this Lizzie indicated a growing interest in religion and hoped that sometime they could discuss the subject together. They had never done this before. Her hope was that she would not long remain in darkness.[36] On May 24 Otis wrote Lizzie a long letter in which he tried to analyze his feelings. He had, he said, long been on the outskirts of Christianity without finding the faith he was seeking. He put down all his faults, all his true motives for performing seemingly generous acts. He knew that his heart was not pure, but, he said, Christ could make it so. At the end of the letter he noted that the Methodists were then holding a revival and that fifteen persons already had joined the church. "The spirit of God is everywhere," was his concluding remark.[37]

A new commanding officer, Colonel L. L. Loomis, a devoutly religious man, attended the Methodist revival and asked Howard to go with him. The first time Howard went he walked out of the meeting when the minister called for sinners to come forward. The Colonel stayed to the end and then they walked home together. Loomis talked with Howard until one o'clock that night and gave him books to read, prayers, hymns and tracts.[38] The next evening Howard went again to the revival, this time alone. The sermon was uninspiring but after the minister called for those who sought religion to come forward, Howard noticed that some young men were laughing at those who rose. This angered him and, as he admits, "more in pride perhaps than humility," he went to the front of the church. He did not experience any emotional resurgence from this but he went back to his quarters determined to find Christ. He took up Vicars' diary and noted how much the English officer's experience was like his own, "how much like me, full of pride & vanity to be overcome." Vicars' inspirational text was "the blood of Jesus Christ his Son cleanseth us from all sin." [39] Then he read the Bible and prayed. And, as he told Lizzie,

I then bore that text above in mind, & said in my heart oh! My Saviour, I know thou canst save me! I made an effort to fully believe my sins washed in the blood of the Lamb, that my dear Saviour had actually saved me at that moment, i.e. had pardoned all my transgressions of the laws of God, & all the wickedness of a corrupt heart —The fullness of the glow of happiness came into my heart, the tugging & burning left me—the choking sensation was gone . . . my mind is as clear as when making out an Ordnance Return. . . . [God] will help me to lead from this time henceforth a consistent Christian life. And you must come along with me—you have as much right & interest in Christ as I.[40]

In the weeks that followed Howard plunged wholeheartedly into the life of a practicing Christian. He led prayers at the Methodist Church, invited enlisted men in to his quarters for morning devotions, conducted a Sabbath school, and assisted in a Bible class. When he entered a home he frequently was asked to lead in Bible reading and prayer,[41] and under Rowland's urging he began to think seriously of joining the ministry.[42] He wanted to know, for instance, how Lizzie would like being the wife of a minister.[43] Lizzie was not so sure she would like it, nor did she wholly approve of what her husband had done. To be sure, she was genuinely glad when she learned that he had found the faith he sought. She heard this just a few days before giving birth to her second child, Grace Ellen, on June 22. Lizzie, it seems, also underwent something of a conversion but she was rather doubtful as to the propriety of what her husband was doing away from home.[44]

But Howard was still in the Army and he would not be able to make any definite decision about a career until he had returned North. At the end of August the order relieving him from duty at Fort Brooke arrived in Florida. His next assignment was to be instructor in mathematics at the Military Academy at West Point, and a day or so after August 26, Howard departed from Fort Brooke to report to his new post.[45] He went directly to Maine from Florida, picked up Lizzie and the two children and reported at West Point toward the end of September 1857.[46]

West Point was then, and remains still, a place of great natural beauty and it offered many advantages to the regular army officer: comfortable housing, proximity to New York City, and social opportunities. Howard especially enjoyed the academic atmosphere, the opportunity to read, to pursue his independent studies, and to engage in Christian service. His duties as an instructor in mathematics, he told his mother, were exacting and demanded some preparation in addition to close attention while in the classroom. Nonetheless, he experienced little trouble with the students, keeping cheerful even when they became vexed; he believed that he got on "admirably." [47]

His students saw before them in the classroom a young man of twenty-six, of dignified bearing, about five feet nine inches tall. His 160 pounds were well distributed and his thick brown hair curled slightly at the back and sides. Like many army men of that day, he wore a full beard. His eyes were dark blue and kindly. The cadets might have thought him grave, but at times his face would break out in a cheerful smile. Some of his students in later years spoke of his kindliness, forbearance, and understanding.[48]

Though the faces he saw in the classroom would change from year to year the regular routine at West Point seldom varied. As late as the latter part of November 1860 Howard could say that it was like a broad prairie with regard to time; the weeks passed with almost no variation.[49] This, of course, was an exaggeration. There was the time, for instance, that Grace, less than a year old, almost swallowed one of Guy's marbles,[50] or the visit to West Point of Edward, the Prince of Wales accompanied by notables in the fall of 1860.[51] Another time Howard had the opportunity of renewing his acquaintance with Colonel Robert E. Lee—the occasion was a court of inquiry.[52]

The Howards spent their summers in Maine and in 1859 took an extended trip through Canada before arriving at Leeds.[53] James Waite Howard was born on December 1, 1860 and in many other ways, trivial and significant, the unusual was mingled with the routine in generous measure, with the result that these were extremely happy years.[54]

Howard had other duties and interests besides his regular teaching. Soon after arriving at West Point he became tutor to the two young daughters of the Commandant of Cadets, Colonel William J. Hardee,[55] and in the winter of 1858 he received notice that he had been promoted to the rank of first lieutenant.[56] Howard became the Academy librarian in the fall of 1859 and received a little additional money for his services which appear to have been far from onerous.[57]

But the most important part of life at West Point for Howard was that which pertained to his religious activities. Here he could take an active role in the religious life of the Academy and the community while at the same time pursuing his independent religious studies. On first arriving at West Point Howard became superintendent of the Sunday school for the children of enlisted men.[58] A short time later he started a Wednesday evening prayer meeting at a small building used by the Methodists and Roman Catholics near the soldiers' barracks.[59] His next activity was a Bible class for enlisted men and civilians. But Howard's most lasting contribution was his founding in March 1858 of a cadet prayer meeting to be held in the half hour of unscheduled time following supper.

All during these years at West Point neither Otis nor Lizzie actually joined a church. Guy and Grace were baptized in the Episcopal church in the fall of 1857 and early in 1858 Howard told his brother Charles that he and Lizzie had decided to become Episcopalians.[60] But only a short time later he expressed an interest in the Methodist church.[61] At the end of the year it seemed as if the Episcopal church had won out, for he confided to his diary that he and Lizzie had had a lengthy discussion of the matter, that she definitely favored the Episcopal church, and that for the sake of harmony in the family he would give in.[62]

At this time Howard began seriously to pursue a definite course of study with the local Episcopal rector with a view to becoming a minister. He had to face Lizzie's opposition. "Lizzie," he wrote in his diary, "likes well enough to have me an episcopalian if she thought I would be a proper one, but fears I will not feel free as now. She dreads my being a minister & opposes it."[63] Despite these few references to his becoming an Episcopalian, neither husband nor wife ever took the step; but Howard did go ahead with his theological studies, particularly the study of Hebrew.[64]

Meanwhile Howard's conversion had led him to even more

intensive introspection than he had indulged in previously. His diary of this period reveals much soul-searching and concern over his tendency to pride. Once he wrote that "the pride & haughtiness of my heart is more than pen can tell, but I believe God will so school me, by failures when I act without Christ, by disappointments & afflictions, as to bring my miserably foolish soul into full subjection to himself. . . . I fear if God would give me success with my heart as it is now, that I would be puffed with pride & thus lose the countenance of my blessed Saviour." [65] There can be little doubt but that, especially after his conversion, Howard frequently had to wrestle with the problem of vanity. His strong urge to excel met head on the Christian virtue of self-effacement, and his public career from this point on would intensify the problem.

Then in 1860 national affairs interrupted the quiet routine of West Point life. The sectional controversy which had agitated the nation for more than two decades was approaching a climax and within a matter of a few months war would break out. Yet Howard, like so many Americans, failed to grasp the gravity of the situation. Shortly after Lincoln's election in November 1860, he wrote to his mother that he would not care if South Carolina did leave the Union. He thought "it would be a good lesson to her people to stand alone for a few years." [66] In the Howard household family affairs tended to push the mounting national tension into the background. December brought snow and sliding for the children, Christmas and Christmas trees; it also brought secession. Howard turned to this latest event with some apprehension and considered the state of affairs "alarming in the extreme." [67]

His interest mounted as the crisis became more acute. Already Major Robert Anderson, in command at Charleston, had concentrated his small force at Fort Sumter, and Americans North and South centered their attention on the island fort in Charleston harbor. Still, there was no immediate anticipation of war. Major Anderson's plight was serious but that did not mean that Lieutenant Howard would have to alter his plans for the future. At this very time, he was contemplating taking a six-month leave from the army to study at Bangor Theological Seminary where his brother Charles already was in attendance.[68] Howard could not believe that there would be actual fighting between the North and South.

Sumter's surrender on April 13 ended Howard's hesitation. Indeed the whole North, for a short time at least, dropped differences and party animosities in its revulsion against the attack on Sumter and the national flag. Howard abandoned the plan to enter the ministry and determined to stay in the army as a regular or volunteer until the war was over.

Harmonizing war and Christianity was no problem. Nine years earlier, while still a cadet, he had theoretically examined this question and concluded that the principle of non-resistance was understandable for individuals, but would not work for the national government. It was a citizen's duty to defend his country just as a father would defend his wife and children from an assassin.[69] Now the country was in danger and the time had come to cast aside personal desires and rally to her defense.

His first move was to try for a commission as colonel of one of the volunteer regiments from his native state. Many of his fellow officers, even some of the first class of cadets, were obtaining commissions in volunteer regiments. Through a friend who had gone to Washington, Howard sounded out the chief of the Ordnance Department, Lieutenant Colonel James W. Ripley, who saw nothing improper in Howard's intended course of action.[70] Ambition for higher rank must have entered into this decision to volunteer. There was nothing to prevent his staying in the regular army, a course which many others followed, and which the War Department desired.[71] Neither did he feel any hesitancy in calling on some of Maine's leading political figures to aid him in gaining the desired colonelcy, for during April and May Howard was in touch with Governor Israel Washburn, Congressman Anson P. Morrill, and James G. Blaine, Speaker of the Maine House of Representatives.

Despite the fact that the men of each regiment elected their own officers, Washburn assured Howard in May that the colonelcy of the Kennebec (Third Maine) Regiment would be his if he wanted it. Here was the opportunity he sought, but it appears that he accepted the offer with just a little reluctance. "I shall expect much hard work & no little annoyance with the volunteers, whereas, here I am quiet & untroubled," he wrote from West Point on May 15, "but if I can do more to advance the right & put down rebellion by changing I am ready to do so. . . . I would prefer a three years regiment for I mean to stay in the army till the war is over if the Lord permits." [72]

Howard secured a seven-day leave and early on the afternoon of May 28 bade farewell to Lizzie and the children. With a full heart he descended the steep bank of the Hudson and took the ferry to Garrison on the opposite shore. There he boarded the New York train and began the first leg of the trip to Augusta where he would take command of the regiment.[73]

Brigade Command

Arriving at Augusta late on the afternoon of May 29, Howard found the Third Maine encamped in a park across from the State House.[1] Hardly a man in the regiment had ever seen Howard before, but on the recommendation of Blaine and Washburn they had elected him their colonel.[2] Thus assured, he had sent in his resignation to Washington knowing that the regiment had immediate need of his services.[3] Howard's younger brother Charles had left theological school to enlist in the regiment and was detailed as aide to the colonel.

Colonel of the Third Maine regiment of volunteers at the age of thirty; before the year was out a brigadier general; and then at little more than thirty-two, a major general. How well equipped in training and temperament was Howard to handle these positions of high command? What kind of man was he that he could rise above so many others in so short a time? What might prevent him from rising higher?

Howard did not have the training to fill high command in the army. Few men in the country did. Yet he had the advantage of a sound education, as good as the nation offered in the midddle 1800's. His West Point background was responsible for his becoming a colonel at the start of the war; it was to be an asset all through the next four years. Yet this alone is not a sufficient explanation for his later success. Only two other members of his class reached the rank of major general in the Union Army during the war,[4] and their commissions were by brevet and came over two years later than Howard's. Few West Pointers of whatever class became army commanders as Howard did. Thus, although the West Point background was of considerable importance, it cannot alone account for Howard's ascent of the military ladder.

Equally important is the fact that Maine politicians, on the state and national level, worked in Howard's behalf. At the start of the war Howard knew personally only Blaine, but he soon gained the friendship of Governor Washburn, and at least an acquaintance with Vice President Hannibal Hamlin and with the Morrill brothers, A. P. Morrill, a congressman, and Lot M. Morrill, senator from Maine. Until late in 1862, Howard was not of sufficient importance to attract much attention from politicians outside his own state; from then on, however, he had a measure of support from the Radical group in Congress and from Secretary of War Edwin M. Stanton. Howard's swing to a more forthright abolitionist stand probably accounts for this support. Still the evidence available indicates that Howard either did not choose, or was not forced, to make any decided effort to protect and improve his position in the army through the pulling of political strings.

There are other reasons why Howard rose above the crowd during the Civil War. Quite apart from his West Point background or his political influence, he had natural abilities that recommended him for promotion. Outstanding was the conscientious way in which he always carried out an assignment. He was attentive to duty, strict in obedience to orders and thorough in their execution. He also had the happy trait of being able to get along well with others, to bury his personal desires for the good of the cause. Consequently, he kept free of petty and major quarrels which so hampered the Northern armies and jeopardized more than one career. Closely related to his ability of working harmoniously with others was an unbending loyalty to the nation and to its civilian and military leaders. He never was a member of a clique nor participated in intrigue; he believed it his duty to uphold his superiors and to deal justly with his subordinates. Courage in the face of physical danger is a necessary quality for a field commander, and it was a central trait in Howard's make-up. Early in the war he acquired the reputation of being absolutely fearless under fire. Indeed, he was even rash in this respect. Naturally, Howard's knowledge of the problems of command—both on the field and in the camp—was more theoretical than real, but he possessed the capacity to learn and to apply what he learned—which accounts in large measure for his steady advancement during the war.

In evaluating the success or failure of Howard's military career one must consider his religious views. For the pious, Howard was the warmhearted Christian soldier; for the worldly-minded his piety was something to ridicule or at best to ignore. After the war General Joseph Hooker, Howard's superior at the battle of Chancellorsville, was quoted as saying in a newspaper interview: "If he [Howard] was not born in petticoats he ought to have been, and ought to wear them. He was always taken up with Sunday Schools and the temperance cause. Those things are all very good, you know, but have very little to do with commanding army corps. He would command a prayer meeting with a good deal more ability than he would an army." [5] It had been the same when Howard had joined the Bible class as a cadet, when he had founded the cadet prayer meeting and the Sunday school as an instructor. His associates found it difficult to believe that a man who was so religious could possibly be a soldier. There was a similar attitude toward Howard's opposition to drinking and profanity which, with some, branded Howard as a prude. In that day, as this, the army was not the place where one normally sought or found opponents of liquor and intemperate language. All of this meant that Howard's reputation of being a Christian soldier hampered his acceptance by both fellow officers and enlisted men. And yet, despite the reputation he had of being sober and prudish, Howard actually did have a lively sense of humor, and he enjoyed good company and close companionship. Especially did he enjoy the company of ladies. But it sometimes took time for his associates to find all this out.

Many wondered what Howard's religion had to do with being a soldier; he himself found it a source of strength. His steadiness and perseverance in the face of defeat and discouragement stemmed from his belief that God would always support a just cause. His fearlessness in combat can be attributed to his trust that God would protect him but that if it was God's will that he should die then that was as it should be. Death was not something to be feared, because Christ had shown the way to immortality.

Howard's religion gave him strength as a soldier; it also affected his manner of waging war. He believed that every soul was valuable in the sight of God. The humble slave, the private soldier, the orphaned child, all were children of God and brothers with Christ. Thus it was impossible for him to be indifferent to civilian suffering during the war. He constantly urged a persistent prosecution of the war as a means of ending the bloodshed, but he ardently opposed extremely vindictive measures that would bring suffering to innocents. As a Christian he had a large measure of compassion, never showing hatred for the enemy.

Howard's equipment for a successful military career, then, resulted from the mingling of several divergent elements. In the early days of the war, however, it was the West Point training which was his greatest asset. At least he knew something of military matters although in the ways of war most everyone was inexperienced, even the West Pointers.

There would be times when his discipline would react harshly on the independent Maine Yankees, or when his religious efforts would go unappreciated. The private soldier is traditionally critical of his officers. Abner Small of the Third Maine recorded his none-too-flattering impressions of the new colonel: "We saw a pale young man, taller than the governor, and slender, with earnest eyes, a high forehead, and a profusion of flowing moustache and beard. Howard talked down to us ('My men—') with the tone and manner of an itinerant preacher. He told us all about himself and his little family and the Ten Commandments." [6] Perhaps because of his inexperience, Howard seemed unaware that any of the men were not enthusiastic about their colonel; in fact he remarked to Lizzie that they seemed to love him.[7]

Since the government needed all available troops to meet the public demand for a move on Richmond, the regiment remained only a few days in Augusta. As was true of so many of the volunteer regiments of 1861, the Third Maine had the equipment if not the training, and so early on the morning of June 5 it started for the "front." A farewell speech by Governor Washburn, and farewells from the families of the departing heroes, some music from the band, the trains loaded and boarded, and the regiment moved away toward the south.[8] Friday evening, June 7, the Third Maine arrived in Washington and encamped the next day at Meridian Hill, a mile and a half north of the White House.[9]

Colonel Howard did his best during the next few weeks to drill his command and to prepare it for combat.[10] Then on July 6 came the order to cross the Potomac into Virginia to a new camp about three miles below Alexandria.[11] On the south side of the Potomac, Brigadier General Irvin McDowell was assembling an army and organizing it into brigades. Among those selected to command a brigade was Howard who had an advantage over many another colonel because of his West Point background which apparently outweighed political considerations.[12]

The pressure from public opinion gave McDowell much uneasiness. Politicians and unthinking patriots demanded action despite the fact that the Federal army was unready for battle. There just were no officers who knew how to handle large bodies of men and few who had seen much action. The best thing to do, McDowell knew, was to take time to drill his men and train his officers. But the Confederate Congress was to meet on July 20 in Richmond, and Lincoln, unable to resist any longer the clamor for an advance, finally ordered McDowell forward. McDowell concentrated his army at Centreville, twenty miles south and west of Washington and only a few miles from Beauregard's Confederate army at Manassas.

Howard's brigade of 3,000 men rested in the vicinity of Centreville all day Friday and Saturday, July 19 and 20, while McDowell was devising a way to get around the Confederate left. Bull Run, a sluggish little stream, ran between the two armies and, as McDowell finally planned the operation, he would cross a sizeable force over the stream to the west and seize an elevated position south of Bull Run on the left of the Confederate line.

The battle of Bull Run was fought on Sunday and Otis Howard did not like that one bit. It seemed wrong to him to profane the Sabbath. Nonetheless he was up with his men early on that fateful morning only to find that his brigade would have to wait several hours while other units took the road. The hot July sun beat down on the nervous and excited men. The brigade finally marched a few miles on a circuitous route only to be delayed again.

Meanwhile the battle had begun with an attack on the Confederate left and for several hours a hot fight went on for possession of the Henry House Hill. About the middle of the afternoon McDowell finally called on Howard's brigade in a desperate effort to gain the victory which was almost his. The brigade began a demoralizing march of several miles through the dust and heat with sights of battle becoming increasingly evident as they approached the field. The wounded were streaming back, crying out in pain, the blood spurting from wounds. Howard who was seeing these things for the first time felt his legs tremble. Then catching hold of himself he begged God that he might do his duty. The weakness left him and by the time they had reached the field he no longer felt any fear, nor did he again for the remainder of the war.

There was urgent need for Howard's brigade and his men were ordered to move up at the double-quick. But by the time Howard tried to form them before advancing up the hill against the Confederate line only about half the men were still in the ranks; the long march had taken a heavy toll. Howard got his first two regiments into line, the Second Vermont and Fourth Maine, and then formed a second line of the Third and Fifth Maine. By now the Confederates held undisputed possession of the hill and Howard's men attacked without any artillery or infantry support. He marched up the first line and, as he later described it, "got them well at work," and then went back for the second line. The attack was bravely made but futile. Seeing that it was useless to try the impossible, Howard ordered a withdrawal and the men gladly complied. Discipline soon broke down and in the wild retreat to Centreville neither Howard nor any of the officers could control the men whose sole thought was to find refuge.[13]

Bull Run was a demoralizing blow to the Union Army. In the days following the battle, Howard wrote of disheartened and sick soldiers, even of discouraged colonels. Not so Howard himself. He commented: "I am in hopes things will brighten soon. I do not lose heart. I try to rely upon the arm of strength." [14]

Howard's performance at Bull Run was hardly spectacular, but he carried out his assignment to everyone's satisfaction, and, all things considered, his brigade acquitted itself well. From West Point came encouraging words from Lizzie expressive of the general feeling of the North after the disaster, "The exaggerated accounts we received last evening were terrific. I find it not nearly so great a loss and disaster. In the language of war, I feel this will be avenged. It seems to be stirring all to more united feeling and action." [15]

The Union army in the vicinity of Washington did not engage in any major battle from July 1861 until the following April. This interval was a period of preparation, too little understood by the impatient citizens, but McDowell's successor George B. McClellan was a cautious commander and insisted on almost complete readiness before starting a forward movement.

Shortly after the middle of August, Howard was ordered back to his regiment. Its efficiency had declined during his absence, but in a few days he reported that "the rusty arms & the irregular & carelessness movements" were disappearing. Not only that, but he believed that the men, who at first had blamed him for all their troubles, were now beginning to appreciate him.[16]

In the meantime, Howard got his commission as brigadier general. His friends must have been working for him. Governor Washburn visited the Maine troops in McClellan's army on July 29 and of course Howard saw and talked with him.[17] About a week later, Senator Lot M. Morrill informed Howard that his name was on the list of those recommended for brigadier general, but that the Senate would probably not act before adjournment.[18] Some time after Washburn's return to Maine, Howard apparently wrote him in an attempt to correct any erroneous impressions that the governor might have received from dissatisfied soldiers and their families. Washburn's reply was most reassuring and at the same time he explained his part in recommending men for brigadier general. It appears that Washburn had, prior to Bull Run, recommended Major Henry Prince of the regular army but that "after yourself & Col. [Charles D.] Jameson [Second Maine] were known as candidates, I wrote a letter to the Sec'y of War doing justice to all, making no preference. . . . No one of all your friends would be more gratified than myself at your appointment." [19]

Howard had felt that being sent back to his regiment was a sign of disapproval. When Colonel John Sedgwick got the command of a brigade and reputedly was on his way to becoming a brigadier general, Howard was aware of a tinge of resentment. "I do not think I desire the promotion," he told his mother, "certainly not for itself, but I do not like any *implied* dereliction of duty, nor incapacity. . . . It is spiritually healthy to be disappointed once in a while when you find your heart beginning to desire worldly distinction—for its own sake." [20] The old conflict was again stirring.

When the commission finally did come, Howard wondered whether it was "better for the country, the cause of Christ & for my poor self to take or decline the position." [21] The indecision did not last long; two days later he accepted. Two weeks after his appointment he was relieved of command of his regiment. On leaving the Third Maine, Howard wrote a pompous farewell order, a stylistic descendent of his schoolboy diary and a sign of lingering immaturity which he later outgrew. The order read in part: "Genl. Howard owes much of worldly notice and position to this regt and he trusts he will never tarnish the reputation given him by any neglect or miscarriage on his part." [22] Finally on September 25 the War Department assigned him to what he described as "a first rate Brigade" in the division of General Silas Casey.[23] Howard was relieved to find that all the officers except those of a regiment from New Hampshire were strictly opposed to drinking. He developed a particular aversion to the use of liquor in the army and a few months later was greatly distressed when McClellan authorized the issuance of a ration of whiskey to the men.[24]

About the only duty that this brigade performed in two months' time was to supervise the fall elections in the lower counties of Maryland.[25] McClellan, giving up all idea of a fall campaign, continued to delay despite the proddings of Lincoln and the country. Howard chafed under inactivity. "Our present officers do not suit me in rapidity of movements," he complained. "I dont want to move blindly but I want to see more activity." [26] The dull routine of camp life was unbroken. It rained hard and the mud became so thick that an advance was now an impossibility.

Howard tried to make the best of things while in camp. In addition to giving his men as much military training as possible, he also tried to foster a religious atmosphere. He held nightly prayers in his tent for himself and any members of the staff who cared to be present; he saw that each regiment had religious services on Sunday, sometimes addressing the men himself if no chaplain was present; he visited the hospitals to pray with the sick and wounded and tried by his own example to raise the moral level of his troops.[27]

Howard's next opportunity to show his fitness for combat command came at the end of March 1862. He commanded a reconnaissance to the Rappahannock River, north of Fredericksburg.[28] The reconnaissance was an indication that at long last McClellan was on the move. From northern Virginia his vast Army of the Potomac was taking ship for the low lying Peninsula to begin a new campaign against Richmond.

Immediately after returning from the reconnaissance to the Rappahannock, Howard's brigade, attached now to the division of General Israel Richardson in General Edwin V. Sumner's 2d Corps, went on board ship at Alexandria and sailed down the Potomac River and Chesapeake Bay to the Peninsula.[29] There at Fortress Monroe McClellan was gathering his army and preparing an advance up the Peninsula between the York and James Rivers toward Richmond.

Prompt action by McClellan would have added greatly to the chances of success for his plan; but he was overcautious and his movements were exasperatingly slow. The days passed. It turned hot and the apple trees blossomed. The army came to a halt against the Confederate works at Yorktown, and Howard, like many others, became impatient. "There is no change in our position & that of the enemy," he wrote. "I dont know what Genl McClellan is doing—I wish he would wake up to the impatience of the country a little & make us move with a little more rapidity." [30] Then on May 4, writing that Sunday morning to his wife, Howard broke off his sentence to say that Yorktown had fallen.[31] Now the way was clear for the Army of the Potomac to move up the Peninsula. Shortly after, Howard commented on the manner in which McClellan had conducted operations thus far: "I believe *myself* & *have* that it would have been better for the country to have attacked the Yorktown works, the next day after arriving & I am sorry that the enemy could be executing a retreat from Wednesday till Sunday & Genl McClellan not know it. But I do not believe he lacks genius for his profession, but I think he inclines too much to *engineering*." [32] Some of the troops by-passed the muddy roads by taking ship to West Point, Virginia, up the York River from Yorktown. Sumner's corps of two divisions, under the command of Generals John Sedgwick and Israel Richardson, reached West Point on May 12 and Howard's brigade moved on to Eltham, about five miles beyond.[33]

Howard's first wartime reference to the slavery issue came in a letter written to his wife on May 17, 1862. Never more than a mild antislavery advocate, Howard still could see that the Negro might be an effective weapon in crushing the rebellion: "I believe if the rebels persevere in rebellion as in New Orleans even after they have a fair chance to return to their allegiance & it is so evidently their interest to do so, I believe the *bone* of contention will have to be destroyed. Genl Hunter has begun to arm & train the negroes under intelligent sergeants & corporals.[34] If every army in the field commences this process & encourages fugitives from 'secession' we shall strike a heavy blow. It will create hate but initiate a policy to weaken the enemy while it will encourage & elevate the black men." [35] Still, he wrote this in confidence and there is no evidence that Howard during the war belonged to the Radical group in the army.

McClellan's army was now so close to Richmond that a battle was almost inevitable. During the last days of May the men of Sumner's corps built two bridges across the Chickahominy in an effort to link the two parts of McClellan's army. On the south bank were the corps of Erasmus Keyes and Samuel P. Heintzelman, separated by a swampy river from the corps commanded by Sumner, Fitz-John Porter, and William B. Franklin. The Union army was in a dangerous position. This became even more precarious when heavy rains on May 30 made passage over the swollen waters of the Chickahominy increasingly hazardous.

About noon on the thirty-first the Confederates began the two-day battle of Fair Oaks by launching a major attack on the Union left. They drove it back with heavy loss and enjoyed a decided advantage for several hours. Sumner sent a reinforcing brigade to assist the hard-pressed troops of Keyes and Heintzelman and he was able to cross his whole command before the day's end. Sumner's prompt action enabled the Federal forces to stabilize the front and thwart the Confederate plan of crushing the Union left. The effort was renewed the following morning until a Federal counterattack forced the Confederate command to decide on a withdrawal.[86]

Howard's brigade had come up late on the afternoon of May 31 and had been placed in a supporting position. At dawn of the next morning Howard had his men in readiness for the expected Confederate attack with the Fifth New Hampshire serving as a skirmishing force in front of the brigade.

Richardson ordered Howard to close a gap in the line with one of his regiments. Soon after, the Confederates launched a determined attack and were having such success that Richardson had Howard throw in his two remaining regiments. Howard put himself in front of his troops and gave the order to advance. The enemy fire was especially severe but the men rose up and moved forward, Howard riding ahead. They had reached a point about thirty yards from the Confederate line when a bullet struck Howard's right elbow. A short time later his horse went down and another bullet hit Howard's right forearm near where the first wound was. He tried to keep going but as faintness began overtaking him he turned over the command and went to the rear to have his wound dressed. By this time it was 11:00 and the second day's battle of Fair Oaks was almost over.[37] The action on June 1 had been less intense than that of the previous day; nor was it any more decisive.

Howard's wounds were severe and there was little choice but to amputate his right arm midway between the elbow and the shoulder. An army surgeon did this about five that afternoon a mile or two behind the lines.[38] The next day, the General, his brother Charles, who also had been wounded, and the brigade adjutant, Frederick D. Sewall, went by freight car to White House Landing. Just as they were on the point of leaving up rode General Phil Kearny and his staff. Kearny had lost his left arm in the Mexican War and as he talked sympathetically with Howard about the loss of his arm, Howard apparently was in a joking mood, for he proposed to Kearny that in the future they buy their gloves together.[39] Using his left arm and in a hand almost impossible to read, Howard scratched a short, pathetic note to Lizzie: "Dearest I am on my way with only my left arm."[40] Howard's temporary absence meant that he missed the severe fighting of the Seven Days battles. It was to be his only extended leave during the four years of war.

During the last days of June, while McClellan's army fought on the Peninsula, Howard was rapidly recovering in Maine. Not that he remained inactive for long. He assisted the governor's recruiting campaign by making an extensive speaking tour throughout the state, urging enlistments and defending General McClellan who by this time had won the enmity of the extreme antislavery element. Then, at the time the Army of the Potomac was returning to northern Virginia from the Peninsula, Howard set out to rejoin his command.[41]

The military situation at the end of August 1862 was confusing in the extreme. John Pope's Army of Virginia was, for a time, in position along the Rappahannock River, between Richmond and Washington. Pope expected to detain the Confederates long enough for McClellan's Army of the Potomac to leave the Peninsula and return to northern Virginia for the defense of Washington.

Sumner's corps arrived at Aquia Creek, a short distance from Fredericksburg, on August 27,[42] the day after Stonewall Jackson's Confederates had first appeared between Pope's army and Washington. Howard joined General Sumner the same day. Another officer had taken his command shortly after Howard's departure, but Sumner gave him a brigade in the division of General John Sedgwick.[43]

The situation developing around Manassas, resulting in the second battle of Bull Run, brought an abrupt change in the plans for Sumner's corps. Hardly had it left ship at Aquia, when the order came to proceed to Alexandria.[44] The corps remained inactive at Alexandria until the evening of August 29 when, instead of reinforcing Pope, General Henry W. Halleck, the general-in-chief of the Union armies directing the troop movements from Washington, ordered it up the river toward the Chain Bridge to prevent a possible Confederate raid on the capital.[45] They carried out this order then retraced their steps to Fairfax Court House and finally marched to Centreville, near Manassas, arriving there about noon on August 31. By this time the battle was over and Sumner's corps had taken no part in the fighting though it had worn itself out in marching. Pope now believed that his only choice was to retreat within the fortifications of Washington, an admission of failure which, coupled with the recent defeats and general lack of confidence in him, cast gloom over the combined Armies of Virginia and of the Potomac. To have command of the rear guard of this retreating army was a depressing assignment, and the job fell to Howard. Some shelling from the Confederates was all that was encountered in that dismal night retreat through Vienna, across the Chain Bridge to Tenallytown in the District of Columbia.[46]

It had been hard campaigning for a man who had recently lost an arm and who had been away from active duty three months. Howard was fully aware of the trials he had been through, but he reported with pride his physical well-being: "I never underwent harder campaigning in my life than I did till I got to Tenallytown, sleeping on the ground, marching nearly all night for two or three nights in succession, eating *what* I could catch & *when* I could catch it, and added to this the responsibility of important commands of troops new to me—and yet I was perfectly well, rode my horse, scolded stragglers, rallied men in panic, & watched the enemy every whit as well as if I had two arms."[47]

Fellow officers of lesser rank could not but respect Howard's abilities. Early in September, shortly after McClellan had resumed command of the Army of the Potomac, some of the officers of Howard's old brigade recommended to McClellan that he promote Howard to the command of a division. "The undersigned officers of the Brigade lately commanded by Brig. Genl. O. O. Howard, do cordially recomend [sic] the appointment of that officer to the command of a Division, believing that if true merit be any qualification Gen'l Howard posseses [sic] it in an eminent degree. During the long period of our service with Genl. Howard, he exhibited in the camp and in the field, all the characteristics of a true soldier & a gentleman, & we do not believe any officer in the service has gained a firmer hold upon the respect & confidence of those under his command. . . ."[48] There follow signatures for thirty-six officers from lieutenant through colonel, including two who knew their business as well as any in the Army of the Potomac:

Edwin C. Cross, Colonel of the Fifth New Hampshire, and Francis T. Barlow, Colonel of the Sixty-first New York. These were men not then serving under Howard but who were still urging his appointment to the command of the corps' Second Division of which they were not a part.[49] The words "during the long period of our service with Genl. Howard" are of some importance. Howard was the type of commander who seldom elicited enthusiastic acceptance from the beginning. But by virtue of his ability, his bravery, his skill, and his concern for the command's welfare, he invariably won the type of affection and admiration illustrated by this letter.

At Tenallytown Howard could reflect on the recent change in command of the army which saw Pope give way to McClellan. "After I got to Centreville I came to the conclusion that General Pope lacked some of the first principles of a good general," Howard wrote in a letter to his wife. "I am heartily glad we are back to McClellan. He will not throw us away through sheer incompetency. He is the only man yet who has the love & confidence of this entire army."[50]

Division and Corps Command

On September 5, Sumner's corps marched northwest from Washington to Rockville, Maryland. Two days later it became generally known that Lee had crossed the Potomac into Maryland and had moved north as far as Frederick.[1]

Lincoln had restored McClellan to command of the troops in the vicinity of Washington and his presence did much to revive drooping spirits. Not only that, but the weather was delightful, the air clear and the days warm. As confidence replaced Howard's earlier lack of trust in McClellan, he began to share the army's enthusiasm at the return of Little Mac. "We cannot help feeling well about the matter," Howard reported from Middlebrook, west of Rockville, on September 10. "His fortifications saved Washington & his system gives us something to hope for, and for some indescribable reason the army loves him. Pope's reckless course has brought McClellan's caution into good repute."[2] Howard, as usual, never showed the slightest taint of political prejudice about any army officer or government official in his letters. He seemed to care little whether or not a man was an abolitionist, a Democrat, or a Republican. He asked of any army man only that he fear God, show devotion to duty, and display ability in the military profession. Pope did not measure up to these standards. Late in September he wrote to Mrs. Howard: "I have learned that Gen Pope has the reputation of being a liar, a profane swearer, & he certainly is a braggart and a failure. . . . I am now glad he has gone overboard & I hope God may spare us from such men."[3]

By the evening of September 14, Sumner's corps had arrived at the eastern end of Turner's Gap which Union troops had forced that day in the battle of South Mountain. The following day part of McClellan's army made contact with that portion of the Confederate army which Lee had with him around the town of Sharpsburg, Maryland on the west side of Antietam Creek.

On the afternoon of September 16 Hooker's corps crossed the

Antietam well above Sharpsburg and during the evening the 12th Corps followed. Hooker opened the battle of Antietam with a brief encounter with the troops occupying the left of the Confederate line, but night brought an end to the fighting. Hooker, under orders from McClellan to attack the Confederate left, renewed the battle very early on the morning of the seventeenth, but though he drove the Confederates through the cornfield between the East and the West Woods in the direction of Sharpsburg, his momentum was soon spent. The 12th Corps then came up to renew the attack. Like Hooker's men, those of the 12th Corps also gained some slight advantage, but at a fantastic price.

Meanwhile, Sumner, commanding the 2d Corps, had put Sedgwick's division in motion over much the same ground covered by the 1st and 12th Corps in their attacks. He formed the division into three double lines by brigades, each line separated from the others by about fifty yards. Through the East Wood, across the cornfield, and over the bodies of the dead and wounded, across the Hagerstown Pike they marched. The division plunged into the West Wood, a grove of oaks with no underbrush, moving straight ahead and completely alone. There was a lull in the fighting all along the front; so far the Confederates had offered no opposition. Sumner did not know that at this very moment strong reinforcements were advancing to the support of Stonewall Jackson who commanded the Confederate left. Howard's brigade was third in line, entering the east side of the wood as the lead brigade emerged on the west side. Just as this brigade was encountering some resistance both from infantry and artillery, the Confederate reinforcements struck the exposed left flank with terrific force, throwing that part of the Union line into great confusion. They also worked around to the rear of Howard's brigade. Many of the regiments were so badly disorganized that they hastily retreated northward on both sides of the Hagerstown Pike, and the efforts of the officers to rally the men were only partially successful.[4]

During this action, which took less than an hour, General Sedgwick was wounded and, by the time the retreat began, had turned over command of the division to Howard, the senior officer present.[5] The disastrous repulse of Sedgwick's division virtually ended the fighting on the extreme right of the Union line for the rest of the day. Later there was heavy action in the center and still later General Ambrose E. Burnside, commanding on the Union left, after long delay, succeeded in crossing the Antietam and forcing in Lee's right; but the timely arrival of Confederate reinforcements from Harpers Ferry prevented any decisive Union victory in that sector.

The battle of Antietam, one of the most significant engagements of the entire war, was a tactical draw but it ended as a strategic victory for McClellan's army. Lee waited a day and then withdrew to the Virginia side of the Potomac tacitly conceding the failure of his first invasion of the North. McClellan's victory gave Lincoln his chance to issue the preliminary announcement of the Emancipation Proclamation which had the effect of changing the character of the war. Antietam also caused the British government to hold off recognition of the Confederacy, a decision which turned out to be final.

Howard's role in this truly decisive battle was relatively minor, but the result was of some personal consequence for him. Not only did he emerge unscathed, but through the wounding of Sedgwick he had risen to the command of one of the best divisions in the Army of the Potomac.

During the remainder of September and into October, Sumner's 2d Corps rested and refitted at Bolivar Heights overlooking Harpers Ferry. The weather was generally good for campaigning but McClellan was, as usual, reluctant to move. About the middle of October, Howard became ill with a fever and took a short leave.[6] On November 8, the day after his return, he learned that Lincoln had removed McClellan from the command of the Army of the Potomac and had appointed Burnside in his place. That evening, from a point near Warrenton, Virginia, Howard confided to his brother Charles: "I should feel safer with McClellan to finish what he had planned & was executing so well. . . . I now feel sorry for McClellan. I fear we hav'nt a better man."[7] And the following day, after describing McClellan's farewell to the army, he wrote: "It is not possible to be associated with Genl McClellan and not love him."[8]

Burnside appeared to act with resolution. One of his first acts was to organize the army into three grand divisions under Sumner, Hooker and Franklin. Each grand division comprised two corps, Sumner having the 2d and 9th.[9]

Howard's division left Warrenton on November 15 and reached Falmouth on November 17. Falmouth is a village on the north side of the Rappahannock slightly above and across from Fredericksburg. Burnside had expected to seize Fredericksburg and its commanding heights, but the pontoon bridges did not arrive with the army and he did not dare risk a crossing without them. Each day of delay gave Lee that much more time to assemble his army and to fortify his position behind Fredericksburg. By December 2, Howard began to show just a touch of impatience: "However we may get impatient," he wrote, "God's ways are not always our ways and he will doubtless regulate us to his own praise. I feel that I am too little dependent on Him, too disposed to be ambitious." [10]

If Howard was becoming ambitious it might have been because of the rumors of his promotion to the rank of major general. Governor Washburn had visited the army during the middle of November [11] and upon his return to Maine had written Howard that he had said a good word for him "in the right place." According to Washburn, who stopped in Washington on his way home, Howard had the reputation "in high quarters" of being "one of the special favorites, pets & confidants" of McClellan, a political conservative who disapproved of Lincoln's Emancipation Proclamation. The Governor continued: "I was glad that I had it in my power to state . . . your precise *status,* & your true opinions, not alone recently, but uniformly for many months, expressed to me, so that I felt that you were now rectus in curia." He indicated that Howard would have his chance after General Hiram G. Berry, another of Maine's favorite sons, had become a major general, and concluded: "I have not the slightest doubt that your great merit will be recognized by the President & Sec'y at an early day, by your nomination . . . as Major General. Whatever I can do to bring about a result so just to you & wise in the Admn will not be neglected." [12]

This letter reveals that Howard had no difficulty in obtaining that political support so helpful in military promotion. This is further supported by a letter from some of Maine's leading politicians to the President, in which Vice President Hamlin, Senator Morrill, and Maine's entire Congressional delegation, all Republicans, urged Lincoln to promote Berry and Howard to the rank of major general.[13] Nor was Howard dependent solely upon political influence for his position in the army. The foe of the Radicals, General McClellan, had on October 27, 1862, recommended him along with seven others to the adjutant general for promotion to major general.[14]

Perhaps to counteract the impression among influential men that he was in sympathy with McClellan's opposition to emancipation, Howard veered around to a stronger antislavery position, as is indicated in his letter of December 7. From snow-covered Falmouth, he wrote his mother: "It is very possible . . . that the very incompetency of our leaders is God's way of blessing the nation. Why? because his object is to humble, disenthral & purify the nation & ours merely to prevent disruption. Slavery, which has given us so much trouble must 'go by the board.' " [15]

He could leave such matters to the nation's civilian leaders. It was the military situation which was his deepest concern. The pontoons at last arrived and Burnside could proceed with his plan. It was to cross Franklin's grand division a short distance below Fredericksburg and Sumner's directly opposite the town. Hooker's center grand division would be sent across as the exigencies of the moment dictated. On Thursday morning, December 11, Howard's men left their camp about half past six and moved down to the river. The Confederate sharpshooters on the opposite bank made things so hot for the engineers trying to lay a pontoon bridge that they had to scurry for safety. The day was almost gone when the commander of a Michigan regiment volunteered to take his men across in boats. Howard agreed to the plan and in a short time this regiment, quickly followed by three more, cleared out the sharpshooters' positions and made it possible for the engineers to complete their pontoon bridge. By night all of Howard's division had crossed and had taken possession of that part of Fredericksburg closest to the river.

When day dawned on December 12 Howard threw forward two brigades and took over the whole town and the ground beyond to the base of the hills which rise just south of Fredericksburg. That day the rest of Franklin's men crossed downstream from the town and the various units of Sumner's grand division took up position in and about Fredericksburg.[16]

The battle of Fredericksburg, on December 13, 1862, was two separate battles fought independently by Franklin and Sumner. Franklin, on the left, made only slight headway against Jackson's corps and in general the fighting in that sector was a defeat for the Union army. Burnside, when he thought that Franklin's attack was well underway, ordered Sumner at about 11:00 A.M. to seize the heights above the town.[17] Between the town and the heights, however, lay a drainage canal and the famous sunken road, the latter heavily manned by determined Confederates. Behind and above the road were more infantry and the artillery.

To storm and take such a position with frontal assaults was beyond human power. Yet acting under Burnside's orders, Sumner threw his men, brigade after brigade, against the Confederate works. First William H. French and then Winfield S. Hancock sent their divisions into the battle while Howard waited in the town. Just before one, Darius Couch, 2d Corps commander, ordered him to support Hancock, which he did with his three brigades. None of the attacks that day, including Howard's, ever reached, much less broke, the Confederate line. There were other attacks by some of Hooker's grand division later but they ended the same way.[18]

Darkness brought an end to the fighting, and though it was not known at the time, an end to the battle, for Burnside withdrew his army across the river the night of the fifteenth. In his report Sumner praised Howard's "judicious disposition" in driving the Confederates from Fredericksburg.[19] Couch, in speaking of the corps' losses, stated: "Howard, coming up late, lost 700 men, besides 150 on the 11th. He did well the part assigned to him." [20] This last statement summarizes Howard's conduct at Fredericksburg.

During the rest of that winter and well into the spring, the Army of the Potomac lay in camp north of the Rappahannock. There was little activity and Howard found time to fulminate about the dissident elements in the North. On the first day of the new year he wrote to Lizzie: "I have felt such a burden for my country, that I have written a hasty article to the times. . . ." [21] The letter to the *Times* confirms the change which had taken place in Howard's thinking apparent in what he wrote his mother on December 7, 1862. While never an out-and-out abolitionist, he now had come around to a stand which undoubtedly reflected the sentiment of many in the North, that slavery would have to go. Howard's promotion was pending and he possibly believed that promotion came more rapidly to those officers who upheld the administration's stand on emancipation. In view of the evident misconceptions prevalent in high circles indicated in Washburn's letter of the previous month, he might have been using this unorthodox method to clarify his position. The letter, printed in the New York *Times* on January 16, 1863, was a plea for an end to apathy at home and for a realization on the part of the home front that the enemy was resolute and unwilling to have peace until the country should be destroyed. Since the rebels would not give up because they insisted on maintaining slavery, then, said Howard, let us have an end to slavery.[22]

If self-interest was a reason for writing the letter Howard might well have saved himself the trouble because, on the same day it was printed, Lincoln sent to the Senate the names of eighteen officers recommended for the rank of major general. Seven of these, incuding Howard, had been on McClellan's list the previous October. In every instance of nomination, report, and confirmation, Howard's name was simply one of a large group, and the Senate apparently confirmed without debate the decision of the President and the Military Affairs Committee.[23]

How much Howard's promotion was the result of political influence, how much the result of recognition of military ability is a matter of speculation. Probably, the influence which he could command was important, but his West Point affiliation and his record in the war were equally, if not more, significant. The army commanders, the Secretary of War, the President, and the Senate had given him only the same consideration as had been accorded a good many other officers. Obviously, Howard was not of sufficient rank or political importance to excite any surprise at his promotion, or to become the center of any controversy.

Late in January, before the Senate had acted on Lincoln's appointments, the President named a new commander of the Army of the Potomac, Major General Joseph Hooker. The country generally approved the change. After Howard had paid Hooker a visit and had received what he called a very warm reception, he revised an earlier hostile opinion of the new commander.[24] Acknowledging that Hooker had always been very friendly toward him, he went on to describe him to Lizzie, as handsome, manly, affable, and self-confident. He especially approved Hooker's strong loyalty to the cause.[25] With the advent of Fighting Joe Hooker the Army of the Potomac took on new life. Under his guidance, the army increased in efficiency and morale. There was little pressure on him for any advance during the winter months, so he had time to perfect his organization.

During this period of preparation and waiting Howard found time to make a quick visit home and to get an artificial arm fitted in Philadelphia. He was quite hopeful of the effects of the new arm, but it proved unsatisfactory.[26] Always, from then on, the empty right sleeve was a distinguishing mark and a symbol of his heroism.

On his return to the army Howard faced a new problem. In a reorganization order of February 5, 1863, Hooker had assigned Daniel E. Sickles to temporary command of the 3d Corps.[27] Sickles was Howard's junior in rank and Howard's pride got the better of his humility. He expressed his objections to Hooker and was promised the 11th Corps provided General Franz Sigel, the Corps' commander, was ordered elsewhere.[28] A short time later Howard received the command.[29]

Perhaps in his anxiety to receive a command commensurate with his rank he had failed to consider all the consequences. Not only would there be increased responsibility, but the 11th Corps presented peculiar difficulties. In the first place, it had a large proportion of German or German-speaking men.[30] These were warmly attached to their former commander, Sigel, who, they thought, had been wronged.[31] Moreover, the 11th Corps had only recently become a part of the Army of the Potomac and was looked upon by the older units with some disdain, despite its having seen considerable action.[32] Finally, a campaign was in the offing and there would be little time for Howard to come to know the officers and men.

Almost immediately upon taking command he became aware that the Germans were behaving cooly toward him. He believed that he could in time gain their confidence, and after about two weeks with the 11th Corps he began to think that he was doing well. President Lincoln came down from Washington for a review of some of the troops and Howard was very pleased by the showing his men made.[33] Yet if he believed that he had already won the confidence of the 11th Corps he was mistaken. The forthcoming campaign culminating in the battle of Chancellorsville would bear this out.

Chancellorsville and Gettysburg

Hooker's Chancellorsville campaign began on April 27 when three of his corps, with the Eleventh in the lead, marched several miles up the Rappahannock, crossed that stream and also the Rapidan, and prepared to descend on Fredericksburg and Lee's army from the west. Other units of the Army of the Potomac followed.[1] General John Sedgwick's 6th Corps remained on the north side of the Rappahannock opposite Fredericksburg ready to cross the river and assault Lee from the rear should the Confederate commander move out to face Hooker.

Hooker, accompanying the flanking portion of the army, on May 1 issued orders for a general advance from his position near Chancellorsville eastward toward Fredericksburg.[2] Hardly had the men set out from camp than Hooker changed his mind and ordered his army to return to its old position of the night before.[3] By ordering the withdrawal Hooker not only failed to get his army out of the thick undergrowth of the Wilderness into relatively open terrain and nearer to Sedgwick's force at Fredericksburg, but, worse still, he surrendered the initiative to his adversary. Had Hooker retained the initiative, the absence of most of his cavalry under General George Stoneman on a raiding expedition in Lee's rear would not have been so serious. Without the cavalry as a scouting and screening force he was courting disaster.[4] The evening of May 1 thus saw the Union army back where it had encamped the night before. The 11th Corps held the right of the line which did not have any natural resting place such as a river or hill to protect the flank. The Rappahannock secured the left of the Union line, but the right of Howard's position was more than two miles from the Rapidan and simply ended in the Wilderness.

Hooker inspected Howard's part of the line early on the morning of Saturday, May 2. On returning to his headquarters at Chancellorsville he learned that the enemy had been seen passing to the west across his front. These troops were Jackson's men bound by a circuitous route to the right and rear of the 11th Corps.[5] At 9:30 Hooker had an aide send an order to Howard and General Henry W. Slocum (commanding the 12th Corps) directing them to be prepared for an attack from the west and reminding Howard that his position needed to be strengthened by additional artificial defenses. The order also directed that pickets be advanced to obtain timely information.[6] This order and a similar one sent just to Howard became the subject of much controversy.[7] Howard claims never to have received these orders, although Carl Schurz, commanding the 11th Corps' Third Division, relates in detail in his reminiscences the circumstances of their receipt.[8] In any event, this was the last time that Hooker expressed any concern for the right of his line. Also, Howard sent a message to Hooker at 10:50 A.M. that he was "taking measures to resist an attack from the west," which indicated that at that time Howard was aware of the danger.[9]

Hooker soon became convinced that Lee, instead of planning to attack the Union right, was actually retreating. He found ample evidence for this belief: the statements of deserters, the direction of Jackson's march which could be interpreted as a retreat to Gordonsville, the expectation that Lee would retreat as a result of the operation of Stoneman's cavalry against Lee's communications, and reports from Fredericksburg that the Confederates were retreating from there.[10] Hooker had all along expected a retreat, so it is not surprising that he interpreted the reports of Confederate columns moving to the west as a withdrawal.

General Daniel Sickles, commanding the 3d Corps, also believed that the enemy was retreating, for about 11:00 A.M. he asked Hooker's permission to harass the Confederate column moving past his front. Hooker readily consented,[11] and later that afternoon he gave positive orders to Howard to detach Francis Barlow's brigade, the only reserve for the 11th Corps, and send it to Sickles' assistance.[12] These orders from Hooker indicate that the commanding general no longer had any fears for the safety of his right flank, and Howard shared the misconception of his chief.[13]

During the day and especially in the late afternoon warnings came to the men and officers of the 11th Corps that the Confederates were doing something other than retreating.[14] There is no reason to disbelieve Howard's statement that reports from subordinates of Confederate activity in their vicinity were passed along to Hooker,[15] but since both Howard and Hooker believed that Lee was retreating this information merely seemed to strengthen their case. Some of the lower-ranking officers of the 11th Corps, however, did not hold to this belief. Consequently, Jackson's attack, though a surprise to Howard, Hooker, Sickles, and others was not unexpected by a considerable number of those in the 11th Corps who had had ample warning of the impending onslaught.[16]

Convinced that Hooker's sources of information were better than his own, Howard made what appears to be inadequate preparation for an attack from the west. He later wrote in his report: "Our front was covered with rifle-pits and abatis." He also claimed to have taken precautions against a surprise: "During Saturday, the 2d, . . . general [Alexander Schimmelfennig] made frequent reconnaissances. Infantry scouts and cavalry patrols were constantly pushed out on every road." [17] Probably Howard did do all that he reported. Yet that was not enough in view of the vulnerability of his part of the line. The rifle pits and abatis mainly faced the south; the officers in command of the reconnaissances must not have been very aggressive; furthermore Howard did not give credence to the reports of his subordinates, nor did he protest personally to the army commander against having his only reserve removed.

By 5:00 P.M. all was in readiness for disaster. At about 5:15, or a little later, Jackson's 26,000 men began their attack. Some of the 11th Corps had their arms stacked and were preparing supper when the attack commenced, but they had time to seize their guns and take their assigned places.[18] From his position behind the lines Howard caught the sound of skirmish firing. Realizing what might be happening he rushed to the scene only to be met by a crowd of fugitives fleeing from the rapidly advancing Confederates. Efforts to stem the tide were futile. Two of Howard's divisions had quickly collapsed and, while some of the men bravely tried to make a stand, others fled in panic.[19] Near corps headquarters Howard was able to form about 5,000 men for a stand against Jackson's on-rushing veterans. This line held for about twenty minutes until it too was overwhelmed in front and on the flanks.[20]

The time was now a little after six. In the gathering dusk of the Wilderness, regimental and even company organization disintegrated, adding greatly to the task of reforming the men for another stand. Still intact was Adolph Buschbeck's brigade which now formed behind the rifle pits constructed for the reserve. Around this nucleus Howard gathered remnants of other brigades, in all about 4,000 men. Here also he placed some pieces of artillery. This so-called Buschbeck line held perhaps a little more than half an hour, though Howard himself put the time at only fifteen minutes. In any event, this last-ditch stand of the 11th Corps held off the Confederate advance for a considerable time.[21] Each minute was valuable for Sickles discovered what had happened in his right-rear and had begun to withdraw from his advanced position; Hooker was able to make preparations for defending Chancellorsville; and night was fast coming on. So far the 11th Corps had fought alone and had resisted an overwhelming force for almost two hours, yielding in that time about one mile.

When the Bushbeck line collapsed the next rallying point was another mile away at a clearing with the high-sounding name of Fairview just west of Chancellorsville. Already formed there was a strong line of artillery and General Hiram G. Berry's division of Sickles' 3d Corps. These men, the remnants of the 11th Corps and other units from the 12th Corps made a strong line and the Confederate advance stalled in the face of this formidable opposition. Further advance was almost out of the question because of the disorganization of the Confederate force and the confusion of the half light of dusk. Stonewall Jackson received his fatal wound at about this time and although he earnestly desired to push on there was little chance for a successful attack.[22]

Late in the evening, with the situation fairly well stabilized, the 11th Corps moved to a position on the left of the line.[23] It had done practically all the fighting on Saturday, May 2, and had sustained about three-fourths of the Union losses that day. Many of its men had fled in panic, but as many or more had fought stubbornly against hopeless odds. Still, that evening's battle tarnished for all time the reputation of the 11th Corps, and to a large extent, that of its commander.

Severe but indecisive fighting occurred on May 3 and 4. Then on Tuesday, the fifth, Hooker decided to withdraw across the Rappahannock even though at a council of war on the night of May 4–5 the corps commanders had voted to stay on the south side of the river.[24] Howard was one of those who voted to stay and fight. His decision was in keeping with the policy he maintained throughout the war, of forcing the fight on the enemy, although in this instance there may have been a desire to vindicate the reputation of the 11th Corps.[25]

Hooker thus acknowledged defeat and in a letter to Lincoln,

written on May 7, intimated that the rout of the 11th Corps was responsible for the loss of the campaign.[26] Hooker was not being honest. He might well have salvaged victory even after the defeat of the 11th Corps. At the close of the fighting on Saturday, Jackson had not attained his objective and the two portions of Lee's army were still separated. Hooker had a great numerical superiority, and a resolute and unshaken commander might have turned defeat into victory at Chancellorsville. His position was stronger on Sunday, May 3, than it had been the day before.[27] It is quite possible, then, that the disaster to his right so unnerved Hooker that he was unable to regain the initiative from Lee, and that despite numerous advantages in his favor, he was shaken to the point of irresolution.[28]

Even though the responsibility for the loss of the campaign was Hooker's, this does not absolve Howard from responsibility for the fate of the 11th Corps. Surprise in battle is not easily written off, and he deserves at least some of the severe criticism of a great majority of Civil War historians. With numerous warnings coming to him throughout the morning and afternoon, he might well have anticipated an attack on his right and rear instead of falling into the error of believing that Lee was retreating. The 11th Corps obviously was not prepared as well as it might have been for an attack from any direction, especially from the west, and this was Howard's responsibility. Nor did he do everything that might have been done to discover the location of the Confederate force.[29] As a new corps commander he should not have been so complacent as he evidently was; and holding a vital part of the line, he should not have been so willing to rely upon his commander's conclusion that Lee was retreating.

Had Howard anticipated Jackson's attack, the 11th Corps undoubtedly would have made a far better showing than it did. Howard, then, was guilty of poor judgment. But this is far different from willful disobedience of orders or of gross negligence. If Howard had been guilty of dereliction of duty, of failure to obey orders, or of any negligence, Hooker could have brought charges against him. Such action was not unknown during the Civil War. The Joint Committee on the Conduct of the War eager to absolve Hooker, its favorite general, of all blame, had no word of censure for Howard.[30] Thus it is unlikely that politics had anything to do with Howard's escaping official condemnatory action. Years later Howard wrote: "My Army Commander at the time had no censure for me. I was not put under arrest. I was not investigated. I was not relieved from the Command of the Corps." [31] Yet Hooker lost little time in relieving from duty a brigadier general of cavalry, William Averell, for "culpable indifference and inactivity." [32]

Though Howard never conceded that he was in any way negligent, he once hinted that at Chancellorsville he was inexperienced and that there he learned a lesson. "When a lad, a larger boy gave me a drubbing, but I grew in size and strength till he could do it no longer. The war experience of some of us was like that." [33] Never again would Howard be surprised as he was at Chancellorsville.[34]

The next weeks were especially difficult for Howard. The newspapers seized on the rout of the 11th Corps and published many distorted accounts of the events of May 2.[35] The New York *Herald*, for instance, castigated Howard along with division commander Carl Schurz when it declared that the two of them were responsible for the "disorderly flight" of the 11th Corps.[36] "My Corps is much abused, but I think in a high degree unjustly," Howard complained to his wife. "I am conscious of having neglected no precaution. . . ." [37]

At Hooker's request Howard went to Washington on May 20 to see Lincoln, Secretary of War Edwin M. Stanton, Halleck, and others. Hooker had conferred with Lincoln a few days earlier and had agreed that his corps commanders should visit Washington and give the President firsthand accounts of the battle.[38] Howard did go to Washington and did call on Lincoln. "Charlie & I met the President in his grounds before breakfast," wrote Howard two days later. "He appointed a meeting with me after breakfast. . . . After about half an hour Chas. & I visited the President. He had a good deal to say about the campaign of nine days & a good many questions to ask. We saw then nearly all the Secretaries—of whom Secretary Chase is my friend & favorite. Then we called on the Sec. of War at his office. . . . I was very warmly received at Washington." [39] (Howard probably did not know that his "friend and favorite," Secretary Salmon P. Chase, had on the fourteenth written Hooker urging the restoration of Sigel in place of Howard, who was said to interfere with "the German ways of the soldiers, from motives of religious duty. . . ." [40]) The outcome of all this agitation was, for the present, nothing. Neither Hooker, Stanton, nor Lincoln considered the matter of sufficient importance to dismiss, or transfer Howard, to bring charges against him, or to break up the 11th Corps. Howard's previous record was such that these men could not seriously embrace the theory that he had been willfully negligent.

The furor over Chancellorsville did not last long. Lee, having reorganized and reinforced his army, was preparing an advance early in June. It took Hooker several days to divine Lee's intent, and it was not until June 12 that the 11th Corps left its camp and marched to Catlett's Station in the vicinity of Warrenton.[41] This was the beginning of the campaign which would culminate in the decisive battle of Gettysburg.

It was during this northward march that Howard received a letter from one of the leading figures of the Republican party in Maine, Nathan A. Farwell, the president of the state senate. The state convention was to meet on July 1, and the party leaders were still looking for a candidate for governor. Washburn, having served two terms, had voluntarily stepped down at the start of 1863. His successor, Abner Coburn, had defeated his Democratic opponent by only a small majority and was evidently not in the good graces of men like Farwell who sought a more attractive candidate.[42] Farwell's letter of June 12 to Howard and one from a Portland citizen, F. B. Gilman, in April, urged him to accept the candidacy.[43] If these flattering offers tempted Howard to enter the uncertain field of politics, he resisted the temptation.[44] The Maine Republicans went ahead with their convention, nominated another man (who won), and never again approached Howard.[45]

On June 24, the same day that Howard wrote to Farwell refusing the nomination, the 11th Corps resumed its march over the Potomac into Maryland and camped at Middletown, just west of Frederick. By this time a part of Lee's army was already in Pennsylvania, causing much confusion there and much anxiety in Washington. While other corps of the Army of the Potomac moved across into Maryland, the Left Wing (1st, 3d and 11th Corps, and John Buford's cavalry division), under the command of John Reynolds, sought intelligence of Lee's army. From Middletown the 11th Corps marched to Frederick and thence to Emmitsburg on June 29.[46] Buford's cavalry and the 1st Corps held the advance position while the rest of the Army of the Potomac was to the south and east.

George G. Meade was now in command, having replaced Hooker on the twenty-eighth, but there is no comment from Howard on the change. It may be assumed that he was happier serving under Meade. Shortly after Chancellorsville, Howard had written to his brother,

Rowland, revealing his personal mistrust of Hooker believing him to be "impure." He hoped that God might convert Hooker's soul.[47]

On June 30, Howard and the 11th Corps were at Emmitsburg; Reynolds with the 1st was some miles in advance along the road to Gettysburg; Buford's cavalry division was already there. Meade's order to Reynolds, sent at 11:30 on the morning of the thirtieth, indicates that the commanding general was aware that the Confederates were advancing eastward from Chambersburg. Meade's order stated that in the event either Reynolds or Howard encountered the enemy's advance they should withdraw to Emmitsburg to which place he would send reinforcements. He was trying, he said, to ascertain the whereabouts of the enemy. "In the meantime, if they advance against me, I must concentrate at that point where they show the strongest force." [48]

Howard was fully acquainted with Meade's orders to Reynolds. He spent the evening of the thirtieth with the latter at a farmhouse on the road between Emmitsburg and Gettysburg, arriving in time for supper. The officers and their staffs had what Howard called "a cheerful conversation on ordnance tactics" while eating, after which he and Reynolds conferred privately to discuss Meade's latest orders. They momentarily expected to receive additional instructions for the following day. When, by late in the evening, none had arrived, Howard bade Reynolds good night and rode back to Emmitsburg.[49]

At eight on the morning of July 1, Howard at Emmitsburg received an order from Reynolds to move up to Gettysburg. The men were all ready to march, and no time was lost in setting them in motion. Howard rode on ahead of the troops to see where Reynolds wanted his corps to camp. Approaching Gettysburg on the Emmitsburg road, he soon realized that a battle was in progress. Off to the west of the town Confederate troops of A. P. Hill's command were engaged with Buford's cavalry and a part of the 1st Corps. It was then about 11:30.[50]

Howard immediately sent word to his command, at Reynolds' direction, to move up to Gettysburg as rapidly as possible and in the meantime he had an opportunity to survey the field from the roof of one of the buildings in the town. Either while there, or just before entering the town, word came that Reynolds had been killed.[51] This meant that Howard, as the senior officer present, was in command of the Left Wing of the army and of the troops then engaged.

Quickly Howard made arrangements for the 11th Corps then

approaching Gettysburg. He directed Schurz, now in command of the corps, to send two divisions through the town to the right of the 1st Corps, and the remaining division, that of Adolph von Steinwehr, to take up a position on Cemetery Hill, south of the town. He also directed part of his corps artillery to be placed on this eminence.[52]

Why did Howard leave one-third of the corps more than a mile from the scene of the action? Obviously, he realized that superior numbers might overwhelm his command before further reinforcements could reach him, and he could easily see that the open country west and north of the town was not suitable for defensive fighting. It would therefore be prudent to have a strong position to which he could withdraw his forces.[53] The wisdom of this decision became readily apparent, for shortly after Steinwehr took up his position on Cemetery Hill, first Rodes' and later Early's division of Richard S. Ewell's corps began to appear on the field, giving the Confederates great numerical superiority.

Howard dispatched staff officers to Sickles and to Slocum asking them to bring up their corps as rapidly as possible. For a time the 1st and 11th Corps more than held their own against the Confederate force opposing them, but as the warm afternoon progressed more gray-clad brigades of Rodes' and Early's divisions appeared on the field. The position north and west of the town, held all day, was becoming untenable with each passing minute. From the Cemetery Howard watched as all along the line the Confederates renewed the attack with great vigor. When the position no longer could be held, Howard ordered a withdrawal to the prepared position on Cemetery Hill, and after the right of the 11th Corps had given way completely, Howard sent Charles R. Costar's brigade from the Cemetery to cover the retreat through the town.[54]

During these terrible moments when the retreat was in progress, Howard was anxiously looking for some sign of the arrival of the 12th Corps. The troops of this corps should have been arriving just at that time. Sickles' 3d Corps was too far away to be of any immediate assistance, but where was Slocum? His corps was close by and though Slocum was Howard's senior and therefore not subject to his order, the emergency was such, and Meade's orders loose enough, that Howard could reasonably expect help from the 12th Corps when it was most needed. Eight days after the battle, Charles Howard wrote: "He [General Howard] had hoped that Slocum would come up to

CHANCELLORSVILLE AND GETTYSBURG 53

assist in the retreat as he was but 2 miles away but he was too willing to demonstrate the fitness of his name *Slow come.* In fact refused to come up in person saying *he would not assume the responsibility of that day's fighting* & of those two corps." [55] It appears, however, that Slocum did order his divisions forward to Gettysburg, and their arrival late in the afternoon not only was a welcome sight to the discouraged Union forces on Cemetery Hill, but probably was a factor in Ewell's failure to attack that position.[56]

During the confusion of the retreat there was the possibility of a Confederate attack on Cemetery Hill where now the only fresh troops were Orland Smith's brigade of Steinwehr's division. But Howard's foresight of the morning became apparent, for the batteries, protected by earthworks, could come into action. Captain Michael Wiedrich, in command of an 11th Corps battery, sent a few well-directed shots into a Confederate force moving menacingly toward the left of the Federal position on Cemetery Hill, giving warning of what could be expected should the enemy attempt to storm the heights.[57] Howard also ordered Buford's cavalry to take position to the west of the town to cover the left of the retreating 1st Corps.[58] Whether or not an offensive action by Ewell at that time would have been successful is one of those questions which will never be decided, but there is reason to believe that Ewell made the right decision in not attacking.[59] Thus with the completion of the retreat through the town, during which the Confederates captured several thousand prisoners, the fighting for the day was about over.

While the fragments of the two corps were falling back to the Cemetery in the dust and smoke of the waning afternoon, and while Howard and other officers were making strenuous efforts to reorganize them, a new figure appeared on the scene. It was General Winfield S. Hancock, commander of the 2d Corps. He announced to Howard that Meade had sent him to take command, to which Howard protested, calling attention to his own seniority in rank. Hancock then offered to show Howard Meade's written order, but Howard declined and closed the discussion by suggesting that it was not time for argument, and that Hancock see to the left of the line (the part occupied by the 1st Corps) while he would take care of the right. Hancock did not press the question of command and with good grace took Howard's suggestion. The two generals worked together harmoniously reforming the lines until Slocum, senior to both, arrived on the field early in the evening.

Meade, at Taneytown, on learning of Reynolds' death at 1:10 P.M., had sent Hancock ahead to assume command of the 11th, 1st, and 3d Corps, and to advise him on the suitability of Gettysburg as a site for the inevitable battle with Lee.[60] Meade probably was aware that Hancock was junior to Howard, but evidently he wanted someone who was well acquainted with his plans to represent him on the field. There is also the possibility, though this is nowhere to be found in any of Meade's words, that Meade had greater faith in his fellow Pennsylvanian than in Howard. Yet, by the time Hancock reached the Cemetery, the action for the day was substantially over, and it made little difference who actually commanded those few hours after about 4:00 when Hancock first arrived.[61]

Hancock, an inspirational leader, rendered valuable service in restoring the confidence of the men.[62] It also seems certain that Hancock ordered Wadsworth's division of the 1st Corps to occupy strategic Culps Hill, thus foiling a Confederate attempt to do the same later in the evening. Yet, Howard's dispositions—placing the artillery, adequately guarded by fresh troops, on Cemetery Hill; stationing skirmishers and sharpshooters on the outskirts of the town; and sending Buford's cavalry to the left—were all decisive factors in discouraging a Confederate attack. Hancock's presence was not of primary importance. His foresight in occupying Culps Hill was of tremendous consequence later on, but not at that particular moment.

Howard acted as if he were in command even after Hancock's arrival. At 5:00 he wrote Meade a dispatch reviewing the events of the day up to that hour. It was a fairly accurate account although Howard made only a brief reference to the retreat and did not indicate the extent of his defeat and losses.[63] Hancock quite correctly believed himself to be in command. At 5:25 he wrote to Meade's chief of staff, General Daniel Butterfield, that he had arrived at Gettysburg an hour before and that at that time the Federal troops had already abandoned the town and that they were now holding a strong position at the Cemetery. Hancock went on to tell Meade that though the right could be turned the 12th Corps was coming up just then to secure that part of the line.[64]

When Slocum appeared both Hancock and Howard turned over the command to him with rather ridiculous formality. Meade, perhaps unwittingly, added further to Howard's humiliation by sending a message at 6:00 P.M. addressed to Major Generals Hancock and Abner Doubleday (no mention of Howard), announcing that if General Slocum were present ("and I hope he is") he of course would take command.[65] Some time that evening, Howard sent a message to Meade which certainly was justified under the circumstances: "General Hancock's order, in writing, to assume command reached here at 7. At that time, General Slocum being present, having just arrived at this point, I turned over the command to him. . . . I believe I have handled these two corps to-day from a little past 11 until 4, when General H[ancock] assisted me in carrying out orders which I had already issued, as well as any of your corps commanders could have done. Had we received reenforcements a little sooner, the first position assumed by General Reynolds, and held by General Doubleday till my corps came up, might have been maintained; but the position was not a good one, because both flanks were exposed, and a heavy force approaching from the northern roads rendered it untenable, being already turned, so that I was forced to retire the command to the position now occupied, which I regard as a very strong one. The above has mortified me and will disgrace me. Please inform me frankly if you disapprove of my conduct to-day, that I may know what to do."[66]

So the day ended on a discordant note for General Howard. He had fought what he considered a satisfactory battle under adverse conditions and had seen the enemy halted in front of the strong position on Cemetery Hill which he himself had selected. Now it appeared as if he had won only the disapproval of his commander, and had to undergo the humiliation of having an officer his junior sent to supersede him. Early on the morning of July 2, Meade at last arrived at Gettysburg and with Howard and others examined the position held by the Union army.

On the second, the 11th Corps, which held Cemetery Hill to the right of the center of the Union line, was not engaged until the very end of the day. The principal action had taken place on the Union left, but toward sundown Ewell's corps, facing the Union right, delivered two attacks. The first was by Edward Johnson's division against the 12th Corps on Culps Hill; the second against Cemetery Hill by Jubal Early. The latter was an attack by two brigades against the position held by Howard's 11th Corps. The assault was temporarily successful, but timely assistance sent by Hancock ended its threat. By this time darkness had covered the field and the fighting ceased on this second day of the battle of Gettysburg. Lee had gained some slight advantage at either end of the line, but the Union army was still holding its position.

That night Meade held a council of war in his headquarters, a small frame house a short distance to the rear of the line. Present were Daniel Butterfield, his chief of staff, the corps commanders, and some division commanders. Meade put three questions to his principal officers: should the army stay where it was or retire; if it was decided to remain, should the army attack or await attack by the enemy; and if the decision was to await attack, how long should they wait? All voted to remain, and it was the general opinion that they should await attack. Howard's vote was to remain, to await attack until 4 P.M. the next day, and then if Lee did not attack, the Union army should take the initiative.[67] The meeting broke up and the generals returned to their commands to await the coming of the new day.

The 11th Corps line was relatively quiet all during the morning of July 3. Early in the afternoon the Confederate guns let loose with a terrific barrage but according to Howard the damage was slight at his part of the line.[68] Pickett's charge which followed went just to the left of the 11th Corps front and struck Hancock's 2d Corps, though the men of the 11th got in some shots at both the advancing and retreating Confederates. There was almost no attempt at counterattack; Meade was glad to settle for a negative victory. The Confederates remained in position the rest of the day but very early on the morning of a rainy Fourth of July Lee pulled back his left from Gettysburg. Units of the 11th Corps moved down from Cemetery Hill and occupied the town.

In the days after Gettysburg, Meade's cautious pursuit of Lee stirred dissatisfaction throughout the country, from the President on down. Howard's reaction was typical. The few letters written between the close of the battle and Lee's final evacuation of Maryland on July 14 hint that he would have welcomed another fight.[69]

There was frequent contact with Lee's rear guard and cavalry yet never a major engagement.[70] On the twelfth, Meade was close enough for a general assault on Lee's position around Williamsport on the Potomac above Harpers Ferry, but at a meeting of corps commanders Howard was one of the few who voted to attack.[71]

On the thirteenth Howard requested permission to make a reconnaissance very early on the morning of the next day, and according to one reporter's account, Meade refused the request.[72]

This refusal was supposed to have permitted Lee to escape unnoticed and brought a sharp newspaper attack on Meade. Actually, there had been reconnaissances the previous day and more were ordered for the fourteenth of which the newspapers took no account. Howard, ever loyal to his superiors, believed that it was his duty to acquaint President Lincoln with the correct story and on July 18 wrote him a letter absolving Meade of all blame.[73] Lincoln replied that he was deeply mortified by Lee's escape but that he still had confidence in Meade.[74]

Howard also had to deal with the continuing problem of the 11th Corps. Both men and officers believed that they had fought as well as any at Gettysburg, but they could not deny that they had retreated and had become considerably disorganized at the close of the first day's battle. Coming so soon after the Chancellorsville fiasco, this new defeat naturally increased the derision heaped on the corps by the rest of the Army of the Potomac and led to proposals for the 11th's consolidation with other units. Howard would like to have returned to the 2d Corps; Schurz wanted an independent command.[75] Out of this emerged clear indication that some of the 11th Corps had come to appreciate Howard. Steinwehr, writing Howard on the subject of consolidation with other corps, said that he hoped that his division would form a part of a corps commanded by Howard.[76] Similar expressions of desire to remain under Howard's command came from Buschbeck and Smith, brigade commanders under Steinwehr.[77] Howard wrote to Lizzie: "The Germans begin to be attached to me." [78]

In August, Howard took leave and visited his family in Maine, seeing for the first time his son Chancey, who had been born during the battle of Chancellorsville. He left home on the twenty-seventh, and stopped off in Washington two days later, evidently with an idea of effecting a change in his current status. Probably he had in mind a new command. "I visited the Sec. of War," he wrote to Mrs. Howard. "He was sorry I came back, said nothing was to be done here right away, wished I would see the President. . . . The President agreed with me that I had better go back to the army." [79] So Howard returned, evidently without much enthusiasm, to the 11th Corps, now reduced to "a mere handful of men." [80] The corps remained some twenty-five miles to the rear of the advanced lines guarding communications.[81]

This leisurely activity came to a sudden halt. With the defeat of the Union army under the command of General William S. Rosecrans at Chickamauga, Georgia, on September 19–20, and the subsequent investment of his army at Chattanooga, drastic action had to be taken to relieve the critical supply problem. On the morning of the twenty-fourth, Halleck sent positive orders to Meade to have the 11th and 12th Corps, under the overall command of Hooker, ready to move by the following morning.[82] Howard was as surprised as anyone by the order, but on the twenty-fifth his corps was assembling at Alexandria, and the advance continued westward that evening.[83] The next day, the twenty-sixth, he followed the last of the troops of the 11th Corps. "I went to see Mr Lincoln the day I left Washington," wrote Howard several days later, "and he gave me a very nice coast survey map—He had a kind of music stand with two maps just alike one over the other. One was mounted—He gave me that, said the other would do for him." [84] This was to be Howard's last meeting with Lincoln.[85]

Reaching Louisville on October 1, Howard wrote to Lizzie: "I feel that I am sent out here for some wise and good purpose. . . . God grant us success and a speedy close to the war." [86] Howard's military career had, as he seemed to sense, come to a turning point. For over two years he had been with the Army of the Potomac. During that time he had learned many valuable lessons and had unquestionably matured. But with the Army of the Potomac he could not have advanced farther. The stigma of Chancellorsville, the jealousies and controversies arising out of Gettysburg, would have continually plagued him. The 11th Corps could probably not have outlived the scorn of the rest of the Army of the Potomac, and its commander could not have extricated himself from the corps' record even if he had wanted to. It was most fortunate for Howard's career that he left the Army of the Potomac. In the West he could begin with a clean slate, leaving behind animosities and prejudices to which the Western armies were indifferent. There, instead of mediocre commanders and defeat, or at best half-won victories, were Grant, Sherman, Thomas, and the prospect of success.

Western Victories

A quirk of geography put Howard and the 11th Corps down in northeast Alabama. This was as far as the railroad from Nashville could take them, still more than thirty miles from Chattanooga. Howard found the region impoverished and he described Stevenson, a rail junction near the Tennessee River, as "a dirty little town with some half dozen miserable houses." Bridgeport, the last stop on the railroad, was so filthy that he had his men go to work cleaning up the place as soon as they arrived.[1]

Hooker's command found the military situation as depressing as the surroundings. The Union army at Chattanooga was in a precarious position because of a shortage of supplies. The Confederates had destroyed the railroad bridge across the Tennessee River at Bridgeport, and supplies for Rosecrans' army had to go by wagon along the north bank of the river to Chattanooga. This one supply route was wholly inadequate. With Rosecrans seemingly unable to remedy the situation, Lincoln called on General U. S. Grant to assume direction of virtually all the Western armies.[2] Grant's first step was to replace Rosecrans with George H. Thomas, and soon he himself arrived to direct the operations around Chattanooga.

Howard had never before seen Grant but of course knew his reputation and after their first meeting wrote down his impressions: "I liked his appearance better than that of any Major General I have seen. He is modest, quiet and thoughtful. He looks the picture of firmness." Then Howard continued with a remark which confirms the fact that during the war Grant abstained from alcohol (a good part of the time at least). "He does not drink liquor and never swears. A member of his Staff told me he never had used a profane oath."[3] All this was to the good. So also was the resolute manner in which military operations were handled.

On October 24, Thomas set in motion the operation by which the supply routes to Chattanooga would be secure. Hooker's command was to play the principal role, crossing the river at Bridgeport and marching directly toward Lookout Valley. The successful completion of this move would not only protect the wagon road on the north bank, but would also open the river to steamboats and thus relieve the Union forces in Chattanooga.

The 11th Corps left Bridgeport on the twenty-seventh, one division of the 12th under General J. W. Geary following. That night Howard made headquarters in the hamlet of Whitesides, a trifle uneasy over a possible surprise attack since they had encountered Confederate cavalry during the day. Perhaps thinking of Chancellorsville, he wrote: "With *pickets well out* and some misgivings we had a fair night."[4] The advance continued the next day (October 28) with considerable skirmishing until they joined a force from Thomas' army sent over from Brown's Ferry.[5] The night of October 28 found the two divisions of the 11th Corps almost to the Ferry, while Geary's division of the 12th Corps was at Wauhatchie. Howard described the events of that night:

We went into camp—Gen. Geary of the 12th Corps encamped about 3½ miles back. A little after midnight terrific firing was heard near Gen. Geary and I got my command under arms with instructions to go to the relief of Geary. It was clear & there was a bright moon—We had hardly got the Corps under way before we were fired on from a range of hills or spurs on our left as we marched along—My troops drove the rebels from these hills and opened communication—The rebels were driven from rifle-pits and by the 11th Corps, and we have received high commendation. . . . God has been good & sparing and given us the victory & we have opend [sic] the river from Bridgeport almost to Chattanooga.[6]

This engagement at Wauhatchie, of some strategic importance, was far more meaningful to Howard and the 11th Corps who knew how necessary it was to make that favorable first impression. They had won a glamorous moonlight victory and had earned the praise of their superiors.

Meanwhile Grant was preparing an offensive against the Confederate army commanded by General Braxton Bragg. William T. Sherman brought up parts of the Army of the Tennessee from Mississippi and the combined Union armies were about ready to try to break the Confederate grip on the mountains to the south and east of Chattanooga. Grant's plan was to have Sherman make the principal attack against Bragg's right, turning the latter's position on Missionary Ridge. Thomas, with the Army of the Cumberland, would simply make demonstrations in the center, while Hooker, at Lookout Mountain, was to have a subsidiary role. Howard's corps, detached from Hooker on November 22, marched to Chattanooga to support either Sherman or Thomas as the exigencies of the moment might demand. Howard thus came under the direct orders of Grant.

Howard's troops did not see much action in the battle of Chattanooga. They engaged in some skirmishing on the twenty-fourth, the day the battle opened, forming a junction with Sherman's right.[7] The morning of the twenty-fifth, Howard's corps moved over to the left of Sherman's line. Only Buschbeck's brigade took part in the attack on the right,[8] but it was Thomas' men who stole the show that day carrying the crest of Missionary Ridge practically on their own initiative.

Bragg, badly defeated, retreated into Georgia, and assumed a strong defensive position. Grant chose not to renew the attack but turned instead to an immediate and pressing problem. Burnside, commanding a small force at Knoxville, was being besieged by the Confederate General James Longstreet and was much in need of help. On November 29, Grant ordered Sherman to take command of an expedition for the relief of Knoxville.[9] Two of the seven divisions Sherman selected for this assignment constituted the 11th Corps. Having had no chance to rest, the 11th Corps began the march to Knoxville without tents, wagons, or provisions. Rapid progress through difficult terrain brought them to Louisville, Tennessee, only about fifteen miles from Knoxville, when Howard received a note from Burnside telling of the raising of the siege.[10] The completion of the Knoxville assignment released the 11th Corps for a return to its former camp in Lookout Valley.

The results of the Chattanooga campaign and the expedition to the relief of Knoxville were of vast significance to the Union cause. All of Tennessee, including the strategic rail center of Chattanooga, was now firmly in the control of the Union armies, and the way was open for an advance into Georgia. The results were likewise of importance to Otis Howard's military career. Not only did Sherman mention Howard in terms of the highest praise in his official report,[11] but he took the trouble of writing him a personal letter of thanks:

I cannot [wrote Sherman] deny myself the pleasure it gives me to express to you the deep personal respect I entertain for you. I had known you by reputation, but it needed the opportunity our short campaign gave me to appreciate one who mingled so gracefully and perfectly the polished Christian gentleman and the prompt, zealous, and gallant soldier. . . . Not only did you do all that circumstances required, but you did it in a spirit of cheerfulness that was reflected in the conduct and behavior of your whole command. . . . Should fortune bring us together again in any capacity I will deem myself most fortunate, and should it ever be in my power to serve you, I beg you will unhesitatingly call on me as a friend."[12]

It seems unlikely that the ardently religious Howard, the opponent of strong drink and strong words, could ever have been the close friend of Sherman, the tough, hard-boiled soldier. According to a story related by Carl Schurz, Sherman and another officer, General Jefferson C. Davis, once had some fun by deliberately swearing quite freely in front of Howard. Howard became uncomfortable and beat a hasty retreat. After he had gone Sherman is said to have remarked, "Well, that Christian soldier business is all right in its place. But he needn't put on airs when we are among ourselves."[13] Yet Sherman was concerned with winning campaigns and battles. He could be indifferent to Howard's peculiarities as long as he was a skilled, cooperative, professional soldier.[14] Howard's attitude toward Sherman was similar. His first recorded comment was: "I feel much gratified that Gen Sherman was pleased with me and the command. . . . He is rather rough in his expressions, but an uncompromising friend of the government."[15]

The coming of winter forced the suspension of active campaigning until spring and the 11th Corps went into winter quarters at Lookout Valley. The men were far from home but they at least had the satisfaction of having vindicated themselves in the eyes of their countrymen.

Howard spent the first days of the new year in finishing his report of the Chattanooga campaign; then toward the end of January he was able to visit with Lizzie and the children in Maine. On returning to camp he found a letter from Blaine containing important information. "I enclose you a copy of the Joint Resolution whose adoption by a unanimous vote in both branches of congress you have doubtless already noticed," said Blaine. "The effect of the Resolution is to recognize you and to permanently record you in the Annals of the country as the Hero of the great Battle of Gettysburgh. . . ."[16]

The original resolution was to extend the thanks of Congress to

Hooker and Meade. Senator James W. Grimes of Iowa then moved to add Howard's name to the resolution. "As I have read the history of that campaign," Grimes said on the floor of the Senate, "the man who selected the position where the battle of Gettysburg was fought, and who, indeed, fought it the first day, was General Howard, and to him the country is indebted as much for the credit of securing that victory as to any other person." [17] Both houses soon after approved a joint resolution giving the thanks of Congress to Hooker, Meade, and Howard for the victory gained in the Gettysburg campaign and Lincoln signed it January 28, 1864. Apparently no one in either the House or Senate objected to the inclusion of Howard's name.[18] Nor is there any indication that Grimes had any ulterior motive in offering his amendment.

Hancock's friends naturally felt offended at the exclusion of their favorite because of his outstanding performance at Gettysburg on each of the three days of the battle. The Philadelphia *Evening Bulletin* published a letter from one, obviously an admirer of Hancock, who charged that the inclusion of Hooker's and Howard's names in the vote of thanks was the result of politics. "This, however," the writer concluded, "cannot be urged as a reason for so grave a wrong against a gallant soldier. Nor can it justify another in accepting honors in a way which has been denominated by the greatest soldier in the land as a '*pruriency* of fame not earned.' " [19] A similar communication to the *Army and Navy Journal* ridiculed the idea of Howard receiving the thanks of Congress and stated that Hancock was the one who deserved recognition.[20]

By the time Howard replied to Blaine he had already seen the *Evening Bulletin* letter. This, he wrote, "seems to regard the resolution as political, and unjustifiable. But my conscience acquits me of any political maneuvering." [21] He wrote to Hancock that he had had no knowledge of how he had come to be honored by Congress and that as far as he was concerned Hancock, too, deserved to be thanked.[22]

Hancock's reply shows that he did resent the action of Congress. "I thought myself," he wrote, "the act of Congress might have been induced by a desire on the part of the Administration to make you prominent, to have an effect, in case it would be thought wise or advisable to use your name and reputation in the coming Presidential or Vice-Presidential campaign." [23] Howard's concern was not politics but the well-being of his soul. The possibility that he might be gaining the reputation of a glory-seeker troubled him. Could a Christian consistently take pride in the praise of his fellow men? The hostile reaction to the vote of Congress might have seemed like a personal warning. "Circumstances have occurred to touch and subdue my vanity and teach me new lessons of humility," he wrote to George H. Stuart, chairman of the Christian Commission. "Oh, that my guiding principle might be 'the honor of Christ!' I am so prone to forget it and enter so heartily into things that are selfish and earthly, that I bow my spirit thankfully when God sees fit to rebuke and chasten me." [24]

What disturbed Howard still further was the report from his friend the Boston clergyman, E. B. Webb, that he had just seen Blaine, and that Blaine and Vice President Hamlin were going to try to get Howard a brigadier's commission in the regular army. According to Webb, "Abe—is well disposed." [25] Howard's friends were looking out for him to the point of his own discomfiture. There is no indication that he had planted the idea in Blaine's head. Webb's statement that he had discussed the matter with Blaine before indicates that the impetus came not from Howard but from his friends. Blaine's and Hamlin's natural motive was to gain recognition for the state of Maine.

The prospect of attaining high rank in the regular army was a strong temptation, and Howard wrestled with his conscience over what his decision should be if the commission were offered. On April 4 he confided to Lizzie:

My friends are secretly at work for me so I have intimations to get me a Brigadiership in the regular army. I cannot regard it in the light of a great favor. On the one hand it is flattering and suspicious [auspicious?]—on the other quite unflattering. There may be danger of my being politically strong and therefore must be disposed of—or I may be unfit for any place but in the army.[26]

This was Howard's way of explaining to his wife how he would react to a possible appointment to high rank in the regular army. He was examining both sides of the question. If he did receive such an appointment he well knew that this would make him more vulnerable to the kind of attack he had just experienced. He might even become "politically strong." Surely this was a natural thought. He had had the offer of the Republican nomination for the governorship of Maine, and the *Evening Bulletin* letter had suggested that his receiving the thanks of Congress was a political move. Hancock had admitted that he believed that the Administration had a political motive in singling out Howard. This was what was "quite unflattering" about the whole idea—the inherent dangers. The remark that he might be "unfit for any place but in the army" was his way of preparing his wife for an acceptance should the offer come his way. If his true place was in the army then, of course, it would be foolish not to seize such a fine opportunity as a brigadier's commission. His permanent rank at the start of the war was that of first lieutenant. The fact that about a year later he did accept the offer would indicate that he was attracted by the prestige connected with a prominent place in the army. Such a position meant recognition, acceptance, and vindication. This was really what he wanted and he would be willing to accept whatever risks came with the high rank. He closed his letter to Lizzie with this assurance:

I mean to go on as much as possible in the even tenor of my way. If a position in the regular army is tendered me, there will be time to consider it, and if there is no such offer, then will I believe that a good Providence points in a different direction.[27]

There really was small danger of Howard's becoming "politically strong," except in so far as he had political friends. There is no evidence that the Republican party in Maine ever again considered Howard as a candidate for political office, or that there was any probability of his becoming a national political figure. At least for the duration of the war he would remain in the army.

When Howard returned to the 11th Corps in Lookout Valley, preparations were in progress for a spring campaign. Grant and Sherman met to plan a co-ordinated attack on the two principal Confederate armies under Lee and Joseph E. Johnston, Bragg's successor. Sherman now had command of the Military Division of the Mississippi, comprising the Departments and Armies of the Tennessee, the Cumberland and the Ohio, commanded respectively by James B. McPherson, George H. Thomas, and John M. Schofield. Before embarking on the new campaign, Sherman and Thomas made certain changes in the organization of the Army of the Cumberland. One of these changes gave Howard command of the 4th Corps, while the old 11th was consolidated with the 12th to form the 20th.[28]

Being given command of such a large and important unit as the 4th Corps was proof of the confidence which Sherman and Thomas had in him.[29] It was a further sign of the fact that Howard was finding himself in the West.

The Civil War grew to a climax during the long summer of 1864. In the East, Grant took over direction of the Army of the Potomac, still under the nominal command of Meade, and slugged hard against Lee's gallant Army of Northern Virginia. The North watched the growing casualty lists and Lincoln's political fortunes reached a low ebb. Out West Sherman, acting in concert with Grant, forced his way gradually into Georgia and inched toward Atlanta which was guarded by the wily Joseph E. Johnston. Johnston was a worthy antagonist for Sherman, but he could not delay the Union advance for long.

The secret of Sherman's success was the flanking operation and fortunately for him he had the men to carry out this maneuver. He repeatedly threatened Johnston's line of supply and gave the Confederates little choice but to pull back; the only trouble was the snail's pace rate of advance. Throughout the Atlanta campaign, with only occasional exceptions, Thomas' Army of the Cumberland formed the center of Sherman's three armies. To McPherson's Army of the Tennessee usually went the assignment of carrying out Sherman's flanking operations. Consequently Howard's 4th Corps, which formed a part of Thomas' command, was generally in the center following a fairly direct line to Atlanta.

The 4th Corps left Cleveland, Tennessee on May 3 and arrived the next day at Catoosa Springs, Georgia, northwest of Dalton where Johnston had concentrated his army. The Confederates had a strong position near Dalton which Sherman did not wish to attack directly. Instead, he sent McPherson and the Army of the Tennessee southward through Snake Creek Gap to fall on Johnston's rear at Resaca. Meanwhile Thomas and Schofield were to keep the Confederates busy. When McPherson failed to cut the railroad at Resaca, Sherman sent his entire force, except Howard's corps and the cavalry division of General George Stoneman, after McPherson and thus forced Johnston to fall back to Resaca.[30] The retreat took place on the night of May 12, and the next morning Howard moved up and occupied Dalton.

It was Howard's assignment to pursue the retreating Confederates and to form a junction with Sherman at Resaca.[31] Approaching

Resaca from the north, Howard came up on the left of the Union line on the afternoon of May 14. He examined the position and then placed a battery, supported by an infantry brigade on the extreme left anticipating a flanking maneuver by the Confederates. At 5 P.M. a heavy column attacked this position and threatened to turn it. Howard sent to Thomas for help and A. S. Williams' division of the 20th Corps arrived in time to save the battery and force the Confederates to retreat.[32] One phase of this action is identical with the battle of Chancellorsville: Howard commanded a flank of the army unprotected by any natural obstacle. At Resaca, just a little more than a year after Chancellorsville, he was fully alive to the danger and made his dispositions accordingly.

Coming up to Johnston's strong position near Allatoona, after several days of fairly constant fighting, Sherman decided to leave the railroad and swing southwestward to Dallas. He found Johnston ready to receive him, however, and after a severe encounter on May 25, reversed the procedure and started reaching out toward Acworth and the railroad to the east.[33] In this maneuver, Howard's assignment was to turn the enemy's right flank. Late in the afternoon of May 27, having marched several miles through rough country, Howard thought he had reached the end of the Confederate line.[34] He reconnoitered the area and saw the Confederate soldiers busily throwing up entrenchments. All indications pointed to the certainty that here was the end of the enemy line, and consequently Howard ordered the attack. The men of General Thomas J. Wood's division moved forward with supports on either flank, but heavy resistance prevented their reaching the Confederate position. A refusal in the line had deceived Howard, and Wood's attack was thrown back with heavy loss.[35]

Sherman had failed to force Johnston from his entrenched position and he resumed the flanking operations hitherto so successful. By moving east, Sherman regained the railroad near Acworth. After weeks of maneuvering, Johnston backed up to Kenesaw Mountain and established such a strong position that it seemed unlikely that Sherman could dislodge him. On June 27, Sherman changed his tactics and called for a direct assault on the Confederate lines. His purpose evidently was to break through what he thought were lightly-held positions on the mountain.[36] To Howard's corps went the task of making the principal assault.[37] John Newton's division, with C. G. Harker's brigade in the lead, went forward bravely but only a few men reached the breastworks. The ground was rough and the Confederates had used every artificial device to impede the Union advance. After the battle had gone on for about an hour, Howard realized that success was impossible and he ordered the troops to resume their former position.[38]

On July 1, Sherman resumed his flanking operations, once more using McPherson's Army of the Tennessee to threaten Johnston's communications and line of retreat. Johnston, to Sherman's surprise, made a stand north of the Chattahoochee in a strong position. On July 4 Howard's corps came up to the enemy at Smyrna Camp Ground, five miles south of Marietta, and Howard assigned David S. Stanley's division the task of dislodging them. Under pressure of the attack, the Confederates abandoned their position and retreated across the Chattahoochee River. On July 7, Howard wrote that from a hill on the north side of the river he could see Atlanta some ten miles away.[39] The Chattahoochee was a formidable natural barrier, and on the east bank was Johnston's army massed ready to oppose a crossing. On July 9 Sherman was able to establish a bridgehead some distance up the river using Howard's corps to achieve this goal. Within a few days all of Sherman's army was on the south side of the Chattahoochee.[40] By July 18 the Union forces were again in motion, McPherson making for Decatur, east of Atlanta, Schofield and Thomas marching to and near Buckhead, directly north of the city.

The failure to check the Union advance caused Jefferson Davis at this critical point in the campaign to replace Johnston with John B. Hood as commander of the Army of Tennessee. Obviously Davis changed commanders in the hope that Hood would demonstrate his characteristic aggressiveness. The hope was soon fulfilled. Hood noted that Sherman had daringly divided his army and he determined to crush its separate components in detail. At the battle of Peach Tree Creek (July 20) Hood struck Thomas with most of his army, the attack falling principally on Newton's division of the 4th Corps and Hooker's 20th Corps.

Hood was unsuccessful in his first attempt, but those who knew him were alert to a renewal of the attack. Howard addressed Schofield early on the afternoon of July 21:

I have one small brigade in reserve, and there is quite a space between my right and Peach Tree Creek. Hood is great for attacking, and I feel that it is necessary for safety to retain this brigade in a movable condition . . . if you can excuse me, I would prefer not to extend farther to the left.[41]

How different an attitude from that of Chancellorsville where Howard saw his only reserve brigade taken from him without strenuous remonstrance! He had learned to expect the worst from his opponents.

Hood did not attack at this point, however, but on McPherson's flank, east of Atlanta. On the night of July 21, he moved the major part of his army to the extreme right of the Confederate line, and the following day assaulted the left flank of the Army of the Tennessee. The three corps which made up that army, hard pressed at times, finally threw back the reckless Confederates in what is called the battle of Atlanta. Once more Hood had failed in his design to crush Sherman.

McPherson was killed early in the action and the command of the Army of the Tennessee fell temporarily to the senior corps commander, John A. Logan, a political general of considerable ability. McPherson's death meant that Sherman had to make an appointment to the permanent command of the Department and Army of the Tennessee. Within two days he selected Howard for the vacancy. Sherman evidently had no regard for rank when he chose Howard; Hooker was senior corps commander in the combined armies. Logan, the temporary commander, would have been a popular choice with the men and he very much coveted the position. There were several other possibilities as well. But Sherman did not like Hooker, and Thomas refused to work with Logan. Besides Logan was not a West Pointer and was politically ambitious.[42]

Sherman selected Howard for the command of his beloved Army of the Tennessee partly because the two leading contenders, Hooker and Logan, were not "available" in the political sense of that word. Yet the choice was positive as well as negative. Sherman recognized in Howard a man of sure military knowledge, one who could handle a large body of men, not just competently, but with energy and confidence. Sherman had noted Howard's performance at Chattanooga and during the march to Knoxville. He had left him alone at Dalton to hold Johnston while the rest of the army struck at Resaca. He had selected Howard's corps to make the principal assault at Kenesaw Mountain. Throughout the campaign Howard had acted with resolution and had demonstrated military competency and a willingness to subordinate himself to the good of the cause. Ability to act harmoniously was surely one of the strongest of Howard's qualities and must have influenced Sherman's decision.[43]

Vindication of Sherman's choice was not long delayed. He waited a few days after the battle of Atlanta and then began a swing to the south in order to cut Hood's remaining lines of communication. In this operation, the Army of the Tennessee was to leave its position on the left, north and east of Atlanta, and march clear around to the west, aiming at the railroad.

The troops were already in motion when Howard took command on the morning of July 27. He was stepping into an extremely awkward and delicate situation. Not only did he replace two successful and popular men, McPherson and Logan, but he took command while the army was executing a difficult and dangerous maneuver. In his general orders taking command Howard sought to offset the first difficulty: "Your late beloved commander was my personal friend, and while I unite with you in profound sympathy and regret for our irreparable loss, it shall be my constant aim to emulate his noble example." [44] Words, however, would have been pointless had Howard been unsuccessful in his first battle.

On July 27, Howard was able to place in position only the 16th Corps on the extreme right of the Union line in open fields near the little rural meeting house called Ezra Church a few miles to the west of Atlanta. As each division came up, it deployed and made ready for any possible attack, for there was always the danger that Hood would assault an exposed flank. The next day Howard continued the process with Francis P. Blair's 17th Corps and Logan's 15th.[45] That morning (July 28) the 15th Corps occupied a wooded ridge facing nearly south. Howard wrote in his report: "I determined not to push farther, and reported to General Sherman that I anticipated an attack." [46] Sherman did not believe Hood would make another attempt so soon, but did not interfere with Howard's dispositions.[47]

It was well that Howard had anticipated an attack and had so cautiously placed his troops in line, prepared for battle.[48] Suddenly the Confederates attacked Logan's corps with great ferocity. They made several rash assaults but did not succeed in breaking the Union line. Howard stood 200 yards behind the lines and watched the slaughter. At one time during the battle the right of his line bent back some thirty yards but in a short while all the lost ground was regained. By about 3:30 in the afternoon the engagement was over, and all night the Confederate ambulances took away the wounded. "Poor fellows," Howard lamented, "they were rushed into the fight without mercy." If he remained uncertain whether or not he could ever fill McPherson's shoes, Howard could be satisfied that his first engagement with the Army of the Tennessee was a success.[49]

The battle of Ezra Church still did not bring the fall of Atlanta, and Hood held on to his rail communication to the south. Sherman's plan to break Hood's only remaining line of supply had thus far failed. He stretched his lines southward, but Hood would not let go his tenacious hold on the railroad. The hot August days passed and there was still no change. Sherman settled down to a siege of Atlanta, but his impatience and the needs of the administration would not permit him to remain inactive for long.

On the night of August 26, the Army of the Tennessee withdrew from its position and marched southward. Its objective was the single railroad line out of Atlanta that branched in two directions a few miles south of the city.[50] The West Point road was more westerly; the other ran southeast to Macon. On August 28, Judson Kilpatrick's cavalry supported by Howard's infantry got on the West Point railroad and for two days thoroughly destroyed the track.[51]

Howard's written orders from Sherman for August 30 were to advance eastward toward the Macon railroad to a point called Renfroe Place, but verbally Sherman told Howard to push farther, if he could, to the railroad at Jonesboro.[52] Intervening was the Flint River. Using the latitude given him, Howard overwhelmed a small band of stubborn Confederates and captured intact a partially fired bridge across the Flint. He was tantalizingly close to the railroad, but approaching darkness made its seizure impossible.[53] Howard was perfectly aware of the advantages to be won by taking the railroad and he wrote Sherman at 3 A.M. on August 31: "I understand your anxiety to get the road; no exertion will be spared as soon as we can see. The Seventeenth Corps will move up at daylight." [54] Sherman answered: "We must have that road, and it is worth to us a heavy battle . . . and if your guns command any reach of the road it will be a great gain, but we want the road itself. . . . understand that my hope of success rests mainly with you." [55]

At the time he wrote these words, Sherman evidently was not aware that two corps of Hood's army, commanded by William J. Hardee, faced Howard at Jonesboro. There was now a greater possibility of their attacking Howard. At 9:10 that morning,

Howard reported to Sherman that the Confederates appeared to be preparing for an attack; since he did not feel strong enough to make a successful one himself, he would await the enemy.[56] Sherman advised Howard to hold his ground and to threaten the enemy as much as possible. Meanwhile he would interpose Stanley's 4th Corps and Schofield's Army of the Ohio between Hardee and Atlanta.[57]

Howard's belief that the Confederates would attack him was correct. About 3:00 on the afternoon of August 31, the Confederates assaulted Howard's line at several points and were repulsed each time.[58] Sherman's plan for the next day was to have Howard demonstrate on the right while Thomas rolled up the flank of Hardee's force by attacking from the north. The plan miscarried because Thomas, who was supposed to start his attack at 11:00 A.M., waited until late in the afternoon.[59]

Although Hardee escaped, Hood found Sherman across the railroad between Jonesboro and Atlanta. To save his force in Atlanta, he abandoned the city on September 1 and retreated south to Lovejoy where he united with Hardee. Slocum with the 20th Corps was thus able to occupy Atlanta without opposition.[60] Finding Hood in a strong position at Lovejoy, and having already captured Atlanta, Sherman decided to let well enough alone and to give his armies a long-needed rest.

The End of the War

The Atlanta campaign was the climax of Howard's military career. Although the March to the Sea and the Carolina campaign, still to come, were of great strategic importance to the final Union victory the strategy was Sherman's and the exploits were largely those of the men. Howard played an important part in both campaigns—he commanded half of Sherman's army—but in few instances did he have to test his tactical skill. The Union armies always had a large numerical superiority over their opponents and there was never any doubt about the outcome of events between November 1864 and April 1865.

The most remarkable thing about Howard's record in the West is its marked difference from his Eastern experiences. The defeat of the 11th Corps at Chancellorsville and of the force under his command on the first day at Gettysburg were sufficient to blur his reputation in the East. But from September 1863 until the end of the war Howard knew little but success and victory. The explanation for this change of fortune is to be found not alone in the change of scene, although that did contribute to it. The principal reason that Howard became a successful commander in the last year and a half of the war is that he had learned. It was not simply mastering the technique of handling large bodies of men; he learned that because he was a good student. It was more the lesson of never making the same mistake twice, coupled with his willingness to make his own decisions. The enemy never surprised Howard after Chancellorsville, and his precautions at Resaca and at Ezra Church show that he had mastered the problem of protecting the flank of a line. As a corps commander at Chancellorsville he was held within bounds by a commander who did not take his subordinates into his confidence. If Howard had placed less confidence in Hooker's conclusion that Lee was retreating and had forced himself to rely on his own judgment he might well have averted disaster. Once authorized to act on his own initiative Howard rose to the occasion. At Ezra Church, Sherman was not expecting Hood to attack; Howard was. His own good judgment averted another defeat and gained a victory.

Sherman came to depend on Howard so much that despite the lull in activity he refused him permission to take leave as many of his other officers were doing. "I would like exceedingly to go home during this rest," Otis told Lizzie, "or to meet you and the children anywhere, but my future movements are so uncertain that I don't think of either just now."[1] And a week later he wrote, "My Corps commanders are still away and Gen. Sherman will not let me go."[2]

The lull was broken late in September when Hood left Lovejoy, swung west around Sherman into northwest Georgia, and attacked the Union supply lines. He hoped to draw Sherman away from Atlanta. For a time he was successful; Sherman chased Hood around northern Georgia and Alabama for almost a month but never caught him. In this futile operation Howard marched the Army of the Tennessee several hundred miles without fighting a major engagement. Sherman tired of this kind of game and began to concentrate his forces. At the end of October, he left part of his command with Thomas, whose duty it would be to watch Hood, and drew in the rest toward Atlanta preparatory to the march to the sea. He divided these troops into two wings or armies. Howard commanded the Right Wing, which included the 15th and 17th Corps, the former under the temporary command of Peter J. Osterhaus during Logan's absence. Slocum commanded the Left made up of the 14th and 20th Corps. Each wing had about 27,000 men, while the cavalry under Judson Kilpatrick brought the total force of Sherman's army to about 60,000.

Howard's last letter home before the campaign began was from Smyrna Camp Ground, just north of Atlanta: "From present appearances we shall be cut off from communication for some little time. I dont know myself where we shall go, but we have stripped for a trip in the enemy's country. You must'nt be anxious if you dont get a letter or have a dispatch from me for a month."[3] The next day, according to Sherman's instructions, Howard's men destroyed twenty-two miles of the railroad running north from Atlanta.[4] Then on November 13 they moved south of the city to White Hall.

The grand march began on November 15, each wing of Sherman's army taking a different route. The Union troops crashed through central Georgia facing no opposition worthy of the name; but in the rich farming country the men found much to destroy. Howard's greatest problem was not enemy resistance but controlling his men, who saw the maneuver as a holiday excursion. The weather was fine and the chances of death remote. The generals in command might have some military purpose in this march to the sea but for the men, who were veterans of many tough campaigns, the objective was to have a good time. Their outing was at the expense of the people of Georgia.

Sherman's armies, according to most accounts, cut a swath sixty miles wide from Atlanta to the sea destroying everything in sight. Certainly, this picture is accurate enough for the prosperous farming country east of Atlanta. But the last half of the march was through the uninhabited pine barrens of eastern Georgia, less promising land for pillage.[5] Wherever it was possible, though, the Northern troops indulged in excessive destruction, as Sherman and others have admitted.[6]

Otis Howard had no stomach for wanton destruction and he did his best to prevent the worst abuses. Only about a week out of Atlanta he reported to Sherman that his troops were burning abandoned homes and looting household valuables. He said that he was taking measures to check the depradations,[7] but the men were not to be controlled by Howard or any other officer. Frequently the worst offenders were stragglers who did not consider themselves under military regulations.

The absence of effective opposition probably accounts for some of the loose discipline. The two wings were almost to Savannah before the Confederates could rally any kind of respectable force. William J. Hardee, whom Howard had known at West Point just before the war, commanded a small army of perhaps 10,000 at Savannah. But Sherman was more concerned about his supply problem than he was in capturing Savannah. Foraging in the vicinity of Savannah was poor and his men were reduced to eating rice.[8] Before leaving Atlanta he had made arrangements for supply ships to meet him somewhere on the Georgia coast; Savannah was always a logical possibility. On December 8, Sherman urged Howard to try to make contact with the fleet by way of the Ogeechee River which reaches the Atlantic some distance below Savannah.[9] The next day Howard detailed his chief of scouts Captain William Duncan and two of his men to perform this hazardous mission. Duncan was three days in getting down the river and past Fort McAllister guarding its mouth.

He found the fleet waiting and thus conveyed to the outside world the first word of Sherman's arrival at the coast.[10]

Sherman had to establish a supply base but Savannah with its harbor facilities was still in Confederate hands and the only other place suitable for receiving supplies, the Ogeechee River, was well guarded by Fort McAllister on the right bank near where the river entered Ossabaw Sound some fifteen miles below Savannah. If the fort could be taken supply ships could enter the river and deliver needed provisions and clothing for all Sherman's army to King's Bridge, a convenient landing place six miles above McAllister.

It was Howard who conceived and executed the plan to capture the fort. On December 10, 1864 he wrote Sherman that north of the Ogeechee all the inlets were covered by enemy batteries but that there was access to Ossabaw Sound from the south bank. He consequently had ordered reconstruction of King's Bridge which the Confederates had damaged and which Howard maintains Sherman had ordered completely destroyed.[1] Sherman must have wanted to isolate Fort McAllister from Savannah but Howard saw the need for the bridge in any plan to capture the fort.

The next day Howard wrote Sherman: "I have given General Kilpatrick four pontoons, and ordered him to cross the Cannouchee and take the fort if possible. If he is unsuccessful I shall march down a division. King's Bridge will be finished to-morrow night, and from there to Fort McAllister there is a good road, without obstructions."[12]

Soon Sherman gave Kilpatrick orders to reconnoitre Saint Catherine's Sound south of the Ogeechee so the cavalry had to abandon its plans for capturing the fort.[13] On December 12 Howard ordered William B. Hazen's division of the 15th Corps, "to proceed against Fort McAllister and take it" as soon as King's Bridge was completed.[14] On December 13, Hazen's division crossed King's Bridge and advanced on the fort defended by only about 200 men. The approaches, however, were difficult; the Confederates had planted land mines and had covered the surrounding ground with ditches, abatis, and other defensive works. Late in the afternoon, Hazen gave the signal to advance and in a single dash his men swarmed over the works and captured the fort.[15]

The next task was the capture of Savannah and its garrison. The Union forces closed in and were able to invest the city except for one road leading north to Charleston. Before this could be cut, Hardee evacuated his force on the night of December 20. The next morning the Union soldiers, finding the works in their front vacant, moved in and took possession of the city. Sherman capped the successful campaign by presenting Savannah to President Lincoln as a Christmas present.

During the brief interval between campaigns Howard tried once again for a quick trip home but Sherman was unrelenting as usual. Howard had to content himself with a few days' rest in the captured city.[16] It was at this time that Edwin Stanton visited Savannah.[17] Howard, who had seen Stanton several times before, now renewed his acquaintance with Lincoln's War Secretary. Howard wrote of the meeting: "The Sec. of war says he & the President think 'I am the right man in the right place.' He spoke warmly & even affectionately to me the few moments I saw him at Savannah."[18] He even took Howard's one hand in both of his and assured him, in front of Sherman, of a high place in the regular army.[19] Apparently Stanton had some appreciation of Howard's services, and yet it is not clear why he should have gone out of his way to do him any favors. Stanton's promise may have stemmed from Blaine's and possibly Hamlin's influence in Washington and from Sherman's recommendation. In any event, Stanton was true to his promise, though the actual appointment did not come for several weeks. Meanwhile the new campaign occupied Howard's attention.

General Hardee's small army was still in the field; to the north lay the states of South and North Carolina, both relatively untouched by the war. Though the capture of Savannah was of great strategic importance, the war was by no means over, and Sherman lost little time in preparing his next move. The Carolina campaign in the winter of 1865, little publicized in the annals of the Civil War, was an important factor in bringing the war to a successful conclusion.[20]

Sherman's plan for the campaign, as outlined to Grant on January 2, 1865, was to feint with the Right Wing toward Charleston and with the Left toward Augusta, but to make Columbia his first objective. By throwing the Confederates off balance he could march virtually unopposed through the heart of South Carolina. Sherman ordered Howard's command to Port Royal, South Carolina, making it appear that Charleston was his objective. But from there the Right Wing would proceed inland to Pocotaligo arriving there no later than January 15.[21] Union forces were already in possession of

Beaufort, on the South Carolina coast, and Howard began to send the 17th Corps toward that destination during the first week of January.

Although the Confederates had only a small force with which to oppose Howard at Pocotaligo, they were strongly located in the midst of swamps and marshes. In this operation Howard showed that he had learned some important lessons in tactics from Sherman's conduct of the Atlanta campaign. With a great numerical superiority he could outflank any position instead of being forced to assault an intrenched line. In this instance Howard's order read: "Major-General Blair will intrench a division strongly confronting Pocotaligo, and with the other two divisions make a detour to turn the enemy's left." [22] This maneuver was completely successful. It was Sherman against Johnston on a smaller scale. Howard's next task was to cross the Salkehatchie River. On the opposite shore was a force of 2,000 Confederates, but the principal opposition came from natural obstacles. Howard adopted the usual tactic of turning the enemy flank although there was some activity in front of the main Confederate position, described by Howard as "the strongest . . . I ever saw in my life. . . ." [23] Of course, 2,000 men could offer little opposition to Howard's army which in that engagement numbered about ten times as many. Yet the difficult natural barriers the Union army encountered in this instance and throughout the eastern part of South Carolina tended to make the odds more equal. It was no little accomplishment to bridge flooded streams and to wade waist deep through swamps.[24]

Sherman's army continued its march, unopposed, into the center of South Carolina leaving a path of destruction in its wake. On the evening of February 16 the Army of the Tennessee camped on the south side of the Broad River, across from Columbia. The next morning the advance guard crossed the river, and a small band of Confederate cavalry beat a hasty retreat.

Soon Generals Sherman and Howard with their staffs entered the city and selected quarters for the night. They noted that some cotton was burning in the streets. Before long many of the soldiers of Stone's brigade, detailed to occupy Columbia, were helping themselves to any liquor they could find—or that was brought to them by grateful Negroes. Some escaped convicts and some Union prisoners, only just freed from the stockades, joined the revelry. By evening most of Stone's brigade was drunk. The men, not wanting to pass up an opportunity to have a good time after having passed through an excessively arduous campaign, looted stores and private houses, and ignored the attempts of some of the officers to keep them under control. During that long and violent day most of the burning cotton was extinguished, but in the afternoon a high wind sprang up and shortly after dark fires broke out in several buildings. Obviously these fires were set and almost certainly by drunk Union soldiers. The troops supposedly guarding the city actually interfered with efforts to extinguish the flames. Howard ordered in an additional brigade and finally all of C. R. Woods' division. A shift in the wind early in the morning checked the flames but only after a large portion of the city had been levelled. The sober men arrested the stragglers and by morning the episode was over.[25]

Several commentaries on this subject accuse Sherman and his officers of deliberately plotting the destruction of Columbia.[26] The authors of such accounts do not substantiate their accusations with positive evidence, and they fail to appreciate the significance of Howard's direct involvement in the episode. If the burning were by premeditated design, Howard would have known about it, as would almost certainly other high-ranking officers such as Logan, Charles R. Woods (division commander), William B. Woods, and George A. Stone (brigade commanders). Yet, in their official reports they all agreed substantially with Howard's account.[27] "Neither the general-in-chief nor any of his lieutenants," wrote Howard, "have ever sanctioned any conduct so evidently against the dictates of humanity." [28]

Throughout the war Howard had done all that one man could to lessen the horrors of war for non-combatants. It is inconceivable that he would have sanctioned the burning of a surrendered city, rendering thousands homeless, and even more inconceivable that he would then have falsified the record.[29] Nor does it make sense that all the other officers concerned would perjure themselves in their official reports. In answer to the question, "Who burned Columbia?" one thing is certain—it was not Sherman nor Howard nor any responsible person. Indeed, the day after the fire Howard issued an order setting up patrols and guards "to prevent at all cost, even to the taking the life of any refractory soldier, a recurrence of the horrors of last night." [30]

The army lingered for only two days in the vicinity of Columbia. In that time, Howard had charge of destroying all the remaining military installations. Before resuming the march, he ordered that five hundred head of cattle be left behind for the destitute.[31] Yet such was the helplessness of many people that several thousand, mostly Negroes, left Columbia in the wake of the army. They formed a long refugee train which Howard organized out of compassion for these unfortunates.[32]

As the 15th Corps marched out of Columbia a local citizen watched them pass. These young, well-equipped soldiers impressed the viewer. He realized then that this army which had marched across Georgia to the sea and through half of the state of South Carolina could go anywhere it pleased. He knew, and many other Southerners must have come to understand that the cause of the Confederacy was hopeless.[33]

From Columbia, the Right Wing marched to Winnsboro, destroying the railroad en route, and then turned eastward across the Catawba and Lynch Rivers. Logan's corps crossed the Lynch on the last day of February and followed Blair, who was proceeding at a leisurely pace toward Cheraw. The Pedee River, just beyond Cheraw, was bridged with pontoons, and on March 8 Howard's army entered North Carolina. At Fayetteville Sherman established communication with the outside world by way of Wilmington (recently taken by Schofield) and the Cape Fear River. Sherman's plan was to take Goldsboro, an important rail junction, and join forces there with Schofield who was advancing inland from New Bern. At Goldsboro he would rest and refit his army.

By this time, the Confederates had assembled a respectable force of some 30–40,000 men and Sherman fully expected Johnston, recently reinstated, to contest his advance.[34] Slocum was, as usual, on the left, and on March 16 he encountered severe oppositon in the minor battle of Averasborough. He continued his march eastward while Howard's column followed roads five or six miles to the south. Because Slocum was deceived about the force opposing him, thinking it was primarily cavalry, Sherman relaxed his guard and ordered Howard to proceed directly on Goldsboro.[35] This meant that Howard got several miles ahead of Slocum, a situation which Joe Johnston was quick to recognize. The Confederate commander rapidly concentrated his forces and on March 19 threw them on Slocum's isolated Left Wing. Sherman did not immediately credit the report that Johnston had concentrated against Slocum, writing to Kilpatrick at 5:00 that afternoon: "General Slocum thinks the whole rebel army is to his front. I cannot think Johnston would fight us with the Neuse to his rear." [36] Because of this interpretation, Howard was allowed to continue on his way until the day's end. Meanwhile, Slocum, though holding his position, was experiencing serious trouble in the first day's battle of Bentonville. At last Sherman ordered the Right Wing to turn back to aid Slocum, Hazen's division making an all-night march and appearing on the battlefield at dawn.[37] Logan and Blair brought up their commands, but Johnston had refused his left flank to resist this new threat and the day ended without a decision.

Johnston's army was still in position the morning of March 21, but there was only slight and indecisive action that day. Then on the morning of March 22 the Union army discovered that the Confederates had withdrawn.[38] This was the last major encounter of the war for Sherman's army and for Howard. Actually the battle was primarily Slocum's; the Right Wing was only lightly engaged.

The Union troops entered Goldsboro on March 25 and there rested and refitted for sixteen days. Just before entering Goldsboro, Howard learned that he had been made a brigadier general in the regular army.[39] On February 25, Stanton had sent the recommendation to Lincoln, and that same day the President referred it to the Senate. The Senate confirmed the appointment on March 3, along with a large number of others.[40]

News of the fall of Richmond arrived on April 6, and Sherman moved quickly to pursue Johnston and prevent his joining Lee.[41] The army moved out of Goldsboro toward Raleigh on April 10. Two days later Sherman published the definitive news of Lee's surrender, and on April 15 an armistice went into effect. Howard's command was just west of Raleigh when they received the news.[42] They waited there while Sherman and Johnston negotiated surrender terms.

On April 17 news of Lincoln's assassination, which had occurred on the fourteenth, tempered the general rejoicing. Howard felt the shock deeply. To his mother he wrote:

President Lincoln has been everything to the nation, and the nation will never cease to do him honor. But to me personally he has been a friend. . . . I anticipated a real pleasure in serving under his administration after the war was over cherishing the same complete confidence in Mr Lincoln that I would in my own father and knowing that he would sustain me in every right course.[43]

President Andrew Johnson and Secretary of War Stanton repudiated the first surrender terms entered into between Sherman and Johnston because they dealt, in part, with non-military matters. Sherman deeply resented the repudiation as well as the abusive press comments. Howard sympathized with his commander, explaining to Lizzie that Sherman had "meant right & the reasons of offering generous terms [were] not rightly set forth. How easy it is to impute wrong motives." [44] On April 26, Sherman and Johnston held another conference, at which Howard was present, and completed the surrender negotiations. Then the army began the march to Washington by way of Petersburg and Richmond.

Early on the afternoon of May 10, just after reaching Richmond, Howard received a telegram from Grant telling him to proceed to Washington and report to the Secretary of War.[45] Howard reported to Stanton on May 12. "Mr. Stanton received me very kindly about the first of May 1865, at Washington, D. C.," he recalled many years later.

> He told me distinctly that Mr. Lincoln, before his death had expressed the desire of having me on duty as Commissioner of Freedmen as soon as my services could be spared from the field. He further said that Mr Johnson, the President, desired to carry out these wishes of the deceased and he gave me to understand that he himself desired it too. So he said take time to consider the matter and then give me your answer as to whether you will or will not accept the detail.[46]

If Howard could have foreseen the stormy future, perhaps he would not have accepted Stanton's offer as readily as he did. The position, as described in the act of Congress, entailed general supervision of four million Negroes during their transition from slavery to freedom with vaguely delineated powers for the commissioner. It is likely that Howard was flattered by Stanton's expressions of confidence and by Lincoln's request that he be assigned to the position. In the last months before the end of the war he had been considering his future plans. At one time he had considered buying a farm in Maine, an indication that he might have wanted to avoid duty in the peace-time army.[47] Then this offer came to him which Howard later called providential.[48] An opportunity of this kind would have its attractions: a chance to serve mankind and at the same time the holding of a prominent public position, still in the army yet not in one of the routine command positions which would involve frequent moves. After four years of war service Howard wanted to settle down with his family in one place.[49]

Sherman, who had special cause for distrusting the politicians in Washington, wrote Howard a lengthy letter on hearing of his appointment. This act was typical of Sherman's kindly manner and Howard might well have heeded his commander's sage advice:

I hardly know whether to congratulate you or not, but of one thing you may rest assured, that you possess my entire confidence, and I cannot imagine that matters, that may involve the future of four millions of souls, could be put in more charitable and more conscientious hands. So far as man can do, I believe you will, but I fear you have Hercules' task. God has limited the power of man, and though in the kindness of your heart you would alleviate all the ills of humanity it is not in your power. Nor is it in your power to fulfill one-tenth part of the expectations of those who framed the bureau for freedmen, refugees, and abandoned estates. It is simply impracticable. Yet you can and will do all the good one man may, and that is all you are called on as a man and Christian to do, and to that extent count on me as a friend and fellow soldier for counsel & assistance.[50]

Howard had one more military duty to perform. The Grand Review of the Union armies took place on two successive days, May 23 and 24. On Tuesday, the twenty-third, the Army of the Potomac paraded up Pennsylvania Avenue from the Capitol. Wednesday was given over to Sherman's Western army. In view of Howard's long service as commander of the Army of the Tennessee he expected to lead it in the review. Sherman, however, wanted to placate Logan and asked Howard to surrender the post of honor to him. Howard graciously acquiesced.

Sherman then asked him to ride with him, and on Wednesday, May 24, a "perfect, cloudless and cool day," Otis Howard rode up Pennsylvania Avenue alongside Sherman at the head of the veteran Western army.[51] This army had marched hundreds of miles through enemy country against stubborn opposition. It had done more to end the war than any other army. Howard had done his part almost without flaw. To Sherman, of course, rightly go most of the laurels, but Howard's contribution was as significant and important as that of any other Union officer of second rank. Yet his reputation at the end of the war, paradoxically, did not rest on his military ability, but rather on his position as a Christian, the most outstanding in the Union army.⁵² This was not altogether satisfactory to Howard. The seeker after spiritual truth was content with his reputation. But the veteran campaigner wanted to maintain an untarnished record. In the years following the war, Howard wrote letters, articles, and an autobiography all stoutly defending his military career. But try as he would, he could not keep the record clear. To this day he is still either the Christian soldier or the incompetent officer at Chancellorsville and Gettysburg. Any attempt to raise Howard's reputation as a military man meets an immediate obstacle: Howard was almost always in the role of a subordinate; on only a few occasions did he handle his command independently.

A cursory glance at Howard's war career in the East associates his name with defeat, and in the Western campaigns he is overshadowed by Sherman. Yet it is significant that he had command of a large and important army at the end of the war. Howard rose from relative obscurity to a position of prominence and great responsibility, in contrast to the record of many Union officers who were tried and found wanting.

Several factors made Howard a successful military commander. He survived; he enjoyed some political influence; he also knew how to learn. His formal military training provided the background, while his experiences on the field of battle added tremendously to his store of military knowledge. Long before the end of the war he could skillfully handle large bodies of men on the march and in the face of the enemy.

Howard's tactical skill, especially in the latter stages of the war, was of the highest order. George W. Nichols, a member of Sherman's staff wrote: "History shows that more battles have been lost or gained at heavy cost because the commanders did not know the nature of the ground they were fighting over than for any other reason. Such a criticism can never be applied to General Howard. He sees the whole field of operations, and has an admirable tactical knowledge of the best use to be made of its advantages." ⁵³ Thomas W. Osborn, of Howard's staff, commented on his "unerring judgment in military operations" an opinion shared by the correspondent D. P. Conyngham.⁵⁴ Howard's experiences in the course of the war taught him what it failed to teach others, that direct assaults on fortified works had little chance of success.⁵⁵ In the Savannah and Carolina campaigns he consistently used the flanking maneuver, except at Fort McAllister where frontal assault was the only choice.

This does not mean that Howard lacked aggressiveness. He was always eager to find the enemy and fight him.[56] At Chancellorsville he voted to remain on the south side of the Rappahannock and fight it out with Lee's army; at Gettysburg he carried on an unequal struggle rather than withdraw in the face of the enemy; at Williamsport he voted in a council of war against the majority to attack Lee. He was impatient at McClellan's dilatory tactics, and throughout his letters runs expression of the desire to get on with the war.

Howard always was loyal to his superiors, he got along well with his associates,[57] and he was fair to his subordinates. He supported McClellan and Meade when these officers were subjects of public criticism. Never was he involved in internal intrigue; he was not a part of any clique. His men soon came to realize that he would look out for them. Thus Surgeon John Moore included in his report of the Atlanta campaign a testimonial to this trait in Howard's character: "no less important than success, in attaching the soldiers of the army to him, is the constant interest which he manifests for their physical and moral welfare." [58] Before setting out on the Carolina campaign, Howard sent back to Sherman two brigadier generals who had been absent during the March to the Sea, not wishing to displace young officers who had "borne the burden and heat of the day." [59] Out of consideration for those who were obedient to orders and had undergone hardships in the mud and swamps of South Carolina, he publicly reprimanded a captain in the 15th Corps for using a number of large size tents for his private comfort when one small tent was all he was permitted.[60]

In four years Howard had matured to the point where he was a far different man from the one who had entered the war in May 1861 as colonel of the Third Maine. Modesty had taken the place of the willingness to indulge in self-praise demonstrated in the farewell order to the regiment. In the latter part of the war Howard made no mention in his letters of whether or not the men liked him—sometimes frequently seen in the first two years. That references to the Deity and to a Kind Providence are not quite so numerous does not mean that Howard had lost any of his faith but simply that he had become less showy about his religious beliefs.

While Howard never reached the heights of civil and military popularity attained by Grant, Sherman, and Sheridan, he received the quiet and deep respect of those who had been under his command. At the close of the war, T. A. Meysenburg, the adjutant of the 11th

Corps, commented on the depth of feeling evoked by Howard: "Your slow and steady promotion is the surest sign, that it was really deserved. . . . It was not the momentary impulse and exaltation over one act, but a promotion on reflection, which it seems to me, makes it of much more value. . . . Believe me, if I assure you that I regard the period of my life which I spent in your association, one of the brightest, which will remain inscribed on my memory for ever." [61]

War causes some men to lose their faith; it intensified Howard's. As in every phase of this life after the weary months of search for a personal religion had been rewarded, Howard fought in the Civil War with the faith that he was serving God in a righteous cause. He knew that God was acting in the affairs of men, and this knowledge sustained him. It made him able to maintain that steady adherence to duty which Sherman was quick to recognize. For his part, he fostered a religious atmosphere about his headquarters; he did all that one man could do to check depredations; he was concerned as a Christian when his men destroyed private property or stole from civilians. Consequently he earned his reputation as "a Christian soldier." There is no doubt that this phrase, which came so easily to newspaper correspondents, won Howard a small popular reputation. And it was this reputation, in addition to his successful record of handling a large army, that recommended him to Lincoln as commissioner of the Freedmen's Bureau.

Early Months of the Freedmen's Bureau

When General Howard assumed the duties of commissioner of the Bureau of Refugees, Freedmen and Abandoned Lands on May 15, 1865 he faced an enormous task. The actual physical facilities he had to start with would have discouraged the most sanguine optimist. Stanton had provided him with a house on the corner of 19th and I Streets for office space and had authorized the Quartermaster's Department to issue desks, chairs, and other equipment. The War secretary also turned over to Howard an odd assortment of documents relating to freedmen's affairs accumulated during the war years. As for personnel, Howard had his own staff plus some clerks assigned by the War Department. On that first day this was all there was to the Freedmen's Bureau charged with the care and supervision of roughly four million freed slaves in the late seceded states.

Though few in the South at that time would admit the necessity for any governmental agency to aid the Negro, there existed a crying need for some kind of supervisory body to guide the freedmen in their transition from slavery to freedom. Many thousands lacked the basic essentials of life; they had been uprooted and they flocked in large numbers to the towns and cities to enjoy new-found freedom only to find that they had no means of supporting themselves. The South's labor system had just been wrenched apart, and the average Southerner questioned the feasibility of a free system based on Negro labor. Slavery had served as the main prop to a social organization, and now there emerged the difficult problem of adjustment for the people of two races forced to live in an entirely new relationship. In May 1865 no clearly defined status for the Negro had as yet emerged. Some Southerners evidently hoped for the emergence of a system which while perhaps not quite the same as slavery, would nonetheless assure the former slave holders of a labor supply and would keep the Negro "in his place" socially. Many questions were still unanswered. Would the Negro, for instance, become an independent farmer, or would he continue to work in gangs as before? Would he be allowed to testify in the courts; would he be eligible for public education? It was to be the responsibility of General Howard, under the broad authority granted in the act of Congress which created the Bureau, to find the answers to these questions. The Bureau was charged with providing emergency rations, clothing, and fuel for the destitute, administering the confiscated and abandoned lands in the control of the government in the South, and controlling "all subjects relating to refugees and freedmen. . . ."[1] In addition to handling the relief and land matters specified in the act, the Bureau also would assume responsibility for the working conditions of freedmen by supervising the negotiation of labor contracts. It had under its control judicial matters involving freedmen if the local courts should fail to grant them equal rights, and it would do what it could to foster Negro education through cooperation with Northern philanthropic societies.

In trying to carry out its mandate, the Bureau could expect to encounter opposition from the Southern white population. While it is difficult to generalize, it is not far from the truth to state that this population in 1865 was not prepared to go very far in according the Negro equality of any kind. The slave might be free but his future status was uncertain. This would prove to be the major obstacle to the harmonious restoration of the Union. Other than this, the fruits of the war seemed assured. The Union was again intact; rebellion no longer prevailed in any part of the country. The Confederate government ceased to exist and, had there been no problem of the freed slave, the return to the old ways of government, to the familiar state-to-state and state-to-national government relations, might have been effected with relative ease. Had there been no problem of the freedman, President Johnson's lenient plan of Reconstruction might have proved effective in the South and satisfactory to the people of the North. And it is doubtful whether the Radical Republicans could have persuaded Northern voters that punishment of the South as a whole, and especially of the leaders of the rebellion, was either justified or desirable. Had there been no problem of the freedman, the old state governments might better have secured immediate representation in the national Congress. But the former slaves could not be forgotten or ignored. What was to become of them? Could their former masters be trusted to acquiesce in the drastic changes which the war had wrought? One of the most telling arguments of the Radicals, an argument which had a strong appeal in the North, was that the white people of the South were not sincere in recognizing the end of slavery.

The problem of the freedman, then, complicated the whole Reconstruction period. Under the Johnson plan the former slave holders, leaders in their own states and communities, would more easily have found some way to preserve the substance of slavery. If one is inclined to doubt this, let him see what was done not only immediately after the war by the Johnson-sponsored state governments, but also what the Southern states succeeded in accomplishing in all the years following the war in reducing the Negro to a semi-servile status. It would have been expecting too much for the Southern whites *not* to have tried to keep the freedman from becoming really free. Few Southern whites had any faith in free labor. Why should they? For years they had proclaimed the superiority of slave labor over free. Was there any reason to believe that their views would suddenly change? Would they not do everything they could to perpetuate the labor system which they believed in and which they believed was the only feasible system for their type of economy? And even if some were willing to accept the former slave as a free laboring man, almost no one had the slightest intention of conceding him political, much less social, equality.

Even if this view of the Southern white attitude is incorrect, it is true, nevertheless, that the abolitionist-Radical group in the North *believed* that the Southern whites intended to perpetuate slavery in some form. To have fought for four years not only to preserve the Union but to free the slaves and then to see part of the fruits snatched away by the very persons who, in their eyes, were responsible for the whole catastrophe was more than they could accept. This group rightly believed that the federal government, having taken upon itself the task of liberating the slaves, had a clear responsibility to see that slavery really was dead and also that aid was extended to the freedmen in the difficult period of transition.

Were *all* of the Northern abolitionist-Radical group sincerely concerned over the fate of the freedman? Probably not; and surely as time went on the concern became less and less until at length only a handful wanted to keep up the unequal struggle. But in 1865, and for a few years after, there obviously was in the North a strong feeling, and especially in the Radical group, that the Negro needed protection from his former masters. Perhaps he did not need that protection (although there is plenty of evidence that he did), but the fact remains that a powerful group in the North *believed* that he did. First, Congress gave the freedman the protection of the Freedmen's Bureau and then, in the Reconstruction Acts of 1867, it gave him the ballot which, it was believed, would ensure him his liberty. The Radicals were wrong in believing that the ballot was the solution to the problem, but were they, this group of persons who were conscious of the government's responsibility to the freedman, wrong in wanting to assure the real and not just the formal emancipation of the slave? In other words, it can be argued, that the effort to raise the Negro population to the level of the white had to be made in order to satisfy the national conscience. When national harmony was at least outwardly achieved after 1877, it was at the expense of a racial minority and never since that time has the national conscience been fully at rest.

Hence the story of Reconstruction is not as simple as some historians would have us believe. The Radicals, some of whom might have been selfish, vindictive, and unreasonable men, did have a genuine motive for much of what they did. The story of the Freedmen's Bureau, as well as the whole story of Reconstruction, must be viewed in the light of this effort to achieve real freedom for the former slave. The Bureau was originally created because some members of Congress believed that the government had a responsibility it could not avoid. It was continued in 1866 because it was clear that the job had only just begun. It was allowed to expire after 1868, with the exception of the educational and bounty-paying branches, because it was believed that the new Reconstruction state governments, at that time in most instances controlled by Republican regimes, would protect the interests of the freedmen. By the time these governments had lost their hold during the 1870's, the enthusiasm for the cause, in Congress and in the North generally, had died down. The Negro, from that time on, was left pretty much to his own devices. Thus the Bureau's life was brief; but it played a key role in the history of Reconstruction and the history of the Negro in America.

In the brief history of the Freedmen's Bureau, General Howard was the central figure. He was the only head the Bureau ever had. From modest beginnings in 1865, under his direction it grew by

1868 into a large and influential organization. Howard then presided over the Bureau's declining but still lively years. He gave it life and direction; its success or failure was largely in his hands. It is hard to imagine anyone else who was as suited for the position of commissioner as was General Howard.

The job called for special, even unique, qualifications. The man who became commissioner of the Freedmen's Bureau almost had to be an army man since the Bureau was an agency of the War Department to be staffed by army officers and because there was no appropriation from Congress. He had to have sufficient rank to deal with his subordinates and with the military commanders in the Southern states. He would have to have a sympathetic outlook toward the freedmen since his main object would be to help them through the difficult transition period from slavery to freedom, and to do this patience, understanding, and freedom from prejudice were essential. The commissioner would also be more effective if he had the active support of the numerous freedmen's aid societies which had long been in the field as abolitionists, distributors of relief, and founders of schools for freedmen, and it was through these agencies that much of the support for the Bureau would have to come. Since a large majority of these organizations was directly associated with the Protestant denominations, the commissioner's task would be easier if he, himself, were a prominent, Protestant Christian. The commissioner of course had to have ability and experience as an executive. Yet equally as important he had to be a man of vision and imagination, someone who saw the Negro not as he was supposed to be in 1865—illiterate, child-like, improvident, inferior—but as a man with the same potentialities as any other man. What was needed was someone who could cast aside the prejudices and preconceptions of the past and visualize the day when all men in this land would be equal before the law and would have the same economic and educational opportunities.

Several men were either considered or were recommended for the position. Among these were James E. Yeatman of the Western Sanitary Commission, General Clinton B. Fisk, General Benjamin F. Butler, and General Rufus Saxton.[2] It is probable that Lincoln first offered the job to Yeatman.[3] If so, Yeatman turned it down. That Howard was the ultimate choice was logical. His high position in the army gave him not only the necessary rank but had gained for him useful executive experience. And he also had attained a reputation, not so much as a man who knew at first hand the problems of the freedmen (for his experience in such matters was limited), but as a humanitarian and a Christian soldier. He was known and respected amongst the freedmen's aid societies which hailed his appointment.[4]

It seems certain that Howard was Lincoln's choice. In an address in Augusta, Maine in the summer of 1865, just a few months after the event, Howard related how Stanton, on offering him the assignment, had said it was made at Lincoln's request.[5] Stanton had waited until Howard's military duties allowed him to leave the army to come to Washington. All the while there was a pressing need for the Bureau to begin its work even though other agencies had been active for some time in trying to meet the problems of the Negro in the South.

Since the first year of the war the federal government had had to cope with the problem of the Negroes who had come into the Union lines. As the armies advanced and took over control of slave territory, various commanders had to feed and care for an increasingly large number of freedmen and their families, especially in such places as the Sea Islands off the coast of South Carolina and Georgia, the area around Norfolk, Virginia, and parts of Louisiana, Arkansas, Mississippi, and Tennessee. Involved in this work were such army officers as General Rufus Saxton in the Sea Islands, Captain Orlando Brown in Virginia, Chaplain Thomas Conway in Louisiana, and General John Eaton in Alabama and Mississippi.[6] Also, in accordance with a confiscation act of Congress, the Treasury Department had come into possession of quantities of "confiscated" or "abandoned" lands in the seceded states, lands which were eventually turned over to the Freedmen's Bureau.[7] What had been done, however, was somewhat haphazard and not according to any plan, nor under single direction. It was Howard's responsibility to formulate a policy, form an organization, and then try to implement his program, all without any appropriation from Congress.

The Bureau's basic policy was related to its opportunity which was as great as its responsibility. The opportunity, and hence the policy, was to help an enslaved people rise from their ignorance and lowly position to take their places in a free society. To do this, fair treatment had to be assured; the freedmen had to be taught the ways of a free labor economy, and above all they needed education. To Howard, the matter was quite simple. Soon after the capture of

Atlanta, Howard made one of his few comments on the Negro which anticipated the policy he would later adopt as Bureau commissioner.

The negroes [he wrote to Lizzie] must be employed & instructed, clothed, and fed, borne with and kindly treated as well as emancipated. God in his wise providence will hold us to it at the north and at the south.[8] [Now in the summer of 1865 he restated the same basic policy to which he adhered throughout the Bureau's history. To his audience at Augusta, Maine he said:] the Government has solemnly promised to them [the freedmen] their freedom and the fruits of freedom. It will keep that promise. . . . I think that all we have to do is to aim at absolute justice to blacks and whites, watching the signs of the times, and keeping a steady rein. . . . I believe that when God sent us forth to liberate this oppressed race, he did not mean that they should be wholly engulfed. He intended that they should be free, and free to some purpose. If we attempt to re-enslave them, or to bind any heavy burdens upon them, he will chasten us again and again.

Just as soon as the white people of one of the Southern states showed evidence of allowing equal justice to the Negro, and of a willingness to care for indigent freedmen then Howard would be willing to have the Bureau functions cease in that state, for, he always asserted, it was not his intention to carry on a perpetual work. He believed that the Southern whites, or at least a sufficient number of them, through their humanitarian instincts and sense of fair-play, or if not that, through enlightened self-interest, would deal fairly and justly with the freedman, would aid in his education, and would give him the same civil and legal rights as the white man.[9]

This, then, was the basic policy which Howard laid down for the Freedmen's Bureau: assure to the former slaves equal rights under the law, extend to them every possible educational advantage, and bring the work of the Bureau to an end as quickly as safety for the Negro would permit. This policy seems reasonable enough, yet its execution in the Reconstruction period met determined and often violent opposition, largely because not many Southerners were prepared to grant equal rights to the Negro. They might grant his freedom from slavery, but they had no intention of allowing him the same legal rights as white men. Here was the source of much of the trouble which grew up between the Freedmen's Bureau and the local white population.

During the last days of May, while the Union armies were holding their grand reviews and the soldiers were making their way home, while the Southland began to struggle back from defeat, General Howard issued a series of circular letters to his newly appointed assistant commissioners laying down the specific policies which would guide the work of the Bureau. In the first of these circular letters, Howard definitely stated that while the Negro's freedom would be protected, "on no account if able to work should he harbor the thought that the government will support him in idleness." [10] Circular number two, dated May 19, encompassed several items: the duties of the assistant commissioners, relief, cooperation with benevolent societies in educational work. And, reiterating the sentiments of the first circular, Howard emphasized that "the able bodied should be encouraged and if necessary compelled to labor for their own support." [11] The third circular of May 22 concerned the rights of the freedmen while cultivating "abandoned" lands,[12] and on May 30, Howard issued a comprehensive circular which was the result of a meeting of some of the recently appointed assistant commissioners brought together to help formulate a uniform system.[13] This circular designated the headquarters for the different assistant commissioners, enjoined the latter to start work immediately, announced that relief would be discontinued as soon as possible, that the freedman would receive protection when necessary, and that if the local law did not give equal justice then the Bureau would have to step in. The freedmen would be free to choose their own employers, would not be compelled to work under an overseer system, and would be aided in obtaining title to land. The assistant commissioners were to obtain all pertinent information about abandoned and confiscated lands, destitution, and schools, and they were told of the requirement of sending in to Washington periodic reports. Finally, this circular made it quite clear that War Department regulations would prevail in the Bureau over both military and civilian personnel.[14] At the same time, Howard asked Stanton to request the President to issue an order which would effect the transfer of land, funds, and records relating to the Freedmen's Bureau from Treasury Department officials and army officers who up to that time had been in charge of freedmen's affairs.[15]

There were numerous freedmen's aid societies in the North, representing primarily the various religious denominations, which had been active in abolitionist work and also in relief measures during the war. These groups, fired by a crusading zeal, eagerly wanted to aid the newly-freed slave. It was important that their enthusiasm be channelled and their efforts coordinated because these groups were to provide most of the teachers and a large part of the financing of schools and orphanages for the freedmen. It was equally important for the commissioner to have the wholehearted support of these bodies. Sensitive to the plight and wants of the freedmen, the leaders and representatives of the aid societies kept an alert watch for any real or imagined wrong to the freedmen. How necessary then to effect a plan of cooperation between the Bureau and these societies and between the societies themselves. In a letter to the officers of the various aid societies Howard urged a union of effort with the Freedmen's Bureau as coordinator. The Bureau would also assist with transportation and rations for their personnel.[16] A union of some of the aid societies did come about with the formation of the Union Aid Commission which, with the American Missionary Association of the Congregational Church, became the most prominent in establishing schools for freedmen. From the beginning it was a central feature of Howards' policy to work closely with the private and denominational aid societies of the North. Without their support the work of the Bureau would have been severely hampered.

While Howard was laying down a basic policy in the early days of the Bureau he was also putting together an organization. He would need competent, experienced men to head the various Bureau departments in the central office in Washington, and men of special talents to take over the positions of assistant commissioner in the several Southern states. Drawing on his army experience, Commissioner Howard divided up the duties of his office and assigned them to staff officers according to the practice of the army. Thus he organized an adjutant general's office under the leadership of an army associate, Joseph S. Fullerton, formerly Howard's assistant adjutant general of the 4th Corps. This office, which Howard called the records division, would handle all the correspondence, orders, and assignment of personnel. It was the vital center of the entire Bureau organization and was handled in the same way a similar office would be conducted in the army. That is, the system of recording letters received and letters sent, forms of correspondence and the like were done according to regular army practice. The chief disbursing officer handled all the Bureau's financial affairs. General George W.

Balloch who had been with Howard in the 11th Corps filled this post during most of the Bureau's history. In addition there were medical, commissary, quartermaster, and land divisions.[17] All but the land division had its army counterpart, and all the division heads had had war experience in their respective fields. Howard's inspector general in the Army of the Tennessee, General William E. Strong, served the Bureau in the same capacity. There was no mistaking the military character of the Bureau's organization.

The Bureau's success would depend in a large measure on the quality of the personnel in the field. Here was a major problem which hampered the smooth functioning of the Bureau throughout its history because trained, efficient, honest, and conscientious agents were not always to be had. One difficulty was that Howard had little choice over the selection of any but his most immediate subordinates, i.e. the assistant commissioners. He did not always select them. Yet it was highly important that the assistant commissioners be competent men. They would have a heavy responsibility to perform and would have closer contact with everyday conditions in the Southern states than would Howard.

Subject to the approval of the Secretary of War and the President, Howard selected for assistants men who were either already engaged in freedmen's work or who were known to him personally in the army. In the first group were some of the men mentioned earlier: Captain Orlando Brown, Chaplain T. W. Conway, and General John Eaton. Brown and Conway were assigned to the states of Virginia and Louisiana respectively, while Eaton was given the District of Columbia and Maryland as his territory. Howard had come to know General Rufus Saxton, a West Point graduate and member of the regular army, in January 1865, while the Army of the Tennessee was on the coast of Georgia and South Carolina. Because of Saxton's long experience in freedmen's affairs, Howard assigned to him the three states of South Carolina, Georgia, and Florida. Later, he had only South Carolina. Several of the other assistant commissioners, Colonel T. W. Osborn, Colonel Eliphalet Whittlesey, General John W. Sprague, and General Wager Swayne, son of the Supreme Court Justice, had all either served under or with Howard during the war. They were assigned respectively to the states of Florida, North Carolina, Arkansas, and Alabama (Sprague had Missouri also). Whittlesey, a Yale graduate and a former Bowdoin professor, had served on Howard's staff in the 2d Corps. Osborn had been his chief of artillery at Gettysburg and for the Army of the Tennessee during the Carolina campaign. Sprague and Swayne had both served in the Army of the Tennessee. General Clinton B. Fisk was known to Howard more by reputation than through personal acquaintance. He had been a successful businessman in St. Louis before the war and had had a creditable war career. Howard assigned him the states of Tennessee and Kentucky. (Assistant commissioners for Georgia and Texas were selected at a later time.)

Shortly after making these appointments Howard told what had guided him in his selections. "I took generally those who had been long in the work," he said, "men who had been successful and who were earnest in securing the rights of the freedmen. When I was compelled to go beyond this class, I took those whom I knew to be men of integrity and with Christian hearts." [18]

Of these original selections, all were relatively successful in carrying out their duties satisfactorily with the exception of Conway and Saxton. Apparently Conway could not keep on good terms with everyone, was wont to be hypercritical of the local civil officers, and was overzealous in championing the cause of the freedmen. When Conway complained to Howard in September 1865 that his salary would not support him in New Orleans, Howard took the opportunity to ask Stanton to relieve him and appoint in his place General Absolam Baird.[19] Baird was a West Point graduate, a regular army man, and had served as a division commander in Slocum's Army of Georgia during the Savannah campaign. He had a successful administration as assistant commissioner for Louisiana.

Saxton proved to be an incompetent administrator although he had the confidence of the freedmen on the Sea Islands. Howard overestimated his ability to handle freedmen's affairs for three states, and following an inspection by Howard's adjutant general, Joseph S. Fullerton, other men were appointed assistant commissioners for Florida and Georgia.[20]

Whittlesey, as we shall later see, was charged with mismanagement, but a court martial cleared him, and Howard called him to the central office in Washington to be the adjutant general of the Bureau.

Had the original appointees, with some few exceptions, retained their positions throughout the life of the Bureau, a better administration would have resulted. Instead, in most every state, there were frequent changes which necessarily meant a lack of continuity and stability. This was no fault of Howard; rather it resulted from the fact that many of the assistant commissioners retired from the army or were transferred to other duties. In some instances President Johnson intervened to effect changes. In all, there were over fifty army officers who at one time or another held the position of assistant commissioner between 1865 and the end of 1868. Some of this rapid turnover was because of the fact that from April 1866 until the fall of 1868 the positions of assistant commissioner and military commander were united in the same person and there was frequent change in military assignments. Prior to the adoption of this policy, there had been considerable friction and overlapping between the two offices.

Despite the numerous changes, the assistant commissioners, with few exceptions, carried out their duties with little cause for complaint from the commissioner. One of the exceptions was General Joseph B. Kiddoo, an officer with an excellent army record but who was also a heavy drinker. While Kiddoo, who was assistant commissioner for Texas from April 1866 to January 1867, was visiting Washington in November 1866, Howard became aware of his drinking habits. When Kiddoo was reported as being at Willard's Hotel under the influence of liquor, Howard wrote him a friendly letter begging him to "reverse the wheels." [21] Shortly after, Howard exacted from Kiddoo a temperance pledge which evidently worked for the short time that Kiddoo remained in Texas as assistant commissioner.[22]

A few of the assistant commissioners proved none too friendly toward the policies of the Bureau. One of these was General Jefferson C. Davis, for a time assistant commissioner for Kentucky.[23] Another was General Robert C. Buchanan, assistant commissioner for Louisiana from January to August 1868.[24] On the other hand there were those who leaned too far in the other direction. For instance, there was General Edgar M. Gregory, assistant commissioner for Texas from the fall of 1865 to March 1866, who was highly unpopular in that state because, according to General Philip H. Sheridan's inspecting officer, General H. G. Wright, Gregory was too prejudiced in favor of the Negro.[25] The case of Conway in Louisiana has already been mentioned. These extremes were the exception rather than the rule. All the assistant commissioners were officers of the regular or volunteer army who had orders to carry out, and who tried to do a conscientious job. There was little fanaticism in this group of men; there was rather practical mindedness, good sense, and correct behavior.

When it came to the Bureau agents below the rank of assistant commissioner, Howard was not so fortunate. He had little control over appointments made by the assistant commissioners. Nor did the assistant commissioners themselves have much voice in the matter of appointments. For the first two years of the Bureau's life, that is, when it was doing its most important work, the great majority of agents were officers detailed to the Bureau from the regular army or from what was called the Veterans Reserve Corps, veterans who had been disabled by the loss of an arm or a leg during the war. To compound the difficulty, regimental commanders naturally gave up to the Bureau those officers who were least desirable to the regiment.

One of the most persistent complaints of the assistant commissioners was their inability to keep enough qualified officers to fill the necessary jobs. As early as June 30, 1865, General John W. Sprague, assistant commissioner for Arkansas and Missouri, wrote to Howard anticipating this difficulty. "I find one of the greatest dificulties [sic] I shall encounter," he wrote, ". . . is to find *men* who have the necessary qualifications for the different positions where men of *zeal* and *discretion* are needed—and as we are obliged to choose from the Army only, when the right men are found and set to work they are liable to be mustered out. . . ." [26] "Under orders received today," wrote Assistant Commissioner Brown of Virginia, "five thousand more of the troops in this Dept will be mustered out which will take about forty of the officers and men now doing duty in the Bureau. I do not know how these can be replaced." [27] Saxton complained that many of his officers were "so entirely unfitted by sympathy and inclination for duty in this bureau that their services can by no possiblity be of advantage to it or this work." [28] And General J. B. Kiddoo, assistant commissioner for Texas, wrote in 1866: "I regret . . . to be obliged to state that the withdrawal and muster out of troops in this State will materially damage the successful operation of the Bureau." [29]

Howard did his best to retain men already detailed to the Bureau, or at least to assure their replacement when they were mustered out. The War Department cooperated in the latter situation,[30] yet the problem was never satisfactorily solved. The commissioner had to work with what he could get, and inevitably some of the officers assigned to Bureau duty proved unsuited to the task at hand. It is significant to note that frequently the Bureau was criticized because some of the agents were alleged to be hostile to the freedmen and overly friendly with the whites. Still, when all the above is taken into consideration, the results were better than might have been expected. These men were still under orders, charged with certain duties, and subject to military discipline. When one takes into account the magnitude and difficulties of the task, the Bureau agents in most cases performed their duties well. True, there were instances of fraud, dishonesty, overzealousness, or lack of interest. On this, Howard wrote in 1868: "Out of over a thousand officers who have been more or less on bureau duty, not more than ten or twelve have been guilty of the charges brought against officers of the Freedmen's Bureau. A very few may have . . . alleged that the negroes would have their master's estates but considering the manner of detail, the constant change by muster out, and the peculiar and delicate duties imposed on them, it is wonderful that so many true men have been found." [31]

The Bureau sometimes employed Southern whites as agents. In the Bureau's first year Howard was reluctant to employ them because he did not want to spend the money on salaries. He did, however, allow individual assistant commissioners to experiment with the practice. The most notable example of this was in Georgia where General Davis Tillson was the assistant commissioner. Tillson, a native of Maine, had spent two years at West Point and had had a favorable war record. As sub-assistant commissioner for the Memphis district in the early months of the Bureau, he had made a reputation of being able to get on well with the local residents. When it was apparent that Saxton was having trouble handling Georgia as well as South Carolina, Howard appointed Tillson assistant commissioner of the former state. In October 1865 Tillson complained that he did not have enough army officers to organize the state, and requested permission to employ local officials, such as justices of the peace, to act without salary as Bureau agents.[32] Howard, who wanted his assistant commissioners to have as much latitude as possible, gave his assent [33] but later he counselled: "They [the civilian agents] will need careful watching and prompt removal in case they do not perform their duty." He also recommended that these agents rely for their pay on fees for making contracts between freedmen and their employers.³⁴ About a year later when Howard's inspector, General Frederick D. Sewall, was in Georgia he reported that the system was not working well because the agents did not make any accounting of fees collected and this had led in some instances to overcharging. Furthermore, wrote Sewall, the freedmen frequently complained of some of these agents either because of their actions or their inactivity. He did concede that some were doing a good job.³⁵ General Sprague tried out a similar system in Arkansas. Howard, through his adjutant, wrote Sprague telling him to go ahead since "at some period the Bureau will have to turn over all its functions to the civil authority, and it would be better before doing so, to test the spirit in which they will receive and execute them." ³⁶

The practice of employing Southerners lasted in Georgia throughout Tillson's tenure, that is until January 1867, when his successor, General Caleb C. Sibley, discontinued the scheme at Howard's suggestion. In his report for 1867, Howard wrote that the Southerners were never fitted for the job and that often they "shamefully abused" their powers.³⁷ General William P. Carlin, assistant commissioner for Tennessee, complained that some of the civilian agents in his jurisdiction sought favor with the "former disloyalists" and really did nothing toward protecting the rights of freedmen.³⁸

As more army officers left the service, the Bureau frequently reemployed them as civilian agents. This became fairly common in 1867 and 1868 although Howard always favored active army men for agents.³⁹ In October 1868 there were in the employ of the Bureau one hundred and forty-one commissioned officers and four hundred and twelve civilian agents.⁴⁰ But many of these civilians were former army men. For instance, in July 1868 in Florida, of the fifteen sub-assistant commissioners, eight were army officers and the seven civilians had formerly been officers in the army.⁴¹

The use of civilian agents was not altogether satisfactory, and they were the cause of much of the criticism directed against the Bureau. They ranged in ability from the competent and judicious to the inept, dishonest, or overly partisan. One difficulty was that they lacked the cloak of authority granted by the army uniform, and they were not under the army's rigid discipline.

Finally, the Bureau employed a few Negroes as agents, but so few that they really were not an important factor. Writing for Howard in September 1865, Max Woodhull, the Bureau adjutant, stated that though one or two colored officers had been assigned to duty in the

Bureau, the practice was not deemed advisable because, he wrote, "they saw through prejudice and caused a hostility hard to overcome." [42]

Never, then, throughout the life of the Bureau could Howard have the assurance of a dependable personnel. Always he had to accept those officers who were sent to him or the civilian agents available for hire, and the results were not always satisfactory. Yet by laying down certain goals and principles he could indicate the general policies to be followed; by frequent inspection and prompt removal of dishonest and unsatisfactory agents he did his utmost to maintain as effective an organization as was possible.

So, during the late spring and early summer of 1865 the Freedmen's Bureau began to take on life. Otis Howard found a few days early in June to visit Lizzie in Philadelphia. Following this brief visit Lizzie went back to Maine for the rest of the summer and Otis stayed on alone in the Washington heat. "I find the house very cool this hot weather," he told his son, Guy, "the repairers are white washing and painting and I am having the gas pipe in my room mended. We have a good cow and I am having the hay made so as to put it in the barn." [43]

Howard was becoming just a bit unhappy about his separation from wife and children. For four years he had seen very little of them, and on a very hot July 22 wrote Lizzie, "I feel too much like a stranger to my family. Everything is so remarkably uncertain now in army and political life, that we *must* be together when we can and lose not a drop of comfort we always derive from each others society. . . . Our wedded life has surely been happy but it seems wonderfully short and I cant help feeling as if there was danger of our getting old & moving off the stage, before we have had a fair portion of life." [44] Before the month was out Otis had left Washington to join Lizzie in Augusta where he stayed for almost four weeks. It was really his first extended leave since the summer of 1862 following the loss of his arm at Fair Oaks.

Relief Work and Land Policy

The summer of 1865 was a time of great distress in the South for whites and blacks alike. The returning Southern soldier was often greeted by sights of desolation, of homes and farm buildings destroyed, of fields unplanted or untended. Some of the Negro population remained on the master's farm or plantation, not wishing to lose what little security remained. Others believed that freedom implied freedom to move around, and in the months immediately following the war many of the freedmen took to the roads. In some areas, such as in parts of Tennessee, Louisiana, and Virginia, this practice had been going on ever since the early part of the war.

The Negroes tended to congregate in the larger cities and in those places held by Federal troops, as for instance on the Sea Islands of Georgia and South Carolina. Wherever this occurred the army assumed the responsibility of providing subsistence for these unfortunates. Now, with the end of the war the task of caring for those who were unable to care for themselves became truly enormous. Thus when the Bureau started its work in the late spring of 1865 the most pressing task was that of relief for the destitute. Now this was an age when it was considered the duty of private philanthropy or local government to care for the poor; surely it was not the function of the federal government. The plight of the freedmen after the war was such, however, that only the government could adequately perform the great relief job which needed to be done. From 1865 to the end of 1868 the Freedmen's Bureau had the difficult responsibility of issuing rations to destitute freedmen and refugees. (Refugees were the loyal whites of the South, and one of the problems the Bureau constantly faced was trying to determine just which whites had been "loyal" during the war.) It was a difficult task because there was the possibility that too liberal a policy would simply encourage the freedmen to go on accepting the government's largesse and never get the idea that they should work if they could. In solving this problem the Bureau did its best to see to it that only those in need received aid. While reports of Negro idleness in the months immediately after the war vary considerably, it is probable that the situation, when it did exist, was a temporary one. Most freedmen appeared willing to work.

Howard was acutely aware of the danger of being too generous with rations and he feared hostile criticism. His early circulars, already cited, warned his subordinates that, if necessary, the freedmen should be compelled to work and that just as soon as possible the Bureau would discontinue all relief. Since the Bureau was only a temporary institution, Howard believed that it was essential that local government and philanthropy take up the burden of caring for the needy, the destitute, sick and aged persons, as well as for orphans. The Bureau's policy was to do what was necessary but no more. Not only Howard but also the assistant commissioners did their utmost to hold down the number of rations issued. In July 1865 Eliphalet Whittlesey, assistant commissioner for North Carolina, wrote to Howard that there were too many able-bodied freedmen on Roanoke Island living off the government, and recommended reducing the distribution of rations.[1] In that same month General Fisk in Tennessee urged a stricter policy and stated that he was not deceived by the type, both black and white, who were taking advantage of the government.[2] In the following year, General Wager Swayne, assistant commissioner for Alabama, admitted that there was some destitution in that state, but said that he was very reluctant to distribute too many rations. Early in 1866 the state legislature had estimated the number of destitute whites at fifty-two thousand, so Swayne agreed to issue fifteen thousand rations daily, increasing the number to over twenty thousand for May.[3]

Howard supported the assistant commissioners in their efforts to keep the issuance of rations under control. For instance, through his adjutant, he issued instructions to a member of his staff, Lieutenant Stuart Eldridge, before Eldridge set out on an inspection tour of the starving areas of northern Georgia and Alabama in June 1866.

The Government must be protected from all kinds of imposition. . . . [the instructions read]

Remember that people who are able to walk from ten to twenty miles, and carry great loads of rations, are in no danger of starving without those rations; and the same exertion that they put forth to draw supplies from the Government, applied to some useful occupation, would earn enough to support wives and children that may be really destitute.[4]

Even though Howard made every effort to protect the government, he was not, as a result, deaf to the pleadings of the unfortunate whether white or black. Between 1865 and September 1869 the Bureau issued over twenty million rations, not simply to freedmen but to destitute whites as well. It also maintained soup kitchens in the larger cities where the number of destitute was great.[5] Strictly speaking, the Bureau was not supposed to help the needy whites, for these were theoretically tainted with the sin of rebellion and thus not eligible for Bureau relief. But it was all too obvious that this class frequently needed help and Howard was quite willing to interpret his authority quite liberally. For instance, in January 1866 the Bureau adjutant, Max Woodhull, explained to General J. W. Sprague, assistant commissioner for Arkansas, that Howard wanted him "to give a liberal interpretation to the word Refugees . . . so that you may issue subsistence supplies to such worthy sufferers as you may consider entitled to Government assistance."[6] In September of that same year Howard appealed to Stanton to permit him to provide relief for the suffering people of Alabama, and in doing so noted that in that state there were two whites who received aid for each colored person.[7] And when, in South Carolina in March 1867, there was some question in the mind of Assistant Commissioner Robert K. Scott about the correctness of feeding other than freedmen or loyal refugees, Howard wired back, "I interpret refugees as liberally as possible to prevent starvation."[8] Thus all classes got relief when it was needed, and in 1867, a year of special need, the Bureau administered a general relief program authorized by Congress and cooperated in by several relief agencies organized in Northern cities.

In addition to affording relief to the destitute, the Freedmen's Bureau also provided hospital and general medical care for the freedmen. Perhaps as many as a million persons received medical aid from 1865 to 1872.[9] The Bureau assisted Northern philanthropic bodies in establishing and maintaining orphanages in several Southern cities.[10] As soon as the local authorities could set up their own establishments the Bureau cut down on these services. Without the aid of the federal government, acting through the Freedmen's Bureau, it is safe to say that many more thousands in the South, white and black, would have died.

Few would deny the success of the Bureau's relief work. Under Howard's direction it performed a difficult task with a minimum of fraud and mismanagement.[11] Those who were genuinely in need of help usually got it, and though inevitably there were cases of the undeserving receiving aid, the officers of the Bureau made a sincere effort to keep the number of these to a minimum.[12]

Relief measures were absolutely essential during the early months of the Bureau's existence. But Howard believed that he had more to accomplish than the temporary alleviation of suffering. He had to try to prepare the freedmen for the future, for the time when there would be no Bureau to assist them. He had to initiate those programs which would be the most effective in gaining freedom for Negroes in America after more than two centuries of slavery.

The best chance that the freedman had of achieving real freedom was by becoming a landowner. Theoretically the possibility existed of granting to each Negro family a tract of land either from the lands of the former owners, confiscated or appropriated by the government during the war, or from the public lands belonging to the federal government. To have divided up the estates of former Confederates would have produced a thoroughgoing economic revolution involving widescale invasion of the rights of property and probably had no chance with a Congress which could not get itself to go that far. Yet something along those lines, though in a milder form, was intended by the framers of the original Freedmen's Bureau Bill. Historians of the Reconstruction era frequently have ridiculed the idea with jeering references to "forty acres and a mule" as if the whole thing were completely illusory, and there is no doubt that the obstacles were great. The former slave had had no experience as an independent land owner; he had no funds to carry him along during the initial years; he was illiterate, and easy prey for unprincipled persons who would take advantage of his ignorance. It was widely believed in South and North that he was improvident and lazy.

For all these reasons the proposal that the federal government assist the Negro in becoming an independent landowner probably had small chance of success even had it been seriously adopted. Yet during the first few months of the Bureau's existence Howard made the effort to carry out the intent of Congress as expressed in the Freedmen's Bureau Bill which stated,

That the commissioner . . . shall have authority to set apart, for the use of loyal refugees and freedmen, such tracts of land within the insurrectionary states as shall have been abandoned, or to which the United States shall have acquired title by confiscation or sale, or otherwise, and to every male citizen, whether refugee or freedman, as aforesaid, there shall be assigned not more than forty acres of such land, and the person to whom it was so assigned shall be protected in the use and enjoyment of the land for the term of three years at an annual rent not exceeding six per centum upon the value of such land . . . At the end of said term, or at any time during said term, the occupants of any parcels so assigned may purchase the land and receive such title thereto as the United States can convey. . . .[13]

Of course, the Congress could have gone further and distributed the land outright, giving immediate title without payment. But except for Thaddeus Stevens and a few others who were sincerely interested in effecting a social and economic revolution in the South, most Congressmen were either indifferent or opposed to such a scheme. Even so, the act was liberal enough with the property of the Southern planters, and had the Freedmen's Bureau been able to carry out its land provisions the social and economic results of Reconstruction might have been very different from what they were. But Howard was never able to carry out this provision of the act mainly because of President Johnson who early showed himself to be a moderate in his reconstruction policies. And part of his program of swift restoration of the Southern states to a normal relationship to the national government was a generous amnesty policy. With the presidential pardon went restoration of property. This in turn meant that the Bureau's land holdings, quite extensive in the early summer of 1865, had dwindled to almost nothing by the end of the year. Howard fought valiantly to preserve this essential part of his program, but he was helpless in the face of Johnson's power to pardon.

For a few months that summer, Howard tried to carry out the intent of Congress by making abandoned and confiscated land available to the freedmen. In June he sent a telegram to each of the assistant commissioners requiring that they send in lists of abandoned lands which they intended to set aside for the freedmen.[14] Confiscation was still going on as late as July, but that month the tide began to turn. As Johnson became more liberal with his pardons, the more apparent it became to Howard that if the present policy were continued, the Bureau would lose not only its major source of income but also the principal means by which the freedman could become a landowner. With considerable confusion prevailing during July and into August, Howard wrote to Stanton for clarification.[15] On July 21, he telegraphed Assistant Commissioner Conway in Louisiana to take all the houses and other property which the Treasury agents would turn over. "We will make use of them," he continued, "until compelled to give them up. File all applications for restoration of lands etc until you receive directions from this Bureau governing the matter."[16] On the 24th he wrote to Colonel Brown, "The matter of Abandoned Lands will soon be settled. Such lands as are confiscated already must be used as the law directs. And perhaps there will be more confiscated, but I doubt it from present appearances."[17]

Before leaving for Maine, Howard framed a circular which was obviously a last effort to stave off the effects of the President's policy. The circular stated that the President's pardon would not extend to property taken by law for the use of the freedmen.[18] It was never issued, because it did not have the approval of Stanton or of Johnson. In August, Johnson ordered Howard to return land in the possession of the Bureau to the pardoned owners with the understanding that the freedmen who had planted crops would be allowed to stay on through the harvest.[19]

How disastrous the President's action was may be seen by the disruption it caused to the plans of some of the assistant commissioners. For instance, Fisk in Tennessee was about to distribute in ten, twenty, thirty, and forty acre lots the plantation of a Thomas P. Brown of Giles County to Brown's former slaves, when he had to make restoration. Fisk had intended to distribute to freedmen lands on several other plantations under his jurisdiction, but decided to suspend his plan while awaiting further orders.[20]

In the first few months of Reconstruction there was little apparent hostility between Johnson and those favoring a stricter Reconstruction policy. Howard was not fully alive to the direction the President's policy was taking and, on returning to Washington early in September, he suggested to Johnson, apparently with considerable hope that his ideas would receive favorable attention, that whenever the President pardoned a man worth more than $20,000 such a man be obliged "to set apart and grant title in fee simple to each head of family of his former slaves, a homestead varying in extent from 5 to 10 acres. to be secured against alienation during the lifetime of the grantee." [21] Johnson pigeonholed the suggestion, and his policy of pardon and land restoration went on without change. The President, responsible for restoring peace and harmony to a divided nation and a conservative in his political and economic views, was unwilling to deprive the Southern property owner of land which had been his at the start of the war. A pardon without complete restoration of property rights would not be a real pardon. In the summer of 1865, Johnson demonstrated that his sympathies were with the Southern white population and that he believed their interests should be cared for even at the expense of the freedmen.

It was at this time that Howard became convinced that Johnson was frustrating the Bureau's land program. "I called on . . . the President last night," he wrote Lizzie on September 9. "Mr Johnson is giving up the law pretty fast and I begin to tremble with anxiety for the freedman. This is *entre nous.*" [22] Four days later, with Lizzie still in Maine, he wrote again, "I have had more frequent interviews with the President and am quite apprehensive, that the freedmen's rights will not be cared for so much as I could wish. Yet," he added, "the President is cordial to me and so are his household officials (a test of good will)." [23]

Thus by the end of the summer of 1865 the President had effectively nullified Howard's efforts to carry out the provision of the Freedmen's Bureau Bill which aimed at making the freed slave a land owner. Howard's subordinates were somewhat perplexed by Johnson's policy. A member of his staff, Lieutenant Stuart Eldridge, wrote at this time from Vicksburg that the belief was circulating that Johnson was not sustaining Howard in the latter's land program. "It appears," Eldridge wrote, "much as if the President was opposed to the Bureau. . . ." [24]

"It seems to me," wrote General Saxton on September 5, "as not wise or prudent to do injustice to those who have always been loyal and true, in order to be lenient to those who have done their best to destroy the Nation's life." He pleaded that he be allowed to go ahead with his plan of seizing more abandoned land and warned lest the government show bad faith to those who already had settled on what they thought was to be their own land.[25] In reply, Howard could only say that they should make the best of a bad situation and especially should they try to help the freedmen purchase lands from private owners.[26]

The land program was deteriorating fast in September. The crucial test would come in the Sea Island areas of South Carolina and Georgia where Sherman, in his Special Field Order number 15 of January 1865, had set aside this region for the exclusive use of the freedmen. Since the beginning of the year, Saxton had been supervising the settlement of the freedmen on abandoned lands in the Sea Island areas of South Carolina and many families had already planted crops. Johnson, however, intended that his amnesty program should apply to the Sea Islands as well as to other areas, and early in October he ordered Howard to proceed with the return of abandoned property there and to go himself to work out a satisfactory arrangement between the owners and the freedmen. In response to this order, Howard went to South Carolina to carry out this painful assignment.

On October 19, Howard met with a large group of freedmen on Edisto Island. He explained to them the President's wishes and urged them to make the best of a bad situation. The freedmen agreed to leave the matter to Howard and yet they stated in emphatic terms their aversion to working for their former masters. If they could not own the land, they wanted to lease it. The best that Howard could do was to arrange for the formation of a board of supervisors, having representation from the Bureau, the planters, and the freedmen with Captain A. P. Ketchum of Howard's staff as the head of the board and charged with carrying out Howard's instructions. Before receiving back their lands, the planters were obliged to agree that the freedmen would get that year's crop, and to enter into labor contracts with the freedmen. If, after two months, the latter failed to make contracts they would thereby forfeit their right to stay on the land.[27]

Still not satisfied, a committee of the freedmen from Edisto Island lodged further protest with Howard who had returned to Charleston. He did his best to allay their fears and to prepare them for the inevitable loss of their lands. "You are right," he said, "in wanting homesteads and will surely be defended in the possession of every one which you shall purchase or have already purchased. The Government does not wish to befriend its enemies and injure its friends, but considers a forgiven man in the light of a citizen restored to rights of property excepting as to slaves." He held out to them the hope that Congress would consider their case, and in the meantime he urged them either to lease or buy land or to contract for wages.[28]

The outcome of the Sea Island affair was that the original owners got back their land and the freedmen became laborers rather than tenants or landowners. Johnson vetoed the Freedmen's Bureau Bill containing a provision confirming the rights of the freedmen to the Sea Island lands, and that provision was dropped from the bill which Congress subsequently passed over Johnson's veto. Howard thus failed in his plan of having the lands of former plantation owners divided amongst the ex-slaves. Whether or not the plan was feasible is open to question. General Davis Tillson, assistant commissioner for Georgia, thought not. "I do not think there are ten freed families on the Sea-Islands of Georgia, to whom their grants of land are of any value whatever," Tillson wrote to Howard the following March. "It is perfectly apparent to any one acquainted with the condition of things on these Islands, that the freed people would be much better off at the end of this or next year to go to work for wages, than to attempt to cultivate the lands assigned them with inadequate means." The report of Howard's inspector, General William E. Strong, a short time later, seemed to confirm this view, but with a significant addendum. Strong wrote that the prospects for those freedmen running their own farms on the islands were poor, but that they preferred to remain where they were rather than to hire out elsewhere. Some, he believed, would do well.[29]

Howard wrote in his autobiography a chapter on abandoned lands in which he deplored the actions of President Johnson, not only in the Sea Islands, but all over the South. The President's policy, he said, negated the intention of Congress and also deprived the Bureau of much-needed income. Yet, at the very end, without any elaboration, he made the wholly inconsistent statement that "After years of thinking and observation I am inclined to believe that the restoration of their lands to the planters proved for all their future better for the negroes." [30] Whatever Howard may have concluded at the time he wrote his autobiography, there is no question but that in the early months of Reconstruction he tried conscientiously to carry out the mandate of the original Bureau bill to afford the freedmen the opportunity of gaining some of the lands in the South which they had formerly cultivated as slaves.

With the settlement of the Sea Island question having gone against the Bureau and the freedmen, the chances of the ex-slave becoming a land holder were slim indeed. Of course, it is important to state that even if all the abandoned and confiscated land had been available to the Bureau for distribution to the freedmen, only a small percentage of Negro families would have become land owners. Would it not have been wise, though, to have afforded as many as possible the opportunity of proving their worth as landowners? The advancement of the former slave to a position of full equality was not aided by having him become solely an agricultural laborer. Had the Bureau been able to settle more than just a few thousand Negro families on their own land the progress of the race could have been more rapid than it has been.

In the fall of 1865 when the President was undermining the Bureau's land program, the notion spread amongst the freedmen that before long, especially at the end of the year, they would come into possession of the lands of their former masters. Such an idea is easily understandable, for had not Congress in the Bureau Bill provided for this? Yet by early fall, Howard realized that the best the freedmen could do was to contract as laborers for the coming year, since Johnson's amnesty program had ended the chance of the Negro becoming a landowner on any large scale. Thus he set about disabusing the freedmen of whatever false hopes they might have had. In a circular to all assistant commissioners, dated November 11, 1865, he noted that the freedmen had been deceived about the government's intentions and that they believed that the lands of the present holders would be divided among the freedmen at Christmas or New Year's. He therefore directed the officers and agents of the Bureau "to take every possible means to remove so erroneous and injurious an impression," and he concluded, "The Commissioner deprecates hostile action and wishes every possible exertion made to produce kind feeling and mutual confidence between the blacks and the whites." [31]

Despite the fact that by the end of 1865 there was no chance of the freedmen gaining possession of the confiscated and abandoned lands, Howard still believed that some means should be found making it possible for the freedman to be a landowner. He believed that men with capital could, with profit, buy up land and sell it to the freedmen on long terms. In March 1866 he replied to a letter of inquiry from an Englishman by saying, "I hope there will be plenty of straight forward, fearless men, who will purchase or aid in the purchase of estates in every part of the South. With such men, or the means they invest, will go industry, thrift, education and civilization." [32] He was ready to endorse every honest plan which would result in the freedman becoming a landowner. "The great want of the colored people is land and homes," he wrote in 1869 to a Philadelphia woman who told Howard of her scheme of buying up land and selling it on easy terms to freedmen.³³ To another individual, in 1870, who suggested that Congress be the purchaser, Howard replied that there was almost no chance of this, and again stated his conviction that private capital should take up the idea. "Establish industrious working men upon farms that will pay for themselves in a few short years, and they will be better off than they possibly can be as the tenants of a man who begrudges them every foot of soil that he has been coaxed or constrained to give up from his darling estate." And, he continued, "let him become an industrious prosperous land owner with every right of citizenship, then the condescending protection of an unwilling patron will not afflict him." ³⁴

To demonstrate his conviction that the freedmen, with encouragement, could become landowners, Howard and a few friends promoted the Barry Farm project. The scheme was a complicated one. Howard took Bureau funds amounting to $52,000 and granted this amount to three of the freedmen's schools supported by the Bureau. These schools agreed to invest the money in a farm of 375 acres (the Barry Farm) on the south side of the Anacostia River in the District of Columbia, the land being held in trust by Howard, Senator S. C. Pomeroy, and a local resident, J. R. Elvans. The trustees sold lots of one acre to some of the more enterprising freedmen of Washington, allowing them two years to pay.³⁵ Most of these paid the full price and thus became landowners. The result was probably not the complete success which Howard, in his usual optimism, claimed for the enterprise, but it did to a small extent help relieve the overcrowded conditions in Washington, and it did illustrate the point which Howard was trying to make, that is, that the freedman was eager to be a landowner, and that by helping him to fulfill his desire, he could best be assimilated into American society.³⁶

There is little evidence that Northern capitalists were quick to emulate Howard's example, but that is no fault of his. Had they done so, had they had the same faith that Howard had, the freedmen undoubtedly would have progressed more rapidly. The fact was, however, that few white people at that time were willing to sell to Negroes, and Howard admits in his autobiography that the seller of the Barry Farm was unaware of the land's ultimate disposition.³⁷

Howard, privately, never was wholeheartedly back of the plan to have the freedman become a homesteader, especially in the West, even though he recommended the idea to Congress late in 1865.

> I consider this [he wrote in December of that year] to a certain extent, an experiment, and do not deem it advisable to carry it too far at present. To remove all the freedmen from the South, would in my opinion, be a great mistake. The feeling of hostility now existing between the two races, I do not regard as permanent. . . . If we can only bring the whites to do the negroes justice . . . I think it preferable that they remain where they are, rather than attempt to colonize in large numbers.[38]

There were still large tracts of federally owned land in some of the Southern states and in June of 1866 Congress enacted legislation opening three million acres of public land in Alabama, Mississippi, Louisiana, Arkansas, and Florida giving to the freedmen exclusive rights to the land until January 1, 1867.

After Congress passed the bill, Howard, despite his personal misgivings, got behind the idea with considerable enthusiasm, urging his assistant commissioners to publicize the opportunity now open to the freedmen.[39] Relatively few freedmen availed themselves of the opportunity to take up homesteads, however. The fees, low as they were, acted as a deterrent, as did the lack of funds for agricultural tools and other requirements of the independent farmer. Much of the land opened to settlement was not suitable for farming. The provisions of the bill expired too early for many freedmen to take advantage of it, and finally in some instances opportunities for employment were so favorable that the tendency was to avoid taking a chance on an uncertain future as an independent farmer.[40]

Thus the freedman, in general, did not become a landowner, despite the efforts of General Howard and a handful of other Americans who had the vision to see that the Negro would advance most rapidly when given the proper incentives. In the light of what did happen after 1865, it would appear that the nation lost a great opportunity to do something truly constructive. The situation in 1865 of four million landless freedmen demanded a bold, imaginative plan for which few Americans were prepared at that time.

During 1865 relief measures and disposal of the land question dominated the Bureau's work. In addition, Howard was responsible for inaugurating a system of contracts between freedmen and planters, for issuing transportation to refugees and freedmen, either returning to their homes or enroute to localities where jobs were available, and for coordinating the educational activities of the various aid societies and extending to them what help the Bureau could in that first year when funds were so limited. Finally, there was the major concern of protecting the Negro in his newly acquired status of a free man, and of reassuring the white population that even though the former slaves were now free, there was nothing to fear in the way of insurrection. Such fears became quite pronounced as the year 1865 came to a close; even President Johnson wired Major General James Steedman, in command at Augusta, Georgia, as early as August, to suppress quickly any insurrectionary move on the part of the Negro population.[41]

From all over the South, the assistant commissioners repeatedly denied that there was any danger of an uprising, and they frequently asserted that the rumors were only an excuse to raise a local military force,[42] or, as Assistant Commissioner Samuel Thomas in Mississippi said, to argue that the Negro was being spoiled and made dangerous under the pampering of the Bureau and that therefore the Bureau must be withdrawn. "They know," Thomas wrote to Howard, "that if they admit that the Freedmen's Bureau has a single virtue, it would endanger the prospect of a total removal of federal authority from this state. If they can once get free of all control, they know they can do as they please with the negro."[43] Christmas and the New Year's Day came and went with nothing resembling an insurrection on the part of the freedmen. Many Southerners would have said that this was no fault of the Bureau; on the other hand, it is reasonable to believe that the Bureau agents, in most cases, represented a restraining influence.

By the end of 1865 Howard had learned what a thankless job he held. Most Southern whites disliked the Bureau with varying degrees of intensity. There were some who recognized the Bureau's worth in having the freedmen enter into labor contracts, or in distributing supplies to needy whites. But because of the very nature of the Bureau, it was certain to arouse the hostility of a large majority of the Southern whites, for its existence implied that they were not to be trusted to deal justly with the freedmen. It also stood in the way of local control of the Negro population.

Criticism by white Southerners was natural and understandable. It also is that which is most often cited in any discussion of the

Freedmen's Bureau.⁴⁴ Yet there was adverse criticism from the other side as well, and Howard was perhaps more sensitive to the strictures of the old abolitionist groups than he was to those coming from the South. The friends of the freedmen frequently were critical of Howard, and the Bureau generally, for failing to do more for the Negro, for carrying out Johnson's program of land restoration, and for failing to give the freedmen adequate protection from their oppressors.⁴⁵

Steering a course between these two extremes was hardly an easy job and Howard was to find long before he was relieved of his task that it was impossible to please everyone. If the Bureau had expired at the end of a year, perhaps he would have escaped relatively unscathed, but the work was scarcely begun. For the Bureau to carry out its program Congress was going to have to enact new legislation. The Republican majority in Congress was prepared to do this. At the end of 1865 almost all the Republicans in Congress including the moderates (those who could not yet be clearly classified as Radicals), were ready to support a new Freedmen's Bureau bill.⁴⁶ There were cogent arguments for such a bill which Howard could logically and convincingly put forth: conditions in the South were still unsettled, and he believed that if deprived of Bureau and military support, the freedmen would not receive equal justice; the system of labor contracts was still new, and in many areas untried; he had hopes that Congress would act in the question of lands for the Negro, especially in the Sea Islands; and he wanted the Bureau to go ahead with its program of helping to establish schools for freedmen.⁴⁷

Early in December, Howard submitted his annual report to Stanton. In this report he made specific recommendations for the ensuing year and requested a sum of eight and a half million dollars to carry on the work of the Bureau.⁴⁸ His recommendations were embodied in bills introduced in the Senate and House respectively by Lyman Trumbull of Illinois and Thomas D. Eliot of Massachusetts. Howard wrote of this action to J. A. Chapin, the secretary of the American Freedmen's Aid Commission, saying, "There are two points on which I feel very urgent, one that the Freedmen, as far as possible, shall have the actual possession of land, and the other that school privileges shall be extended to them and secured." ⁴⁹ He was confident that Congress would do this much. To help the bills along, Howard kept in touch with Congressional leaders and apparently he had no doubts about a new Freedmen's Bureau bill becoming law.⁵⁰

The feeling among Republicans in Congress was that Johnson would sign the bill which by February 6, 1866 had been passed in both Senate and House by large majorities, virtually every Republican voting for it.[51] But the President, apparently influenced by Secretary of the Navy Gideon Welles and following his own essentially conservative bent, instead prepared a veto message.[52]

Some of the factual data for the message came from Joseph S. Fullerton, a brevet brigadier general in the volunteer service. Only a few days before he submitted to Johnson a detailed statement of objections to the new Bureau bill, Fullerton had been on duty at Bureau headquarters in Washington.[53] He had been Howard's adjutant in the Fourth Army Corps and also during the early months of the Bureau's existence. Howard had helped him to get his promotion to brigadier general and the two men had worked closely together for many months.[54] Fullerton's views on reconstruction were more conservative than Howard's and he had become aware through an inspection trip to South Carolina and Georgia and through a short tour as temporary assistant commissioner in Louisiana during the fall of 1865 that there were inefficiencies in the Bureau's administration. He had also favored Johnson's policy of land restoration.[55] Johnson thus had a convenient source of information for his veto message.

On February 19, Lyman Trumbull, seated in the Senate chamber, in a hasty scrawl wrote Howard: "The President's veto message has just come in—Have not read it."[56] Howard had just returned from a two weeks' speaking tour in the New England states, and this piece of news was undoubtedly a surprise, although Johnson's hostility to the Bureau had already become apparent.[57] Two days later, after the Senate had failed to pass the bill over Johnson's veto, Trumbull wrote again to Howard encouraging him with the hope that "something will yet be done for the Bureau."[58]

In the meantime, while awaiting further Congressional action, Howard wrote to the assistant commissioners warning them that they must expect increased hostility from the Bureau's enemies, but stating also that the President had assured him that under the original law the Bureau could continue to function for at least another year. He complimented them on a job well done and urged them to continue in the same good work, "so as to demonstrate to the people of your District the good intentions of the Government and the complete practicability of the system of free labor." Howard concluded with an injunction to "give a thorough inspection of every agent for whom you are responsible," and added, "Immoralities, corruption, neglected duty and incapacity are sometimes complained of against Officers and Agents of this Bureau." Howard directed the assistant commissioners to take swift action against anyone found guilty of these charges.[59]

In view of Johnson's veto and his unwillingness to carry out the land provisions of the original bill, Howard's letter to Davis Tillson, assistant commissioner for Georgia, written only a few days after the veto, reveals a certain political naïveté on Howard's part which can only be explained by the fact that Johnson's resistance to Congress' role in reconstruction was only just beginning to manifest itself. Howard told Tillson that because cases of "crime and misdemeanor continually multiply" in the South "the President will be obliged to use us as an arm of strength to him, to keep the peace." Then Howard added the peculiar statement, "He never has been an enemy to the Bureau, but his southern friends, many of them, are. He has expressed himself as satisfied with its conduction." [60]

But Johnson was not satisfied with the Bureau's "conduction." In mid-April he launched a covert and indirect attack on the Bureau hoping to frustrate passage of another Freedmen's Bureau bill. This he attempted to do by sending General Fullerton, recently retired from Bureau service but still on active duty in the army, and General James B. Steedman, a long standing friend of President Johnson,[61] on an alleged inspection tour through the South. Perhaps it was at the suggestion of Montgomery Blair that Johnson took Fullerton into his employ. In any event, soon after Blair made the suggestion to Johnson, Steedman and Fullerton were off on their tour.[62]

Accompanying Steedman and Fullerton were reporters for the New York *Herald*, a Democratic paper, and as the tour proceeded they sent back stories of alleged misdeeds and corruption or other criticism of the Bureau.[63] This was especially true of North Carolina where the assistant commissioner, General Eliphalet Whittlesey, and several other Bureau officers were accused of a variety of misdeeds. Some states, such as Georgia and Florida, got off with no adverse criticism, yet the inspectors left behind the desired impression. Steedman wrote to Johnson from Jackson, Mississippi in June frankly admitting the purpose of the trip. "The strong hold which I knew the institution [i.e. the Bureau] had upon the religious and sympathetic people of the North . . . ," wrote Steedman, "convinced me we would be more likely to produce effect upon the public mind and secure candid attention, by exposing the abuses and frauds, and peculations of its officers, than by attacking the system." According to him most of the Bureau officers, with few exceptions, "constitute a Radical close corporation, devoted to the defeat of the policy of your Administration." [64]

Over a year before, Sherman had warned Howard of this very thing. The Freedmen's Bureau had become a political football and inevitably Howard's administration would come under criticism, not because there was any real desire to set things right, but because it was politically profitable to pick on every flaw no matter how inconsequential. Howard took the criticism hard and protested with some feeling both to Stanton and Johnson.[65] He was especially upset when Steedman and Fullerton made accusations through the *Herald* against several of his subordinates in North Carolina before the War Department or he himself had been notified. The tour continued, however, as long as it could serve Johnson's political purposes. Then, when Congress enacted another Freedmen's Bureau bill and passed it over Johnson's veto on July 16, Steedman and Fullerton cut short their inspection of Bureau affairs in Texas and never went to Arkansas or Tennessee.[66]

In August Howard sent a nine-page letter to Johnson which amounted to a detailed refutation of the formal Steedman and Fullerton report. He complained again of the release of the preliminary reports through the press stating, "The effect of this course has been to concentrate the attention of the public upon certain individual acts of officers, and agents, or accusations against them carelessly drawn, in such a way as to keep the faults committed, and not the good done, prominently in view." Of course, this was the very thing which the tour was supposed to accomplish. Howard knew this and said as much to Johnson. "From the course pursued by the Inspectors," he wrote in the same letter, "I suspect the object of the inspection, as they understood it, was to bring the Freedmen's Bureau into contempt before the country, and, to do this, they have endeavored to prove maladministration." He closed this lengthy letter with a plea to the President for his "full and hearty sanction" and said that "if the Government would keep good faith with its new made citizens, some sort of United States agency must be maintained in the Southern states until society shall have become more settled than it now is." [67]

The Steedman and Fullerton affair ought to have been a warning to Howard to be especially careful to avoid any semblance whatsoever of corruption in the Bureau. Despite his repeated warnings to subordinates, questionable practices were permitted to exist, as for example Whittlesey's employment of freedmen on his own cotton plantation. When Steedman and Fullerton exposed this activity, Howard ordered it stopped but asserted that Whittlesey had not done wrong.[68] He would never admit that there was anything wrong with his administration of the Bureau, but it is not unfair to say that he did not govern with a firm hand, and he was too trustful of his subordinates, too unready to believe that they might not have the necessary talents of competent administrators. His defense of his agents in North Carolina is illustrative of this shortcoming. Conditions there might not have been as bad as Steedman and Fullerton had asserted, but neither were they as free from wrong as Howard tried to maintain.[69] Howard rightfully pointed out to President Johnson and to Assistant Adjutant General E. D. Townsend the many errors in Steedman's and Fullerton's charges. He noted, for instance, that their charges often involved agents and officers long since dismissed, or who never were in the Bureau but instead were attached to the commissary department.[70] Yet the impression persists, despite the fact that Howard had an inspector general in the field most of the time, that there was a certain laxness present in the Bureau administration.

Johnson had failed in his effort to prevent the Congress from enacting new Bureau legislation. Under the provisions of the new bill the Bureau had statutory authority to continue another two years, assistant commissioners for Maryland and Kentucky were authorized, and the Bureau was empowered to handle cases involving freedmen when they did not receive equal rights in civilian courts. The bill also strengthened the educational work of the Bureau. Omitted was the provision for granting to freedmen title to Sea Island lands which had been a part of the earlier bill. Most important was enactment in the summer of 1866 of an army appropriation bill which supplied close to seven million dollars for the Bureau.[71]

The Bureau could be assured now of solid Congressional backing, legal authorization for its varied activities, and adequate funds to carry out its program. The Bureau in its first year had been mostly concerned with relief measures. Now, despite the failure of the land policy it could proceed with the remainder of its program with new confidence. Particularly important in the first year was the Bureau's effort in helping the freedmen and white employers adjust to a system of free labor. In this field the Bureau enjoyed considerable success.

Labor and Legal Matters

When Howard became commissioner in 1865 the labor situation in the South was in a state of disruption. Through Lincoln's Emancipation Proclamation the Negro in most parts of the South had become free, but the Thirteenth Amendment prohibiting slavery everywhere in the country had not yet become a part of the Constitution. The future status of the freedman as a laborer was still very much in the air. There is considerable evidence which shows that some Southerners, usually former slave holders, hoped that though slavery itself was officially dead, there still might be some way of continuing its essential features in practice if not in theory.[1]

That this was so should occasion no surprise. The Southern agriculturalist knew the Negro, with some few exceptions, only as a slave, and was quite convinced that he would not work as a free man. For instance, the provisional governor of Louisiana, J. Madison Wells, wrote to President Johnson, "your knowledge of the race Mr President must convince you that if left to themselves they [the freedmen] will not work."[2] If the Negro could not be a slave, then the next best arrangement was to have strict supervisory laws which would greatly restrict his freedom of movement and freedom to bargain for wages. During the fall of 1865 the legislatures of most of the former slave states adopted what were generally called Black Codes for the regulation of the freedmen. These varied in severity from state to state but generally they placed restrictions on the freedom of Negroes not imposed on whites. In particular, they provided for the hiring out of unemployed freedmen to white employers (sometimes referred to as "masters"), and in some instances even prescribed how the freedman should behave toward his employer.[3] In every instance the intent was obvious: the Negro was not to be treated as an equal but rather as a subservient being with few of the rights the whites enjoyed. The freedman was not to be completely free.

Here was a situation which demanded the Bureau's attention and not alone because it was its function to protect the Negro from such treatment. The Bureau was under constant pressure from the anti-slavery, abolitionist group in the North which would never allow the former slave holders to get away with what was considered an attempt at re-enslavement. And this group still could be heard in the halls of Congress and in the Northern press. Even those in the North who denied the Negro equal treatment, both legally and socially, became incensed at Southern mistreatment of freedmen. What they did in their own states was one thing, what the defeated Southerners tried to do in perpetuating slavery in any form whatsoever was quite another matter. The attitudes and actions of Northerners were inconsistent but they are understandable.[4] The alleged reenslavement of the Negro was the great issue which prevented the Reconstruction of the South from being a relatively peaceful, harmonious period in American history. Without this issue there was a good chance that the seceded states could quickly and easily have been restored to their former places in the Union. But how could the national government, having assumed the responsibility of liberating the slaves, simply turn its back on them when only technical emancipation had been conceded? In most cases the leading citizens of the South and the white population in general apparently did not fully understand what liberation meant and had no intention of allowing the freedmen political and legal equality, much less economic and social equality. Had the Southern states in the months between the end of the war and the meeting of Congress in December 1865 showed their willingness to grant the freedmen the same rights as white men and to permit educated Negroes to vote and even hold office, then the people of the North and the Republicans in Congress might have been more willing to accept the South's protestations of good faith toward the national government and assurances of having accepted the results of the war. And why did not the Southern states adopt these reasonable and politically judicious steps? It was because the men who were the political leaders in the South again failed, as they had failed in the years before the Civil War, to face unpleasant reality. They would have had to inform the people of the South that the war had brought more revolutionary changes than simply the freeing of the slaves, and that the Negro would now have to be conceded basic equality. Only a few could bring themselves to do this. Responsibility for the unhappy experience of Reconstruction lies as much with these people as it does with Radical Republicans bent solely, so it has been maintained, on consolidating their political grip on the national government. The result of the failure of Southern leadership was a defiant attitude on the part of the Southern white population and especially of the state legislatures. They were determined to retain as much control over the Negro population as was possible, and inevitably they saw the Freedmen's Bureau as an obstacle in their path. So the Bureau early came to be hateful in the eyes of probably a large majority of the Southern whites. Its principal crime was that it refused to sanction the relegation of the freedmen to a position of economic or legal inferiority.

Howard very early showed his unwillingness to countenance any system resembling slavery. A circular of July 12, 1865 to the assistant commissioners and Bureau agents stated this most emphatically.[5] Howard did not let the matter rest there but constantly reiterated his position both as regarded state laws and local regulations. In December 1865 he had occasion to write to a resident of South Carolina: "I believe no system of slavery could be adopted much preferable to the one just abolished, and therefore with all my mind and might I oppose any substitute founded on the same ideas of compulsion." The thing to do, he advised somewhat unrealistically, was to forget the color of the workers.[6]

Because few Southern planters could forget the color of the skin of their former slaves it was inevitable that they would continue to think of them either as slaves still or at least as persons inferior to white laborers. To eradicate all vestiges of slavery would be no easy task, and Howard conceived his responsibility to be that of implanting the idea of a free labor system in the short time that would be available to him. Once the white employer could see that the Negro would work as a free man the transition would be virtually complete. It was primarily for this reason, but also to encourage him to work and to protect the landowner, that the Bureau sponsored in every insurrectionary state a system of labor contracts. These were entered into voluntarily by both planter and freedman, and the Bureau agents urged their use for the protection of both parties. Howard wanted wages to be regulated by local conditions, insisting only on a fair contract. He even disapproved of minimum wages, preferring to give the assistant commissioners discretion to decide for themselves whether or not a labor contract was satisfactory.[7] To cover the cost of paper and printing the Bureau agent could charge a fee of ten cents for each contract.[8]

The contract provided either for wages to be paid the freedmen or for a division of the crop. Because of the scarcity of cash and because the planter would naturally not want to be committed to paying wages in poor years, the tendency was to make an arrangement for crop sharing.[9] The Bureau thus might have been guilty of helping to saddle this iniquitous economic system on the South. Yet it is difficult to see how any different system could have emerged from the conditions as they existed in the years right after the Civil War.

At a time when there was mutual distrust between employer and laborer, the Bureau rendered important service in assuring the beginnings of the free labor system in the South. Both parties needed a measure of supervision, and this the agents of the Bureau provided. Of course there were instances of partiality. If the Bureau agent was overzealous in his efforts to protect the freedman that is understandable; and yet there is evidence to show that at other times he tended to approve a wage scale detrimental to the freedman and in other ways showed a willingness to side with the planter.

A number of Bureau agents in the summer of 1865 evidently were doing this, or so thought the president of the Western Sanitary Commission, James E. Yeatman. Howard replied to Yeatman that he was aware of the practice on the part of "many agents" to fix wages too low. "A sort of morbid sympathy obtains," he wrote, "from constant contact with those who really feel that they have lost everything in losing their Confederate money and their slaves." The trouble is, he continued, that these same people have no realization of the fact that they might owe something to the freedmen for past labors. Though recognizing that injustices sometimes existed, Howard repeated his determination to avoid setting minimum wages.[10] He was also concerned lest the freedmen fail to live up to their side of a contract, and he sought ways of keeping them at work. This was especially difficult in the fall of 1865 when rumors of a division of land went the rounds among the freedmen.[11] It was not to be tolerated, as Howard many times stated, that the freedmen would be allowed to do nothing for their own subsistence. Consequently, early in October he ordered that state vagrancy and apprenticeship laws, when these applied equally to whites and blacks, be recognized by the Bureau.[12] Frequently, however, these laws applied only to the freedmen. In January Howard had to tell Osborn in Florida not to recognize the validity of a Florida law permitting the use of the whipping post for Negroes. There would be no distinction in punishments because of race; that was the broad principle which he constantly tried to enforce.[13]

All things considered, the Bureau agents did succeed reasonably well in seeing that the employer as well as the employee received the same consideration in the fulfillment of labor contracts.[14] Naturally, from Washington, Howard could do little in this respect, but his instructions to subordinates were clear: to protect the rights of both parties.[15]

Howard was always convinced that the Bureau did an important work in this field. As early as March 1866 he was writing that the Bureau had demonstrated to the planters that a free system would work and had helped the planter group by getting the Negro to work in the difficult days of 1865 and by assuring the employer of a labor supply.[16] In December of the same year Howard, in a supplementary report to Stanton, told the War Secretary that the contract system had worked well and that the assistant commissioners wanted to continue it. He did not mean that there had been no problems but that, generally speaking, both sides were living up to the agreements fairly well.[17]

The contract system was effective for only about two years, or at most three, and never did have anything approaching universal application. After the practicability of free labor had been demonstrated there was less need for supervision by an agency such as the Freedmen's Bureau, and both freedmen and planters seemed to prefer to enter into agreements on their own.[18]

If progress was being made toward a solution of the labor problem, in 1865 and 1866 there existed, Howard believed, an increasingly difficult situation with regard to outrages against freedmen. There is a large amount of evidence in the records of the Freedmen's Bureau which makes it fairly certain that outrages were common throughout the South in the years following the war. That this was so should not be surprising. The Negro was no longer a slave, but the white population, generally speaking, had no intention of allowing the freedmen to assume an equal social status. To inflict physical violence on a free Negro was a far different matter from doing the same thing to a slave who was a piece of property; and in a land where physical violence was not uncommon, and where normal society was so badly disrupted, there is no reason to doubt that there were numerous instances of violence against freedmen, just as there were in the years following Reconstruction.[19] It is only a question of how widespread was this violence and how exaggerated were the reports which reached the North.

This is a matter of considerable importance, because outrages against freedmen provided a major argument supporting passage of the Reconstruction Acts of 1867 which undid most of what Johnson had done and instituted a different plan for readmission of the former Confederate states.[20] Johnson and his supporters, of course, denied that conditions in the South warranted continued federal interference. Their contention was that in any postwar period there is bound to be some social disruption but that in this instance the states were perfectly able to maintain order and provide for the safety of all persons. They charged the Republicans with enlarging and fabricating atrocity stories to give them an excuse to intervene.[21]

On the other hand, the Radicals maintained that conditions in the South were unsafe both for loyal Union men and for the freedmen. Reports of atrocities appeared frequently in the Northern press giving rise to the impression that society in the South was thoroughly disrupted and that military control was absolutely essential to safeguard life and property.

While it is difficult to judge accurately not only the motives of those who played up the accounts of atrocities but also the authenticity of the accounts, there is so much substantiating evidence in the Bureau records that it is probable the number of outrages was greater than is often conceded and that by no means all or even a large proportion of the reports submitted by agents of the Bureau were fabrications.[22]

The Bureau had hardly started before the complaints from Negroes began to come in. One of the earliest was from a group of Virginia freedmen who claimed to have been driven from their homes by their former masters.[23] A Bureau agent in Charleston told of the hatred and prejudice of the former slave owners, charging that they were "constantly trumping up fictitious charges against [the freedmen], dragging them before the courts, robbing them of what little they may possess, and then sending them to prison." [24]

Davis Tillson, assistant commissioner for Georgia, was one of the most conservative of the assistant commissioners. He was no alarmist and his sympathies were frequently on the side of the white population. Yet, in November 1865, he wrote of the dangers to the freedmen from those white men in the South called "regulators," those who inflicted punishment on Negroes who would not remain in their place. He urged the necessity of retaining troops in Georgia, arguing that only a show of force would impress the white population and that unless military occupation continued the government would be failing in its duty to the freedmen.[25] This was at a time when President Johnson's plan of readmitting the Southern states was nearing completion.

All during the year 1866 reports of outrages of one kind or another against Negroes continued to pour into the Bureau's Washington office. The most dramatic incidents were the race riots in Memphis and New Orleans. According to General Fisk, assistant commissioner for Tennessee,

[Negro] Laborers quietly returning to their homes with the implements of their industry in their hands were shot down like dogs—defenceless old men and women were butchered in the streets and their own houses—Dwellings were burned by the dozen. . . . The freedmen's churches and schoolhouses were reduced to ashes.[26]

Fisk's report was concurred in by Howard's special investigator, Major F. W. Gilbreth.[27] The New Orleans affair resulted in the deaths of some forty Negroes.[28] While responsibility for this loss of life was variously placed, it was the firm conviction of the Bureau's assistant commissioner for Louisiana, Absalom Baird, that the municipal officials of New Orleans, including the police, deliberately planned and carried out the massacre.[29]

The Memphis and New Orleans riots were publicized widely in the Northern press as examples of the state of lawlessness prevailing in the South and of the unwillingness of white Southerners to treat Negroes with justice. But there were less spectacular occurrences which seemed to lend support to these assertions. For example, the assistant commissioner for Texas, General J. B. Kiddoo, wrote Howard in August 1866 of the increasing lawlessness in his state. Unable because of lack of troops to afford adequate protection to the freedmen, Kiddoo said that he was *"sick at heart"* and that he would have to have more troops if his duties were to be "a *reality* instead of a *farce*." [30]

Then, in September 1866, A. P. Ketchum the Bureau adjutant

asked the assistant commissioners to send in a record of murders of freedmen which had occurred in their states "to test the truth of statements that have been publicly made touching this matter, and to enable General Howard to give the facts." [31] The time of this request, only a few weeks before the crucial Congressional elections, is worthy of note. It is probable that Republican leaders hoped that a public statement concerning atrocities against Negroes would help to swing the elections in favor of their party. On January 18, 1867 General Grant, general of the United States Army, in a confidential letter asked Howard to send him

a list of authenticated cases of murder, and other violence, upon Freedmen, northern or other Union men, refugees etc. in the Southern States for the last six months or a year. My object in this is to make a report showing [that] the courts in the states excluded from Congress afford no security to life or property of the classes here referred to, and to recommend that Martial Law be declared over such districts as do not afford the proper protection.[32]

Likewise, Stanton, at the request of the Senate, ordered Howard to prepare a list of violations of the Civil Rights Act.[33] Here was a fine opportunity for Howard and his subordinates to paint a lurid picture of murder and violence in the South, and this political tie-in puts a stigma on the atrocity reports which Howard submitted to Stanton and Grant. If a political motive were involved, it turned out as was anticipated, for Howard's reports aided in the adoption of the Reconstruction Act of March 2, 1867 which established military government throughout the former Confederacy except in Tennessee.[34]

Stanton presented these reports to a cabinet meeting on February 15, 1867. The recorded comments of Navy Secretary Gideon Welles, and of the Secretary of the Interior, Orville H. Browning, show the incredulity of these two members of Johnson's official family. Welles called the report an "omnium-gatherum of newspaper gossip [and], rumors of negro murders. . . ." It was, he said, "wholly unreliable." Browning set down in his diary the belief that the reports were exaggerated and constituted a wicked plot on Stanton's part.[35]

That such reports could serve a political purpose is undeniable, but it is also a fact that Howard was genuinely concerned over conditions in the South. On September 4, 1866 he had written in a private letter, "The condition of the freedmen in many parts of the South is simply horrible. It is hard to believe that there exists so much downright murder in the human heart, as every day appears."[36]

Even a sympathetic attitude toward the plight of the mistreated Negroes would have been of little consequence had the reports been largely false. Undoubtedly, the Radical press did exaggerate atrocity reports from the South. But Howard was not dependent on the newspapers for his information. It came to him from responsible army officers and in such voluminous amounts that it is difficult to discount it simply as unfounded rumor.

The reports which Howard received in the late months of 1866 and the early part of 1867 were not in every case as specific as one could hope. Assistant Commissioner J. W. Sprague of Arkansas gave the date and place of twenty-nine murders, but in some instances failed to include the names of the principals. But Sprague expressed the belief that this was only about half of the total number of murders of freedmen in Arkansas.[37] It is not easy to dismiss a report as rumor when the details are spelled out. So, for instance, General Kiddoo reported from Texas the murder of a freedman, Martin Cromwell. The local agent in Victoria on May 30, 1866 told of how "Martin Cromwell, formerly a slave of Mr. Alex. Cromwell, and a man over 50 years of age, was wantonly shot, and killed by Alex. Cromwell Jr. a young man of about 21 yrs on Sunday evening the 27th inst. on the plantation of his father."[38] Or take another example the report of General Joseph A. Mower, assistant commissioner for Louisiana. He stated that up to February 20, 1867 seventy freedmen had been killed by whites in that state and the number might have been as much as twice that. In addition there were two hundred and ten cases of freedmen being shot at, whipped, beaten, and stabbed. He gave a brief account of each murder and stated that in almost every case the guilty ones had gone free. The whole report takes up thirty pages. One report of an attack on a freedman follows:

May 27th 1866. Lieut. Rollins, Lake Providence reports that about 10 o'clock on Sunday morning in the town of Lake Providence, Martin Day, "freedman,"—for answering a white boy quickly—was knocked down by M. Kingsley (white) taken thro' town and across the Levee, and there stripped and terribly beaten, with raw-hides by Kingsley, and some 6 or 8 other men, who put a rope around his neck nearly choked him, jumped upon him etc. Civil Authorities took no notice of the affair, and on arrival of the military the parties left the Parish.[39]

Labor and Legal Matters

One further example is worthy of note; it is the report of General Jefferson C. Davis, assistant commissioner for Kentucky. Davis was a conservative who could be counted on to submit a report as free from padding as possible. Yet he sent in a list of nineteen murders for the period to October 1, 1866, giving, in every instance except one, the name, the date, and the county in which the murder occurred. He reported also two hundred and thirty-three cases of freedmen being badly maltreated. "In none of these cases," wrote Davis, "was any action reported by the state Civil Authorities to punish the offenders." [40]

There is no need to credit every report of outrage. Furthermore, there evidently were areas of the South where atrocity was infrequent or not known. Osborn, for instance, reported from Florida in November 1865 that cases of personal violence of planters against freedmen were of rare occurrence.[41] One individual wrote to Howard in the summer of 1866 stating that he had opened a Sabbath school for freedmen but that he feared without government protection it would be broken up. Howard's adjutant forwarded the letter to the assistant commissioner asking for a report. The answer was that the complainant had no reason whatever for any fear.[42] Apparently the Bureau agents could and did show common sense and restraint and did not jump to conclusions. For every complaint, Howard would first get in touch with the assistant commissioner responsible to discover the facts in the case. He did more than that. His inspectors were constantly in the field giving detailed accounts of conditions in the various parts of the South. His most trusted inspector was F. D. Sewall, who did not hesitate to report everything, favorable and unfavorable.

Sewall had a good deal to say about atrocity reports. In September 1866 he was on a tour of inspection of Kentucky and Tennessee and told of the relative calm of some areas of Kentucky. He remarked that the region about Louisville was free of outrages and that the colored people were being treated well. There were some counties, however, where these conditions did not prevail, an assertion borne out by General Davis' report. "It is well known," wrote Sewall, "that in these counties an organized band exists, whose object is to persecute and drive out Union men and freedmen." Yet he conceded that in Tennessee the freedmen received fair treatment.[43]

Another of Howard's close associates, General Whittlesey, made a tour of inspection into Louisiana and Arkansas in February 1867. His account of the treatment of freedmen in those states probably was true of all areas of the South: in some places the freedmen got on well with the whites; in other places there were terrible outrages. This, he said, is the reason for "the conflicting accounts which reach the public through the newspapers." [44]

In his annual report for the year 1869, Howard wrote on this general subject of outrages and gave a reasoned explanation of what had been taking place. There had been so many stories of murder and other physical violence, he wrote, that the general impression conveyed was that the whole white population was "engaged in a war of extermination against the blacks." Careful investigation, however, showed that the outrages usually were the work of a relatively few lawless men who got away with their crimes because civil government was not strong enough to arrest the guilty parties. Only the Bureau and the military, Howard continued, provided any protection for the freedmen. Then Howard added a pertinent statement, the validity and truth of which, no one can test but which is nonetheless worthy of attention. "And the evils remedied," he wrote, "have probably been far less than the evils prevented. No one can tell what scenes of violence and strife and insurrection the whole South might have presented, without the presence of this agency of the government to preserve order and to enforce justice." [45]

It seemed to Howard, to the assistant commissioners, and to the friends of the Negro everywhere that the Southern people could not be trusted to refrain from outrages against freedmen except where federal troops were stationed. It was useless and dangerous, they believed, to trust the local law enforcing agencies to administer impartial justice. Just so long as these conditions prevailed, Howard believed that Bureau agents and Bureau courts were needed. As a result, the Freedmen's Bureau entered very extensively into the legal field. Howard first entertained the hope that the Southern people would grant to the freedmen equality before the law. To him the whole matter was so simple: "I mean, a black, red, yellow or white thief should have punishment for his theft without regard to the color of his skin," he wrote to a subordinate in June 1865.[46] Since the policy in the South during slavery had been not to admit Negro testimony in courts and also to have a separate legal code applicable to Negroes there was little likelihood that the new governments formed during the early months of the Johnson administration would radically alter the former laws except under compulsion. Public sentiment was too generally opposed.[47]

To assure fair treatment for the freedmen, Bureau agents first made use of provost courts, but these military tribunals proved unsatisfactory in some instances because of prejudice against Negroes.[48] Soon the assistant commissioners were instituting Bureau courts manned, in most cases, by the Bureau agent himself. Howard relates how, while on an inspection trip into Virginia in September 1865, he created a new kind of court, a three-man body composed of representatives of the planters, freedmen, and the Bureau.[49] This type of court thereafter was used most extensively in Virginia.[50] Bureau courts received legislative support in the Civil Rights Bill, and the second Freedmen's Bureau Bill and up until the end of 1867 handled minor cases which frequently involved contract fulfillment and crop division. That these courts were impartial is open to serious question, but that they were as one-sided in favor of the Negro as has been charged is doubtful.[51]

Knowing that these courts were temporary expedients, Howard from the beginning wanted to see the regular courts handle cases involving freedmen. The condition was that these courts admit Negro testimony even in cases involving white persons and that they show impartiality. He was so eager to prove the practicality of a system of equal justice that when Swayne was able to obtain the consent of the Alabama authorities for the admission of Negro testimony Howard agreed to have the Bureau courts abandoned in that state. He explained his views to Clinton B. Fisk, assistant commissioner for Tennessee, stating that though he expected that there would be some abuse of the system "yet it is a recognition of the rights of freedmen to justice," and once the principle becomes established and recognized in the state laws, the results "can hardly be other than satisfactory. . . ."[52]

About a month later he told Whittlesey in North Carolina that whenever the state government was "prepared to do simple justice" to everyone then the Bureau could be dispensed with there. But one requirement was that everyone should have the right to testify and sue in the courts, and that if ever the courts refused to take a freedman's testimony then Whittlesey was to withdraw his recognition of that court.[53]

It was not long before Howard began to be suspicious of the good faith of those persons in the South responsible for the execution of the laws. In September 1865 the provisional governor of Mississippi William L. Sharkey had assured the assistant commissioner, Samuel Thomas, that the freedmen could sue or be sued, and could testify in any state court.[54] Yet two months later, Howard's adjutant, Max Woodhull, was writing to Thomas that he should try to persuade the Mississippi legislature to enact laws ensuring the rights of freedmen, and also that such laws as were passed should be viewed in their operation before general approval was granted.[55] A month later, Woodhull again wrote to Thomas, at Howard's direction, stating that in the event the legislature should enact bills at variance with Bureau policy, then Thomas was to use all his power to protect the freedmen's rights. Should the courts admit Negro testimony and afford equal treatment, then the Bureau could, in cases involving freedmen, act simply in a supervisory capacity.[56] Obviously, Howard was not impressed with Governor Sharkey's earlier protestations.

At about this time several of the assistant commissioners wrote to Howard expressing their reluctance to do away with Bureau courts. Osborn wrote: "the prejudice of a half dozen generations must be overcome before comparative legal justice can be done the freed people."[57] Tillson, in Georgia, right after Johnson had vetoed the Freedmen's Bureau Bill, expressed to Howard his fear that the President might interfere with his system of Bureau courts. "If he does," said Tillson, "all hope of justice to the freedpeople, for the present, will be lost. I shall decline to act in my present position when no longer able to protect the freed people—it would be too mortifying to be endured."[58]

Howard hoped that the Civil Rights Bill, passed over President Johnson's veto on April 9, 1866, would "enable us to regulate the judicial features of our work without difficulty."[59] This bill provided that officers and agents of the Bureau should be "specially authorized and required" to start proceedings against those who violated the Civil Rights Bill.[60]

The authority granted in the Civil Rights Bill and in the new Freedmen's Bureau Bill, passed in July, was not sufficient to assure unqualified judicial equality to the freedmen. Cases could still be handled by regular judicial procedure, and only when the freedmen did not receive impartial treatment did the Bureau or the military authorities step in. A major difficulty was that while in most instances no distinctions as to race existed in the law, in practice the freedmen were not treated with equality. The assistant commissioners made frequent complaint of this throughout 1866 and 1867. General Kiddoo, for instance, wrote to Howard in June 1866 that prejudice was so strong in Texas that a freedman's trial before a civil court was *"worse than a farce."* [61]

Assistant Commissioner Robert K. Scott of South Carolina stated that even under the best circumstances freedmen did not receive the protection necessary to keep them from reverting "to a condition differing little from their former slavery—save in name." [62] Howard reported to Stanton in January 1867 that the objectives of the Civil Rights Bill were being defeated because even though the Southern states had impartial laws, impartial justice was seldom administered, especially by juries and inferior courts.[63]

Despite all the evidence of unequal treatment, Howard's policy regarding separate Bureau courts was that they should be discontinued if there was any hope that equality would be granted the freedmen. Hence he advised Scott in January 1867 to have just as few Bureau courts as possible so as not to provoke unnecessary opposition.[64] By 1867 not many of these courts were operating and when, at the end of 1868, statutory authority for most Bureau activities expired, the Bureau courts ceased altogether. From then on the freedmen had to depend on the civil courts.

The Freedmen's Bureau had helped the freedmen in gaining a start on the road to full status as Americans by insisting on equality before the law. Howard knew full well that until this was obtained the emancipation of the slaves would never be truly accomplished. In three years' time it was not possible to undo the thought patterns of centuries, yet the all-important start was made. The Bureau had tried to check atrocities against freedmen and had, with greater success, obtained for them, in theory at least, equality before the law. But it was all too apparent that the white population of the South was not prepared to translate the theory into fact. This was an important reason for the passage of the Reconstruction Acts of 1867 which plunged the Bureau into the maelstrom of politics.

The Controversial Bureau

As reconstruction policy developed into a controversial issue between President Johnson and Congress from the time that Congress held its first postwar session in December 1865, the Freedmen's Bureau became a political football. The dispute over restoration of land to pardoned rebels in the summer and fall of that year was only a mild foretaste of what was to come in the veto of the Freedmen's Bureau Bill in February 1866, the Steedman-Fullerton affair and the Bureau's participation in the implementation of the Reconstruction Acts of 1867. Followers of Johnson, and Democrats generally, seized on every opportunity to flail the Bureau while the Republicans in most cases defended it. Its enemies naturally saw the Bureau as a major element in the program of Radical Reconstruction and General Howard's administration of the Bureau was under constant surveillance. On two occasions Johnson came close to dismissing Howard and refrained from doing so only because he realized that to do that would make matters worse between him and his adversaries in Congress. While Howard retained friendly surface relations with the President, underneath there was a good deal of bad feeling on both sides. Johnson's position was so at variance with Howard's that he could not help but see the Bureau as the peculiar tool of the men in Congress who sought to defeat his reconstruction policy. When the occasion offered he did not hesitate to interfere with Bureau action or to find cause for complaint.[1] The President was only one of a great multitude, mostly in the South, which found the Bureau not to its liking. Of all the charges made against the Bureau—that it was an incubus on the South, that its very existence was unnecessary, that it cost too much money, that it ruined the chances for satisfactory race relations in the South through the officious meddling of fanatic and corrupt agents—the one which has been the most persistently applied and the most uncritically accepted is the charge of political partisanship.

For a little less than two years, from the passage of the First

Reconstruction Act in March 1867 through the presidential election of November 1868, the Freedmen's Bureau became active in the political life of the South. Until March 1867 there was no political life of any consequence in which to be involved for the Negro could not and did not vote; after the end of 1868 the Bureau functions were so curtailed it could not have had any appreciable political influence. Thus the oft-repeated charge that the Bureau became a political organ of the Republican party applies only to about twenty months out of a total life of seven years.[2] In several states where elections and conventions were not held until late 1867 or the first half of 1868 the time available for political activity was even less. Although this was undeniably a crucial period, it hardly gave enough time to build an effective political organization.

Other factors which would have hampered the designs of anyone attempting to transform the Bureau into a political machine were the rapid turnover in personnel and the haphazard and irregular method of recruitment. Nor was the Bureau's manpower sufficient to cover adequately the whole South. So, for instance, in May 1867 there were only twenty-eight Bureau agents for all of Arkansas' fifty-seven counties, and the novelist John W. De Forest, a Bureau agent in South Carolina, had three large counties in his jurisdiction.[3] Though the agent might have been willing to promote Republicanism amongst his charges and while it was possible for one effective man to have considerable impact on a wide area, he would find the physical handicaps rather formidable to say nothing of the demands on his time from routine, non-political duties which were overwhelming and taxing.[4]

Finally, if the Freedmen's Bureau were to be an effective political tool for the Republican party it would be essential for the man in charge to be willing that this be so, and furthermore that he personally take a hand in organizing and directing the Bureau personnel so that they could better carry out their political duties. But Howard was not a politician and he did not think and move as a politician. His primary concern was in protecting the rights and interests of the freedmen and not in building up the Republican party in the South. That Howard saw the Republican party as a preferable political power to the Democratic party is quite true and this led Howard into some questionable actions, but this is far from saying that he deliberately used the Bureau as a political tool.

The fact that a good many Bureau agents and officers did come to occupy civil offices in the Southern states during the years of the carpetbag governments was not in itself reprehensible. Even if it had been, the commissioner of the Bureau cannot be made responsible since most of this occurred after 1868 (when most Bureau activities ceased) and in almost every instance of Bureau officers entering politics during 1867 and 1868 their official connection with the Bureau ended when they accepted either the nomination for office or the office itself. Major M. S. Hopkins, Bureau agent in Gordonsville, Virginia was told that he could run for office if he wanted, but that if he were elected he would have to resign from the Bureau.[5] In October 1867, Howard turned down the request of an agent in Bainbridge, Georgia to employ a clerk to take his place while absent at the state constitutional convention to which he had been nominated as a delegate. The reply was that if elected, his resignation would automatically follow.[6] Adjutant Eliphalet Whittlesey telegraphed to Assistant Commissioner Robert K. Scott in South Carolina in November 1867 an order to discharge any agents elected to the state constitutional convention.[7] A month later General Wager Swayne, assistant commissioner for Alabama, asked for advice (this being the first case of its kind to arise) in the case of General John B. Callis, a captain in the regular army and a Bureau agent who had been nominated for Congress. Howard's reply by telegraph was to relieve Callis should he accept the nomination, and a short time later Callis was ordered to report to the adjutant general.[8]

Not always was Howard so prompt to act. The assistant commissioner for South Carolina, Genreal Robert K. Scott, became a candidate for governor of the state in the early spring of 1868. Howard did not order Scott to decline the nomination even though earlier he had told him that he did not like to see officers "using their official position to lift themselves into power or position." He did not object to Bureau officers gaining civil office, "but it will never do," he warned, "to encourage officers of the Freedmen's Bureau to seek office through their official strength. I refer particularly to officers of any considerable importance."[9] That Howard was not annoyed over Scott's election is apparent from a remark he made to the assistant commissioner for Virginia, General Orlando Brown, at the end of April 1868, to the effect that the Republicans in South Carolina could get on well by themselves.[10] Scott may have dispelled any misgivings Howard possibly had by his letter of May 2, in which he stated that he had declined being a candidate but had been nominated anyway.[11] Scott began his term as governor in July when he was still assistant commissioner of the state, but his place was taken early in August by Colonel John R. Edie.[12] The example of Scott is exceptional and it may even be true, as Scott asserted, that he had not used his position in the Bureau to secure the nomination for governor of the state of South Carolina.

Keeping tabs on Bureau agents seeking political office was not so difficult. It was almost impossible to regulate the speech and actions of those who would use their Bureau position for partisan purposes. This became a serious problem following the passage of the Reconstruction Act of March 2, 1867. In this act the Congress ignored the actions of the Johnson administration, divided the former Confederacy, except Tennessee, into five military districts and provided for the calling of state constitutional conventions which were to fulfill certain requirements before Congress would consider admitting representatives from the Southern states. The act specified that all adult males who were not disqualified because of participation in rebellion be eligible voters. This in effect enfranchised the freedmen. The military governors found the Bureau a convenient agency for explaining to the freedmen their rights under the Reconstruction Acts, especially the intracacies of the electoral procedure. Since it was obvious that the power to instruct was also the power to indoctrinate, Howard directed

that officers and agents of the Bureau while in discharge of their duties should refrain from *party* discussion and addresses. It is the duty of all such officers to instruct the freedmen as to their rights, and to protect them in the exercise of those rights, but it is not proper to take those occasions for partizan addresses. It subjects the Bureau to censure and not infrequently defeats the good objects intended to be accomplished.[13]

Despite Howard's admonition it is probable that some Bureau agents did try to indoctrinate the Negro with Republican ideas. But the fact that so frequently the agent was an army officer detailed from his regiment for Bureau duty who sometimes was more friendly to the whites than to the Negroes or who might be a Democrat would necessarily greatly reduce the Bureau's efficiency as a political machine. There was never a poll of the agents to determine which ones were Republicans and which ones actively tried to make Republicans of their charges; hence an assumption of pro-Republican bias on the part of the Bureau personnel must remain that. The simple matter of instructing the freedmen in their rights and functions as voters was a perfectly legitimate Bureau activity. If an agent conscientiously instructed freedmen concerning their voting rights and urged them to register and to vote, could this not seem to be partisan political activity especially when it turned out that the freedmen voted Republican? So thought Robert K. Scott, assistant commissioner for South Carolina who in December 1867 wrote to Howard, "even this legitimate and proper effort to enlighten an ignorant and downtrodden race is sufficient to provoke the most bitter animosity of a class of Rebels who will never cease to oppose the elevation of the Freedpeople." [14] But would not the Negro have voted for the Republican candidates anyway, regardless of any indoctrination? The logical answer to this question is yes. Undoubtedly there were instances of freedmen following their former masters, yet since the end of the war they had had ample opportunity to discover which party was serving their interests.[15] So if the Negro voted overwhelmingly Republican, as he did, was it not because this was what he would normally have done rather than because of any indoctrination on the part of agents of the Freedmen's Bureau?

While Howard urged his subordinates to eschew partisan politics, he sometimes allowed his own political preferences to shine through an outward show of neutrality. An early example of this occurred in May 1867. At that time the assistant commissioner for Louisiana, General Joseph A. Mower, reported to Washington that he had reassigned two Bureau officers who had attended public political meetings and who had advised the Negroes on how to vote.[16] He then ordered that all agents in Louisiana stay away from political meetings. On receiving word of this, Howard wrote Mower:

While I agree with you fully as to the necessity of our officers never mixing themselves up in politics, yet I think the officers ought to attend public meetings of every kind, whether political, judicial, or religious, with a view of ascertaining everything possible with regard to the people with whom they have so much to do.

Howard went on to suggest that Mower write a private letter to each agent warning against becoming active in politics but not prohibiting attendance at political meetings.[17]

Mower's reply is revealing. He stated that the two officers had advised the freedmen to vote for their "old friends," that is, their former masters and that he could not allow that. "I thought it the best and quickest method in order to prevent the freedmen being thus influenced," Mower wrote, "to issue an order forbidding all interference in political matters as I could not of course in a public order direct Agents to advocate the views of either party; but where I find that the Agents were all right,—when I find they are not a willing tool in the hands of the planter . . . they are instructed to teach the negro in political matters, and to impress upon him the fact that he owes his freedom to the Government of the United States, and that *that* Government represents the Great Union [Republican] Party, the Party now in power. . . . I fought General in this war, and I assure you that I am the last person who would desire ever to see our enemies gain political ascendancy." [18]

There is no evidence that Howard ever corrected Mower on this point probably because Howard, himself, thought along the same lines. For instance in March 1868 he instructed the assistant commissioner for Alabama, General Julius Hayden, to assign a particular person to duty in that state. This man had been relieved from his position for speaking out in favor of Congressional reconstruction. Howard reminded Hayden that "every officer and Agent should use his influence in favor of law and not against it. . . . expressing political opinions is not deemed sufficient reason for the discharge of any one." [19]

Nonetheless, a few months later, Howard had occasion to reprimand a Bureau agent in the same state for expressing his political opinions.

I have testimony . . . that you have been calling up the negroes and advising them against trusting to *union men* (carpet baggers, etc.) [Howard wrote in a confidential letter to the offending agent, Captain E. H. Weirman] and that you have advised negroes to become democrats, taking active political grounds. I am disappointed, and if this be true—deceived. I do not wish to control your politics, but know that the sympathy of the negroes at Mobile will be, if not already, alienated from you. . . . I must have somebody at Mobile in full sympathy with the colored people.[20]

Two months later, Captain Weirman was returned to his regiment.

One of the assistant commissioners who gave Howard some trouble on this point was General Alvan C. Gillem in Mississippi. Gillem was not a Radical, in fact was a friend of the President. He had apparently incurred the wrath of Thomas Conway, former assistant commissioner for Louisiana and currently working for the Republican National Committee. Gillem got wind of Conway's criticism and sent off a crusty letter to Howard stating that he resented the charge that he, Gillem, needed reconstruction, that he was as loyal as any to the United States, but that he would not meddle in the politics of Mississippi.[21]

Howard replied, "However your sympathies may be politically, of course, they must be on the side of the Government, or against all who would destroy the government." Gillem should understand that he must do everything possible to enable the freedmen to vote and to understand the issues. "The army cannot be a political machine," he concluded, "yet Congress has given the work of reconstruction into its hands, and the law, like every other, must be executed by the army with energy and good faith. The Freedmen's Bureau is a branch of the War Department, and closely connected with the army in this work." [22]

Howard did not openly speak out for the Republican party in the years when he was commissioner of the Freedmen's Bureau, but he did lend what support he could to others who were working for that party. If it was not that, he failed to restrain, as conscientiously as he should have, the political activities of his subordinates. Of this there is little doubt. Howard did not reprimand Wager Swayne, assistant commissioner for Alabama, for participating directly in the constitutional convention of that state. Swayne admitted that this transcended his official duty but that he felt obliged to do this because the "success" of the convention seemed to him "essential to the restoration of the country." [23] Orlando Brown, in Virginia, could remark to Howard, "we can carry the state on an out and out Republican ticket by twenty thousand majority," [24] without a word of protest from the commissioner.

The use made of John L. Langston, a Negro speaker of recognized ability, is another case in point. In the crucial political years of 1867 and 1868, Langston did a great deal of speaking in the South in behalf of the Republican party all the while being in the pay of the Bureau as an inspector of schools. Howard was careful to specify that Langston's official appearances be limited to non-political matters, his Bureau duties being to encourage the freedmen to support schools and in general to further their progress.[25] But Howard must have known that Langston was a valuable political asset to the Republican party. Requests for Langston's services came to Howard from various Republican aspirants who seemed to think that Langston's presence would materially aid their chances of being elected. In one instance there was a request that Langston help out in Ohio because of the closeness of the political contest there. At this time Langston was on leave. Howard allowed the leave to be extended so that Langston could speak in Ohio giving as a reason the sickness then prevailing in the South.[26]

Langston himself was under no illusions as to his function. In that singularly self-centered autobiography written in the third person, Langston wrote that while on duty with the Bureau "he acted by special engagement as the representative and duly accredited advocate of [the Republican] party. Nowhere . . . did he fail to present and defend . . . its claims upon the support of the newly emancipated classes. . . ."[27] Howard must have known just what Langston was doing yet he made no real effort to stop him.

Howard gave his unofficial blessing to the Union League, a Radical organization which sought to recruit the freedmen for the Republican party. Though he protested that the Bureau had nothing to do with the activities of the League he smoothed the way for the League's traveling agent, Thomas W. Conway, formerly assistant commissioner for Louisiana.[28] Conway's letters to Howard are unashamedly frank in the admission of recruiting members for the League. In April 1867 he told Howard he had organized "a fine state council" in Virginia, and that some of the Bureau officers had become officers of the council. The next month from Alabama he reported that Bureau officers generally were "devoted to the great work of our League."[29] Possibly Conway was more enthusiastic than he should have been. Assistant Commissioner Scott of South Carolina wrote Howard in December of that year that no agent of the Bureau in that state was a member of the Union League "or any other organization of a political character."[30] It seems evident that Howard permitted officers of the Bureau to be active in the Union League if that is what they wanted to do. He would not go out of his way to urge them to join, nor would he stand in the way. After all, the Union League treated the freedmen equally and supported the policies he was attempting to further.

In summary, Howard presented a correct official attitude and yet he could scarcely hide his sympathies. Sometimes he allowed the Bureau to aid the Republican party; he never knowingly allowed it to do anything for the Democrats. But this does not mean that he actively sought to make the Bureau an instrument for the use of the Republican party. The distinction is admittedly a fine one, yet it does exist.[31] In the Bureau records and in Howard's private correspondence there is no evidence that the central office of the Bureau was the headquarters for a vast political network spreading out over all of the South with agents receiving frequent directives as to their political duties. Nowhere does it appear that the commissioner was not first of all concerned with the prosecution of his work amongst the freedmen, the same non-political work that had absorbed his energies all during the first, non-political, years of the Bureau's existence.

If it had been otherwise, had Howard seen the Bureau as a useful political tool, he would have wanted to see its life extended just as long as possible. But his policy was just the opposite. Beginning in June 1867, the very time when the freedmen were beginning to be active in Southern state politics, he began to cut back by half the number of civilian employees in the border states.[32] Six months later he ordered all Bureau activities closed, and all officers and agents discharged in the states of Maryland, Kentucky, West Virginia, and Tennessee with the sole exception of the superintendent of education.[33] As for the other states of the South, Howard ordered in September 1867 a drastic reduction in personnel. Where an inspector could handle the work, the local agent should be allowed to go. Use dispensaries instead of hospitals, he directed. Agents who have been helping in registering should be discharged when that job was completed.[34] In his annual report for 1867, Howard explained why he was moving toward an early end to the Bureau. His decision was, he said,

based on the belief that each of the several States where the bureau exists or has existed will be completely reconstructed by next July [when the Bureau Bill of 1866 would expire]; and the freedmen, having all the rights of citizenship, can protect themselves with such aid as the United States military forces may be able to render, the only bar to this result being the ignorance of those who have not yet been reached by the influences of education. This ignorance will be remedied gradually by the States establishing and setting in operation thorough systems of common schools.[35]

Early in 1868 Howard began to have second thoughts about discontinuing the principal functions of the Bureau so soon. For one thing, interested persons, colored leaders, and Congressional delegations in particular, raised loud protest over Howard's order shutting down the Bureau in Maryland, Kentucky, and Tennessee. The Senate adopted a resolution calling on Howard to furnish documents relating to this matter.[36] In addition, Howard soon realized that frequently when the Bureau withdrew from a certain area the number of atrocities increased there, consequently, in February 1868, he recommended that the Bureau continue for another year, "till matters settle; till the new governments shall be not only established, but in particular operation, and be able and willing to afford the protection and relief which the United States government has rendered and is now rendering through its instrumentality."[37] Would the Bureau also be a valuable asset to the Republican party in the forthcoming presidential election? Howard never made any such admission. Instead, thinking as usual of how events would affect the freedmen, he remarked to Senator Henry Wilson, "The pending state and presidential elections are apt to increase or develop the elements of disorder in the South, by efforts on the part of employers to restrain by threats or punish by discharges, their colored employees from casting their votes as freemen."[38]

Howard's hope of seeing the Bureau continued during the election year of 1868 possibly stemmed from Radical pressure or from his own desire to see a Republican victory in the fall. But, if he did have a political motive he went about carrying out his scheme in a most peculiar way. Despite postponements and a revision of the original order, Howard did arrange for a drastic reduction in the Bureau's activities in Kentucky in July.[39] At the same time he approved Scott's plan for reducing the Bureau force in South Carolina, and urged him to replace all civilian agents with army officers who were far less dependable as potential political workers.[40] A few days later he sent similar instructions to General C. H. Smith, assistant commissioner for Arkansas. Put in army officers for civilians and have as few officers as possible were Howard's orders.[41]

Two acts of Congress, the one of July 16, the other of July 25 (when it was passed over Johnson's veto) first extended the Bureau's life for a year and then ordered it to cease as of the end of December 1868. Only the education and bounty paying duties of the Bureau would continue. The second of the two acts also specified that Howard should remain as commissioner since there were reports that Johnson had a replacement in mind.[42] Even then, the business of curtailing the Bureau's activity continued, not only through the reduction of force but also by having army officers take over the duties of civilian agents.⁴³ The restoration of seven Southern states to representation in Congress and their domination by Republican governments undoubtedly eased Howard's mind. This action, reflecting his prior concern for the freedmen, bears out the assertion that Howard's motives were not basically political. Had they been, he would not have plugged away so consistently at cutting back the Bureau's activities. Maybe Bureau agents and officers assisted the Republican campaign effort in the summer and fall of 1868 but, from all the evidence available, they were not actively supported by the Bureau commissioner.

When Howard permitted the Bureau to become tainted with partisanship it was to try to better the chances of the freedmen in making their way in an unfriendly world. This is also why he eventually came to favor Negro voting. By 1868 the salvation of the freedmen seemed to Howard to rest on the franchise. At first he had trusted in the land program, but that was now a thing of the past. It did seem that if the Negro were not to go backward in his march toward betterment he would have to have some means of protection. The federal government could not give its support indefinitely; Howard, as most others in the second half of the 19th century, was opposed to an intervening central government and, as has been pointed out, he foresaw, indeed he urged, an early end to the Bureau. Yet it would not be just, nor honorable to abandon the freedmen to the mercies of their former masters. By 1867 there was enough evidence on hand, harking back to the Black Codes, to convince any reasonable person that the Negro was not going to have any kind of equality in the Southern states. How obvious a solution, then, to give him the vote. If he had political power, then his protection would seem to be assured.

Howard was interested in Negro suffrage, then, not for the isolated purpose of giving the Republican party control in the South and hence the nation as a whole, but rather for what it could accomplish for the freedmen. He believed that it would assist the Negro in being assured equal rights and enable them to have their own schools. Through education they would have the opportunity to achieve material prosperity.⁴⁴ At least the Bureau ought not to oppose the work of the Republican party in the South. But it was Congress, not the Bureau, which finally arranged matters so that freedmen in the South could vote. The Bureau was responsible only for carrying out the laws of the land.

Did the fact that the Bureau in some instances unofficially lent its support to the Republican party negate the beneficial aspects of its work? It is difficult to believe that this was so. The partisanship displayed by some of the Bureau agents undoubtedly disgusted Southern whites in general and added to their hatred of the Bureau. But this was nothing new. Long before the Bureau had even the opportunity to become involved in political affairs it had become odious to most Southerners. It had been that practically from the beginning and it most certainly was by March 1867. Some more perceptive Southerners, it is true, recognized the need and the benefit of the Bureau, but the overwhelming majority very naturally resented its very existence. This is not difficult to understand. After all, the Bureau was an agency of the United States government, and especially was it a branch of the army; it had the specific function of promoting the interests of the freedmen, who were in the eyes of the Southerners best off in a slave status; it sought for the Negro equality before the law and an opportunity for education which Southerners saw either as foolish or dangerous; it interfered with whatever hopes they had of perpetuating slavery under some other name; and some suspected the Bureau even of fostering the social equality of the races.[45] Even if the Bureau had been one hundred per cent pure and never had any taint of political activity, Southern whites would still have hated it. The political activities of the Bureau in 1867 and 1868, such as they were, could not possibly have nullified the accomplishments of the preceding years, nor could they materially have impaired those of 1867 and after.

Hostility to the Bureau because of alleged political partisanship was especially rife in 1867 and 1868. Hostility on general principles started as soon as the Bureau did. Inevitably there arose, to some extent in the North, more especially in the South, the charge of partiality toward the freedmen and prejudice against the Southern white population. Equally troublesome to Howard was criticism from those Northerners who charged the Bureau with failing to look after the interests of the freedmen. The chances of the former occurring were considerably greater simply because of the mandate the Bureau had from Congress.

President Johnson was one of the Bureau's earliest critics. In the summer of 1865 he asked General George H. Thomas to investigate charges that Bureau agents in Pulaski and Nashville, Tennessee were illegally taking property from white persons. Johnson told Thomas that he feared "the operations of Treasury Agents and the Freedmen's Bureau are creating great prejudice to the Government and their abuses must be corrected." [46] General Grant in August 1865 asked Secretary of War Stanton to remove General Edward A. Wild, ranking Bureau officer in Georgia, because Wild had, without just cause, accused some civilians of concealing a supply of gold.[47] Grant stated that Bureau agents should "not always be guided by prejudice in favor of color." [48] The Governor of Alabama, R. M. Patton, writing to President Johnson in September 1866 accused the Bureau of "doing much mischief." [49] A Union man in Louisiana complained to Howard in February 1866 that the Bureau agents he was familiar with were either more interested in making money than in caring for either the whites or blacks, or were "well-meaning but fanatical enthusiasts, entirely and totally wrapped up in the negro and ignoring the white altogether." [50]

Of course, certain individual agents were overzealous on behalf of the freedmen. It was natural, too, that general criticism of the Bureau should eminate from such as Governor Patton of Alabama. It is, however, a little-known fact that Howard and his subordinates often got criticism from the other side, from the Radicals, from the church groups and others concerned about the freedmen. The charge usually was that some individual Bureau officer was acting not on the side of the freedmen but of the whites, or that he was actually mistreating the freedmen. General Joseph Fullerton was assistant commissioner for Louisiana for only a few weeks, yet it was enough time for Northern papers to attack his administration as being unfriendly toward the freedmen.[51] The Cincinnati *Commercial* charged Samuel Thomas in Mississippi with not securing justice to the Negro.[52] The New York *Tribune* blamed Assistant Commissioner Absalom Baird for the deaths of two hundred freedmen in the New Orleans race riot of July 1866. The correspondent complained of Baird's "slow feebleness," and "reluctant action." [53] Tillson, in Georgia, felt that he had to defend himself from attacks appearing in the New York *Herald*. The accusation against him was that Negroes were forcibly being taken to Mississippi and Arkansas from Georgia by Bureau agents with the aid of the military.[54]

Nor was it solely the press which was critical of the Bureau for not defending the rights of the freedmen or even for mistreating them. In January 1866 Congressman Thomas D. Eliot of Massachusetts sent Howard a House resolution calling attention to a form of contract adopted by planters for use in some parts of South Carolina which seemed to give the former master considerable control over his ex-slave.[55] Howard had an explanation for this but the point is that the Freedmen's Bureau had to beware of hostile criticism from Congress.[56] Senator Henry Wilson of Massachusetts, a man vitally concerned over the condition of the ex-slave, wrote Howard about a report he had received from Grenada, Mississippi that the Bureau agent there had denounced Congress, had associated with rebels and had done other reprehensible things.[57]

As one final example of what Howard was up against, there was the complaint from the president of the American Iron and Steel Association, E. B. Ward, who wrote to Howard in October 1868 at the time of the election campaign. Ward said that he and others who had traveled in the South were convinced that "in many places the Bureau agts have been more willing to feed & aid the traitors than the loyal men. . . ."[58] Howard was greatly disturbed by Ward's letter and wrote a lengthy rebuttal in an effort to convince Ward that the Bureau was not aiding traitors. He insisted that, with only a few exceptions, the assistant commissioners were "first class men, and men politically right. . . ."[59]

The officers of the aid societies frequently joined in the criticism of the Bureau. They complained that the Bureau did not do enough for the freedmen. The corresponding secretary of the American Freedmen's and Union Commission, J. M. McKim, actually accused Howard of demonstrating "an evident leaning toward the Executive [Andrew Johnson]—charged by some with undue deference & even submissiveness in that direction. . . ."[60] That meant of course that Howard was not zealous enough in behalf of the freedmen. In November 1866 J. R. Shipherd wrote to the Reverend George Whipple (both men were secretaries of the American Missionary Association, an adjunct of the Congregational Church) that Assistant Commissioner Wood in Mississsippi was all wrong in using local agents in the Bureau, the implication being that the Mississippians could not be trusted to do justice to the Negro.[61] Thomas Conway, a frequent critic, wrote Howard in the summer of 1868 that the Bureau in Louisiana, where he had originally been assistant commissioner, had been for the past months "a *Copperhead* concern."

Conway urged Howard to do his best "to have it cease being a mere agency of the enemies of our country."[62] This occurred during General Robert C. Buchanan's tenure as assistant commissioner in Louisiana and apparently Buchanan actually did do more for the Democrats than the Republicans because, after General Edward Hatch had succeeded Buchanan, he wrote to Howard that many of the Bureau agents had been active in the Democratic clubs.[63]

At about that same time, Howard received a complaint that the Bureau agent in Suffolk, Virginia had been associating with rebels, drinking with them and had neglected the freedmen.[64] Howard had to face other types of criticism than the charge of political partisanship, or that of pampering or mistreating the freedmen. He frequently had to deal with the agent who was dishonest or whose private life made him an undesirable Bureau officer. That more than just a few agents became involved in corrupt practices, were grossly incompetent, or over-indulged in liquor is all too evident. General Edward Hatch, assistant commissioner for Louisiana, commented, "I find in closing the Bureau, many of its agents in this state are thoroughly dishonest."[65] Nonetheless, Howard did keep up a constant battle against this type of officer.

In one of his early letters of instruction to the assistant commissioners in June 1865 he warned, "It is absolutely necessary to have officers above corruption" and as soon as evidence of corruption came to his attention he took immediate action.[66] The procedure was to have the assistant commissioner make an investigation and then to dismiss or arrest the offending officer, and withhold his pay if embezzlement were involved. For instance he ordered General John W. Sprague, assistant commissioner for Arkansas, to investigate charges of fraud on the part of Bureau agents and to remove those who were dishonest.[67] In another instance, he told Brown in Virginia to find out about a case of bribery and to have the man "thoroughly dealt with" if guilty.[68] For a time Louisiana had a special school tax collected by Bureau agents. Howard's adjutant, A. P. Ketchum, instructed Assistant Commissioner Baird to hold to a strict accountability any officer unable to make a proper return.[69] In the last years of the Bureau there were several cases of embezzlement arising out of the payment of bounties to Negro veterans with which Howard had to deal and which caused him no end of trouble. As in the former cases he did his best to correct the wrong that had been done. Wrongdoing of any kind pained him and he would never cover up for anyone even though in one instance the guilty party was a professing Christian. "Their professions cannot screen them from the punishment they deserve," he told the assistant commissioner who had reported the case.[70]

In his letter to E. B. Ward, Howard had said,

I have removed a dishonest man at once, as soon as discovered. A man of bad habits, drunken, licentious or profane, has been promptly discharged, when the facts have been proved. Scarcely one instance has occurred for a year, where the Government has been defrauded. Some bad Agents have swindled the people, and have been caught and made to suffer. Perhaps two or three have escaped. I hold the Asst. Commrs responsible for their subordinates. It is customary to underrate any man's ability who tries to serve his God, and to impute to him special weakness but I wish you could take my administration of the brigade—division—Army Corps—and Army of the Tennessee—& then of this "misrepresented bureau," and give to them a thorough examination from 1861 to Oct. 1868, and then tell me if I have not understood *men* and accomplished the purpose intended.[71]

Any insinuation that he lacked firmness or that he had good intentions but was a poor administrator always made Howard extremely annoyed.

Some Bureau officers liked to drink too much. A Bureau surgeon believed this was because the pay for civilian agents was so low that few sober men, and few men of intelligence could be induced to enter the Bureau's employ.[72] In any event, drunkenness was a frequent problem and, as in the case of dishonesty, Howard dealt with it swiftly and decisively, more so, since the sin was usually more easily detected and proved. In one instance the Bureau officer in charge of one of the districts of Virginia wrote about one of his subordinates in the following manner, "Lieut Hite is cutting up badly, drinks like an old sucker, gets crowds of negroes at his office nights and with fiddles & wine get up a shameful *'Hullaboloo,'* till long after decent hours."[73] Assistant Commissioner Orlando Brown asked that this man be relieved and Howard forwarded the request to the adjutant general.[74] On another occasion Howard wrote to General Kiddoo in Texas relaying the accusation that one of the Bureau agents kept a mistress and was a hard drinker. "You know," Howard told Kiddoo, "this Bureau must be pure enough to withstand all sorts of accusations. . . . A drunkard and a debauchee are not fit to be officers of our government."[75]

All this merely demonstrates that in these, and in numerous other examples not recorded here, Howard bent every effort to root out the undesirables and the misfits. He did more than that of course. Constantly he was at his assistant commissioners to correct some mistake, make an investigation of some situation, or simply to be more active. "Have you an energetic officer on duty at Charleston," he telegraphed General Saxton very early in the Bureau's history, "a great many complaints come from that quarter."[76] A few weeks later, in July 1865, he had occasion to get after Samuel Thomas, assistant commissioner for Mississippi, urging him to expand the Bureau's work into every part of the state. "Get officers and Non Commissioned Officers from Dept Commanders and set them to work," he told Thomas. "Keep inspecting Officers and Agents in motion."[77] When reports came to him in December that Gregory in Texas was being too unfriendly toward the whites, he asked General Philip Sheridan, division commander, to make an investigation.[78] Shortly after this, with a good deal of exasperation, he told Saxton in South Carolina to "do something" about the outrages occurring in that state.[79] In March 1867 he wrote a confidential letter to General Carlin in Tennessee following a tour of inspection into that state telling Carlin to get some life into the Memphis office which he described as "dirty" and "uninviting." "Please see to it" was his concluding remark.[80] Wager Swayne in Alabama was a man of considerable ability but he was, for a time, performing double duty as assistant commissioner of the Freedmen's Bureau and also as department commander. Politely Howard asked, "Do your officers make regular reports, and do they do their work efficiently and to your satisfaction? . . . I wish you to stir up all the officials and energize them as you used to your regiment in the field."[81]

Not only did Howard deal with incompetents and misfits with dispatch, not only did he keep after his assistant commissioners by corresponding with them directly, but he also kept inspectors almost constantly in the field. Howard, himself, on several occasions made extensive tours through the Southern states.

In the early history of the Bureau, the inspector general for the Bureau was Howard's former staff officer, William E. Strong, but for the longest period of time, Frederick D. Sewall had that position. Both Strong and Sewall were competent inspectors and were objective and fair in their reporting. Sewall never hesitated to point out wrongdoing, irregularities, improper records, or any other shortcoming on the part of a Bureau agent. For instance, in his report on Swayne's administration in Alabama in 1866, Sewall called attention to the poor system of records, the failure to make proper reports, and the lack of activity on the part of some of the Bureau officers. On another occasion he was critical of Wood's administration in Mississippi, charging that there had been many errors in the transaction of business there.[82]

Finally there were instances where it was very apparent that the Freedmen's Bureau was a military organization and that a military man was in command. Following Grant's Southern tour in the fall of 1865, Howard issued a circular to the assistant commissioners reminding them that they were still subject to the orders of the War Department and that any agent or officer who acted contrary to those orders would be tried by court martial.[83] A court martial in North Carolina convicted a Bureau agent of accepting graft money; another in Mississippi sentenced a civilian agent to a year in prison for malfeasance in office. Another court martial in Mississippi convicted a civilian Bureau agent for accepting exorbitant fees in several different law suits brought before him.[84]

On most occasions Howard dealt with his subordinates on a personal basis, and the tenor of most of his letters is non-military, but this was not always true. On receiving the report of a state inspector, Howard, through his adjutant, swiftly issued orders that a certain agent be dismissed, and another transferred. This sharp letter concluded: "You will acknowledge the receipt and obedience of these instructions." [85] In another case he asked the adjutant general to muster out a Bureau officer "for delay and hesitation in obeying orders." [86] His approach could, then, be strictly military and the military character of the Bureau could be and was useful in enforcing discipline and in eliminating undesirable agents.

It is hard to see how Howard as commissioner could have done more than he did to remove incompetent, corrupt, or intemperate agents. He demanded devoted attention to duty from his subordinates, he kept inspectors busy throughout the life of the Bureau, and he was willing to use the military authority at his disposal. Naturally he did not catch every misdeed nor was he able to get all the assistant commissioners and other Bureau officers to keep the best of records, but when one takes into account the vast scope of the Bureau's activities and the great number and variety of its agents the wonder is that it operated as efficiently and as honestly as it did.

Even assuming that the above estimate is correct, there is still room for criticism of Howard's administration of the Bureau. His subordinates in the Washington office enjoyed his confidence to the point where they had little supervision from the commissioner. Thus General George W. Balloch, the Bureau's chief disbursing officer, had a free hand to carry on the entire financial administration of the Bureau. This was to prove an embarrassment to Howard later on. It can be argued that the assistant commissioners were not subjected to tight enough rein from the central office and it is apparent that after the inspector general had made his report, as for instance of incomplete or poorly kept records in some Bureau office in the field, there was not enough follow-up. Such criticisms are difficult to evaluate. More clear-cut was Howard's loose way of interpreting the law to fit his needs. He frequently was too ready to follow the spirit rather than the letter of the law. In most cases this produced no harm; in fact it can be argued that to interpret his authority liberally was not censurable because in so doing Howard was able to accomplish results not otherwise attainable. But in some instances it would have been wiser to have adhered more closely to the letter of the law so as to have avoided all criticism.

Some examples will serve to illustrate the point. The Bureau was not empowered to pay teachers of freedmen, rather the various aid societies did that. Yet Howard at times circumvented this restriction because he was so eager to promote freedmen's schools. In September 1866 he had to tell Swayne to stop paying teachers because there was no appropriation for such payment. He explained that his disbursing officer, General George W. Balloch, said that he had authorized the employment of teachers in this case "by special instructions," but that they could not be found. Howard finished up the letter by saying, "However that may be, we will now have to conform to the law." [87]

About a month later a situation arose in Macon, Georgia in which a group of Georgians wanted restoration of property formerly belonging to the Macon Free School. Howard wrote the assistant commissioner, Davis Tillson, that under Bureau law such a restoration could not be made legally but that since the object of the law was to promote education he told Tillson to go ahead and make an "informal" restoration of the land and buildings, the formal title remaining with the government.[88]

Other evasions of the law emerged from Howard's willingness to construct school buildings even though the Bureau had at first only the authority to rent or repair buildings. In January 1867 he told Joseph B. Kiddoo, assistant commissioner for Texas, to proceed with the erection of certain school buildings with the following warning, "You must embrace everything under the head of 'rent' or 'repairs,' temporary structures being merely a liberal interpretation of the term, covering the object intended, though not specifically named in the law." [89] Later, after Congress had appropriated funds for actual construction, he explained to Caleb C. Sibley, Tillson's successor in Georgia, that he could "arrange under the head of 'construction,' to secure a building already erected." This would be proper, said Howard, since it would save the government several thousand dollars.[90]

Another tricky device was for the Bureau to construct a school building, call the construction rental or repair, and then ostensibly pay rent to an aid society for the building the Bureau had built but actually pay a salary to the teacher. As General W. P. Carlin, assistant commissioner for Tennessee, wrote Howard, this "would hardly bear investigation as a legal question." [91]

Something else that Howard did was to use the various funds at his disposal for praiseworthy ends but in rather questionable, at least not always strictly legal, ways. As we shall see later on, he juggled Bureau funds in such a complicated way that he ended up helping such institutions as Howard University, the Congregational Church in Washington, and the YMCA. Another time he asked the Second Comptroller of the Treasury about the legality of using the "Destitute Fund" to pay freedmen to work on the new streets of Washington rather than issue direct relief. Howard's purpose was to encourage industry, provide relief, and render a public service all at the same time.[92]

In most instances Howard got approval of his interpretation of the law before proceeding with any bizarre scheme of his own.[93] Nor did he always seek to stretch his authority. To C. C. Carpenter, superintendent of the Lookout Mountain Institute, he wrote that even to furnish transportation for teachers going to the school demanded a very liberal interpretation of the law and that he could not permit payment for transportation back to their homes.[94] Again, he denied funds to Berea College until after it was legally incorporated because the law forbade doing otherwise.[95] In other words the assertion that he liberally interpreted the law ought not to be exaggerated. He did try to carry out the spirit of the laws establishing and continuing the Freedmen's Bureau because, he believed, that was the way he could best promote the interests of the freedmen. There is no evidence to show that Howard's motive was personal gain. Still his actions caused comment and criticism because that was a time when there was a great deal of dishonesty and corruption in public life. Some persons could not believe that a man who twisted the law to mean what he wanted it to mean could be anything but corrupt.

Howard's administration of the Bureau was to come under the close and sometimes hostile scrutiny of two investigating boards and while he was publicly exonerated on each occasion there lingered a feeling that his control over his subordinates was lax, his records were sometimes incomplete, he was careless in money matters, and especially was he too willing to take liberties with the law. That all of this should brand him as a poor administrator is hardly fair. In its brief existence the Bureau with an everchanging personnel, operating over a vast area, among a hostile white population, and with only three years in which to accomplish its major goals (the education program excepted) performed near miracles. One reason for the success of the Bureau was the undeviating determination of Howard to work constantly for the good of the liberated race and not to allow extraneous matters to come in the way. This is the explanation, too, for the Bureau's successful effort in the field of education.

Education

At the end of 1868, all Bureau activities ended, with the exception of the payment of bounties to Negro veterans and their families and the furtherance of Negro education. The educational work of the Bureau was of especial importance during the year and a half from January 1869 to July 1870 when appropriations from Congress for educational purposes ceased. It was during that period that a superintendent of education replaced the assistant commissioner as the ranking Bureau officer in each state and that the number of employees declined to the point where only a few agents and clerks carried on the work of the Bureau in the South.

Before 1869 the Freedmen's Bureau had already accomplished much in the field of Negro education. In one of his first circulars Howard had urged the importance of education, and from that time on he put this work in the forefront of Bureau activity.[1] To have such a strong feeling about the necessity of education for the freedman it was necessary to have the conviction that he was worth trying to educate. Howard had that conviction in no small degree, because from his own observation he was convinced that the Negro had the same capacity for learning as the white man. "What possible use is it," he asked an audience made up of members of the New England Society a couple of years after the establishment of the Bureau, "for some of our scientific men to demonstrate the inferiority of the African to the Anglo-Saxon and to the other races, when practically you can breath[e] into him the breath of real life and make him stand forth with all the five senses unimpaired and showing all the faculties of a man capable of education and development?"[2]

Howard was not so optimistic or naive as to believe that a comprehensive public school system could be established for the freedmen in the Southern states in the short time the Bureau would be in existence. He did believe that the Bureau could work toward specific goals which in the long run would provide such a system.

Most important, he believed that it was essential as an initial step that the Bureau, in cooperation with the various aid societies, demonstrate the "pressing necessity" of education to those who saw no reason to educate the Negro, or who doubted that it could be done.[3] By seeing schools in actual operation, Howard wrote to Senator William P. Fessenden of Maine, in May 1866, "a large number of persons who were skeptical upon the subject of education have been and will continue to be stimulated to an examination of the benefits accruing and in acquiescence in them."[4] If the Southern people could be convinced that Negro education was in the best interests of all concerned, then they would proceed to establish a system of public schools which would aid in the uplifting of the colored people. Howard was firm in his belief that without education the freedmen could never compete successfully in the economic world.[5] He did not permit the subject of segregation in the public schools to stand in the way of his primary concern which was to expose as many freedmen as possible to the benefits of education.[6] The schools run by the various Northern philanthropic organizations were open to all, but in practical operation they served only Negroes. Howard believed that the two races could learn together as well as separately (the charter of Howard University, framed in 1867 with Howard's aid, made no distinction as to race and the university has never been one exclusively for Negroes) but he was quite willing to go along with segregated schools on the practical assumption that this was all that could be had at that time. In behalf of the principle of equality he stipulated that when the Bureau disposed of its school properties and buildings to the aid societies that the buildings would always be used for educational purposes and that no person should ever be excluded on account of race.[7]

Howard and the Bureau were not directly involved in the establishing of publicly supported schools. This would be the work of the Reconstruction or carpetbag governments formed after passage of the Reconstruction Acts of 1867. While the establishment of such schools was Howard's ultimate goal, in the first three years after the war there was no choice but to work through the various Northern aid societies which maintained their own schools for freedmen. For one thing the Bureau had no appropriation in its first year and it was a question of using the societies' funds, facilities, and personnel or not having an education program at all. Besides, the societies had been in the field since 1861 and already, in several

EDUCATION 159

places, operated flourishing Negro schools. Still, the Bureau could render valuable assistance.

Howard helped to negotiate a merger of many of the non-denominational societies, an action which was finally consummated in May 1866 in the formation of the Freedmen's Union Commission.[8] This with the American Missionary Association and some smaller, denominational bodies (for example, the American Baptist Home Mission Society) carried on most of the educational activities amongst the freedmen during the years of Reconstruction and it was these bodies with which Howard worked in comparative harmony until the Bureau ceased its education program in 1871. The Bureau also was able to provide transportation and rations for the teachers of freedmen and in some instances provide temporary buildings, confiscated Confederate properties, or surplus army barracks and warehouses.

When the Bureau was still new, Howard promised J. R. Shipherd, corresponding secretary of the American Missionary Association, that he would not only help them in this fashion, but also that he would aid them, and other agencies, with "every dollar that can be spared after the absolute necessary expenditures are met. . . ."[9] After Congress provided an appropriation for the Bureau in July 1866, Howard was able to assist in the construction of school buildings, defray the costs of teachers' salaries, and in other concrete ways promote the cause of Negro education. The Bureau ended up spending over five million dollars for the education of the freedmen between 1865 and 1871.[10]

The Bureau, holding the purse strings, could set the basic policies for Negro education. Howard did not exercise direct control over the freedmen's schools, although John W. Alvord, inspector and later superintendent of schools for the Bureau, did travel extensively throughout the South assuming a general supervision of educational activities; he did have influence over the type of education which the aid societies offered the freedmen. Over and above the elementary schools, which provided only the rudiments of learning, and which of course would form the core of the program, Howard promoted vocational training, normal schools, and institutions of higher learning.

To give the freedmen vocational training was so obvious that Howard does not deserve any special credit for promoting this type of education. Southerners favored it as did Northern philanthropists.

Since some Bureau critics have been of the opinion that freedmen's schools devoted too much attention to academic, non-vocational subjects,[11] it should be noted that Howard strongly favored vocational training. "This education must of course extend rather to the practical arts," he wrote in October 1865.[12] At another time he told a correspondent, "There is no institution that seems to be more useful in aiding the colored people in the transition state, than the industrial school." [13] During the time that he was commissioner, Howard was responsible for large grants to such industrial schools as Hampton Institute and Tougaloo University.[14] All the other Negro colleges and normal schools to which the Bureau lent assistance had departments in which vocational subjects were taught.

For vocational schools and more especially for the great number of Negro elementary schools springing up all over the South increasing numbers of trained teachers were needed. But the demand far exceeded the supply. The aid societies furnished as many teachers as possible but it was soon obvious that Negro teachers would be essential for the long range needs of Negro education in the South. Consequently Howard devoted much of his effort toward the founding of normal schools.[15] All the Negro colleges founded during this period either had normal departments or were exclusively normal schools. To aid in this indispensable work and to supplement the assistance the Bureau could give, Howard solicited aid from the Peabody fund, the different freedmen's aid associations, and individual philanthropists.[16]

Vocational schools and normal schools were necessary and Howard gave them his unqualified support. But he realized that even these were not enough. There must also be some institutions of higher learning to train professionals in the fields of teaching, law, medicine, and theology, and also to serve as examples both to the freedmen who needed the inspiration and to the white people of the country who needed to be shown that a Negro was capable of college work. He knew that not many freedmen were prepared for such work at that time, but he did insist that the facilities be available to the few who were and to those who in the course of the years would have been made ready for higher education. Consequently the Bureau aided a considerable number of "colleges" in getting a start, and the fact that these institutitions were called colleges and sometimes even universities bears witness to the courage, foresight, and vision of men like Howard who could see beyond the immediate present and the depths of ignorance of the great majority of Negroes and envision the time when higher education for the Negro would not appear so out of reason.

In 1871, after the Bureau had closed its educational work, Howard remarked that the framework he had had in mind from the beginning was a system of common schools at the base, "as many as possible," then academies, normal schools, and colleges, and finally, at the summit, a university, "with all departments." He went on to say that gradually this work was going forward "and it may sometime be brought to some degree of completion—perhaps not in my lifetime."[17] His basic purpose was to make a start, to build slowly toward a long-range goal. There was no idea of providing a college and university system for Negroes full-blown, and the picture of large numbers of freedmen in the Reconstruction period eagerly but futilely struggling with Greek, Latin, and other esoteric subjects is not an accurate one. Howard was aware that those few who were ardent pursuers of the classics, theology, and law might better be doing something else. But he was liberal enough to open the doors for these students and let them have their chance. In answer to a critic of this policy who especially found fault with a graduate of Howard University professing to know Greek and Latin and passing on his knowledge to other students, Howard said that at the University they were more than once faced with the problem of whether or not to "take in this class & do the best we can with them," or to exclude them. The policy was, of course, to let them in and give them the best training possible.[18] Some few, then, did pursue a regular classical course but it was many years before any one of the "colleges" advanced far beyond the high school stage. For example, Talladega, a Bureau-aided "college" of the American Missionary Association chartered in 1869, did not have even the barest beginnings of a college department until 1879 and did not grant a single degree until 1895. As late as 1932 the number of students in the college course was less than fifty per cent of the enrollment. In 1878 the Freedmen's Aid Society of the Methodist Episcopal Church supported five so-called colleges, but the total number of genuine college students in all five colleges was only seventy-five.[19] During the early years of these institutions the great majority of students were in the elementary or preparatory departments. Many were in what was usually called the normal department in which students, who had received a rudimentary training in reading and writing, learned to become teachers of these subjects.

Therefore, there were very few legitimate college graduates leaving these newly-formed colleges and universities during the time the Bureau was in existence. Yet, and this is the important point, there were a few and these, in most cases, went on to train others to serve as an inspiration and an example. This is exactly what Howard had wanted to see happen. W. E. B. DuBois tells of a survey made in 1900 of 1600 Negro college graduates over the period from 1850 to 1900 and of these 53 per cent were teachers or school administrators, 17 per cent were clergymen, and 17 per cent were in other professions, especially medicine.[20]

To many in 1865 the thought of using government money to support Negroes in college was not only laughable but poor judgment, but despite the inevitable scorn and criticism Howard went ahead and, as often and as generously as he could, aided in the establishment of colleges for freedmen and furthered their endeavors. Among the many institutions which the Bureau helped, either through the purchase of land, the erection of buildings, or outright endowment grants, were Hampton Institute, Atlanta University, Fisk University, Lincoln University, and Howard University.[21]

To get this program of higher education started took more than the mere allotment of money. The Bureau officials had to know that the new institution had responsible trustees and adequate support, usually from some aid society, that its location was suitable, and that there was a reasonable chance of its success. More than that, this program demanded conviction, vision, and sympathy together with a degree of cooperation with the philanthropic societies not usually appreciated. In June 1869, General Samuel C. Armstrong, former Bureau officer, and at that time head of the struggling Hampton Institute, wrote Howard after having received $7,500 from the Bureau, "You have always stood most kindly and heartily by us and shall always have the right to feel that you have 'a large part' in whatever success may be achieved here."[22] Both the Bureau with its funds and coordinating powers, and the aid societies with their enthusiasm, personnel and donations, were essential to the founding of Negro colleges. It was a co-operative effort and, in view of the almost insurmountable handicaps, a remarkable success.

It took great tact and patience on Howard's part to work

successfully with the various denominational groups and philanthropic non-sectarian societies. The problems became especially delicate when he was dispensing fairly large sums. Inevitably the charge of favoritism arose and it was all that he could do to keep peace in the Christian family. Howard, a Congregationalist by association, was catholic in his views on Christianity. It annoyed him, for instance, when the Reverend Lyman Abbott, and J. Miller McKim, both officers of the American Freedmen's Union Commission, found fault with him because he had supported the establishment of a normal school in Raleigh, North Carolina [23] founded by the Episcopalians. Howard could only say that he tried his best to be impartial and to avoid aiding schools which had a sectarian bias, and that each school charter had to be "entirely free from the narrowness complained of." Then he expressed himself rather forcefully: "with my view of things," he told Abbott, ". . . Liberal Christians are as sectarian as Episcopalians. . . . It does seem to me that some of our friends take too much pains to search out and worry themselves about the fences that separate the different lots, instead of . . . 'caring for the sheep in the lot.' " [24]

The reason for this impatience with Abbott and McKim probably was the fact that for the last few months he had had to try to arbitrate a factional struggle between Congregationalists and a Unitarian by the name of Edwin M. Wheelock, Bureau school superintendent in Texas. An American Missionary Association agent in Texas criticized Wheelock because he showed a lack of enthusiasm for his work and also because he was a Unitarian, who would necessarily, in the eyes of a Congregationalist, be unfit for educational work. All sorts of charges and counter charges went around. McKim accused the assistant commissioner for Texas, General Charles Griffin, who had criticized Wheelock's work, of being a sectarian, and his subordinates "hungry wolfish bigots." Howard's reply to McKim stated his views on the whole question very simply, "I do not enter into your theological difficulties, but try to act as a consistent follower of Christ." [25] On the other side, J. R. Shipherd, secretary of the American Missionary Association, practically demanded that Howard dismiss Wheelock, described by Shipherd as a "profane, indolent, scoffing ex-Unitarian preacher, whose record for five years is one continuous narrative of malfeasance and misfeasance." [26] Griffin, at approximately the same time, was writing to Howard complaining of all the interference and asking that he be allowed to handle the matter in his own way.[27] Yet a month later Shipherd was still stewing about Wheelock who, despite all the fuss, retained his position.[28] It was no easy matter for Howard to keep the peace among all the warring factions yet he succeeded in doing so with remarkble success. Equally important, he retained the good will of all.

In July 1870, as the educational work of the Bureau was coming to a close, James B. Simmons, the corresponding secretary for the Baptist Home Mission Society, recipient of a large amount of the Bureau's bounty, but inclined to be somewhat touchy when it came to the apportionment of funds, wrote a letter of thanks to Howard for having been fair in his treatment of the different denominations. Simmons said that he understood now "that you do not help *any* class of religionists, *as such*. But that those who work, you help; & those who do the most, you help most. That is right. Sorry we had not known it earlier." [29] No doubt Howard was sorry too.

Howard had to be diplomatic in his handling of the different groups because they were absolutely essential to the success of the Bureau's educational program. Still, he did not hesitate to criticize when criticism was in order. For instance, after he had been on a tour of inspection through most of the Southern states in 1868 he wrote to the Reverend E. P. Smith of the American Missionary Association, who had asked for help in founding a normal school in Beaufort, South Carolina, that the American Missionary Association had more than it could handle successfully without taking on more burdens. On his trip he had noticed that a good many of their schools were not first class schools, and found that the teachers in a number of instances were not qualified. These schools need, said Howard, competent principals "who know what a good school is, and who have the ability to organize and control. Such men must be paid, and you cannot pay them if you attempt to employ too many." [30]

Neither did Howard refrain from criticizing his own subordinates. In September 1868, for example, he complained to the assistant commissioner for Florida about the failure of the Bureau there to fulfill its promises regarding school construction.[31] Some months later he got after the general superintendent of schools, John W. Alvord, telling him to "stir up" the school superintendents. "Tell them to *work, work, work* or let somebody take their places who will," he said.[32]

Naturally, the criticism from those within the Bureau was mild compared to the denunciations from those on the outside who opposed Negro education. Bureau schools were subjected not only to verbal complaints but also to outright physical hostility. There is some question as to how widespread the opposition was but some objected on theoretical grounds, that Negro schools were useless, others on social grounds, that an educated Negro would be more difficult to keep in a subordinate position, and still others on political grounds that a Negro educated by Northern teachers would probably vote Republican and hence become a political enemy. Negro schools and pupils could survive such criticisms. It was another matter when the school building was burned down or the teacher driven away.

Despite Howard's realization that there were enlightened persons in the South who saw the necessity of providing education for the Negro, he was convinced that freedmen's schools needed federal protection because, as he wrote Senator Henry Wilson, "The minds of white men have been so long enslaved by prejudice and habit, that it will require time and education to bring them to a respectable degree of enlightenment." Howard wrote these words in the fall of 1865 and at the time he realized that in the South hostility to Negro education was as widespread as before the war.[33] He did, however, think that in ten years a change would occur and that Southerners, in general, would see the benefit of educating the freedmen. Until that time the protection of the United States government would be necessary.[34]

Southerners believed they had ample cause for opposing, even to the point of burning, Negro schools founded and operated by Northerners with Bureau support. There is some reason to believe that if the teachers had been Southern whites the degree of hostility would have been considerably less. In other words, the opposition was not so much to the idea of education for the Negro as to the geographical origin of the teachers and the nature of the subject matter taught. But the field was usurped by Northerners since Southern whites, with some exceptions, shied away from the whole field of Negro education.[35] This meant, for practical purposes, that Yankees would continue to teach the freedmen just as they had done in isolated places during the war, and that the Freedmen's Bureau had very little choice in the matter.

Inevitably the Northern teacher was to prove unacceptable to the Southern whites. These blamed the Northern school teachers, especially those from New England, with being fanatics on religion, with teaching their charges a hatred of the South, and conversely, teaching them to consider only Northerners and Republicans as their true friends. There obviously were grounds for criticism. Even Davis Tillson, assistant commissioner for Georgia, spoke out against some of the female school teachers because of their inability to take criticism and because of a tendency to play up to the press. He concluded his remarks to Howard by saying, "I don't wonder at the disgust with which they are regarded by the Southern people." [36] No doubt there were some teachers who instilled certain political and social beliefs in the minds of the Negro children and this aroused hostility but it is not known how widespread this practice was. The Yankee teachers were suspect simply because they taught Negroes. The basic trouble arose from the fact that the teachers saw the freedman as one who had the right to equal opportunities and who was not to be treated, even socially, as an inferior. The overwhelming majority of Southern white people had quite another view, that aside from the desirability of educating the Negro, there could be no acknowledgement of his social equality.

Howard's sympathies were with the teachers. He defended those who lived and ate with Negro families, in most cases the only ones who would take in a Yankee. He praised the Northern teachers in the South because he knew how much they had suffered. "Despised, misrepresented, called mercenary, ostracised by persons of less culture than themselves," he wrote to Erastus Colton of the Freedmen's Union Commission, "these teachers have suffered no obstacle to thwart, no hatred to make them hesitate, but have energetically and earnestly demonstrated by their success, the true nature of their mission." [37]

Much as Howard applauded the work of the teachers sent South by the aid societies, he knew that they would never be a permanent fixture. Nor would the flow of financial assistance from private philanthropy continue indefinitely. In due time, Howard expected to see the Negroes themselves reach the point where they could sustain their own educational institutions with financial aid and with teachers coming out of the normal schools and colleges which the Bureau had assisted in founding.[38] He also foresaw the development of a locally supported public school system. "I do prefer," he wrote the Reverend J. Brinton Smith, at the end of 1865, "for any state, a regularly established system of free schools, to the methods now operating. . . ." ³⁹ Howard was especially hopeful following the elections of 1868 which resulted not only in Grant's becoming president, but also in many of the Southern states having Republican regimes. At about this time, Howard said, in the course of some written remarks on the subject of Negro education, that with these benevolent administrations, immigrants would flock to the South because of its land, climate and "boundless resources." A "new life and energy" would emerge and then, "established school systems [would] gradually be set in active operation." ⁴⁰

Howard knew, however, that the Southern whites were not prepared mentally or financially to establish an adequate public school system, so he proposed to the Secretary of War toward the end of 1869, when it was becoming clear that the Bureau's days were numbered, that the education division of the Bureau be united with the government's Department of Education in the Department of the Interior, the new agency to be empowered "to establish schools by coöperation with Benevolent, State and local agencies where no such systems exist." This, Howard believed, would overcome the prejudice against schools and lead to "the gradual assumption of the school work by the States themselves." He did not, therefore, have objection to a permanent system of federal aid to education. He anticipated opposition on the grounds of cost and of a dangerous tendency to centralization. His answer was,

That education is generally the best possible investment that can be made in a free government; intelligent citizens, as every one knows, in all their varied occupations make constant returns to the government largely in advance of the money expended by it for their education. To the second objection it is sufficient to oppose the well known fact, that the general education of the masses always tends to the procurement of the largest liberty consistent with good government, thus counteracting all centralizing tendencies.⁴¹

When Congress failed to act on Howard's recommendation, he made one final effort to have the government carry on the work he had helped to start by suggesting in his annual report for 1869 that Congress provide for the continuance of the schools already established and the organization of additional ones.⁴² By this time, however, interest amongst the people of the North had waned considerably. There was no public demand for such action and the Republican majority in Congress seemed willing to relax its efforts on behalf of the freedmen especially since Republican regimes were in control in a majority of Southern states. So the educational work of the Bureau, practically speaking, closed with the exhaustion of the appropriation from Congress at the end of June 1870. Alvord, the superintendent of schools, stayed on until October but then even he left the Bureau's service.[43]

Howard admitted in his annual report for 1869 that only one tenth of the freedmen children who were eligible were in school at that time.[44] The Bureau had not been the first agency to enter the field of education and it had needed the assistance of the aid societies. Still, of all the work performed by the Bureau that of the educational branch probably had the most lasting results and benefits. Thousands of freedmen did receive some semblance of an education; they had set precedents for the future which could never be undone. Howard believed that schools were a significant factor in "passing from slavery to freedom with so little . . . disturbance. . . ."[45] And many years later in assessing his work as commissioner of the Freedmen's Bureau he wrote,

My glory, if I ever have any, consists in results attained; and the results in the case of the Freedmen's Bureau are, for me, more marked than those of the war. . . . It is a pleasure to know that Institutions of learning like Howard University, Hampton Institute, Atlanta University and others in whose incipiency I bore a part, are now constantly increasing in power and influence, and will continue their good work long after I am gone.[46]

In an age when materialism was supposedly rampant it is remarkable that some persons were looking to the future, to the uplifting of a people who never before had had the advantages of school and college, and who in the eyes of a good many Americans were not worth the trouble to try to educate. In the decades following 1870 there has been proof enough that Howard, the Bureau, the aid societies and those Americans who had faith in the freedmen's capacity to learn and the necessity of affording him an education were right.

Howard University

All the while the work of the Freedmen's Bureau was going forward, Howard was active in a variety of other pursuits, all of which had some relationship to his position as commissioner. While it will be necessary to treat each of these as a separate topic, it should be understood that these projects were in operation simultaneously and were acting upon each other. Thus, during his stay in Washington, Howard helped to found Howard University and became its president in 1869, he promoted the Barry Farm project, was one of a group which founded the First Congregational Church, and was the center of a violent interparish dispute related to the race question.[1] Howard's effort in behalf of Howard University was by far the most important unofficial work with which he was connected in this period of his life. He had a signficant role in its founding and he successfully guided it through its first stormy years. Without his inspirational leadership, farsighted vision, and the assistance he was able to lend as Bureau commissioner it is hard to see how this great university in the national capital could have become the important institution it has grown to be.

Howard's plans for the freedmen embraced a university at the apex of the educational structure which he was attempting to build during his tenure as Bureau commissioner. This would afford the freedmen the opportunity to obtain instruction in the various professions, especially the law, medicine, and theology. The chance to put this part of his plan into effect developed unexpectedly during his second year in office.

Shortly after he returned from his Southern tour in November 1866, an idea took shape in the minds of some of the leading members of Washington's First Congregational Church which eventually developed into the creation of the kind of institution Howard had in mind. At an evening prayer meeting on November 19, the Reverend Benjamin F. Morris, who had earlier that day been present at an examination of some Negro candidates for the ministry at a Baptist seminary in Washington, suggested that the preparation of freedmen for the ministry was a suitable field for the Congregationalists. Others thought well of the idea and Deacon Henry A. Brewster invited those interested to meet the next evening at his home.[2]

On November 20, at Brewster's home at 1823 I Street, Northwest, a group of eleven men, of whom Howard was one, all Congregationalists, agreed to support the founding of a theological school and appointed a committee of three, including the Reverend Doctor Charles B. Boynton, pastor of the church, to prepare a detailed plan. This committee reported on December 4 and it was during this third meeting, at which were present two Senators, Samuel C. Pomeroy of Kansas and Henry Wilson of Massachusetts, that it was decided that the training of teachers be included in the scope of the new institution, and that the name be Howard Theological Seminary.[3] According to Howard the name was adopted over his protest. "I thought I could do more for the Institution under any other name," he is reported to have said in 1899.[4] His protest notwithstanding, on January 8, 1867 the founders decided on the name of Howard University.[5] Three interested members of Congress, Pomeroy, Wilson, and Representative Burton C. Cook of Illinois, became a committee to obtain a charter from Congress.[6] Senator Wilson introduced in the Senate on January 23, 1867 a bill for a university charter, and a revised measure became law on March 2.[7]

Before the final action on the charter, Howard had been able to have the scope of the institution enlarged so as to have it include preparatory, collegiate, law, agricultural, and medical departments. As commissioner of the Bureau he would be in a position to give it substantial financial aid, since the obvious intent was to have this a university for the freedmen even though the charter as it finally was approved made no mention of race but stated merely that the purpose of the university was to provide "for the education of youth in the liberal arts and sciences. . . ." Nor was there any restriction as regard to sex.[8]

Howard, with his usual impatience to get on with the job, had already on December 12, 1866, ordered General Balloch, chief disbursing officer of the Freedmen's Bureau, who was also treasurer of the University, to invest twelve thousand dollars of the Veteran Retained Bounty Fund in a building and a three acre lot on the east side of Seventh Street, north of the then boundary of Washington

City within the District of Columbia. The land was to be rented to the University.⁹ The buildings on this plot of land had formerly housed a beer garden and dance hall, and it was here that the first informal class was held, probably in February 1867. A board meeting on January 29 had voted to have the normal department start at an "early day." ¹⁰ The first students were four white girls, daughters of two of the founders, the Reverends Danforth B. Nichols and Ebenezer W. Robinson.¹¹ These first classes could not have amounted to much because later in March Howard wrote that the normal department "goes into operation immediately." ¹²

The first formal meeting of the trustees, following the passage of the act of incorporation, took place on March 19, 1867 at the home of the Reverend Charles B. Boynton on the corner of N Street and Vermont Avenue. Howard and his brother Charles were among the seventeen trustees who named Boynton the first president of the University.¹³ On May 1, the normal and preparatory departments formally opened,¹⁴ but another year passed before the opening of the collegiate, law, and medical departments, and it was more than three years before the theological department had its start.¹⁵

The trustees wanted, as a permanent home for the University, a tract of land large enough to accommodate all departments. Howard and General Eliphalet Whittlesey became a committee of two to find a suitable site. They encountered hostility because of the reluctance of land owners to sell to a Negro institution,¹⁶ but at length they found an available tract. This was a farm of 150 acres within the District of Columbia, beyond the settled region and located on a summit overlooking the city. But the owner would sell only the entire tract and 150 acres were more than needed.

One day in the early spring of 1867 Howard and Whittlesey sat in the living room of the owner of the farm trying to persuade him to sell them just fifty acres. He would not do it. Furthermore he was asking a thousand dollars an acre and the sum which would be involved seemed to be beyond reach. Then Whittlesey suggested that the unneeded acres could be sold off to pay the purchase price. Howard joined in with this plan and impulsively then and there offered to buy the entire tract. Howard and Whittlesey had thus committed the University to a purchase price of almost $150,000 at a time when it had scarcely any available funds.¹⁷

Howard met the first payment by taking $30,000 from the Refugees and Freedmen's Fund, money which had been collected from rental of abandoned lands, fines, sale of crops, and so forth, a miscellaneous fund which sustained the Bureau in its first year of operation.[18] The step was characteristic. Of course he was not only a member of a site committee but he was also commissioner of the Freedmen's Bureau with considerable government funds at his disposal. Howard believed that he had the authority to use the Refugees and Freedmen's Fund under the act of March 2, 1867, but actually that act stated that the fund could aid "educational institutions actually incorporated for loyal refugees and freedmen." Since the charter of Howard University made no reference to refugees and freedmen, Howard was certainly stretching a point in this case.[19] Here is a typical example of his willingness to place a liberal interpretation on the laws of the United States government. No doubt in this instance the alternative was to pass up the chance to buy a choice site for the University; the money was available so why not use it as long as the purpose was defensible? Then, too, the University, not needing all 150 acres, could regain the purchase price by the sale of lots at advanced rates.[20] This is exactly what happened. Within a few months Whittlesey reported the sale of $110,000 worth of lots [21] and by 1870 the University had taken in $172,234.[22]

Howard was one of the first to start building a home in this new residential development. At a trustees' meeting on April 8, 1867, the secretary, E. M. Cushman, moved that they donate to General Howard an acre lot on which he could build a private home.[23] Later, in 1870, when a committee of the House of Representatives investigated Howard's connections with the University, it came out in testimony that perhaps the suggestion of the donation had come from Howard himself to the Reverend Charles B. Boynton, president of the University and also pastor of the Congregational Church.[24] According to Boynton, the feeling was that a fine house built by Howard would be a great stimulus to the sale of lots in an undeveloped section of the city and would enhance the value of the property.[25] Boynton stated that he had no objection whatsoever to Howard's receiving a lot as a gift but he had feared that the transaction might possibly involve them all in difficulty and that he had advised Howard to pay for his lot.[26] Whether or not it was at Boynton's suggestion, Howard in August 1867, declined the gift and in December agreed to give his note for $1,000 to pay for the lot.[27]

More significant was the development of the University proper through the assistance of the Freedmen's Bureau. Even before the consummation of the purchase of the University land, the trustees had asked Howard, in his capacity as commissioner, to "erect such buildings on the grounds purchased . . . as may be practicable" for the use of the University. Howard's endorsement of this request was that he would "erect such buildings as his means will allow." [28] The Bureau thus could be counted on to grant important aid to the fledgling university. It paid for the construction of several of the principal buildings and gave help in other ways. Yet Howard University could not depend solely on the federal government. It also needed substantial private support to pay salaries and to provide for the general expenses of an educational institution. Even with the aid of the Bureau and Northern charitable organizations the Negro colleges were not able to cover all expenses without charging the students at least nominal fees, and one of the biggest problems these colleges faced was that of finding a way for students to defray costs of tuition, room, and board.

In an effort to assist deserving students Howard became entangled in an ill-starred venture—the manufacture of a patent building block. Howard, his brother Charles, General Whittlesey, school superintendent John W. Alvord, and several others who were in some way connected with the Freedmen's Bureau formed a company which purchased from the inventor, George E. Van Derburgh of New York, exclusive rights to manufacture the building block in the Washington area. Howard's primary reason for backing the scheme was to provide jobs for needy students since the plan was to make the blocks on the University grounds. Furthermore this building material was cheaper than the best grade of brick and equal in cost to common brick.[29]

The building block in question, called the American Building Block, was made by steaming a mixture of sand and lime and molding it under pressure. The theory was that the block would harden as time passed because of the formation of silicate of lime.[30] The block was about three times the size of an ordinary brick and cost about three times as much.[31] The promoters intended to have the block used in the construction of the University buildings and quite obviously thought that there was a chance that the company would make money. That this was so, is evident from a letter to Howard from Henry R. Searle, architect for the university, and the principal promoter of the project.[32] In this letter Searle mentioned the names of persons who would like to invest some money in the enterprise, saying that if he, Howard, did not care to enter the company, as he had intimated in conversation, that his brother Charles, with some others, including Searle and General Whittlesey, might like to form such a company.³³ Howard replied that he had no objection to being in the company.³⁴ Next day he wrote to Whittlesey before leaving Washington on a short trip that he was eager to get on with the formation of the company because he could not hold up construction of his house much longer nor did he want to delay going ahead with the University buildings. He offered the possibility of having the freedmen become the owners of the block-making machine but concluded, "it would be much better for the company to raise the money and do the work entirely independent if possible." ³⁵

There is no question, then, but that Howard was active in the creation of the company. According to the testimony of the Reverend C. B. Boynton during the House investigation, Howard borrowed $10,000 from the firm of Jay Cooke to purchase the building block machine.³⁶ Actually, Howard put up $7,500 to obtain the right of manufacture, loaned the company, which went under the name of the D. L. Eaton Company, five hundred dollars, and bought two shares of stock at a thousand dollars a share.³⁷ Later, seeing the impropriety of being an interested member of the company and at the same time commissioner of the Freedmen's Bureau which would bear the cost of constructing the University buildings, Howard sold out to the other members of the company.³⁸ Where Howard's desire to aid needy students had given way to a selfish interest in profits is impossible to tell. Certainly no one grew rich from the building block company, least of all Howard, but it was the kind of thing which created misunderstanding and caused no end of trouble. Had Howard been trying at all cost to avoid the least suspicion of wrong doing he would never have allowed his name, or that of his Bureau associates, to be linked with that of the company they formed, but he seems not to have thought it extraordinary that the commissioner of the Freedmen's Bureau would be assisting with sizeable funds an institution of which he was a prominent official, and indirectly a business enterprise which he had been instrumental in founding.

Oblivious to the dangers inherent in the scheme, Howard, as commissioner, proceeded to enter into a contract with the builder. The contract specified that the walls of the University buildings were to be constructed of the American Building Block.³⁹ The contract did not specify that the building material had to be purchased from the D. L. Eaton Company but since the nearest supplier other than that company was in Philadelphia ⁴⁰ it amounted to the same thing.

Now all this was ill-advised at best; but to make matters worse, neither Howard nor any of his associates really knew enough about the block to have complete confidence in it. One of the University trustees, Dr. S. L. Loomis, expressed doubts to Howard as early as June 19, 1867,⁴¹ and Howard, though he tried to reassure Loomis, must have been somewhat uneasy himself, for in November of that same year he instructed the architect to approve any accounts of *"good* material delivered by the Building block Co." Could it have been that some of the material delivered by the company was not good? ⁴² Howard was willing to have the block used in the construction of his own house,⁴³ yet to a correspondent who inquired about the block, he admitted,

My experience with it has been so short, that I cannot give it an unqualified recommendation. . . . My opinion is that where the proper proportions of lime and sand are secured, the mixture skilfully made, and the block finished by a good machine, the material will prove all that the seller of the patent claims for it." ⁴⁴

The building blocks used in the University Building were of good quality and the builder, who later testified against Howard, admitted that this building was of sound construction with very few cracks.⁴⁵ What did cause some concern was the appearance of cracks in the tower which probably resulted from a settling of the foundation which was not of the building block construction.⁴⁶ The condition of the tower was such that some of the workmen refused to work on it, but this too was completed without mishap.⁴⁷

At this time other buildings were going up or had already been erected on the grounds of Howard University: Miner Hall, a dormitory; the hospital and medical school building; and the homes of Howard, D. L. Eaton, J. W. Alvord, and G. W. Balloch.⁴⁸ All these buildings were of the building block construction. Because of various delays, the builders did not complete the hospital building by the middle of November, the time called for by the contract.⁴⁹ From December 10 to 15 there was a spell of very cold, freezing weather followed by a warm period during which the temperature never went below freezing. This caused the disintegration of some of the building blocks in the unfinished hospital building and on the afternoon of December 21, 1868 the east and west walls collapsed.[50]

The very next day Howard reported to the Secretary of War, General John M. Schofield, that he was appointing a committee to investigate the accident.[51] Van Derburgh came down from New York [52] and preparations were made for extensive tests of the building block by impartial authorities.[53] One of the men Howard called on was Alfred B. Mullett, supervising architect for the Treasury Department, who condemned the use of the building block in these words, "I do not believe an experienced architect would have ever advised you to use such trash or that a good architect or engineer could be induced to live or stay long in a building constructed of such material." [54] Mullett also sent a "card" to the New York *Tribune* disclaiming any connection with the Howard University buildings and saying, furthermore, that the building block was, in his opinion, "utterly worthless." [55]

Howard, ever ready to defend himself, sent a lengthy rebuttal to the Washington *Chronicle* insisting that the brick had proved satisfactory in his home and the University Building. He explained that he severed his connections with the building block company because he had not wanted "to incur any censure or criticism on account of my official position if the block was used in the University buildings." He closed his letter with a defense of those government officers and officials who had invested in stock companies saying "They must do something to support their families. . . ." [56] The case is comparable to the investment by Bureau officers in cotton lands and plantations in the South, a practice condemned by Steedman and Fullerton and condoned by Howard. The ill-advised nature of the building block company seems never to have occurred to him. Did this company advance the cause of Negro education? Howard believed that it did. Would it materially benefit some of those who were in a position to fix the terms of the contract? Maybe so, but a man has a right to earn some extra money through investments. That, apparently, was the reasoning, and no wonder there was criticism.

Not long after the accident, Howard left Washington on a speaking trip in the West and while he was away, J. W. Alvord, Bureau superintendent of schools, trustee of Howard University, and a partner in the building block company, kept him up to date on the latest developments in the growing controversy. He reported that Mullett had partially changed his opinion of the block, but he also mentioned that the builders were repairing Balloch's house, also being constructed of the building block, and that the walls of Howard's house were bad on the north side and might have to come down in the spring.[57]

On February 22, 1869, Howard's brother Charles reported on the results of a trustees meeting held the night before. Charles said that seven of the ten members present were satisfied with the building block. Two architects who had reported against that material had influenced the University president, Dr. Byron Sunderland, to be somewhat hostile. Charles was willing to discount their findings, however, because they were *"Democrats."* Furthermore, he went on, Mullett was not really a professional architect but owed his position with the Treasury Department to political influence. Finally, Mullett had an interest in a stone quarry and would naturally oppose the use of a competitive material.[58]

The various opinions and reports seemed to accomplish little except to confuse the issue further, for there was much difference of opinion. A committee of the University trustees, which included President Byron Sunderland, could come to no agreement and simply made a report of its findings.[59] At a meeting on February 15, 1869, Charles Howard moved that the report with accompanying papers be referred to another committee "to present a summary of their contents and suitable conclusions or a result to be published." [60] Howard was not present at that meeting but his friends were looking out for his interests because the most resolute opponent of the building block, Dr. Silas L. Loomis, was conspicuously not included in the second committee and the only member in any way hostile was President Sunderland.[61] According to Sunderland's testimony during the House investigation the following year, this second committee published a report in the Washington *Chronicle* without his consent, an action which apparently had something to do with his resignation from the presidency of the University a short time later.[62]

The report in the *Chronicle* was favorable to the building block. It told of tests made at the Navy Yard and the surgeon general's office, the results of the tests indicating that if made properly under the correct conditions, and that if allowed time to harden, the blocks could withstand many times more the amount of pressure to which they would be subjected in the wall of a building. The blocks used in the University Building had been made properly and were of good quality. They concluded that the hospital walls had collapsed because the blocks were too new and had been subjected to alternating freezing and thawing which caused them to crumble.[63]

The other report was that of the committee of six which Howard had appointed and which was headed by James A. Hardie, inspector general of the Army, and which included two builders and a mason. This group interviewed the architect, builders, and masons who had worked with the material; they called in the owner of the patent, George Van Derburgh, and they conducted exhaustive tests. Despite Van Derburgh's contention that the freezing of the mortar in the joints of the interior or "cross-walls" pushed the exterior walls out, an occurrence which could happen with any brick, the committee in a confidential report submitted March 15, 1869, concluded that the brick used in the hospital (as opposed to that used in the University Building) was of inferior quality. The sand had too much loam in it, the mixture did not include enough lime, and the bricks had not had enough time for drying and setting. The block, they concluded, if made properly, was a satisfactory building material.[64]

That was about all there was to it. The hospital was rebuilt with common brick and some inside supports were added to the University Building [65] but there was no prosecution for negligence because no negligence was evident. The building block company ceased operations after the hospital's collapse and the investors never earned any profits from the venture.[66]

The building block controversy reached a climax just at the time Howard faced some important decisions affecting his career. Coincident with these events of March and April 1869 came the inauguration of General Grant as President and Howard, in part as a matter of courtesy, and possibly too because he was not eager to remain in a position which no longer was as important as it once had been, tendered his resignation. At first it appeared that the resignation would be accepted and that Howard would leave Washington to accept an army command in the field. Sherman, who never liked the idea of an army man doing the kind of work Howard was doing as commissioner of the Freedmen's Bureau, ordered Howard to take command of the Department of Louisiana.[67] Howard's resignation had caused much consternation in the ranks of the benevolent associations whose members urged him to stay on and see the job to the end.[68] The governor of Massachusetts, William Claflin, and

Senator Henry Wilson were among those who objected to his leaving the Bureau.[69]

Just at the time that this question of reassignment was being resolved, Dr. Byron Sunderland resigned as president of Howard University and immediately the board of trustees named Howard to fill the position.[70] The first president had been the Reverend Charles B. Boynton, pastor of the First Congregational Church and one of the founders of the University. He served for only a few months, from March to August 1867.[71] His successor, Dr. Sunderland, apparently did not approve of the link between the University and the building block company[72] and there must have been some threat to resign, or perhaps a falling-out with Howard, for the latter, in January 1868, was trying to persuade General Samuel C. Armstrong, former Bureau officer, and at that time founder and head of Hampton Institute, to be president of Howard University.[73] Armstrong declined as he did two years later when Howard once again tried to lure him from Hampton.[74]

In September 1868 the trustees had appointed a committee of three, including Senator Pomeroy, to offer Howard the presidency of the University.[75] Since no action was taken until April of the following year it may be that, before renewing the offer, the trustees wanted to know whether or not he would still be in Washington at the start of the new year, following the close of the Bureau proper, and at the start of the new administration. Once it was known that Howard would remain in Washington they tendered him the office.

Howard now had to make the decision of whether to accept the trustees' offer, continuing in Washington as Bureau commissioner and undertaking the difficult position of president of Howard University, or of pressing on President Grant his desire to take an active military command. It did not take Howard long to make up his mind. On April 8 he wrote a friend, "The prospect . . . is at present that I shall remain at the head of the Bureau."[76] Not only that, but he also accepted the presidency of Howard University with the understanding that it would not interfere with his official duties.[77]

An important factor in Howard's decision was the request of President Grant and of his Secretary of War, John A. Rawlins, that he remain at the head of the Freedmen's Bureau.[78] If ever he believed that he was needed or that it was his duty to undertake some task there never was any hesitation and there was little doubt but that Howard University needed him right at that time.

Even before taking over the presidency of the University Howard had been mainly responsible for the progress already made. It was his boldness and imagination which secured the large tract of land; it was in his role as Bureau commissioner that he was able to divert large sums to the University's buildings and real estate holdings. Obviously all concerned looked to him for guidance and support.

For nearly five years Howard served as president of Howard University, giving it the advantage of wise leadership at a crucial time in its young life. During his relatively brief tenure he added to the University's physical plant, saved it from the restrictive bonds of sectarianism, and maintained high academic standards in the face of pressures to lower them to the level of many of the applicants for admission. He also raised funds for current expenses and an endowment.

While he was president the University plant increased by the addition of two new buildings. One of these was Clark Hall, a dormitory for men named for David Clark, a Hartford, Connecticut philanthropist who gave $25,000 for this building. The other new building was Spaulding Hall, built to house the normal school.[79] Furthermore Howard, as commissioner, turned over to Howard University the buildings which the Bureau had already built, the University Building, the dormitory, and the hospital.[80] This was in keeping with Howard's usual practice, and as soon as the University Building was ready for occupancy the Bureau moved its offices there from downtown Washington and paid rent to the University at an annual saving of $2,000.[81]

It was not just buildings which he gave, however. Added to the prestige of his name was the wise leadership he provided. The trustees had early adopted a resolution that any person in an official position had to be a member of an evangelical church.[82] Besides, all the original board members were Congregationalists. But by the end of 1868, because of their desire to add to the law school faculty John M. Langston, who was not a member of any church, they rescinded that rule and before long there were even Unitarians on the faculty.[83] Howard was much in sympathy with this and wrote in 1869 soon after becoming president, "our only desire is to have Christian teachers, and all instructors assent to the truth enunciated in the words of the Scripture: 'For there is none other name under Heaven, given among men, whereby we may be saved.' "[84] Disagreement over what brand of Christianity to emphasize in the theological school had held up establishment of that department until after Howard became president. He was annoyed by the denominational squabbles and wrote in his report to the trustees in 1870, "A lengthy preliminary discussion and complete detail of arrangement are difficult, if not suicidal in this connection. Practically, Christians can run in the same pasture without conflict, but theoretically the points of difference grow by discussion."[85] The American Missionary Association was willing to pay the salary of a professor of theology, and finally the original purpose of the founders took concrete form.[86]

Obviously the level of instruction could not, at first, be high. That is why, for instance, there were so few students in the collegiate department in the early years.[87] Consequently most of Howard students were in either the normal department or the preparatory department. The curriculum of the preparatory department was similar to that of any academy which prepared students for a classical course in college but there was some temptation to lower standards in order to enlarge the school. This Howard would not do. In his first report to the trustees he emphasized his determination to maintain high standards both in the preparatory and collegiate departments.[88]

He wanted so much that others might see the progress the students were making that he issued many invitations. ". . . we can here demonstrate," he wrote in 1869 to John W. Forney, "nay we do it daily, that the dark color of the skin does not of itself unfavorably affect the intellect. This is often considered 'enthusiasm' or 'fanaticism' on my part, but it is by those who have never yet been here to examine for themselves."[89] Somewhat later he recorded in a diary, which he kept for a short time in 1871, "It is curious to see how puzzled . . . visitors are at the evident intelligence of the students. It evidently goes so against the prejudices of a life time—but the proof of the pudding is in the eating—and of the bridge in the crossing."[90]

The inability of many of the students to pay the tuition, board, and room fees was a constant problem. Howard, both as Bureau commissioner and as president, constantly sought ways of giving them employment. When the University first acquired its tract of land it was necessary to grade the land, put in roads and make other improvements. Here was a chance for students to earn money. Some, for a time, operated a farm on University land and sold produce. Others worked for the building block company. When the company ceased operations following the collapse of the hospital building, another scheme was attempted, this time by the financial agent of the University, John A. Cole, who obtained the right to manufacture the "Barry Bed Lounge." The manufacture of this article went on for a few years in the basement of Spaulding Hall but stopped at the time of the panic of 1873.[91] There were students who worked in government offices, particularly those of the Freedmen's Bureau, or who taught school in the evening, or who were employed as janitors and watchmen by the University.[92]

There was talk for a time of a shoe factory, a paper mill, and a tannery, but nothing came of these.[93] No doubt the would-be promoters thought also in terms of profits for themselves, but surely the need to provide employment for students was a major consideration. This is indicated in Howard's report for the year ending June 1872 in which he stated that the industrial and agricultural departments had not been self-supporting. "Destitute students flock in upon us and beg for work," he wrote, "that they may earn something towards their support. We have tried agriculture, gardening, sewing-classes, lounge-making, and a variety of other experiments, but as yet have had no well planned, well organized and well endowed department." [94]

There was a solution to the problem, of course, and that was to have philanthropists provide scholarship money and endow chairs. To this end, Howard devoted much of his spare time using his fund-raising talents to good advantage. In David Clark of Hartford, donor of Clark Hall, he found a generous benefactor who, in 1869, gave a thousand dollars for scholarships.[95] That was at the time Howard was trying to raise three hundred gifts of a thousand dollars each to provide a permanent endowment for the University so that it could some day be "completely free to all pupils." [96] There is no indication that he ever was able to raise anywhere near that much even though he himself pledged $10,000 to endow a chair in the law department.[97] Howard, as a fund raiser, would try anything. For instance he approached General Joseph Hooker asking him if he would endow a professorship to carry his name.[98] Hooker was not at all cooperative, writing, "I presume that this compliment will involve the use of some money. In this event, the state of my

Mrs. Oliver Otis Howard, *nee* Elizabeth (Lizzie) Ann Waite, married Second Lieutenant O. O. Howard in 1855, and survived him.

Bowdoin College in the 1840s when Otis Howard was a student.

West Point—in 1850 O. O. Howard was graduated 4 in a class of 46; in 1881 and 1882 he Superintendent of the Academy.

exchequer will forbid my entertaining this proposition for one moment." [99] Howard even wrote to Queen Victoria asking her to help with the endowment although there is no indication that the request met with any response.[100]

He threw himself into the work with enthusiasm and raised considerable sums for the University. Probably as important, however, was the wise guidance he provided during these early years of the University's existence. To him the others turned for help, not only in financial matters, but also in harmonizing differences and settling difficulties.[101]

Howard brought some innovations to the University. Convinced that the men students who lived on campus needed training in health, neatness, and discipline he instituted a military regime similar to what he had known at West Point.[102] It seems rather strange that at an essentially civilian institution so strict a regimen should have been introduced, but that is the case. There were reveille, marching to classes, saluting, roll calls, and inspections for the "cadets." [103] Howard believed that all this was productive of good but it is significant that the military department was quickly dropped soon after he left the presidency.[104]

In addition to the theology department, already mentioned, Howard was instrumental in establishing a music and a commercial department. The latter held classes at the Congregational Church for a few years; then it too fell by the wayside.[105]

As president, Howard entered actively into the life of the University. Each morning except Friday he conducted a chapel service for all the students, reading the scripture and leading in the prayers. "Our chapel room is pretty well filled," he once described the scene "perhaps two hundred students boys on the north & girls on the south side facing west, look up to me at the desk and the teachers ranging right & left along the raised platform. Oh, such congregational singing—nothing excels this—'There is resting by & by,' 'Nearer my God to Thee'—'Jesus, Lover of my soul' & such hymns make your heart swell & the tears come." After chapel, he would go directly to his office in the same building and start the day's Bureau work.[106] He also held Bible recitations for an hour every Monday morning.[107]

At the end of 1873 Howard resigned from the presidency because he expected soon to have an active army command,[108] and he suggested that Langston, as vice-president, have the position of acting president. The trustees, refusing to accept Howard's resignation, granted him an indefinite leave and also followed his suggestion concerning Langston.[109] Langston never did formally become president and this, plus financial troubles brought on by the panic of 1873, the end of Bureau aid, and the absence of Howard's stabilizing influence all contributed to a period of grave troubles for Howard University which continued at least until the end of the decade.[110]

Howard never ceased being interested in all that concerned the University and he was an active trustee until three years before his death.[111] As late as 1891 he was involved in raising money for the University and in 1907 he served on a committee which selected a new president.[112]

Howard University was always dear to the heart of its principal founder, but no less was he proud of and interested in the other educational institutions which the Bureau helped during the Reconstruction era. In his autobiography he devoted the best part of a chapter to what he called "institutions of the higher grade," enumerating these, noting progress made since their founding, and demonstrating clearly that he believed them to be his most prized achievement as Bureau commissioner.[113]

Bureau-related Activities: the Barry Farm and the Freedmen's Bank

Simultaneously with the purchase of land for Howard University and the formation of the building block company, that is, during the spring of 1867, Howard became involved in another venture, a plan to allow the freedmen of Washington to purchase land and to build homes of their own. The purpose was admirable and the result satisfactory, but the appearances were not favorable. The venture, already described briefly in an earlier chapter, was a settlement on individual acre plots on the outskirts of Washington of about three hundred Negro families who wanted to own land but found it impossible to buy any from white persons in the District of Columbia. The project came to be known as the Barry Farm.

Because of the large number of colored persons living in Washington at the close of the war, the conditions under which they lived were often squalid and unsanitary. The Bureau had an especially difficult task in caring for these people, providing them with food and shelter, and trying to find employment for them. For a time, some had housing in military barracks, but since these were frequently on private property and this property was eventually returned to the owners, many of the freedmen were hard pressed to find a place to live.[1]

Sometime in the early part of 1867 Howard faced the problem of caring for those people who were about to be evicted from barracks on land privately owned.[2] He went to these tenements on Meridian Hill, where he had brought the Third Maine back in 1861, and called together the freedmen to discuss the matter with them. Several spoke up and said what they wanted was land of their own.[3] Senator Pomeroy, a fellow member of the Congregational Church, was also interested in the plight of these people,[4] and the general and the senator together concocted a scheme which not only would help relieve the housing problem but would also demonstrate to the white people of Washington and in all the country the feasibility of selling land to Negroes. This plan was consistent with Howard's belief that the freedman would make a better place for himself in the community if he could own his own land and that the best way to get this program going was to have the Bureau set the example.

As always, the question of money arose. The Bureau had no funds earmarked for such a project, but since the cause was just, Howard was able to get around that difficulty. There was on hand the Refugees and Freedmen's Fund which already had done service for Howard University. Howard took $52,000 of this fund and, as commissioner of the Bureau, transferred that amount to a board of trustees, acting in behalf of three educational institutions: Howard University, Richmond Normal School, in Richmond, Virginia, and St. Augustine Normal School in Raleigh, North Carolina. These would be the beneficiaries of the fund administered by the trustees, but first of all the trustees would invest the money in land in Washington for the relief of the poor colored people who would rent or buy the land. It was stipulated that any proceeds from the investment would be distributed annually to the three institutions.[5]

Thus he would be accomplishing two purposes with one expenditure. Was this legal? Pomeroy and Howard discussed the matter and concluded, before making the purchase, to consult the Second Comptroller of the Treasury, Joseph M. Brodhead, who would have to approve the accounts of the Bureau and pass on their legality.[6] Assured by Brodhead that there was nothing illegal about their plan, they, along with another Congregationalist, John R. Elvans, a local hardware merchant (the three of them forming the board of trustees for the fund), were able on April 23, 1867 to purchase a tract of 375 acres known as the Barry Farm on the east side of the Anacostia River just north of Saint Elizabeth's Hospital. Elvans made the original purchase to disguise the fact that colored persons would eventually occupy the land.[7]

Once in possession of the land the next step was to divide it into acre plots and sell them on time to the freedmen who were enterprising enough to want their own homes. Pomeroy made up a form of contract which would ensure that the original purchaser would retain the land.[8] The price of the land ranged between $125 and $300 for an acre, the average being $225,[9] and payments would be about ten dollars a month. This was apparently about what the freedmen were currently paying for their tenements in the city.[10] Once they had paid for their land in full, the freedmen received title to it. By October 1868, according to Charles Howard, agent for the trustees, there were three hundred lots which had been sold, with only fifty-nine unsold at that time.[11]

In addition to selling desirable plots of land on easy terms to the freedmen, the trustees also provided seventy-six dollars worth of lumber to each plot owner who then had to construct his own house.[12] Some of the lumber was taken from the razed barracks owned by the War Department [13] but a large amount of it was purchased in Bangor, Maine from J. B. Foster, Charles Howard's future father-in-law. Charlie went to Maine late in June 1867 and by July 1 had completed the transaction.[14] In a two-year period Foster sold over $60,000 worth of lumber to the Barry Farm project, which, according to Charles' statement, amounted to a saving of almost $8,000 over Washington prices.[15]

As the freedmen made their payments the fund once again began to fill up and the trustees were obliged to distribute it to the three institutions devoted to Negro education. The board of trustees on October 1, 1868 voted to allot $10,000 to each of the three institutions but since there was only $23,000 in the fund at the time, Howard University's share was short by $7,000 to be made up later after more money had been paid in.[16] But neither the Richmond Normal School nor the St. Augustine Normal School actually received $10,000 in cash. Instead they invested the money, the one in bonds of the First Congregational Church and the other in a piece of land in Washington.

Ralza M. Manly had been the Bureau superintendent of education for Virginia since 1865, but he was also superintendent and a trustee of the Richmond Normal School. In September 1868, according to Manly, Howard asked him to come to Washington to receive the money due the Normal School from the Barry Farm fund.[17] Howard suggested to Manly that instead of taking $10,000 in cash the Normal School invest the money in the bonds of the First Congregational Church. Manly agreed to do this because, as he later explained, the school had no immediate need for the money and had planned to invest it anyway with the purpose of using the donation later on for a larger school building. He insisted that, though

Howard made the suggestion, the decision was entirely his (Manly's) and that the trustees later approved his action.[18]

The investment in land by the St. Augustine Normal School is a little more complicated. The Reverend J. M. McKim, corresponding secretary of the American Freedmen's Union Commission, wrote Howard in October 1866 that a donation of money had come from England and he was looking for suggestions as to how to use it.[19] Howard finally came up with a plan in July 1867. It was to use the donation, which was worth about a thousand dollars, to buy land which could be sold to freedmen.[20] This was about the time the Barry Farm project was getting under way and Howard believed that this could help some of the poor colored people of Washington get homes of their own. Howard bought a square of city land on Capitol Hill for about $10,000 using the money from England plus a borrowed thousand to meet the initial payment.[21] The rest of the money, eight thousand dollars, was to be paid over a five-year period.[22] Because the location seemed unsuited for the purpose,[23] Howard decided to sell it. The buyer turned out to be the St. Augustine Normal School, J. Brinton Smith, principal.

Howard, passing through Raleigh, North Carolina in September 1868 had asked Smith if, instead of taking his installment from the Barry Farm fund in cash, he would instead invest it in that piece of Washington real estate on the condition that if the trustees did not find it satisfactory, he, Howard, would take it off their hands.[24] The trustees of the Normal School agreed to take the land at a price of $8461.75, money which they never saw but which went from the Barry Farm fund to the holders of the notes for the land.[25]

Such were some of the intricate transactions surrounding the Barry Farm venture which was one of the first, if not the first, government venture into the field of public housing.[26] As General Balloch wrote Howard many years later, it was the first opportunity the freedmen had had in Washington to buy land "and thus become citizens in fact as well as name." [27] Howard himself called it "a wonderful success." [28]

Howard was directly involved in the Barry Farm project and was to a large degree responsible for its reputation. He was not directly responsible for another more notorious institution of this period of American history: the Freedmen's Savings and Trust Company. What came to be known as the Freedmen's Bank had, for a period of a few years, an unofficial connection with the Bureau, and the failure of the Bank has incorrectly been linked with the Bureau, much to the detriment of the latter's good name.

What ultimately ended in disaster had started auspiciously. The Bank received its charter at the same time the Congress passed the Bureau bill. Its principal purpose was to provide a depository for the savings of the freed people, and there is no question but that the idea was a laudable one.[29] Howard believed that this was a fine opportunity for the Bureau to support a worthwhile institution and to promote the welfare of the colored people. Hence he did all he could to aid the Freedmen's Bank. For instance his endorsement of the Bank appeared on the passbooks, referring to it as "an auxiliary to the Freedmen's Bureau."[30] In 1867, the commissioner ordered his subordinates to rent office space for the Bank,[31] and he also allowed the Bank inspector to be on the Bureau payroll as a school inspector. He did this because he wanted, as he put it, to "do what I can for an institution so important to the interests of a people just struggling out of poverty."[32]

Later, he arranged for the payment of bounties to colored veterans through the branches of the Bank. Some of the Bank's cashiers became Bureau agents for this purpose without pay.[33] In 1871, when the Bureau was hard up for funds, Howard turned to the Bank for aid in the payment of bounties, wherever possible using Bank personnel and thereby reducing Bureau expenses.[34]

The Freedmen's Bank was not officially a part of the Freedmen's Bureau, but there was a close relationship. Some of the Bureau officers also were officers or trustees of the Bank, the most prominent being John W. Alvord, Bureau superintendent of schools who for some years was president of the Bank. Howard was twice elected a trustee of the Bank, in 1865 and again in 1872. The first time he declined to serve stating that he could best serve the interests of the Bank by remaining unidentified with its operation.[35] In 1872 he resigned on attending his first meeting and he never, at any time, had anything to do with the management of the Bank or the determination of its policies.[36] The next year when it came to his attention that the Richmond papers were associating his name with the Bank, he wrote to a friend there urging him to inform the local press that "the bank is in no way, shape, or manner connected with so bad an individual as they believe me to be."[37] He was a depositor and did make several loans, but these were as an individual and not as a government official.[38]

The Bureau's support of the Bank, until 1870 at least, was cause for commendation and not criticism. Until that time the Bank could invest its funds only in government securities, but an amendment to the charter in May 1870 permitted investments in real estate. From this time until its forced closing in 1874 the Bank became the victim of highly questionable practices, improperly secured loans, and careless, if not corrupt, management.[39] Even though the Bank eventually was able to pay 62 percent of its obligations,[40] the whole episode left a bad impression on the Negroes who were now disillusioned about savings banks,[41] and on the country in general which saw the Bank from the beginning to end as one big swindle. Of course, this was far from the truth. Unfortunately, however, the collapse of the Bank confirmed in the minds of those who would believe the worst about the Freedmen's Bureau, that somehow the Bureau was to blame and that here was further evidence of the rottenness of all schemes involving aid to the former slaves. The public could easily confuse the Bank with the Bureau and Howard's reputation suffered accordingly.[42]

Had the Bank been a success, as it promised to be until the general financial collapse of 1873, no one would have thought to criticize the officials of the Bureau for lending support to the Bank.[43] But the Bank failed in 1874, two years after the Bureau had completely stopped functioning, and the enemies of the Bureau seized this opportunity to strike another blow at the already defunct organization. In the interest of historical accuracy, the fact must be made clear that the Freedmen's Bureau was in no way responsible for the failure of the Freedmen's Bank, that the Bank, a wholly worthwhile enterprise during the life of the Bureau, deserved the Bureau's support, and that no blame should be attached to General Howard for lending that support.[44]

...ders Library, Sixth St. gate, Howard University, Washington D. C.; University named for ... Howard, president 1867–1873, who obtained the charter of 1867 for preparatory, **collegiate**, law, agricultural, and medical departments, with no restrictions of race or sex.

Grant-Lee Hall, Lincoln Memorial University, Harrogate, Tennessee, memorial to Abraham Lincoln—founded and directed by O. O. Howard in the late years of his life.

Church Dispute and House Investigation

The Barry Farm did not occupy a great deal of General Howard's time during these years of Reconstruction; the Freedmen's Bank not at all. That he should give unstintingly of his valuable time to Howard University is quite understandable, and that the same should be true of his church is equally patent. Howard had not lost any of his religious zeal since his conversion in 1857; it had become less obvious during the war years but, if anything, it had deepened. During the war he had had no opportunity for regular church attendance; now finally settled in one place with his family he could engage in the kind of religious activity which had occupied a part of his time during the years he was an instructor at West Point. He and Lizzie had been members of a Congregational church in Auburn, Maine for a short time, and they naturally sought the association of fellow Congregationalists in Washington even though there was no formal church organization there in May 1865.

In the summer of that year a group of Congregationalists began to discuss the possibility of forming a regular church. On August 17, 1865 this group started an informal society and just a month later they held their first public service.[1] The minister who conducted this service and who was to be the church's first pastor was the Reverend Doctor Charles B. Boynton, a native of western Massachusetts, but more recently the pastor of the Vine Street Church (Presbyterian) in Cincinnati. He had come east to write a naval history of the Civil War and to be on the staff of the Naval Academy. Subsequent to his arrival in Washington he became the chaplain of the House of Representatives.[2] Boynton had been prominent in antislavery circles and was a noted speaker. He is the same man who was president of Howard University from March to August 1867.

Howard became a member of the governing committee of the church Society on September 14, 1865.[3] Following his trip to the Sea

Islands that fall, he became active in formulating plans for the erection of a church building. In December he became one of a committee of two to negotiate with the central organization of the church, the Congregational Union, for a grant of money to purchase a building site.[4] Then in February Howard was placed on the building committee of the Society.[5] The Society purchased seven lots on the corner of 10th and G Streets, Northwest for a little less than $17,000 the largest part of this sum having been supplied by the Congregational Union. In April 1866 the building committee approved a plan of the architect Henry R. Searle and excavation began on June 23.[6]

Shortly before that Otis and Lizzie became official members of the First Congregational Church. They had their membership in the High Street Congregational Church, Auburn, Maine, transferred to the Washington church, and at the same time Howard was chosen a deacon.[7]

There was a cornerstone laying ceremony on October 4, 1866 at which Howard delivered one of the principal addresses telling of the early history of the church.[8] Up to this time all had apparently gone smoothly. There was a growing membership and Boynton attracted large crowds either to the hired halls where the church met while the building was going up, or, while the Congress was in session, to the hall of the House of Representatives.[9] Furthermore Howard was having considerable success in raising money for the building, which was expected to cost close to $100,000.[10] He had started in May to write letters to associates, friends, and likely prospects pleading for a Congregational church to be a place of worship in the nation's capital, "to meet the wants of the thousands of temporary residents who are necessarily comparatively poor." [11]

Beginning in February 1867 were signs of trouble between Boynton and some members of the congregation. There were those who objected to having their pastor preach in the House of Representatives. They wanted a minister who could perform all the pastoral duties which Boynton obviously could not do and they wanted the full-time use of a building which the Capitol did not afford.[12] Howard was not a part of this controversy.[13]

In May, shortly after the Society had elected Howard president for a two-year term, both men attended a Congregational gathering at Henry Ward Beecher's Plymouth Church in Brooklyn. The Washington church still needed about $30,000 to meet the building

CHURCH DISPUTE AND HOUSE INVESTIGATION   193

costs [14] and at this meeting each man made a plea for funds. According to Howard's account of the episode, he told how some friends in Maine had offered him a personal gift of money in appreciation for his war services, just as friends of Grant and Sherman had presented them with gifts. At the time of the offer, he had urged that the money go to the widows and orphans, but now that he had an opportunity to help in the building of a church in Washington he would change his mind and accept a present. Boynton apparently interpreted this to mean that Howard was trying to make the First Congregational Church a personal monument,[15] although he did not at the time show his displeasure. Howard's efforts to raise money for the church were indeed such that a prejudiced observer might conceivably think that he was trying to minimize the work of others and to take the credit for building the church. Howard did have the friends, the reputation, and the money-getting ability that could make the campaign a success. Without his efforts it is difficult to see how the church could ever have raised the money it did. But in throwing himself so wholeheartedly into the project he inevitably excited jealousy on the part of those who could not do as well as he. There might have been times when his self-esteem outshone his Christian humility and undoubtedly some of his words conveyed the wrong impression to such as Boynton. It was an unfortunate development for surely no one tried harder in a cause than did Howard for this church. In fact early in May 1867 he was begging to be relieved from the burden of raising the money needed at that time, but when no one appeared to take over the work he went right ahead as before.[16]

Failing to obtain a loan of $25,000 in New York, Howard met the church's obligations by pledging his own securities until such time as the church could raise the funds.[17] That is why he was eager to have the Society get full title to the land from the Congregational Union so that it might borrow money on the land.[18] Nor did he stop there. He sent out a letter to every Congregational church and Sunday school in the country asking each to contribute ten dollars toward the completion of the church.[19] This appeal brought response from over three hundred churches and Sunday schools.[20]

The pastor and Howard would most certainly have resolved any difficulty arising from the money-raising campaign. The thing which drove them apart permanently was a dispute over the race question. In the early days of the church's history this was quite obviously an academic matter, for all the members were white. Most had antislavery associations and theoretically believed in equal opportunity for all, especially in the church. By the spring of 1867 the Sunday school included some colored children although as yet there were no Negro members of the church.[21]

During that summer, while Boynton was absent from the city on a vacation, an incident occurred which this time split the church in two. It seems that Howard, a teacher in the Sunday school, thought that there were not enough scholars, and to boost attendance he offered a prize to those pupils who brought in the most new students, regardless of color. The competition and enterprise must have been tremendous for this little device resulted in a great influx of new students, including one hundred and twenty colored children. Theoretically this should have made no difference, but there was a group in the church, a majority as it turned out, which objected to that kind of action. They saw it as an attempt to dictate policy without first consulting the other members. This group even went so far as to charge Howard with doing this to advance his own political fortunes, although the charge came later after an open break had developed between the two groups.[22] This incident probably explains Boynton's resignation from the presidency of Howard University on August 27, 1867.

There were other troubles which the struggling church had to meet. Early in July a heavy wind blew over the partially erected west wall of the church and the financial strain grew so great that, once having gained full title to the property in September, the Society authorized the issuance of up to $40,000 worth of bonds.[23] Howard was feeling the weight of the responsibility. "This church presses heavy upon me," he wrote to the father of his West Point classmate, Edwin Greble of Philadelphia.[24] In the immediate future the pressure was going to increase.

During the middle weeks of November 1867 Howard went west to Nashville, St. Louis, and other cities, and while he was gone there were sensational developments in the controversy within the First Congregational Church. Three colored adults, two men and one woman, applied to the church for admission as members. One of these was John A. Cook, a Bureau employee. A committee of the church examined them and found them eligible for admission.[25] In an informal discussion following the examination, the pastor expressed himself on the subject of the future of the Negro race, stating that he believed they would progress better if they remained a distinct group. It is possible, also, that he touched on the subject of amalgamation of the races.[26]

The white members of the church and their pastor now were faced with reality rather than theory. On November 17, 1867, the Reverend Doctor Charles Boynton, an avowed enemy of slavery, preached a remarkable sermon titled, "A Duty Which the Colored People Owe to Themselves" in which he expanded the views expressed in his discussion with the colored applicants and which seemed to be aimed directly at them. The gist of his remarks was that the colored people are different, they have been made so by God, and hence God must have in mind a separate destiny for them. Each race must make its own contribution, and if the colored race is left to develop by itself it can and will do its part for humanity and Christianity. He stated very definitely that any qualified colored person applying for membership would be welcome; the doors were open. If there were no colored churches available to them, they should be encouraged to join this church. But when there were colored churches available he could not conscientiously advise them to avoid these "and bury themselves in a living grave, an unheeded little company in the larger masses of the whites." [27]

This sermon had very immediate results. Two of the colored applicants promptly withdrew because they understood Boynton's sermon to mean that they were not wanted.[28] The third, a woman, however, was admitted to full and equal membership in the church.

At a meeting of the congregation, about a week following the sermon, Professor William F. Bascom offered two resolutions strongly opposing Boynton's remarks.[29] As it turned out, Howard and Bascom were the leaders of the opposition to Boynton, and gradually they were able to win over a majority of the congregation though not without many unpleasant scenes and bitter words. Howard really had no choice but to oppose Boynton. His position as commissioner, in addition to his very strong convictions, made it inevitable that he could not accept the pastor's stand, mild and conciliatory as it appeared to be. For despite Boynton's protestations, and despite his motives and undoubted sincerity, he still was pleading on behalf of segregation, he still was hoping to see each race go its separate way. This Howard could not for one moment countenance. Not only did he wholeheartedly disagree, but had he gone along with Boynton's view, he would have sacrificed the confidence of most of the freedmen and also that of many of the religious groups in the North on whom he depended for advancing the education of the Negro. Indeed, the very financial support of the First Congregational Church was in jeopardy because of Boynton's sermon. Despite the fact that Bascom failed to get his resolutions adopted,[30] a fact which showed that, at that time, Boynton had the support of a majority of the congregation, there was a strong reaction evidenced in the Congregational churches to the north. A Congregationalist of Oberlin, Ohio asked, "Have we given our money to strengthen prejudice and caste?" and the pastor of the Congregational church at Staffordville, Connecticut flatly refused any contribution to the Washington church because of Boynton's sermon.[31] These are but two examples of letters of a similar nature which came to Howard at this time.

Articles appeared in the press of the Congregational Church, the *Advance* of Chicago and the *Congregationalist and Recorder* of Boston, attacking Boynton. Boynton in a church meeting on January 28, 1868 and in a letter to Howard on February 3, stated that these articles misrepresented his views, but in spite of his earnest denials he could not dispel the impression, correctly formed from his sermon and subsequent explanations, that he would prefer not to have colored persons as members of the First Congregational Church.[32] Boynton, at the church meeting, restated the same views he had expressed in his sermon, and resolutions supporting the pastor and his stand were drawn up, adopted and sent off to the above named publications.[33] This was hard for the anti-Boynton faction to take since many of their number were not present at that meeting and because it was claimed that the vote on the resolutions was unanimous.[34] Desiring to have their side clearly presented, Howard and his friends drew up a protest against the action of the majority stating that the pastor's views were not theirs.[35] From this time on their purpose seems to have been to oust Boynton from the pastorship of the church.

Boynton was not without weapons in his arsenal. He had a son, General Henry Van Ness Boynton, a volunteer officer in the war, and at this time Washington correspondent for the Cincinnati *Gazette,* a Republican paper. General Boynton came quickly to his father's defense by attacking Howard and he kept up the attack long after the church matter had been settled. In fact this man was directly or indirectly responsible for most of the attacks made on General Howard from this time on.

General Boynton's opening move was to give his account of why there was trouble in the First Congregational Church. According to his story published in the *Gazette,* a small number of Howard's Bureau associates wanted to encourage racial amalgamation and their scheme was to have first a few and then many Negroes apply for admission to the church. His father's sermon upset these plans and the applicants, who were a party to the scheme, indignantly withdrew. This plan, according to the younger Boynton, did not have Howard's sanction.[36] The next day after this story appeared Howard wrote a confidential letter to Boynton, the correspondent, saying, "As I have hardly canvassed the subject [of amalgamation], and have expressed no opinion *pro* or *con* it is better not to commit me further." [37]

The elder Boynton joined the attack on Howard. At the communion service on February 2, 1868 he said that those who opposed him were not ready to take communion, at which point Howard spoke out in defense of himself and of his friends.[38] Boynton then suddenly turned to Howard and asked him his views on amalgamation. Howard related the story of an army officer from Virginia, a widower, who took as his housekeeper a young Negro woman who was deeply attached to him and bore him several children. It was Howard's contention that in the sight of God this man and woman were man and wife. Boynton had to agree that he would marry this couple. After that the service was completed without further interruption.[39]

The next night at a meeting of the Howard University trustees, Howard, in an informal discussion, must have said something to the effect that he favored amalgamation.[40] Howard later maintained that it was said "sportively." Even if he had not spoken in earnest he was most unwise to leave a chance for misunderstanding because amalgamation was a touchy subject. To his old friend, the Reverend George Whipple, he more fully explained his position which was too liberal for that time:

. . . As to amalgamation, I said sportively to several brethren one night, that I was in favor of it. I now turn to Webster's dictionary, and I find that the word means mixing of things, or mixing of races. I know races have been mixed for some time, but what my good friends mean by "amalgamation," I do not know. They sometimes put the question to me in this way: "are you in favor of your daughter marrying a negro?" I do not know why they should worry themselves about my daughter. She is yet a little girl, and her father loves her very much, and I would a great deal rather wait several years before talking about the marriage, or even thinking of it. . . . the question of amalgamation has never come up at all in my bureau operations, and I do not think it will arise. As to amalgamation being a doctrine of the Congregational Church, I have simply to say that I do not think the church is called upon to pronounce upon the subject. The pastor may have some trouble, but it strikes me that it would be well for him to wait for a case to arise, rather than call up an imaginary one. So far as the church is concerned, I have simply planted myself upon the ground, "love thy neighbor as thyself." I do not wish to see our church a German church, a French church, an Anglo-Saxon church, nor an African church, but simply a church of Christ, with its doors wide open; and I do not care an iota whether the brethren and sisters believe in amalgamation or not. I consider this subject entirely foreign to our controversy, and only put into it, with the hope of exciting prejudice against me and my friends by the use of a word, in precisely the same way that prejudice used to be excited against anti-slavery [men], by the use of the word "abolitionist." [41]

The day after Howard wrote this letter, the Cincinnati *Gazette*, General Boynton's paper, published an item from Washington to the effect that Howard, at the trustees meeting, had "avowed himself in favor of amalgamation." [42] Howard's friends in Congress who were trying to push through a new Bureau bill became anxious as to his stand and Congressman Thomas D. Eliot asked him for a denial of the charge.[43] This Howard did in categorical fashion. He called the charge of favoring the intermixture by marriage of the races "absurd" and concluded: "whatever words I may have used the charge is untrue." [44]

General Boynton compounded the confusion by introducing Howard to his readers as a possible presidential candidate and then describing the movement (which, he said, existed only among Bureau officers) as weak and "almost farcical." [45] Although some admirers of General Howard had from time to time suggested that they would like to support him as either a presidential or vice presidential candidate there is absolutely no evidence that there ever was a concerted move on his part or that of his friends to advance his candidacy. Who knows? The flattering suggestions of his friends no doubt set his mind to working, but that can happen to anyone who has even a remote chance of getting on the national ticket of one of the major parties. There is not a word from him or from any of his friends to indicate that he for one minute seriously thought of himself as a candidate. It seems evident that the younger Boynton was only trying to bring ridicule upon Howard, his father's opponent in the church controversy.

Between March and June (at the same time as the impeachment proceedings against President Johnson), the majority group, backing Boynton, arranged for a special committee to try to bring about a settlement. The committee, composed entirely of members of the majority, made a sincere effort but the minority was far from satisfied. Meanwhile the minority failed in its efforts to have the congregation call a mutual council which would be composed of delegates from other Congregational churches.[46] Next the minority turned to the plan of an *ex parte* council, called by one side only.[47] But the reply of several churches was a hope that both sides would agree to a mutual council. The dispute remained unsolved during the summer months.

The younger Boynton, unwilling to let matters rest, returned to the attack at the end of June with a scathing article denouncing Howard and the Freedmen's Bureau "ring" and "clique" for gaining possession illegally of large amounts of valuable Washington real estate, and for their connection with the building block company. He again charged Howard with favoring amalgamation in an effort to secure political preferment.[48]

Howard saw this attack while traveling in the West and wrote to the editor of the *Gazette* stating that Boynton's article was "false in spirit and false in fact" and that he "would be glad to have an investigation at any time." He admitted that he was having difficulty with the correspondent's father, "and his son takes this wicked way of giving a stab. Coming from a Republican," he concluded, "it will of course be calculated to do great harm." [49]

During that summer of 1868 two prominent members of the majority, Hiram Barber and James S. Delano, called at Howard's home and in a generally friendly conversation suggested how much better it would be for the church if he and Dr. Boynton would reconcile their differences. Barber spoke of the way the controversy was damaging Howard's standing in the religious community and he spoke of the power of the press in making and unmaking reputations. He made some mention of the correspondent, General Boynton.[50] Later, during the House investigation, it became apparent that

Howard believed that Barber's suggestions were a thinly veiled attempt to blackmail Howard into submission and perhaps his belief was well founded. In any event this incident further enforced Howard's feelings against the Boyntons and his determination to proceed to a showdown.

Early in November the majority agreed to a mutual council but the six men appointed to the committee to make the arrangements were all of the Boynton faction.[51] The majority was trying to cut the ground from under the minority which had, on October 24, sent out a call for an *ex parte* council. Of the fourteen churches invited, nine sent representatives. This council met on November 18, 1868 and sat until the 20th. It received written statements from both sides as well as oral testimony from a number of persons. The council's report condemned the "repellent attitude" of the church to the colored race and believed that on the basis of the evidence it would be expedient for the pastor to withdraw. Yet, since there was still some hope for reconciliation, it advised the minority to await the outcome of the mutual council called for January even though at that time their recognition as a group was not assured.[52]

At the last meeting of the *ex parte* council, as those present were leaving the church building, an unpleasant scene occurred between General Boynton and Howard. There are conflicting reports as to what exactly took place but apparently after some rather caustic words had passed between them (Howard always had trouble controlling his temper), Boynton said something to the effect that if Howard had only two arms he would strike him. Howard's reply was: "You ought not to belittle me," and the two men went their separate ways.[53]

Obviously the chances of bringing about a settlement were by this time nonexistent. This was even more obvious after the publication by the majority of a pamphlet directed against Howard. Among other things the pamphlet stated that it had been a mistake to have allowed the church to have come under the influence of one man on whom they depended to raise money. Mention was made also of the communion scene and the Sunday school episode.[54] Here it stated that neither Howard nor his friends should "think it strange that some regarded this [effort to bring in colored pupils], however unjustly, as a first move on the political chessboard." [55]

The mutual council, to which eleven Congregational churches sent representatives, opened its deliberations on January 13, 1869. (This was shortly after the collapse of the hospital building of Howard University.) The minority seems to have won a partial victory at the beginning for it was represented by a committee, and the majority had to consent, against its will, to the discussion of the desirability of continuing the pastoral relation.[56] Howard had a chance to refute the charges against him asserting that there never entered his mind any idea of seeking the presidency or vice presidency. He also claimed that the personal differences between him and Dr. Boynton could be easily disposed of, but that the matters of church policy could not so readily be dismissed and he preferred to let the council handle these.[57]

The council's report was an almost complete vindication for Howard and his minority group. Especially did it uphold his stand on the race question, stating that the Master cares nothing of color but simply "the character of the heart." And while the report criticized each side for issuing inflammatory pamphlets, and the minority for calling an *ex parte* council, it applauded the good character of those on both sides.[58] It described Howard as one "whose past career as a Christian soldier has endeared him unspeakably to his country, while his efforts in behalf of this church have been from the first a principal source of its strength and success." Finally, the report hoped that there might still be a chance of reconciliation but thought this unlikely and hinted that Boynton should resign.[59]

The victory for the minority was not readily apparent for Boynton remained on as pastor. Howard left almost immediately on a lecture tour into the Middle West not yet knowing who would have eventual control of the church nor what would be the outcome of the hospital collapse. These cares plus the added burdens of nightly lectures each in a different city brought on an attack of homesickness. He found the lecturing, at one hundred dollars per lecture, *"trying* upon strength, nerve, & *self*-respect. I know it has humbled me," he wrote from Toledo early in February, "& perhaps this is well. If I was a woman sometimes I would sit down, look out of the window & when nobody but God was looking into the windows of my soul I would cry. I do say God be merciful to me a sinner' [sic] for I know I am nothing but a poor publican."[60]

When Howard returned home at the end of February there was still no decision. But at the annual meeting of the Society on April 6, 1869, on a motion to elect new members the old minority was able to muster a majority of two. Following the election of fifty new members most of whom apparently were of the anti-Boynton persuasion, W. F. Bascom was elected president succeeding Howard.[61]

The next week Howard reported to the Society for a committee charged with negotiating with the pastor concerning his salary for the coming year. The committee offered $1800 while Boynton said that he would have to have $3000. A resolution stating that the most they could afford was $1800 passed by a vote of 36–29.[62]

At the church meeting on April 22, 1869 Dr. Boynton, because of the Society's action, offered his resignation as of May 1 and stated his position so positively that the church accepted his resignation unanimously. The conclusion to this long and unseemly church fight came immediately following the vote on Boynton's resignation when the pastor's friends asked for letters of dismissal. In all, over a hundred members followed Boynton into a new church.[63]

Boynton preached his last sermon on April 25,[64] and after that there was peace in the First Congregational Church. Howard still had a job to do, however, for the church was not yet out of the financial woods. That summer a mortgage of close to $9000 fell due with no funds available. Howard came to the rescue and scraped together the money the day the note expired. A short time later at a Society gathering he told what he had done and right then and there enough was pledged so that only a thousand dollars was left owing to Howard.[65]

Dr. Jeremiah E. Rankin, a friend of the Negro and an able speaker and writer, was called to the church's pulpit from Charlestown, Massachusetts in August and he preached his first sermon in October.[66] Rankin was most acceptable in every way and the church prospered and grew under his inspired leadership.[67] Even the indebtedness seemed not to cause any great problem although to help pay off the bonds issued in 1867 Howard pledged five hundred dollars a year for ten years.[68] Outstanding bonds were twice extended but the last one was retired in 1903.[69]

The conclusion of the church dispute was only the introduction to an even more disturbing and unfortunate episode in General Howard's career. He now had an enemy in General Boynton who could not easily forget his father's defeat. For his next move in the war against Howard, Boynton found a useful, if unlikely, ally in Congressman Fernando Wood of New York. Through their attacks on Howard and the Freedmen's Bureau they permanently damaged the record and reputation of both.

Attacks on the Bureau were nothing new. As far back as 1866 and the Steedman-Fullerton investigation Howard and his subordinates had known the hostility of powerful enemies. The white South and Northern Democrats had naturally found the Bureau an attractive target. Now Boynton's attacks in the press exposed the alleged machinations of Howard and the Freedmen's Bureau "ring." Boynton was a Republican and it was therefore a strange alliance that developed between the younger Boynton and Wood, the machine Democrat from the teeming wards of New York City. Boynton's motive must have been personal; Wood's was undoubtedly political.

Fernando Wood already had had a colorful career as mayor of New York and as a representative in the national legislature. Once a strong Tammany man, he had broken away to form a rival organization, Mozart Hall, but regardless of local disputes, he was on the national scene a partisan Democrat. The most colorful episode connected with his career was his facetious proposal in 1861 to have New York become an independent city. During the Civil War he was known for his Copperhead sympathies and his support of peace proposals in 1864.[70]

Wood was a leading Democrat in a House which numbered but relatively few members of that party. Up until the spring of 1870 Wood had shown no particular hostility toward Howard or the Bureau. He did not know Howard and had never even seen him.[71] But to use the Freedmen's Bureau as a means of attacking the Republican party could easily have been in the back of his mind for some time, and it is just possible that he chose to attack at the time he did because the House was on the point of passing a bill to transfer to the Bureau of Education the remainder of the Freedmen's Bureau appropriation (a sum in the neighborhood of $600,000), and its bounty-paying function to the War Department. Samuel M. Arnell, Republican of Tennessee, had reported the bill on March 30, 1870 from the Committee on Education and Labor.[72] The next day there was debate on this bill with Thompson W. McNeely, Democrat of Illinois, a member of the committee, attacking the measure as a disguised effort to continue the Bureau under different names. He stated that Howard had made "nice property speculations with the funds of the bureau," and also that this bill was simply a scheme to cover up for the Freedmen's Bureau and allow it to escape examination. During an exchange over a motion to table the bill, Wood made some remark in scarcely audible tones from his seat to the effect that this was "a bill to enable . . . Howard, who had grown rich out of the bureau, to control 'six hundred thousand more.' " [73]

The next morning Howard saw a report of this in the newspaper. He rose to the bait and wrote Wood a letter denying that he had grown rich and expressing doubt that Wood had made these remarks since the bill proposed to remove the Bureau funds from his control. "I have discharged the trust committed to me with fidelity," he concluded, "as you yourself would say if you should give *every* transaction the most thorough examination." [74] This was just the opening Wood needed and early the next week he asked to see Boynton in the lobby back of the Speaker's chair. After this preliminary meeting there were others, Boynton turning over to Wood the articles on Howard, the Bureau, and the University, which became the basis of Wood's attack.[75]

On Wednesday, April 16 shortly after the House session opened at noon, Wood arose to ask unanimous consent in order to make a personal explanation. There being no objection, he started out by referring to his aside remark of the past week and the letter which this brought forth from Howard. A clerk read Howard's letter and then Wood went on to say that through his Bureau connection Howard had grown rich and that he thought the bill under discussion was intended to give Howard control over $600,000 more. Since that is exactly the opposite of what the bill provided, Wood must have been desperately seeking an opening for presenting his charges. He read the first charge, that more than $500,000 of government funds had improperly and illegally gone to Howard University, successfully overcame an objection by Eugene Hale of Maine, and went on to read fourteen more charges. These dealt with the First Congregational Church, the building block company, the block itself, the collapse of the hospital building, Howard's salary as an army officer, commissioner, and president of Howard University, the Washington YMCA and the Barry Farm, the mismanagement of the Bureau, and a final charge that Howard belonged to the Freedmen's Bureau "ring." He concluded with a resolution that the Committee on Freedmen's Affairs, an all-Republican committee, investigate these charges. Several members objected to having Wood present a resolution while making a personal explanation, but the feeling among the Republicans was that since these charges had been voiced the only thing to do was to go ahead and investigate them.[76]

CHURCH DISPUTE AND HOUSE INVESTIGATION 205

Half a dozen men came to Howard's defense but not one seemed to suspect what Wood was undoubtedly trying to pull off. Wood must have known that a Republican dominated House would clear Howard of these charges. If they did not, so much the better for the Democrats; if they did there would still be the doubts raised in men's minds as to the integrity and honesty of leading Republicans and the management of the Freedmen's Bureau. They had really nothing to lose.

It was anomalous to say the least for Wood, a politician whose integrity, loyalty, and patriotism were suspect, to be maligning Howard, a war hero and a man of standing and reputation in the community and in the country. The trouble was that Wood's charges had the ring of authenticity and for that Howard had only himself to blame. After his Steedman-Fullerton experience, if not before, he might have realized that the Bureau would be wide open for attack by the opposition party and that the only way to escape embroilment, if then, was to conduct his operations so that there could not be the slightest doubt as to the propriety of every move by himself and by his subordinates. Certainly the way in which he manipulated the finances of the Bureau, the church, the University, and the Barry Farm, regardless of whether or not they were legal, was lacking in good sense if not downright foolhardy, knowing the political situation as it then existed. His connection with the building block company, the purchase of lumber from Maine, the acceptance of a lot from the University all were such as to arouse suspicion on the part of anyone who was willing to believe the worst about a man. The investigation which finally was held by the Committee on Education and Labor was the inevitable outcome of a policy which was admirable perhaps from the standpoint of benefits to humanity, but naive and inexcusably unrealistic from the standpoint of the political facts of life.[77]

On April 8 the committee held a meeting with Howard and Wood to agree upon a mode of procedure. The ten-man committee was made up of the chairman, Samuel M. Arnell of Tennessee, seven other Republicans and two Democrats, Thompson W. McNeely of Illinois, and Anthony A. C. Rogers of Arkansas. Wood had counsel although he took direct part in the questioning of witnesses whereas Howard's attorney, Edgar Ketchum of New York, did all the interrogating for the defense.[78]

It was a sunny spring morning when the investigation got underway in a House committee room at the Capitol.[79] Howard had received, and was to continue to receive, a flood of letters from friends offering aid and prayers and assuring him a complete vindication.[80] These strengthened in him the already firm conviction that he represented the forces of good against evil. Wood's counsel, Joseph H. Bradley, began the investigation by calling witnesses who could testify about the purchase of land for Howard University. When he completed his questioning the committee members had their turn and finally Ketchum was able to cross-examine. Howard was present for each session but remained silent except for a voluntary word of explanation here and there. At the end of the proceedings he made a formal statement.[81]

Wood and Bradley continued to call witnesses for the next seven weeks and although there were occasional recesses the sessions were practically continuous. Wood's and Bradley's object was to demonstrate the alleged illegal actions surrounding the financial affairs of the University, the church, and the Barry Farm particularly, and they devoted a great deal of time to the building block company and the collapse of the hospital building.

In his cross-examination Ketchum constantly hammered at the reliability of witnesses' testimony and extracted unwilling admissions of uncertainty as to facts. He also tried to establish the existence of a conspiracy which he and Howard believed included the Boyntons and other Congregationalists who had sided with the pastor during the church fight. He seemed to think there had been several meetings at Boynton's house about four weeks before Wood made his charges when plans for the attack on Howard were formulated. But he was never able to get anywhere with his attempt, except to show that General Boynton was obviously the source of most of Bradley's and Wood's information and the guiding hand behind the investigation.[82]

When finally the defense had its chance Ketchum first called J. M. Brodhead, Second Comptroller of the Treasury, who attested to the legality of Howard's use of Bureau funds. When asked what limitation there was on Howard the answer was, "None, whatever." In other words, Congress had granted the commissioner such wide powers that he could do virtually as he pleased with the Bureau's money.[83] This proved to be the most significant piece of testimony in the entire investigation. Besides calling on other witnesses to establish one point or another, Ketchum also had Senator S. C. Pomeroy give an account of the origins and purposes of the Barry Farm.[84]

When the defense rested on June 9, there were still the reports to be prepared, so several more weeks passed before the committee issued any statement. Howard probably did not worry over the outcome because throughout the investigation it was obvious how the Republican majority would vote. Soon after his ordeal at the Capitol was ended he wrote to a cousin that the investigation, now about over, "amounts to nothing" and that "it is Boynton's republicans that hurt & not democrats or the democratic press." [85] At the end of the investigation Howard was as convinced as he was at the start that General Boynton was at the bottom of the whole business, and to a friend he confided, "I have tried hard, my Heavenly Father Knows, to do my duty and nothing can be gained by Republican Newspapers misrepresenting me." [86]

Finally on July 13, 1870, Arnell submitted the report of the committee to the House but there was no debate, simply an order for both the majority and minority reports to be printed, with the testimony.[87] Howard naturally was pleased by the report of the eight-man Republican majority which upheld him at every turn. After they had come to charge 11, the one accusing Howard of misusing federal funds in behalf of the YMCA, the majority stated that they could not help noting that the charge against Howard of "grave frauds committed upon the public treasury, not for his own personal gain, but in the interest of a Congregational church and a Young Men's Christian Association, is . . . quite novel in the history of such investigations." [88] In the final paragraphs of their report, they become quite eloquent.

Has the Bureau been a success? [they rhetorically asked and proceeded to answer.] Success! The world can point to nothing like it in all the history of emancipation. No thirteen millions of dollars were ever more wisely spent; yet, from the beginning this scheme has encountered the bitterest opposition and the most unrelenting hate. . . . yet, with God on its side, the Freedmen's Bureau has triumphed. . . . the Commissioner has been a devoted, honest, and able public servant. . . . his great trust has been performed wisely, disinterestedly, economically, and most successfully.

They went on to intimate that Wood was not the real instigator of the charges, made a veiled reference to Boynton, and concluded by recommending the passage of a resolution in praise of Howard, declaring that "he is deserving of the gratitude of the American people." [89]

It is hard to believe that the two members of the Democratic minority listened to the same evidence for, while the Republicans had no fault to find with Howard's actions, the Democrats stated that the charges were sustained on all but one count, the charge that Howard received three separate salaries. They spoke of the Bureau as "this excrescence on our body politic," and found a motive for Howard's actions in his desire to become vice president.[90] Each report is excessively one-sided but of the two, the majority report bears the closer resemblance to the testimony. At least, that was Howard's view. To the editor of the Philadelphia *Evening Bulletin* he said that it was "incomprehensible" how the minority could have written "such barefaced untruths against evidence. . . ."[91]

Howard had to wait until March for House action on the committee report and in the meantime Wood and McNeely had another chance to stab at him. This came during a debate on the deficiency appropriation bill. The Bureau sought funds to complete the fiscal year and Wood moved to strike out a $5,000 appropriation for the Freedmen's Hospital. He went on to denounce the Bureau and spoke of the "plunder" those in charge had gained at the public's expense. When McNeely backed up Wood it was more evident than ever that the investigation had done nothing to silence Howard's enemies. A member of the committee, Washington Townsend of Pennsylvania, came to his defense as did a representative from Maine, John A. Peters.[92] A short time later Arnell was able to bring up his resolution acquitting Howard of the "groundless and causeless" charges brought against him and stating that he deserved "the gratitude of the American people," and on March 2, 1871 the House passed it by a vote of 134 to 52.[93] The fact that it was a strict party vote might have detracted some from the victory but it was all that Howard could ask.

Despite his tactical defeat, Wood had succeeded in stamping on the public mind an impression of Howard and the Bureau which would outlast his own lifetime. If he had deliberately set out to undermine the Bureau and its leader, to ridicule the agency which had worked in behalf of the freedmen, and to score a point for the Democratic party, as he undoubtedly did, he could feel satisfied that his plan had succeeded.

Peace with the Apaches

For the year following the House vote on the report of the committee which investigated Fernando Wood's charges, Howard continued to conduct the affairs of the Bureau in routine fashion. When in Washington, Howard went to his office every day at the University and conducted what Bureau business there was. Most of this concerned the payment of bounties to Negro veterans. Since General Balloch performed practically all of this work, there really was little for Howard to do. Then in September and October came the first inklings of trouble ahead. General Balloch was unable to make a proper accounting of all funds put at his disposal for paying bounties and this eventually resulted in another investigation of Howard's administration of the Bureau. This will be the subject of the next chapter.

During the summer he was concerned with the establishment of the theological department of Howard University. In October he attended a meeting of the American Missionary Association in Hartford and he continued to lecture extensively. Congress no longer was appropriating money for the education of the freedmen and one of Howard's duties was to raise funds for Bureau schools. From the middle of November until a few days before Christmas he travelled west to Wisconsin and Minnesota on such a mission.

Howard went to Massachusetts for two days in the middle of February 1872 to deliver some lectures. On the evening of February 28 he and Lizzie held a reception at their home for the graduates of the law and medical departments of the University. But that very day he had had a communication from Secretary of the Interior Columbus Delano, asking him to come to the department either that same day or the next morning because of "a matter of some importance to the public service. . . ."[1] The matter was of some importance. It was a matter of peace or war in the far off Arizona Territory where Apache bands threatened a general Indian war. Clashes between the various bands of Apache Indians and the white settlers supported by the United States Army had grown more frequent in the years since the start of the Civil War.[2]

The settlers found it impossible to sympathize with the Indians, in fact called for their complete suppression. Thus there was little local condemnation of what is called the Camp Grant massacre in April 1871. Eighty-five Indians, all but eight, women and children, were slaughtered by a party of whites and Indians from the vicinity of Tucson. They believed that the Arivaipa, Pinal, and Yavapai Indians, who were supposedly living at peace near Camp Grant, had been ravaging the neighboring countryside.[3]

News of the massacre quickly spread over the country and was in part responsible for sending to New Mexico and Arizona a special peace emissary, Vincent Colyer, secretary of the Board of Indian Commissioners. This Board, established in 1869, was President Grant's answer to the demands for a more humane policy toward the Indians. As might be imagined, news of Colyer's appointment was greeted with ridicule and derisive criticism on the part of the more "practical" citizens of Arizona and New Mexico.[4] Long and bitter experience had convinced these hardy frontiersmen that all ideas of justice and fair play toward the hostile Apaches were just so much sentimental nonsense.

Colyer lacked tact in dealing with the people of New Mexico and Arizona and he failed to win the confidence of General George Crook, commander of the Department of Arizona, who took a far less optimistic view of the good intentions of the Apaches than did Colyer. Still Colyer did bring together about half the warring Apaches onto reservations.[5]

Colyer's failure to bring about a permanent peace in the Southwest became evident soon after he returned east. Cochise, leader of the Chiricahua band of Apaches, had been on the warpath intermittently for more than ten years and his raids became even more frequent in the fall of 1871. Colyer had not even been able to persuade Cochise to attend a conference because that chief at a previous meeting several years before had been tricked and made a prisoner.[6] He was justly suspicious of white men and remained far removed from them in his stronghold in southeast Arizona while his braves made bloody incursions on white settlers and travelers.

Even the Indians Colyer had gathered on reservations did not all stay put. Rather they too slipped away in small groups to raid far and wide throughout central and southern Arizona and western New

Mexico.⁷ The *Alta California,* a San Francisco newspaper, in November 1871 published a letter from the Governor of Arizona, A. P. K. Safford, condemning Colyer's policy and urging that the military commander, General George Crook, have a free hand in dealing with the hostile Indians.⁸

General Crook, West Pointer, veteran of the Civil War, and already recognized as a doughty Indian fighter had taken command of the Department of Arizona in June 1871. He immediately began preparations for an active campaign against the Apache tribes still at war, convinced that the only way the Indians could be brought to a peaceful condition was through force. Crook's views meshed easily with those of the white population of Arizona who believed that an end to the Indian troubles was at last in sight.

Crook was unable to put his plans into effect during the time of Colyer's presence because this special commissioner had powers exceeding those of the department commander. During the summer and fall of 1871 he did get his command in readiness for what he considered the inevitable campaign against the Apaches as soon as Colyer's peace plan had proved ineffective. In this he had the support of his division commander, General John M. Schofield, who in November 1871 ordered Crook to put all roving Indian bands on reservations and to keep them there by means of a rigid enforcement policy.⁹ Crook set February 15, 1872 as the deadline for the Indians to be on reservations. After that date he intended to wage war on all who were at large.¹⁰

Such was the situation in February 1872. Apparently there would be a vigorous renewal of the Indian wars in Arizona and a general abandonment of the peace policy of the President. It was at this point that the Secretary of the Interior, Columbus Delano, decided to call in General Howard to make one final effort to end hostilities before they began, to review the whole reservation question, and especially to bring Cochise's band of Chiricahua Apaches onto a reservation. Delano conferred with President Grant on the evening of February 28 requesting Howard's services and the next day consulted Howard and Secretary of War William Belknap.¹¹ The Secretary of the Interior apparently had no trouble persuading Howard to take the assignment which was admittedly difficult even to the point where the President saw little chance of success no matter who took on the task.¹²

That same day, February 29, Delano issued instructions to Howard stating the purpose of the mission and clothing him "with full power and a general discretion, to be exercised as your own good judgment may dictate, in carrying into effect [the Interior Department's] views in relation to these Indians. . . ."[13]

Howard turned over his Bureau work to General Whittlesey and on March 7, 1872 left Washington. In San Francisco Howard conferred with General Schofield who offered to cooperate to the best of his ability and instructed Crook to do likewise.[14] Howard proceeded by steamer around the tip of Lower California and then up the Colorado River as far as Fort Yuma in the Arizona Territory.[15]

Having made some temporary provision for a demoralized little band of friendly Yumas,[16] Howard with his party moved on by wagon to Fort McDowell in central Arizona where he was to meet General Crook. Howard's relations with Crook were cordial and the department commander gave every evidence of willingness to cooperate. Crook, whom Howard described as "kind, quiet in deportment & very energetic,"[17] put at Howard's disposal the facilities of the department and, without publicly expressing his displeasure, suspended active operations against the Indians while Howard was in the territory. Howard in his reports to Grant and Schofield expressed thorough satisfaction with Crook. "I would ask for no better officer to work with me in carrying out what I understand to be your Indian policy," he told Grant.[18]

Crook, while maintaining a correct attitude towards Howard, unquestionably nursed hurt feelings within. He resented Howard's coming to Arizona at all and he had little faith in any efforts to achieve peace with the Apaches other than his own. He had little use for Howard, believing him to be conceited and sanctimonious. "He told me that he thought the Creator had placed him on earth to be a Moses to the Negro," Crook wrote about Howard in his autobiography. "Having accomplished that mission, he felt satisfied his next mission was with the Indian."[19]

Crook, as was true of so many others, failed to read Howard correctly. He failed to see that behind this apparent smoke screen of religious idealism was a goodly measure of straight thinking and realistic common sense. Howard talked a somewhat different language from the hard-boiled Indian fighter, and yet their aims were virtually the same. The major difference between them was that Howard believed that it was worthwhile treating with the Indians, trusting them to keep their word, and that too great an emphasis on force would defeat the end in view. Crook wanted first to reduce the Indians to submission and then treat them with justice and humanity.

Despite his hopes of being able to make a peaceful settlement of basic difficulties, Howard could not escape the reality that a good many Indians in Arizona were actively at war with the whites. Many of these were Indians who were supposed to be on reservations. Consequently, early in May he told Crook—who hardly needed to be told—"there is no course left but to deal with them with vigor, according to your discretion, until the murderers and robbers, and those who sympathize with them, whatever tribe they belong to, be made to feel the power of the Government to punish crimes." Crook's orders called for the prevention of any collision between troops and Indians while Howard was in the department. Howard now relieved him of all restraints.[20]

Howard's principal accomplishment during this first visit to the Southwest was a general settlement of problems at Camp Grant amongst certain Apache, Papago, and Pima tribes. To a three-day council he called in chiefs and other representatives of these tribes, the governor of the Territory, General Crook, and other army officers. The major results of this council were the establishment of a new reservation at a healthier location, the conclusion of a general peace arrangement with the Indians represented at this council, a promise by the Indians not to molest white settlers and travelers, and their offer to aid in the apprehension of those who still committed depredations. Reporting the results of the council to Secretary Delano, Howard closed his telegram by saying, "good men rejoice while the bad are active. Success seems now sure."[21]

During this visit to Arizona and also to southwestern New Mexico General Howard visited the different Indian reservations, talked with the chiefs in solemn councils, heard their complaints, and made changes and recommendations. He went to the principal towns, talked with representatives of the press, and addressed the citizens. Of course he was in close touch with General Crook and his subordinate officers at all times during his stay in Arizona. He traveled hundreds of miles over desert country and experienced all the discomforts of frontier life in the American Southwest. He became convinced before this mission ended that he was still capable of active campaigning and thus was determined to remain in the Army rather than seek retirement as he had thought of doing before leaving Washington.

There was one part of his assignment unfulfilled: to find Cochise and get him to end his war against the whites and to take his band of Chiricahua Apaches onto a reservation. Soon after meeting General Crook at Fort McDowell in April, Howard asked Crook to arrange a meeting with Cochise, but all efforts to persuade Cochise to come to a council failed. Consequently Howard temporarily abandoned his plan of meeting with Cochise and returned to Washington, taking with him a group of Indian chiefs. This was a common practice in that day, the idea being to impress on the Indians the greatness of the Americans and to demonstrate the peaceful intentions of the government.[22] They travelled eastward by way of Santa Fe and arrived in Washington June 22, 1872.

The trip with the Indians to Washington, New York, and Philadelphia was a successful one with many amusing occurrences. Yet Howard's work was not finished. Cochise was still at large and conditions in southeast Arizona were as bad as they had ever been. Howard was not satisfied with what had been accomplished and knew that he would have to go back to Arizona.[23] On July 3, Grant issued the order for him to return.[24]

Howard's primary concern was to find Cochise, and from Camp Apache in eastern Arizona scouts went out to try to communicate with the Indian leader. For several weeks there were no results from these efforts.[25] Finally, when Howard was at the Tulerosa reservation in western New Mexico, he met Thomas J. Jeffords a well known scout who, it was reputed, was the only white man who could take him to Cochise.[26]

Jeffords was an unusual man. Born in New York State in 1832 he had come to the Southwest in 1859 and served as a government scout during the Civil War and after. In 1867 he visited Cochise and earned the chief's friendship and respect. At first Jeffords was somewhat prejudiced against General Howard because, as he later said, "of his well known humanitarian ideas, and, to my mind, posing as a Christian soldier." [27] Jeffords soon changed his view when Howard told him he would be perfectly willing to go to Cochise in the Indian's stronghold without military escort. Of all the Indians of the Southwest at that time none had a bloodier record than Cochise, none had as notorious a reputation for taking vengeance on all white men. The soldier who would walk straight into the enemy's country might be a little foolhardy but he was also brave. Jeffords now knew his man and set about making the necessary arrangements for this hazardous expedition.

Jeffords did not try to do the job alone. He spent several days trying to reach two of Cochise's band who would be able to take them to the Chiricahua chief. These two were Chie and Ponce, sons of close friends of Cochise. Ponce knew both the Indian dialect of the Chiricahua band and Spanish and so could serve as an interpreter; both men were necessary to the success of the expedition.[28] They belonged to bands which were supposed to be on the Tulerosa reservation but they had been raiding in the neighboring country. In order to secure their services, Howard had to promise that their families and people would not be disturbed by the military while they were off on this mission. Consequently, Howard issued an order to the commanding officers of the two nearest forts giving permission to these people to range about the neighboring region.[29]

Jeffords, Howard, his aide, Captain J. A. Sladen, the two Indians, an interpreter, and two mule drivers made up the original party, but as they approached the Chiricahua country and came into contact with the outposts of Cochise's band these latter three men were dropped. As the remnant moved westward from New Mexico into Arizona they saw increasing evidence of Cochise's band and were visited from time to time by scouts sent out by the wary chief. Finally they arrived at an Indian encampment in the very heart of the Dragoon Mountains where it was expected they would see Cochise. Still the great chief did not appear. In the morning after their arrival there was much bustle heralding the coming of whom they thought would be Cochise, but the first dignitary to arrive turned out to be his brother. Shortly after this Cochise with his wife, sister, and son made their entrance into the little canyon which was the site of the encampment. Howard, a short time later, described Cochise as

a man fully six feet in height, well proportioned, large, dark eye[s], face slightly painted with vermilion, unmistakably an Indian; hair straight and black, with a few silver threads, touching his coat-collar behind. . . . when conversing upon all ordinary matters he was exceedingly pleasant, exhibiting a childlike simplicity; but in touching upon the wrongs of the Apaches . . . when he considers himself to be specially on duty as the Chiricahua chief, he is altogether another man.[30]

Chie and Ponce, convinced of Howard's peaceful and sincere intentions, were able to persuade Cochise that this was not just another white man's trick. Cochise next asked Howard whether or not he would stay while he called in his captains to consult with them. Howard replied that he would stay as long as necessary.[31]

After several more days of waiting the Indians held a council which was a combination of a religious ceremony and a lengthy discussion of the peace terms Howard offered. Near the conclusion of the council it became apparent that though peace would prevail the Chiricahua Apaches would insist on a reservation in the region where they then were rather than at Canada Alamos where Howard wanted them to go. Another condition was that Jeffords be their agent. In return they agreed to end the war, to return stolen property, and to guarantee the peace of the surrounding area.[32]

On October 12, 1872, Cochise with his captains, Howard, Jeffords, and officers from Camp Bowie met at a place called Dragoon Springs to make a final peace settlement. The result was an agreement which fulfilled almost all of Howard's hopes. He did admit to Crook that there were some hostiles whom Cochise did not control, but he reminded Crook, "You know how to deal with them." [33]

Just as General Howard was about to leave for home Cochise went up to Howard, put his arms around him, and said in English, "Good-bye!" [34] The two men had grown to trust each other and as long as he lived Cochise was true to his trust.[35] Immediately the war in southern Arizona ceased [36] and a few weeks later Governor Safford wrote Howard, "We have not had a difficulty with the Indians in Southern Arizona since you brought Cochise on the reservation. . . . No one can but admire the energy and persistence on your part in finding him and getting him on a reservation and whether it proves lasting or not you have done your duty nobly." [37]

In the days and years to come there would be much criticism of what Howard did from both the civilians and the military in Arizona. As he passed through Tucson on his way home, Howard was aware that the local press was charging that he had protected the Indians from deserved punishment and was predicting that when spring came Cochise and his band would leave the reservation.[38] It was soon charged that Howard had also granted permission to Cochise to raid into Mexico and that members of the Chiricahua tribe were taking advantage of this provision of the agreement. Crook went so far as to characterize the peace policy in Arizona as "a fraud." He was most skeptical of Cochise's willingness to keep the peace and predicted constant trouble as long as this band of Apaches was allowed to occupy the Chiricahua reservation.[39]

Quite obviously there were raids into Mexico, but whether these were the work of Cochise's men, as Crook and others maintained, or the work of renegade Indians from farther north, who took advantage of the presence of the Chiricahua reservation (this was Jefford's contention), is not certain.[40] Howard, when confronted with the assertion that he had specifically granted permission to Cochise to make raids into Mexico, emphatically denied it.[41]

Crook wanted to enforce Schofield's order which called for daily roll calls and to have general supervision of the Indians on the reservations. He was thus extremely annoyed to find that Howard's agreement with Cochise exempted the Chiricahua reservation from this kind of supervision. Crook claimed that at one time he had been in a position to take control of Cochise's reservation, and then discovered from Cochise this provision of his agreement with Howard. Whereupon Crook asked to see the written agreement only to discover that there was none.[42] Crook's complaints eventually appeared in the *Army and Navy Journal* and were brought to the attention of the Secretary of War. By this time the treaty with Cochise was being called "disgraceful," "a corrupt bargain," and "this infamous treaty." [43] Jeffords was attacked as one who formerly had sold ammunition to the Indians, and there was complaint that the military had no authority on the Chiricahua reservation.[44]

All these charges eventually reached Howard who made a lengthy rebuttal. He explained to the Indian commissioner that there never was a formal treaty with Cochise and that the same conditions applied on his reservation as on others. After defending Jeffords he went on to detail exactly the terms of the agreement with Cochise: he did not grant permission to make raids on Mexico, nor did he promise immunity from military intervention but rather said he would merely present to the President Cochise's request for a diminution of troops on the reservation. Then Howard let loose his feelings against what he called "the wholesale abuse that has been heaped upon me for risking life and reputation, to save the lives and property of the citizens, and promote peace and good will amongst men." And towards the end of the letter he resorted once more to the religious theme and wrote words which might just as well have not been written because it was certain they would be misunderstood. "By the Divine help," he wrote, "something was done. Envy, hatred, malice, covetousness, revenge, and falsehood, are very lively, but they cannot overturn one grand fact, viz: that the wildest Apaches may be met, and conquered, without arms, by Gods help." [45]

It is only fair to point out here that Crook had a chance to reply to Howard's explanation. There should have been a written treaty, he said, because oral agreements can too easily be misunderstood. The situation on Cochise's reservation is not the same as on others, as Howard maintained, because on the latter there is much closer supervision. Crook obviously was still suspicious of Jeffords, and he charged that Cochise was harboring the perpetrators of the raids into Mexico. Finally, he ridiculed Howard's assertion that the treaty was made by the Grace of God, because similar treaties which Howard had made with other Apache bands had been broken and the Indians had had to be forcibly subdued.[46]

Undoubtedly, Howard did not do a perfect job. By having the southern edge of the Chiricahua reservation coincide with the Mexican border there was too great a temptation to raid across that border and whether or not it was Cochise's men who led the raids the very presence of the reservation at that location encouraged them. Howard's reason for doing this was that Cochise claimed that about one half of his tribe would refuse to leave that region, and so Howard made the concession to enable the chief to have control over the whole tribe. Yet some more satisfactory southern border might have been arranged. Also, it was a mistake not to have put in writing the agreement made with Cochise. A formal treaty with all provisions made clear would have prevented a great deal of later misunderstanding, especially on the part of those who were not present at the time the treaty was made. Finally, Howard probably gave too much freedom to Cochise to be exempt from control by the department commander. It may be that this was necessary in order to get Cochise to agree to any terms and to persuade Jeffords to take the thankless job of agent, a job he did not want but which he had to take if there was to be peace with Cochise. The result, however, was misunderstanding and resentment from Crook who did not trust either Jeffords or Cochise.

Yet when everything has been said one cannot help but he impressed with the results. By a bold maneuver Howard accomplished in a few days what no one else had been able to do in thirteen years, and there is ample evidence to prove that, at least on American soil, Cochise kept his promise to remain at peace. A region which was dangerous in the extreme for travelers and settlers suddenly became safe.[47]

Tom Jeffords in his report for 1873 said that he doubted if there was any one other than Howard who could have performed the job as well; no one could have done it better.[48] And some years later an inspector for the Indian Office wrote to Howard praising him for his work in Arizona. "It is enough to have lived a whole life time for," he wrote. "Few men do as much toward the cause of Christian enlightenment, in the sum of the allotted years of life. . . . If you were to come through this country now—the Indians from far and near would come to see you—and greet you as their best friend." [49]

Indian wars continued sporadically in Arizona until the late 1880's, proof enough that Howard did not solve all problems. Still it would be a gross misrepresentation to minimize his accomplishments and to maintain that his efforts negated those of Crook. By persuading Cochise and his hostile Apaches to cease their depredations and to remain on a reservation, and by demonstrating the feasibility of dealing with these Indians, he materially improved the chances for peace in Arizona.

Bunoty Paying, Court of Inquiry

At the time that Howard first set out for the Southwest, in March 1872, the Freedmen's Bureau was on the point of closing down. Ever since the end of 1868 the only Bureau activities had been the promotion of Negro education and the payment of bounties to Negro veterans. After the middle of 1870 there was little done for education because of a lack of funds. Thus bounty paying constituted the only signficant Bureau function during its last two years.

Many colored veterans had various sums coming to them from the government and early in its history the Bureau had done what it could to aid them in collecting their claims and especially in avoiding the clutches of unscrupulous bounty agents.[1] In March 1866 Howard ordered the establishment of a claims division.[2] Then in 1867 Congress turned over to the Bureau the complete responsibility of acting as agent for Negro veterans and for paying them bounties, pensions, and other claims. Congress passed this bill at the suggestion of some of the officials of the Treasury Department and Howard agreed to assume the added responsibility. Hence his later difficulties arising out of the payment of bounties were in part the result of his own action.[3]

Howard turned over to his disbursing officer, General George W. Balloch, the duty of paying these bounties. Balloch, a former civil engineer and graduate of Norwich in Vermont, had served throughout much of the war with General Howard as assistant commissary of subsistence. Howard asked for Balloch's services soon after the founding of the Bureau and, not only did they share in that work, but they were also associated in the activities of the Congregational Church and Howard University.[4]

Balloch soon established a system for the payment of bounties which apparently worked fairly well. There was ample room for error, however, since in the first place it was especially difficult to establish the correct identity of the claimant and in addition there were numerous instances of false claims and of the manipulations of clever claims agents. Since the law specified that the bounty money was payable to Howard in person and he in turn was to pay the rightful claimants in cash, this placed on the commissioner and his agent, the disbursing officer, a heavy burden of responsibility. Howard, who had other duties to attend to, especially prior to 1869, had Balloch take complete charge of making bounty payments.[5]

One particular pitfall was the ever-present possibility of paying the wrong claimant. With the Bureau paying out, for instance, between April 1867 and March 1868 over two million dollars in bounty payments, inevitably there would be an error here and there. In that period of time, however, Balloch reported only five wrong payments, and, he said, "they were all cases of gross frauds."[6]

Assistant Adjutant General Eliphalet Whittlesey was so impressed with the success of the Bureau's bounty-paying system that he wrote in 1868 to a member of Congress that the machinery was so perfect "that payments are made without loss to the claimants. The Bureau Agents," he said, "can identify the parties better than any other persons, and defeat the schemes of fraudulent Claims Agents."[7]

Actually, of course, the machinery was not that perfect. The Bureau records indicate that there had to be constant vigilance to prevent frauds which nonetheless occurred. For instance, in 1870, Howard appointed a three-man board to investigate alleged bounty frauds. This board of three Bureau officers reported that the system then in effect was satisfactory but that there must be a very rigid and thorough inspection system to keep frauds at a minimum.[8]

Howard always followed up every report of dishonesty amongst his subordinates. His instructions to Balloch and to W. P. Drew, the chief of the claims division, were explicit on this point.[9] In December 1869 he appointed a commission to investigate complaints against Bureau agents in Tennessee and Alabama,[10] and to a correspondent who directed a charge of fraud against one of his agents he replied: "I will give you every opportunity to show the dishonesty of any agent of mine and will thank you. Not one instant will I keep any man in office that would defraud a man of *one dime*."[11] The mere report of dishonesty was naturally no proof of its correctness and apparently there were instances of false or erroneous charges.[12]

In addition to instances of wrong payment and outright fraud, there were indications that the mechanics of the Bureau system were not all they should have been. For example, Howard's inspector, F. D.

Sewall, in 1869 reported that the records system of the claims division was too intricate, so much so that records were "unavailable for reference to any body except one initiated into the mysteries of this system." [13] Later on, toward the end of the Bureau's existence, the adjutant, Whittlesey, complained to G. A. Seely, Bureau agent in St. Louis, that there should not be report of payments without accompanying receipts to show that the money had actually been paid to the claimant. He also said that had the system which was at that time in effect been operating earlier "much trouble and loss would have been avoided." [14]

The system, then, was not quite perfect. Yet when one considers the enormity of the task and the unusual opportunities for fraud against the government on the part of agents scattered throughout the South, indeed throughout the country, the Bureau's record is a commendable one. In five years the Bureau paid out over $7,500,000 with a loss of less than $50,000.[15] Some of this was unrecoverable from dishonest agents; some represented payments to unqualified claimants.

Congress appropriated the money for the bounty payments and these funds were deposited in the Treasury and drawn upon as demand warranted. Howard also had in his custody a fund which he called the Retained Bounty Fund. This was not government money but represented bounties authorized by a few Northern states during the war to be used in recruiting Negro soldiers in the South. These soldiers helped fill state draft quotas. On the order of General Benjamin F. Butler these bounty funds, amounting to slightly more than $100,000, were withheld at the time of enlistment and thus when the Freedmen's Bureau began operation in 1865 they fell into the custody of the commissioner. In 1867 Congress made Howard the trustee for this fund and authorized its investment in government bonds.[16] This investment of course earned interest and undoubtedly gave Howard the idea for the investment of the regular bounty fund, money appropriated by Congress, to cover losses incurred by making double payments on bounty claims. When an agent made a payment to the wrong claimant the rightful claimant still had to be paid. But since the act of Congress making the Freedmen's Bureau the agency for bounty payments made no provision for double payments somehow the difference had to be made up.

On January 27, 1870 Howard addressed a letter to J. M. Brodhead, Second Comptroller of the Treasury, stating that he wanted to invest a trust fund "of a public nature" in government securities and asking whether "security sixes" were a good investment.[17] Brodhead's reply was that since the government was ultimately responsible this investment would be "as safe as any other." It is probable that in addition to this brief written exchange, there was also some oral discussion of the matter during which Brodhead assured Howard of the complete legality of such a move since he was the payee of the Treasury and not simply the payor.[18]

For more than a year Balloch continued to pursue this policy of investing money held by the Bureau for bounty payments in government bonds. At length in September 1871 a Treasury official noted that Balloch did not actually have as much money on deposit in his account with the Treasury as he claimed. He so informed the Secretary of the Treasury, George S. Boutwell.[19] Balloch's explanation was that he had invested $279,000 of bounty funds in government bonds, $50,000 worth of which he had on deposit in a private banking institution so that he might more easily cut the coupons.[20]

Balloch heard a rumor that he was to be arrested, appealed to Howard, and the two of them immediately went to see Boutwell and also W. W. Belknap, the Secretary of War. Howard gathered from a subsequent conversation with Belknap that the secretary wanted Balloch dismissed, and Howard complied on October 7, 1871.[21] That same day he wrote Boutwell asking his opinion on the correctness of the bond purchase. Boutwell's reply was that "it is illegal, and certainly it is irregular."[22] After further consultation with the Treasury Secretary, Howard reconverted the bonds into currency and deposited that in the Treasury.[23]

Such a revelation of course could not be kept from the press and papers gleefully told of Balloch's "defalcation." One reported that he had taken $15,000 of bond interest for his own use and had a deficiency of $500,000 in his accounts.[24] Worse was to follow.

In the meantime Howard quickly rallied to Balloch's defense. To his friend Edgar Ketchum he expressed confidence in Balloch's integrity and ability to make a complete explanation. He attributed this latest difficulty to "the same infamous cabal that tried to ruin me. . . ."[25] Also when orders came through separating Balloch from the Army, Howard thanked his disbursing officer for his labors and expressed his satisfaction with Balloch's "fidelity" and "integrity of purpose" in disbursing millions of public funds.[26]

Howard's old antagonist from the House of Representatives,

T. W. McNeely of Illinois, wanted to know more about Balloch's dismissal from the service. The House adopted McNeely's resolution on December 18, 1871[27] and shortly thereafter Howard wrote a lengthy explanation to the Secretary of War. He went over the bond purchases, Belknap's disapproval and Balloch's dismissal. He stated that there was no evidence of any deficiency in Balloch's accounts or dishonesty in the discharge of his duties.[28] When Boutwell and Belknap reported to the House early in 1872 the press carried the story. The New York *Tribune's* account so impugned the integrity of the Bureau officials that Howard appealed to Whitelaw Reid, the *Tribune's* managing editor, to desist. "I assure you on my word of honor as a man," he told Reid, "that I speak the truth. God willing, the Government never shall lose a dollar by me. Suspicion is so rife that unadulterated honesty is suspected."[29] Public interest in Bureau matters subsided for a few months but the Balloch affair would crop up again to embarass not only Balloch but Howard as well.

Meanwhile it was becoming increasingly difficult to carry on the work of the Bureau. Congress, once open-handedly generous in appropriating funds for freedmen's affairs, now was showing signs of stinginess. Instead of appropriating the requested $187,500 for the fiscal year ending June 30, 1871, Congress lopped off $100,000 of that.[30] This necessitated a reduction in the clerical force and meant that the Bureau was unable to fulfil school construction obligations.[31] Those who stayed took salary cuts and in order to carry on the payment of bounties Howard called on the branches of the Freedmen's Savings and Trust Company to aid in this work.[32]

The work of the Bureau was as yet unfinished but Howard, in his annual report, recommended that the War Department itself take over the paying of bounties and that the Bureau's one remaining hospital, that in Washington, be turned over to the government of the District of Columbia. He believed that the Bureau should cease its operations at the end of the current fiscal year, that is on June 30, 1872.[33]

Just before leaving for Arizona on March 7, 1872, Howard wrote to Congressman C. L. Cobb, chairman of the House Committee on Freedmen's affairs, giving an estimate of the funds needed to close up the Bureau's work. The total came to $98,800.[34] Apparently he never got this money for only two weeks later, after Howard's departure, Whittlesey was begging either for an adequate appropriation to see him through, or for an immediate end to the Bureau. On March 15,

1872, Whittlesey, without funds, relieved from duty all the bounty paying agents in the field and most of the remaining clerks in the Washington office.[35]

When Howard returned from Arizona on June 22, Congress had already, on June 10, enacted a law calling for the transfer at the end of the month of the remaining Bureau activities, its funds and its records to the War Department proper.[36] Whittlesey had tried to get an appropriation and an extension of time so that the records could be put in proper order and so that Howard himself could be present for the final closing operations. He had supposed that he had been successful but the Congress in the end did not grant his request. Whittlesey believed, with some justification, that this was Belknap's doing.[37]

The upshot of all this was that in the last months of the Bureau there was not enough clerical help to keep up with the written work. Furthermore, there must have been much confusion and carelessness attending the transfer of the records from the Bureau at Howard University to the War Department. Howard always claimed that the War Department employees were extremely careless in the handling of the records, which were dumped haphazardly into wagons without proper care.[38] This, he believed, was the principal reason why Assistant Adjutant General Thomas M. Vincent's force of clerks had so much difficulty in straightening out the Bureau records and why they were unable later to find some of them.

Howard, busy with a group of visiting Apache Indians and in Washington for only a brief time in the last days of June, was unable to direct the closing of the affairs of the Bureau. On July 9, 1872 he again left Washington for the West not to return until early in November. During this second extended absence Vincent and Moody, his chief clerk had an opportunity to begin to look into the Bureau records. When they and Captain James McMillan, who had immediate charge of paying bounties, began to find, for instance, that the records of bounty payments were both incomplete and in some instances erroneous, or that colored veterans were asking for bounty money which had ostensibly been paid, they turned over their findings to Belknap.[39] From Tularosa, New Mexico early in September Howard wrote to Lizzie expressing his surprise at Vincent's seizing his safe. "It does seem," he said "as though they might treat me rightly while away." [40]

During the summer and fall of 1872 Vincent continued to turn up matters which to him indicated irregularities especially in General Balloch's accounts. A missing record book, some missing vouchers, and discrepancies between moneys accounted for and actually turned over to the War Department were the principal findings.[41]

The first official indication which Howard had of storms ahead came in the form of a letter from Vincent to the adjutant general referred to Howard for his comment. This was on November 29, 1872. The letter concerned Balloch, so all Howard did was send it along to him. Three days later he sent Balloch's endorsement to the Secretary of War.[42]

Congress convened December 2 and soon after the session got underway Fernando Wood introduced a resolution that the Secretary of War furnish the House with a copy of the charges Vincent had made on the subject of the Freedmen's Bureau.[43] How did Wood find out about all this? Howard had no doubt but that General Boynton had visited the War Department before the session began, learned of Vincent's investigations, and had relayed the information to Wood.[44]

Whether or not Howard's belief was correct, he was thoroughly convinced that a cabal was after him. Leader of the cabal was, of course, Boynton who, as Howard believed, had never forgiven his father's defeat in the Congregational church dispute.[45] Vincent disliked Howard because as Howard put it, "I mortified [his] pride by flooring him on his former charges."[46] But why should Belknap be aligned against him? Howard gave a clue to the answer to this question in his autobiography. He told how during the Civil War, when Belknap had command of a division in the Army of the Tennessee, Howard gave him an order the execution of which entailed considerable danger. Belknap appeared to be on the point of going directly to Sherman to have the order countermanded when Howard delivered a terse message to Belknap to the effect that he had better carry out the order or there would be someone else in his place who would. According to General Howard's son Harry, Belknap never forgave the implied insult and held a grudge against Howard from that time on.[47] Howard also attributed these attacks on him to his work in behalf of the Negroes, and to his efforts to carry out President Grant's Indian policy which neither the Secretary of War nor the Attorney General liked.[48]

This predilection to assume that others were his enemies was a consistent characteristic with Howard. From the time he was a cadet at West Point he seemed to have enemies who, of course, were always in the wrong. Usually he believed that his enemies disliked him because of his views on religion, the Negro, or temperance. In this instance it does appear as if Belknap and Vincent did go out of their way to be hard on Howard. Starting in November 1872 they relentlessly pursued these Bureau matters until 1874 and then, when a military court had exonerated Howard, civil suits were instituted. By that time Belknap had fallen by the wayside, himself a perpetrator of fraud and embezzlement, but for Howard there was no rest until 1880.

Some time in March 1873 a certain J. W. Shaw, who according to Howard had in 1868 been dismissed from the army for embezzlement,[49] had voluntarily approached Vincent with information critical of the Freedmen's Bureau and especially the manner in which the office was staffed and appropriations disbursed.[50] At this, said Howard, Vincent instituted a search for irregularities in Bureau records "extending it far beyond his province."[51]

In the early months of this investigation, throughout much of 1873 and into the early months of 1874, Belknap and Vincent bombarded Howard with letters, often barely civil, calling for information which Howard frequently could not supply.[52] These letters do not make interesting reading but they do show that the year 1873 must have been a continuous nightmare for Howard. At times he did get away to raise money for the University, of which he was still president, but a large part of his time was spent, with the aid of a clerk, in tracking down missing records, corresponding with former Bureau agents and officers, and getting statements from them as to the manner in which they conducted Bureau business and the condition of their affairs at the time the Bureau closed.[53] The replies quite naturally made it plain that the Bureau records were in the best possible condition up until the time of transfer except for some unfinished back work which resulted from the failure of Congress to appropriate enough money to provide adequate clerical help.[54] During the summer the pressure eased somewhat,[55] but at the year's end, Belknap and Vincent were after Howard as much as before.[56]

As the case against Balloch developed, Howard began to have doubts about certain aspects of his former disbursing officer's affairs. Some things Balloch just did not adequately explain and Howard was worried, because the War Department officials obviously believed Balloch to be dishonest. Concerned lest Balloch be concealing some important information, Howard appealed in a letter to him to make a clean breast of everything or else come up with satisfactory replies to the unanswered questions. The letter shows clearly that Howard had given Balloch a free hand in conducting his office, that he had trusted him completely and had never had any reason to question his integrity. Indeed, Howard admitted that Balloch had been instrumental in restraining Howard "from a too liberal interpretation of the law that I might not err against the side of safety." [57]

No answer to this letter is in the records, and it is probable that Balloch never did reply because he was that kind of man—silent, reticent, and morose. His unwillingness or inability to give a satisfactory explanation was of major concern to Howard. What it boiled down to was this: was Howard responsible for the acts of his disbursing officer and other agents, or did these have to answer personally for any illegal transactions or funds unaccounted for? Howard believed the latter. "Why," he asked a Treasury official, "are not the paymaster gen. the Qr. master General & other Bureau Heads held pecuniarily responsible for their disbursing officers . . . ?" [58] Belknap and Vincent believed that the commissioner, according to law, was personally responsible and thus all these matters involving Balloch were first submitted to Howard. They built up such a case that in December 1873 Belknap addressed a formal communication to the Speaker of the House, presenting a list of items involving alleged irregularities in the conduct of the Freedmen's Bureau while Howard was commissioner.[59]

As soon as Belknap's letter was read in the House, Fernando Wood introduced a resolution that this letter relating, as he said, to the defalcations of General Howard, be submitted to the Committee on Military Affairs which should be instructed to report a resolution calling for the court martial of those officers implicated. The Republicans had the latter part of the resolution removed and were able to insert the word "alleged" in front of the word "defalcations." [60]

During the next few days Howard appeared before this committee to which he addressed a formal statement to the effect that he sought "the fullest possible examination." Never, he said, had he shrunk from any trial and he was confident that he could prove that he was not guilty of the secretary's charges. "Certainly it is against the usage of every department of the Government," he wrote, "to hold me pecuniarily accountable for the defalcations of subordinate officers where no collusion whatever is even claimed." [61]

It was the middle of February 1874 by the time Wood's resolution was formally adopted. By that time it had been altered in Howard's favor so that instead of a court martial, it called for a special court of inquiry to be appointed by the President. Even this favorable turn of events failed to check Howard's unwonted despondency. He admitted to his brother Charles that the whole current of his life had changed. His zest was gone; no longer did he take an active part in church, University, and YMCA affairs. He had not made any calls on New Year's Day. "When anybody sees me, he thinks of the charges & inquires about them & I talk. Afterwards I wish I had not done so." [62] A week or so later he wrote his other brother, Rowland, that this depressed feeling had left him, that God had given him "much recuperation energy" and that he was "apt to be light-hearted." It all seemed so simple. "Integrity is mine," he told Rowland. "If I possess it, I possess it; no examination can make or unmake it. Settle this and still the question of administration remains." He believed his administration had been successful. The losses of his Bureau had been "probably less than in any other under the government." [63]

The Balloch matter still troubled him. He had some doubts as to Balloch's ability to make a completely satisfactory explanation. "I am deeply chagrined at it but believe I am not at fault. . . ." he told Rowland a few days earlier.[64] On February 17 he had written Balloch a coldly formal letter ("Dear Sir: Please explain in writing . . .") concerning the interest money on invested bounty funds for which Balloch had not accounted.[65] Yet he could not quite satisfy his conscience on this whole business and he openly expressed his inward doubts to Rowland, a clergyman. He told how difficult it was to accuse Balloch "who is my neighbor, who was long superintendent of our Sunday School & is now a member of our church, prominent & active. Is not his soul as important as mine in the sight of God [?]." When an irregularity turned up in Balloch's accounts, he had fired him, Howard pleaded. When there was strong suspicion of wrongdoing he had reported this immediately. There had been no effort to cover up, and further, no one knew certainly that Balloch was guilty, despite his inability to account for about $20,000 of interest money.

God knows my heart & my life [he told Rowland]. It is better to go to prison than to attempt to deceive Him. I have *not* always done right, even in Bureau matters. In many things I ought to have been more careful. In one or two matters which were presented to the other investigation Committee and in which they exonerated me I am not sure that I sufficiently scrutinized my motives. Had I been more rigid & exacting & stuck to the literal rendering of the laws Balloch would have doubtless been kept straight, but then there would have been no schools etc. etc. I really *depended* on him & other Disbursing officers to hold me in check. I *was* working with my might & energy for the interest of my charge & gave the most sanguine & literal interpretation to every law. It was but a step—a moment of temptation for him to go beyond me. I hope yet he can plainly show that he has not done so, but I assure you it is no easy task for me to undertake to prosecute him.

Still, if Balloch's accounts were wrong, if there were to be suits brought, then Balloch and not Howard should be held responsible. But, "If I must be crippled & broken—if God has no future use for me why so be it— If He has I will cheerfully, by his help, perform my part." [66]

Howard was not to be "crippled and broken," but the next weeks proved to be a strenuous ordeal. From March 10 when the Court of Inquiry began formal sessions, until May 9 when it presented its opinion Howard faced and attempted to turn back a barrage of charges. It seems as if Vincent and the judge advocate who "prosecuted" the case were determined to make Howard's administration of the Freedmen's Bureau appear in the worst possible light. The Judge Advocate, Asa Bird Gardner, was a native of New York City who had attended the New York University Law School. He had served as a junior officer in a New York regiment and in 1873 President Grant appointed him a judge advocate with the rank of major.[67] Howard's was his first important case and, no doubt, he was eager to impress his superiors, the Judge Advocate General, Joseph Holt (who had gained fame as the prosecutor of the Lincoln conspirators), and the Secretary of War, Belknap. Quite naturally Gardner did not endear himself to Howard during the next two months and some years later he had occasion to say that during the hearings Gardner had "showed great personal feeling and marked disrespect." [68] Apparently, too, Gardner came to receive a bad name amongst other army officers of rank. In 1880 General John M. Schofield wrote, "The well known reputation of Major Gardner in the Army deprives his false and slanderous accusations of any injurious effect upon those against whom they are made, at least among their military associates." [69] Howard would have to expect the worst, then, from Gardner.

The court itself was a different matter. He could be very grateful that President Grant had selected Howard's old commander and friend, General Sherman to be president of the court. Among the other members there was no one who could be counted an enemy; indeed a few were close friends. The rest of the original detail was made up of Major General Irvin McDowell of Bull Run fame, Brigadier General M. C. Meigs, the quartermaster general; Brigadier General John Pope who is best remembered for his role in the Second Battle of Bull Run; and Colonel J. J. Reynolds, onetime assistant Bureau commissioner for Texas.[70] Shortly after, two more officers joined the court. They were Colonel George W. Getty, 3d Artillery, and Colonel Nelson A. Miles, 5th Infantry.[71] Miles also had served as an assistant commissioner and early in the war had been an aide on Howard's staff. Howard expressed himself as "much pleased" with the court as well he might.[72] Throughout the proceedings these officers gave countless indications that they, while technically remaining impartial, leaned in Howard's favor.[73]

Howard had as counsel his old friend Edgar Ketchum of New York and Ketchum's son, Alexander P. Ketchum, who had earlier served under Howard in the Bureau. He also retained George W. Dyer of Washington, D. C., a Bowdoin College graduate, and Henry D. Beam.[74] Edgar Ketchum and Dyer appear to have done most of the work.

Gardner had to establish Howard's moral, technical, and legal responsibility for the alleged offenses with which Belknap had in so many words charged Howard in his two letters to the House of Representatives on December 1873 and January 1874. Specifically these charges, or what amounted to charges, were that certain colored claimants had ostensibly been paid by the Bureau but actually had not received their money even though vouchers had been filed with the Treasury that they had; that three of the disbursing agents of the Bureau were guilty of defalcation to the extent of several thousand dollars; that Balloch had attempted to cover up wrongdoing on the part of a Bureau agent; that there had been illegal double payments of bounties and failure to account for interest funds; that money appropriated by Congress for one purpose had been misapplied by the Bureau for other purposes; and finally that erroneous balances had been maintained at the Treasury.[75] For thirty-three days Gardner tried to prove that not only was there a large sum owing to the government because of various irregularities but that Howard was personally responsible.

Howard's counsel, in cross-examination and later in summoning a few witnesses, attempted to establish the fact that Howard was not personally responsible for his subordinates' disbursements as long as he had exercised due diligence in supervising their activities, that he had done this, and that he had maintained satisfactory records. Particularly helpful to Howard was the testimony of several Treasury officials, especially that of J. M. Brodhead, the Second Comptroller, who had sanctioned the investment of Bureau funds in government bonds and who emphasized the unusual degree of latitude Howard had in handling the funds of the Bureau.[76]

On the first of May, Howard, acting on his own responsibility, read a long statement concerning the charges made against him. He stated, among other things, that the investigation was a predetermined effort and not the result of what the Secretary of War called "certain developments," and that Belknap's references to "complaint after complaint" created an erroneous impression of mismanagement and fraud which was harmful to his reputation. He had, he maintained, sought the fullest possible investigation and he read aloud a lengthy letter to Sherman, written the previous November, requesting active duty with the army and a chance to answer his critics. Continuing his statement, Howard said that for too long the secretary had kept him in the dark regarding the specific charges against him and that his efforts to obtain them were met with evasion. He then went on to take up Belknap's charges one by one and to refute them. He had handled faithfully the Retained Bounty Fund; there had been no misapplication of funds; the three defaulters had already been brought to book; Treasury officials had sanctioned the investments in government bonds; and records had been faithfully kept.[77]

Dyer, on May 5, summed up for the defense, ably presenting his argument.[78] The judge advocate two days later delivered a long and technical summary which primarily attempted to establish the fact of Howard's personal responsibility.[79] Gardner believed that he had substantiated all the War secretary's charges, but the court thought otherwise and in its opinion stated that Howard had not "violated any law of Congress, regulation of the Army, or rule of morals, and that he is 'not guilty,' upon legal, technical, or moral responsibility in any of the offenses charged." Although the legality of the investment of public funds was, they believed, doubtful, the fact that the Second Comptroller, when consulted, had approved of the investment, exonerated Howard. Finally, they concluded, after "thirty-seven days of careful and laborious investigation, the court finds that General Oliver O. Howard did his whole duty, and believes that he deserves well of his country." [80]

One might think that this would have ended the matter once and for all. Not so. President Grant submitted the findings and opinion of the court to the Judge Advocate General, Joseph Holt, who wrote an extensive commentary in general disagreement.

Holt's findings sound plausible and there can be little doubt but that Howard paid more attention to the general supervision of his Bureau than to the specific details. Undoubtedly Balloch's administration of the disbursing office was somewhat lax as to procedure and offered opportunity for dishonesty. Howard might well have devoted more time than he did to the supervision of the monetary affairs of the Bureau and, as Holt pointed out, mere good intentions do not sufficiently excuse what he called "the manifest violations of law" attributable to Howard.[81] Grant, however, failed to agree with Holt and, without comment, on July 2 simply approved the findings of the court.[82]

Howard failed to appreciate Holt's review of the case. He admitted that in personal relationships Holt had always been friendly but that he "nearly always sided against me judicially." He tried to explain why Holt should have done this and he concluded it was to sustain the Secretary of War. Holt's review, he believed, was simply "an ex parte argument written by subordinates, signed by himself, sounding precisely like our disappointed Judge Advocate's harangue." Behind all of this was Belknap, whom Howard described as

the moving spirit against me all the time. He has bad associates—foul-mouthed men—Kentucky democrats—meets them at night. He is not really a republican, not in favor of the Peace policy with the Indians— He deceives Gen. Grant. . . . The President is represented by Belknap, Babcock etc.[83] His vigorous, independent self does not appear much. Sherman says often to me ['] I don't wish to crowd myself upon him. Others have his ear ['] and such like expressions, show [ing] that Gens. Sherman & Grant are not as intimate as they once were. He has uniformly shown me courtesy. The conspiracy was to destroy me. Belknap, Schriver,[84] Vincent, Moody & I fear Babcock were in it. This thing now reacts. Judge Holt's review which was under the law wholly unnecessary & substantially against the Presidents promise that my accuser should not appoint the Court, nor review the proceedings, was the only source of justification for the conspirators.[85]

The "conspirators" were not through with Howard, however. Vincent continued relentlessly to plug away at the same charges, incorporating these in his annual reports to the Secretary of War.[86] This perseverance eventually resulted, in 1878, in civil suits brought against Howard for the recovery of certain sums for which the War Department claimed Howard was personally responsible. All during the intervening years Howard longed for relief. "Why can not they stop" he cried out to a friend.[87] "It is strange that I should be so persistently followed! Where lies the wicked offense I have committed [?]" is what he wrote to Sherman in 1875 when the civil suits began to take shape.[88] Sherman answered this with his own explanation as to why Howard got into this mess. "The motive dates back to that old assignment of you to the Army of the Tennessee— when vengeance on both of us was resolved on, and will never let up as long as we live," wrote Sherman. "The same agent Boynton is used in both cases, and this winter will tell the tale. You will be assailed in the Courts and I in Congress."[89] Possibly there was something to Howard's belief in a conspiracy.

Howard even went so far as to ask President Grant in February 1876 to appoint a special board of arbitration to settle all questions of law and equity between him and the government.[90] Soon after, the Belknap case broke. The Secretary of War had apparently accepted bribes and though the Senate later in impeachment proceedings voted not to convict because of Belknap's prior resignation and the consequent belief that the Senate did not have jurisdiction, all but a handful believed Belknap guilty.[91] Howard wrote General Whittlesey that he felt "a sudden feeling of relief" when he heard of Belknap's resignation, and yet he did not "rejoice" in his misfortunes but rather felt sorry and ashamed for him. Still, he noted: "The suits that originated in his unfriendliness are still pending against me in the courts here," and indeed there was to be no immediate benefit derived from Belknap's departure.[92]

A month later he tried a new tack. This was to get Vincent transferred to some other duty. He hoped that maybe General Meigs would be able to convince the new Secretary of War, Judge Alonzo Taft, that Vincent was pursuing Howard for no good reason. Vincent was well aware, wrote Howard to Meigs, that these charges were groundless. "He knows I have disobeyed no order. . . . He knows that I spent every dollar for *educational* purposes in exact accordance with law. Yet he says the opposite or implies it in the story he attempts to tell the country. May the good Lord never visit him with the anxiety, sorrow & trouble he has been able to visit upon [me]. . . ."⁹³ Nothing came of this request. Early in the following year he repeated it to Sherman. "There must somehow be some end," was his plea.⁹⁴ Sherman replied that he, too, had his troubles and that there was little that he could do. When he charged Vincent with persecuting Howard, Vincent "disclaimed any personal animosity" and said that he simply was doing his duty which was to report every irregularity turned up in reviewing the records of the Bureau.⁹⁵

Finally, Howard hoped that the Soliciter of the Treasury, Kenneth Raynor, could be persuaded to withdraw the suits.⁹⁶ Raynor, though sympathetic, was unable to do this and so in February 1878 Howard was in Washington for the last chapter of this lengthy story.⁹⁷

There were three suits, one involving $134,000, and the other two $22,000 and $23,000, which were connected with the Retained Bounty Fund, and the alleged misuse of interest on invested government money. On March 12, 1879, after hearing testimony from Howard and Balloch, the judge directed the jury to return a verdict "for the defendant." This the jury did. Judge and jury repeated the same performance with the second suit on the following day at which point the district attorney withdrew the third and final suit.⁹⁸ This was the anticlimactic ending to the whole affair.⁹⁹

Two investigations and the civil suits had cost Howard much money. Legal expenses and other costs of the Court of Inquiry alone he estimated to have amounted to $7,000, and though he tried, he could obtain no relief from Congress.¹⁰⁰ The cost was great also in damaged reputation, to himself and to the cause for which he had worked. The mere fact that charges of corruption, inefficiency, and fanaticism had been tossed around left the impression that there must be something to these charges despite the fact that every time Howard had complete vindication. Had Boynton, Fernando Wood, Belknap, and Vincent not assaulted Howard and the Bureau as they did both the Bureau and Howard would have appeared before posterity in a far more favorable light, and their positive achievements rather than their admitted shortcomings would stand forth more clearly than they do. Thus though the attackers failed to win the individual battles, in a very real sense they won the war.

Washington, D. C.

The concluding events connected with the Court of Inquiry brought to a close Howard's career in Washington. He could look back with mixed emotions on the past nine years. These were not altogether happy years; there was too much unpleasantness, too much harassment, to count this period happy, but at least Lizzie and Otis were together much of the time; and their home life compared happily with the distresses of Howard's public life.

When the Howards moved to Washington in the summer of 1865 the family numbered six. Guy, Grace, and Jamie had arrived before the war; Chancey was born at the time of the battle of Chancellorsville in 1863. Then in June 1866 Lizzie gave birth to a fifth child, and fourth son, John.[1] Three years later came Harry Stinson Howard, named for Otis' aide, and nephew of Mrs. James G. Blaine, a young man who died in 1866. The last child, Bessie, was born in September 1871.[2] By the time Harry came along it was time for Guy to start preparing for college. In 1869 he entered Philips Andover Academy and two years later went on to Yale. Guy's choice of Yale was a bitter disappointment to his father who had hoped he would follow him to Bowdoin. Then Grace had her chance and left home to go to Vassar. Thus the family seldom was together but Lizzie and Otis tried hard to keep it united in other ways and were eminently successful in doing so.

For almost three years the Howards lived in the downtown residential section of the city but in 1868 they moved to their new home on the present site of Howard University on an eminence overlooking Washington. It was a large house, made of the near-white brick of the building block company.[3] Its mansard roof and general appearance are typical of the architectural style of that era. It must have been a comfortable home to live in, although it was something of a burden for Lizzie to maintain.[4]

During these years Howard enjoyed fairly good health. Occasional attacks of neuralgia and rheumatism marred an otherwise good record but his overall healthy constitution was well demonstrated by his ability to stand up under the rigorous testing of the expedition to Arizona and New Mexico in 1872.

The Howards ought to have made out reasonably well financially but Otis was openhanded, generous, and sometimes too trusting. He listed in 1871 his contributions that year to church and YMCA, a total of eight hundred and sixty dollars, five hundred of which was to pay off the church debt.[5] He pledged $10,000 to Howard University to endow a law professorship and he had to meet constant demands from penurious friends and acquaintances. His troubles were further compounded by his readiness to sign notes for other people. While Howard was in Arizona in 1872, several of these came due and the creditors turned to the endorser. Lizzie became so distressed over the demands made on her that she half jestingly wrote to Otis that when he got back she would have a guardian appointed for him. "I dont think you are capable of taking care of us and yourself," was her comment.[6] Though Howard resolved not to endorse other notes in the future, he was constitutionally unable to keep the pledge. Throughout the remainder of his life he constantly was involved in the financial problems of others, the result of his generosity and faith in his fellow man. Some would call this financial incompetency but Howard preferred to err on the side of openhandedness rather than excessive caution.

Howard dabbled some in Washington real estate and he owned properties in such scattered localities as Buffalo, New York and Nebraska. Most of his investments proved unprofitable, however, because of the nationwide depression which set in in 1873. Hence he left Washington in rather straitened financial circumstances,[7] and his pledge of $10,000 to Howard University was still unpaid.

While in Washington Howard kept up a torrid pace of activity. His official duties, of course, occupied most of his time, but he was involved in a great number of extracurricular interests. Until 1869, the First Congregational Church had probably first call after the Freedmen's Bureau; then when he became president of Howard University that institution was of primary concern. In each instance Howard carried his interest beyond Washington itself for he was an inveterate fund raiser. His friend A. P. Ketchum called him "the most successful man in the world in the securing of money for educational and religious purposes."[8]

The Young Men's Christian Association movement was another of

Howard's interests. He aided in the organization of a company, of which Chief Justice Salmon P. Chase was president, to erect an income-producing YMCA building with auditorium and offices. This building was built at the corner of 9th and D Streets, Northwest, and was opened for use in September 1869.[9] Unfortunately the outcome was anything but happy and the trouble which arose from the mismanagement of the enterprise by Henry D. Cooke, brother of the financier Jay Cooke, plagued Howard for years to come. Mismanagement and the depression of 1873 rendered almost worthless the stock of the company which Howard had induced several institutions, including Hampton Institute, and several of his friends, to buy. This caused him much embarrassment as well as financial loss. At length in 1887 the building burned and the property was sold. Something was realized on the stock but as late as 1888 Howard was sending former Bureau Assistant Commissioner Robert K. Scott twenty dollars a month because he felt responsibility for having induced Scott to purchase several thousand dollars worth of the stock.[10]

Howard also had a more than passing interest in the temperance movement and as commissioner of the Freedmen's Bureau had temperance pamphlets and pledge blanks distributed amongst the freedmen. When he discovered that the Sons of Temperance practiced segregation he gave his active support to the Lincoln Temperance Society formed especially for the Negroes but on the understanding that whites would not be excluded.[11] That his efforts were very effective is doubtful. John W. De Forest tells in the account of his experiences as a Bureau officer in South Carolina of his futile and even laughable efforts to get the freedmen to sign temperance pledges. He got not a single signature, "nothing but snickers and guffaws."[12] Howard believed, though, that the cause deserved his support and he kept right on as an active temperance man long after he had left Washington.

While it could be argued that Howard's finger was in too many pies, it was inevitable that, being the prominent man he was, he would be called upon for service from several different directions. And Howard was not one to flinch from what he considered a duty. Some men are capable of accomplishing more than one thing at once. Howard was such a man.

Because he held an important position in Washington he frequently had occasion to associate officially with the President, cabinet officers, and Congressmen. For a time he conferred frequently with

President Johnson. Oddly enough his relations with Johnson were friendly long after one would have thought that nothing but bad feeling could have existed. At the end of August 1866 after Johnson had twice vetoed bills for the extension of the Freedmen's Bureau, and following soon after the Steedman and Fullerton affair, Howard had an interview with the President which lasted an hour and a half at the end of which Howard said they "parted very good friends. . . ." [13] By 1868, however, Howard privately concurred with those who sought to oust the President through impeachment proceedings. He sincerely believed that Johnson's reconstruction policies were evidence of disloyalty to the nation and he wanted to have the country in the hands of an administration which would deal justly with the freedmen.[14] Shortly before Grant's inauguration in 1869 Howard commented on Johnson's retirement from the presidency in typically charitable fashion, "I do not wish him ill but I do wish my country well." [15]

Howard had far greater faith in Grant, because Grant was, he believed, "on the side of loyalty, reconstruction, and freedom." [16] Following an interview with Grant in 1871, Howard wrote in his diary, "No thoughtful man who comes near him, can fail to be impressed with his honesty of purpose & clear, decided judgment upon questions that are now affecting the public mind." [17] The corruption of the Grant regime of course troubled Howard a great deal. He especially felt crushed at the scandal connected with Senator S. C. Pomeroy's attempted re-election to the Senate. Pomeroy had been his friend and associate for seven years and Howard had known him as a God-fearing man, upright in his private life, and connected with many a good cause. Yet he conceded that all men were imperfect and sinners and that if any had sinned God would know it and bring them to repentance.[18] Howard could not believe that a man who led an upright private life could deviate from the path of rectitude in his public affairs. Yet this was an age when such inconsistency was common enough and the type of dishonesty illustrated in the case of Senator Pomeroy, who tried to bribe certain members of the Kansas legislature in order to gain re-election to the Senate, though not altogether condoned by the public was nonetheless viewed generally with a certain resignation and apathy. No wonder, then, that Howard who would uphold a man who was sober, a regular church attendant, and a loyal Republican did not find it easy to condemn Pomeroy or others of that age accused of corrupt practices. That he himself was caught up in the general free-for-all of incrimination and accusation which characterized the Grant administration is proof enough of the overall indiscriminate nature of the charges bandied about. Howard had good reason to sympathize with Pomeroy and to uphold Pomeroy's good name despite overwhelming evidence against the Senator.

Howard's work as Bureau commissioner, his travels over a large part of the country, his lecturing and fund-raising activities, his service as president of Howard University, and about all his ordeal in the two investigations contributed inevitably to the enrichment of his character. No longer was he the sensitive, reward-seeking, somewhat inmature young officer of the early war period. Heavy responsibilities accompanied by frequent attack and criticism had reduced the self-adulation to manageable proportions. This is not to say that he had altogether lost the unattractive traits of character which he had been burdened with up to 1865. It is merely that he had brought them more under control. They would still be in evidence throughout the remainder of his life, but Howard had learned much from his Washington experience.

Take, for example, a relatively unimportant occurrence in October 1873. Howard attended in Toledo the annual convention of the Society of the Army of the Tennessee. Most of the big names were there: President Grant, Secretary of War Belknap, Governor Rutherford B. Hayes of Ohio, Sherman, Sheridan, and Logan. In the course of the program Logan gave a history of the Army of the Tennessee and never once mentioned Howard's name. The next day Otis confided to Lizzie, "I watched my heart—I found a little bitter [sic] there. . . . The natural & excessive sensitiveness to praise & blame that is in me God will enable me to check & master as it is discovered." [19] Ability to stand up to such slights still took much self-discipline but at least he was aware of the problem. In other words, Howard still struggled with the same dual forces of pride and humility. Never was the former completely under control, but as the years passed he tempered it with a larger proportion of humility.

Looking back from 1874 to 1865 he could count up a large number of lasting friendships formed, of truly beneficial goals attained, but he could also review a political record of some naïveté and poor judgment as in his laying himself open to criticism in the building block and Congregational Church affairs. As far as the Freedmen's Bureau is concerned, especially the establishment of institutions of higher learning, he could rightfully claim a major accomplishment.

In the summer of 1868 while on a tour of inspection Howard visited the Storrs School for colored children in Atlanta. He, as was his custom, gave a short talk to the children and then asked them if there was any message they might have for the people up North. A boy about twelve, wearing a clean white jacket, with teeth just as white, and intelligent, bright eyes got to his feet, raised his hand, and said, "Tell 'em, Gen'l, we're risin'." The episode had a certain symbolic significance and years later this same boy, whose name was R. R. Wright, became the president of the Georgia State Industrial College and Minister to the Dominican Republic.[20] The "risin' " had many more years to go but at least the movement had had a start and Otis Howard knew that the impetus had come partly through his efforts.

Despite Howard's positive accomplishments during his years in Washington, they did not altogether still a feeling of restlessness which stemmed most likely from the fact that he was a professional soldier not doing a soldier's work. Sherman more than once had reminded him of this. Another reason was his desire to get away from the unpleasant atmosphere of Washington into something more wholesome and desirable. He even once tried to resign from the army. This was in January 1872.[21] But he changed his mind once he found, during his two exacting experiences in the West that summer, that he had retained much of his old physical vigor. He was, as he wrote to Lizzie from Fort McDowell, "getting too strong for the *shelf*." [22]

This thought of retirement from the army was not the first time he had seriously considered leaving the military service. He had, in 1860 and 1861, made plans to enter the ministry but the war had interfered. In 1868 he had the opportunity of becoming president of Union College but declined because of his unfinished Bureau work. For the same reason he asked to be excused from taking an active command in Texas in 1871. In this decision to stay with the Freedmen's Bureau to the end he had the concurrence of both the President and the Secretary of War despite Sherman's strong wish that Howard "take his share of duty." [23] In June 1872, between trips to Arizona, he wrote to the Secretary of War stating that the Indian commissioner wanted him to return to New Mexico and that therefore he would like to withdraw his resignation.[24] Then, just about the same time that Howard returned from his second trip west, General Meade died leaving vacant a major-generalship. Every brigadier had his eye on the position. Howard's resignation and its withdrawal had not yet been acted upon and Howard feared lest he be given the promotion and, at the same time, retired. This, he wrote to Sherman, "would look as if it was simply a riddance, and not a reward of service." [25] Sherman replied that he had read Howard's letter requesting withdrawal of his resignation to President Grant and that that was all he could do. Sherman gently reminded Howard that it would have been better for his career and chances of promotion had he taken an active command two years before as he had then urged.[26] Grant apparently agreed to the request for the next day the adjutant general notified Howard that the Secretary of War had approved the withdrawal.[27] Sherman, as General of the Army, had contemplated assigning Howard to the command of the Department of the Lakes, but he never carried out the idea. Because of the unfinished business of the Freedmen's Bureau, the call for information and explanation by the adjutant general, the Secretary of War, and the Congress, Howard remained for almost two more years in Washington on something less than active duty.[28]

In April 1873 Howard admitted to an officer of the New York Life Insurance Company that he was thinking of entering the business world "if a favorable opportunity presented itself. . . ." [29] Nothing came of this nor of a subsequent correspondence with a business man of New York City, Hiram Barney. Howard explained to Barney that his reason for wanting employment other than in the government was solely financial. "It will not do for me to remain here or in the service till I become bankrupt," he told Barney at a time when the panic of 1873 had already begun to leave its mark and when Howard faced increasingly difficult and annoying dealings with the Secretary of War.[30]

Right at the time of Barney's noncommittal reply, Howard made a formal application to President Grant for active duty. He gave as reasons the accusations against him and his consequent unwillingness to leave the service while these "are rife in the country against me" and because of the prospects of a war with Spain just at that time.[31] He wrote a lengthy, impassioned plea to Sherman putting forward the same arguments and calling on Sherman for his aid in restoring him to active duty.[32] Sherman's reply, as always, was kind and generous, yet it also alluded once again to his disapproval of

Howard's having been connected with the Freedmen's Bureau. He assured Howard, however, that if consulted, "which now is rarely the case," he would assign him to an appropriate command.[33]

Shortly after this exchange with Sherman came the Court of Inquiry. This lasted until Grant's final approval of the finding of the court on July 2, 1874. At almost the same time Howard was ordered to proceed to the West Coast and take command of the Department of the Columbia.[34]

Service in the Northwest

Otis Howard had a feeling of great relief at last to be away from what he called "our Babel capital." [1] No wonder. He had had too many unhappy experiences there in the years since 1865 to have harbored any regrets at being sent to the West Coast. Besides having the obvious advantage of distance from the nation's capital, Portland, Oregon was also a pleasant place to live. Here the Howard family was to be for a little over six years.[2]

For over two years Howard found his duties somewhat routine. The Department of the Columbia embraced all of Washington and Oregon, part of Idaho, and all of Alaska. The one thousand men making up the command were scattered around at various posts, while department headquarters were at Vancouver Barracks near Portland. The major problem of the department commander was to keep watch over the score or so of Indian tribes and to be ever watchful for any outbreak of warfare. Alaska presented peculiar problems of administration since that territory did not yet have a civil government. Until the outbreak of the Nez Perce War in 1877 Howard did not have to take the field with his troops. He did, however, make extensive tours of his department including an inspection trip to Alaska in the summer of 1875.[3]

Meantime he took up the usual round of church and YMCA activities. Soon after arriving he reported to his brother Rowland that "much wickedness" was to be found in Portland.[4] It was not long before he became president of the local YMCA and each Sunday in addition to attending church he took charge of a Bible class.[5] He even did some preaching although, showing uncharacteristic caution, he took pains to limit such engagements lest it be thought he was neglecting his official duties.[6]

Largely to revive his drooping financial fortunes, Howard began in his spare time to write for periodicals, to lecture, and to put into book form his own boyhood experiences. The result of these latter efforts was *Donald's School Days,* a book for boys which was quite obviously autobiographical.⁷ Later he wrote a sequel, *Henry in the War*, and, after the conclusion of the Nez Perce War, an account of his experiences in that campaign.⁸

Howard also was constantly trying to improve his mind. Two or three evenings a week, when able, he and some of his officers would gather at Howard's office at Vancouver Barracks to read aloud such authors as Scott and Dante. By himself Howard read Macaulay, Dumas, and other authors.

Guy Howard, the oldest child, was graduated from Yale in 1875, then came west to live with his parents. He worked for a time in a Portland bank, seemed not to like it, and asked his father to get him a commission in the army. Such things apparently were easily arranged in 1876, for Sherman, in immediate response to Howard's telegram, said that the President would grant the request.⁹

Though a continent's width away from the capital, Howard did not lose touch with affairs back East. In addition to the continuation of his law suits arising out of the payment of bounties which took him to Washington in 1878, he naturally retained a lively interest in the affairs of Howard University.¹⁰ But he was equally concerned over the fate of the country. The Congressional elections of 1874 went against the Republicans and for the first time since before the Civil War the Democrats controlled the House of Representatives. This was a serious blow to Howard¹¹ and he deplored still further the apparent willingness to appease the South at the expense of the Negroes. Murder and riot in Louisiana, Mississippi, and Arkansas were met, in his opinion, by a policy of weakness. "I have no bitterness," he complained, "but I do feel sad at the want of courage in our public men." ¹²

When Rutherford B. Hayes received the Republican presidential nomination in 1876 Howard wrote a congratulatory letter to his friend and promised his support saying that he was not "willing to surrender the Administration into the hands of the Confederates yet awhile." ¹³ Still, following the resolution of the disputed Hayes-Tilden election, the new President, Hayes, proceeded to try to win over the conservative South by withdrawing regular army units from the support of the last of the carpetbag regimes in South Carolina and Louisiana. Howard was helpless to do anything at all to aid the freedmen now virtually abandoned by the government. Besides he had problems of his own in the Department of the Columbia. In these same first months of the new administration General Howard became involved in one of the most remarkable and dramatic campaigns in all American history—the Nez Perce Indian War of 1877.

In the 1870's the Nez Perces [14] inhabited a wide area covering portions of Oregon, Washington, and Idaho; their hunting lands extended into Montana. Since the days of Lewis and Clark they had been at peace with the white man, and in 1855 a formal treaty with the United States established a generous reservation area for them. As more and more white people entered this region, especially after the discovery of gold there, friction developed between Indians and whites, and in 1863, at the demand of the whites, the size of the reservation was considerably reduced. Although a good many chiefs would not agree to the reduction, the government took the position that since Lawyer, the principal chief, plus a number of lesser chiefs had signed the new treaty their action was binding on the entire tribe.[15] Those who did not accept the treaty of 1863 and who continued to remain off the reservation were henceforth designated as nontreaty Nez Perces.

One important band of nontreaty Nez Perces was that led by Joseph who claimed as tribal domain the Wallowa Valley in northeast Oregon. Here during the summer months his people would come to hunt and fish and graze their stock. But it was not long before difficulties arose between these Indians and the white settlers. In the summer of 1876 two settlers killed an Indian in the Wallowa Valley and from then on there was a strong possibility of a clash between the whites and the nontreaty Nez Perces.[16]

The Indian Bureau, attached to the Department of the Interior, was at this time pursuing a policy of placing all Indians on reservations and attempting to teach them the ways of the white man.[17] Hence it is not surprising that both the commissioner of the Indian Bureau and the agent at the Lapwai Nez Perce reservation, John B. Monteith, disapproved of allowing the nontreaty Nez Perces to roam about a four-state region while still refusing to acknowledge the sovereignty of the United States over lands the Indians claimed by right of inheritance.

Pressure from the Indian Bureau and from white settlers supported by Governor L. F. Grover of Oregon [18] made it virtually inevitable that the nontreaty Nez Perces would not be able to continue in their accustomed ways. From a purely practical standpoint the only solution was for them to consent to go onto a reservation, but this they did not want to do.

Following the murder of the nontreaty Nez Perce Indian in the summer of 1876, Howard recommended that a commission be appointed to try to effect a peaceable settlement before actual warfare began.[19] A committee of five was eventually named by the Secretary of the Interior. Its chairman was D. H. Jerome of Saginaw, Michigan; two of the other four members were Colonel H. Clay Wood, assistant adjutant general of the Department of the Columbia, and Howard.[20] The instructions to the commission stated that its purpose was "to visit the Nez Percé and other roving bands of Indians in Idaho, Oregon, and Washington Territory, with a view to secure their settlement upon reservations and their early entrance upon a civilized life. . . ."[21] As long as the Indians refused to accept the idea of a reservation the only alternative would be to use force. The commissioners reported that "Joseph and his band firmly declined to . . . make any arrangement that looked to a final settlement of the questions pending between him and the government." Hence they recommended that a military force occupy the Wallowa Valley to preserve the peace there, and that the agent of the Nez Perces (Monteith) should try to get these nontreaty Indians onto the reservation. If this were not done in a reasonable length of time then force should be used.[22]

In January 1877 the Department of the Interior instructed Monteith to carry out the recommendations of the commission, that is, to place the nontreaty Nez Perces on a reservation. At the same time Howard was ordered to send a force to the Wallowa Valley to aid the Indian Bureau if called upon.[23] Early in February Monteith gave Joseph until April 1 to go onto the Lapwai reservation in western Idaho,[24] but Joseph would not accept this decision as final. He requested an interview with General Howard.[25]

Up until this time the decision to move the Indians onto the reservation and its execution were officially the concern of the Indian Bureau. In fact, General Sherman, commander of the Army, and Major General Irvin McDowell, in command of the Military Division of the Pacific of which the Department of the Columbia formed a part, made it very plain to Howard that he must merely aid the Indian Bureau in carrying out its instructions, strongly implying that he should not initiate any action.[26]

Failing to get Joseph's co-operation, Monteith next turned to Howard as his instructions indicated he should. Rather than ask the military to use force, he requested Howard to try his luck at persuading Joseph. Monteith believed that if Howard could talk with Joseph, "the desired result would follow in a short time." [27] A council was held at Fort Lapwai from May 3 to May 7. Present were Monteith, Howard, his aides, officers from Fort Lapwai, and on the other side, Joseph, and various other Indian leaders, including some of the so-called dreamers. These religious leaders, who were bitterly hostile to the whites, had a strong influence over the nontreaty Nez Perces. The most outspoken of these dreamers was Too-hul-hul-sote (there are various other spellings of this name) who, said Howard, was "a large, thick-necked, ugly, obstinate savage of the worst type." Throughout the meetings he harangued the assembled group and finally became so troublesome that Howard had him arrested and placed in confinement.[28]

The Indians were loath to submit to the inevitable and persisted in claiming that they could not be separated from the lands of their fathers. Monteith and Howard listened to these arguments, but they could reply only that their instructions were explicit, that the Indians must go onto the reservation, and that the sole question was whether they would go peaceably. At the end of the third day of deliberating the Indians yielded.

During the next three days (May 8–10, 1877) Howard and the various Indian chiefs, particularly Joseph, White Bird, and Looking Glass, went over much of the Lapwai reservation. The Indians, according to Howard, were in a friendly mood apparently having thrown off the ill-feeling which had existed throughout much of the council.[29]

Howard's work with the majority of the nontreaty Nez Perces seemed over. He, himself, believed it as did Monteith.[30] It seems also that Joseph had every intention of fulfilling the agreement, for with eleven days still remaining before the expiration of the established thirty-day limit he had gathered his band on the southwest edge of the Lapwai reservation.[31]

Still there was dissension among these nontreaty Nez Perces, and it was only by extraordinary pleading that Joseph was able to convince a dissident portion of the band that they must go on the reservation. There were taunts of cowardice from the dreamers; White Bird, a principal chief, spoke out for war, and the younger braves were eager for a chance to demonstrate their prowess.[32] Some of these, according to Joseph's own admission, had been storing up ammunition; he also concedes that Too-hul-hul-sote was the leader of the war party.[33] Any incident might easily result in defiance of Joseph's peace policy and plunge the whole band into war.

A few of the younger members of White Bird's band who objected strenuously to going on the reservation and who wanted to avenge past insults rode off from the Indian encampment, killed three white men, and wounded others. Riding back into camp they exultantly boasted of their exploits and urged war. The war party was now in control; the peace advocates, confronted by a *fait accompli*, had little choice but to accept the fact of war and to close ranks with their own people. This at least is Joseph's explanation.[34]

The nontreaty Nez Perces quite clearly started the actual fighting. That there was strong provocation is not to be denied but it is unfortunate that when the reservation idea was on the very point of becoming a reality a few hotheads precipitated a war which could only end in defeat and a worse fate for the Indians. Joseph seems to have been well aware of this but he was willing to throw in his lot with the war party.[35]

Following the Lapwai council, Howard returned to Portland but left there again on May 30, 1877 with Colonel E. C. Watkins, inspector of Indian affairs for the Department of the Interior, to handle certain other Indian matters at the Yakima Indian agency and to meet with other nontreaty Nez Perces. When Howard arrived at Fort Lapwai the information he received about the Nez Perces was all good; there was no reason to doubt their willingness to comply with their promise of the previous months to go peacefully on the reservation.[36]

About noon on June 15 word arrived at Lapwai of the murders already mentioned above.[37] The settlers in the vicinity of Mount Idaho were thoroughly aroused and begged help from the commander of the fort.[38] Since Howard was present when this news was received, he immediately assumed direction of affairs and his actions were prompt and resolute. After verifying the report of the murders, he immediately realized that an Indian war was in progress and that he must bring together such forces as were available to him, appeal to the division commander for additional men, and, most important at the moment, relieve the settlers.[39] He ordered Captain David Perry to proceed at once with two companies of the 1st Cavalry, ninety-nine men, to the vicinity of Mount Idaho for the protection of the settlers and to deal with the troublesome Indians.⁴⁰ In reporting this action to General McDowell, Howard remarked, "Think we shall make short work of it." ⁴¹

The campaign began in disaster. Captain Perry's force met the Indians some 75 miles southwest of Lapwai at White Bird Canyon on June 17. There the Nez Perces thoroughly defeated the regulars who retreated in disorder to Grangeville, in the vicinity of Mount Idaho. One officer and 33 men had been killed in the rout.⁴² There was nothing for Howard to do now but to wait for the rest of his troops to come up in sufficient numbers so that he could take the offensive against Joseph and the Nez Perces.

Following Perry's unhappy experience, it was imperative that Howard proceed with greater caution. Yet he had to be active, for the civilian population clamored for revenge and certain elements became critical of Howard for his seeming inactivity while he awaited reinforcements.⁴³ Howard's plan was, first, to protect the civilian population by placing at Fort Lapwai the troops under his immediate command; then, to prevent the Indians in southern Idaho from joining the renegade Nez Perces or to intercept them should they retreat southward, he would interpose a force moving out of Fort Boise under the command of Major John Green; ⁴⁴ and finally, it was his purpose to harry the enemy until peace was restored. To enable him to take the field and at the same time to protect the settlers and to keep an eye on the then peaceful Indians on reservations he needed additional troops. To supply the need the 2d Infantry was ordered from Georgia.⁴⁵

On June 22, 1877 Howard's force of some 225 men took the field. For the next two and a half weeks there was some futile chasing around over rough country, crossing difficult streams in flood, and it was not until July 11 that Howard finally caught up with the enemy. Meanwhile another subordinate had suffered defeat. A lieutenant and ten men comprising a scouting force were killed in an ambush.⁴⁶

By the time the two forces met in battle on July 11, Howard's army numbered about four hundred men, while the size of the Indian force had been variously estimated at from fewer than a hundred to more than three hundred.⁴⁷ The encounter took place on the east side of the South Fork of the Clearwater River, a tributary of the Snake, on July 11 and 12, 1877. On the first day neither side was able to inflict much damage on the other. Howard formed his troops in a semicircular formation and engaged the Indians from behind hastily erected barricades. On the 12th some spirited charges by the infantry broke through the Nez Perce lines and forced a rapid retreat across the river to the Indian camp. This two-day battle was a decided success for Howard. It had all the features of a much larger engagement: troop movements, flanking operations, the use of artillery (on the one side only), and sharpshooters. Howard had to draw on all his experience to match the skill and bravery of his opponents. His own troops fought well and suffered casualties of thirteen dead and twenty-four wounded.

Victory came none too soon. There were rumors that the Cabinet was considering the removal of Howard from command, but the Clearwater battle scotched such rumors.[48] Howard's adjutant in Portland, Colonel H. Clay Wood, telegraphed the news of victory directly to President Hayes, and when McDowell's aid, Major B. B. Keeler, who had been present at the battle, wired McDowell the news of what he called "a most important success," and the opinion that "Nothing can surpass the vigor of General Howard's movements and action," these too were relayed to the President.[49]

The battle of the Clearwater proved to be of decisive importance, at least to the campaign in Idaho, for it ended the danger to the civilian population of that region.[50] It also seemed to bring to an end the accession of volunteers from the treaty Nez Perces. The Nez Perces, having suffered losses in manpower, supplies, and prestige, had no chance now of returning to the Wallowa Valley, nor could they remain where they were. There was no choice but to retreat into Montana in hopes that, having abandoned Howard's department, there would be no pursuit.[51]

Howard's next move was to try to get behind the Nez Perces on the Lolo Trail which leads across the Bitterroot Mountains into Montana, before the Indians moved out of their camp near Kamiah on the east side of the Clearwater. The troops had barely started to move when it became evident that the Indians were aware of the stratagem; they had already broken camp and had started toward the Lolo Trail. Since Howard's flanking maneuver necessitated a roundabout route, the Indians would be in the lead; so he abandoned the plan and returned to Kamiah.

Howard's return was also prompted by the report that Joseph (Howard believed that he was the head Nez Perce chief) wanted to surrender. The negotiations were carried on through an Indian messenger. Ostensibly Joseph would not accept Howard's demand for an unconditional surrender; but it may have been that the surrender offer was simply a ruse to gain time. In any event, nothing came of the talks except that about forty of the reservation Indians who had joined the hostile Nez Perces now surrendered.[52] Major Edwin L. Mason followed the Nez Perces along the Lolo Trail for two marches and then abandoned the pursuit since he was unable to break through the Indian rear guard with his small force of cavalry operating in a most difficult terrain.[53]

What Howard had done, then, was to follow up the retreating Nez Perces after his victory on the Clearwater, see that they were leaving Idaho for Montana over the Lolo Trail, and then settle down to wait for reinforcements. General McDowell believed that Howard made a mistake in not immediately pursuing the Nez Perces over the Lolo Trail.[54]

Howard's next plan was to take an alternate route over an easier trail to the north of the Lolo Trail which, he hoped, would take him to Montana before the Nez Perces. But there were reports that the Indians were returning to raid, and he had to quiet the fears of the local population before removing the major portion of the troops. The territorial delegate from Idaho, S. S. Fenn, complained that there were new outbreaks and that the troops should stay. Howard promised Fenn that he would not leave until Major Green's command had arrived from southern Idaho.[55] Howard believed that as long as there was the danger of a hostile force operating in the region of the recent depredations he had the obligation and responsibility to see that the civilian population was protected.[56] Hence he delayed the start of his pursuit.

Another reason for delay was that Green took longer to arrive than Howard had expected. Still, he believed that Colonel John Gibbon, commanding the District of Montana in General Alfred H. Terry's Department of Dakota, would be able to check the Indians when they debouched from the Lolo Trail in the Bitterroot Valley of Montana.[57] But Howard was not entirely convinced that the Nez Perces definitely intended to continue into Montana. This is evident from his instructions to Major Green, warning him to be prepared should the Indians try to return through south central Idaho,[58] and by a report of McDowell's aide, Major B. B. Keeler, that Howard believed they would end up in eastern Washington.[59]

Not willing to postpone the pursuit further, Howard evolved a plan whereby he divided his command into three columns. One, under his direct command, would take the Lolo Trail to Missoula, Montana in hopes of coming upon the Indians from the rear while they were confronted by troops from Gibbon's command. Colonel Frank Wheaton's 2d Infantry, plus some cavalry, would also set out for Missoula but by a route farther north. Wheaton's principal task would be to hold down the various Indian tribes of eastern Washington. Major John Green would command a reserve column whose job would be to guard the region of north-central Idaho (Mount Idaho, Grangeville, Kamiah, etc.) in the absence of Howard's command.[60]

It was not until July 30 that Howard began the trek over the Lolo Trail. By that time the Nez Perces had almost reached the Bitterroot Valley in Montana at the opposite end of the trail.[61] There a small force of some forty regulars under Captain Charles C. Rawn of Gibbon's 7th Infantry, plus more than a hundred civilian volunteers prepared to check the hostiles' advance. When the Indians promised to pass through the region without molesting the whites these citizen soldiers deserted Rawn. Then the Nez Perces passed round Rawn's fortified position and since he was by that time so greatly outnumbered he decided not to risk an engagement.[62] All this occurred between July 25 and July 28 before Howard had set out from Kamiah.[63]

Howard took no wagons over the Lolo Trail; the way was much too rugged for anything but horses and pack mules. His column took ten days to get over the Bitterroot Mountains into Montana, and when he reached Rawn's abandoned fortification and saw its strength, he was sorely disappointed that a stand had not been made.[64] Yet it is difficult to see how his own command could have arrived in time to be of any assistance.

While Howard's column toiled over the Lolo Trail, Colonel John Gibbon, commanding the 7th infantry, was responding to Howard's and McDowell's urgent request to check the Nez Perce advance.[65] By August 4 he had concentrated a force of about one hundred and sixty regular troops at Missoula and set out in pursuit of the Nez Perces who were reported moving up the Bitterroot Valley in a southerly direction.[66] He overtook the Indians in the Big Hole Basin on the eastern side of the Continental Divide, and early on the morning of August 9, 1877 delivered a surprise attack driving the hostiles from their camp. The rout at first seemed complete but the Indians made a rapid recovery and, having numerical superiority, were able to retake their camp and drive Gibbon back to a wooded crest. Here his men hastily threw up breastworks. The soldiers had suffered many casualties in killed and wounded, and, since the Indian sharpshooters could reach their position, and the supplies which they had expected had not yet come up, the outlook for the small command of regulars and civilian volunteers was gloomy in the extreme. But late in the evening of the 10th the Indians suddenly withdrew and the battle of the Big Hole was over.[67]

Before Howard had left the Lolo Trail, he received on August 4 a message from Captain Rawn which stated that the Nez Perces had gone past him and were moving leisurely up the Bitterroot Valley. Howard, then, had reason to hope that he could still effect a junction with Gibbon, moving from Missoula, and together they could meet and crush the Indian force. Taking about two hundred cavalrymen he left the infantry behind and moved ahead by forced marches to try to join Gibbon.[68] As they passed through the village of Corvallis, Montana, on August 9, they heard reports that three days earlier the Nez Perces, and then Gibbon's command, had gone through.

Howard now became concerned about Gibbon, and on the morning of August 10, when the latter was being besieged, he moved out ahead of his force with a picked detachment of twenty cavalrymen plus seventeen Indian scouts. On the road they learned from civilian stragglers about Gibbon's encounter with the Nez Perces and about his unfortunate plight. When Howard's advance force arrived at the battle scene on the morning of August 11, the Indians had already gone.[69] Howard's approach undoubtedly saved Gibbon's command by forcing the Nez Perces to abandon the siege.[70]

Howard waited for his whole force to close up, and then, joined by fifty of Gibbon's command, he set out once more in pursuit of the elusive Nez Perces. He thought he had an excellent chance of trapping them since probably they would go east through Yellowstone Park to buffalo country and he could then head them off at Henry Lake, just west of the park.[71] He had some doubt whether this was the Nez Perces' intent, for, after they moved south from Big Hole, they recrossed the divide into Idaho and could have proceeded westward once again back to their home territory.

Howard wrote of all these matters to General McDowell on August 14 from the Montana town of Bannock City (now Bannack).

He said that should the Indians return to central Idaho then he and Green together could "surely destroy or capture the greater portion." But, he asked, if they should escape eastward "is it worth while for me to pursue them further from my department unless General Terry or General Crook [72] will head them off and check their advance? . . . Please advise me, that I may not wear out our troops to no purpose. We have made extraordinary marches, and with prompt and energetic cooperation from these eastern departments, may yet stop and destroy this most enterprising band of Indians. Without this cooperation, the result will be, as it has been, doubtful." [73] Here Howard made two mistakes which McDowell quickly noted. His first was to request additional orders after he had already been explicitly told that he was to pursue the Indians without regard to department or division lines.[74] On July 29 Sherman had told McDowell (who sent this message to Howard) that he wanted Howard "to follow them up, no matter where they go. If these Nez Perces come to Montana, order the troops to follow, regardless of boundary lines. If the Indians can find food, the troops can also." [75] In replying to Howard's request for further instructions McDowell (through his adjutant) made obvious his impatience with Howard by saying that he had had instructions enough and that he was expected to continue the pursuit.[76]

Howard's other mistake was his implication of lack of co-operation and of the possibility of not receiving co-operation from the departments to the east. This was unfair to Gibbon, Terry, Sheridan (commanding the Military Division of the Missouri), and their subordinates, who had done everything possible to lend aid to Howard. McDowell somewhat caustically told Howard "to be less dependent on what others, at a distance, may or may not do, and rely more on your own forces and your own plans." [77] Before Howard received this reply, he had to undergo another annoying and frustrating experience at the hands of the Nez Perces, the affair at Camas Meadows.

Howard had yielded to the insistence of settlers that the best route to Henry Lake was not the most direct. So he moved south a short distance and then turned eastward. He hoped to catch the Indians before they crossed the north-south stage road just south of the Montana-Idaho border, but on his arrival at that point (Dry Creek Station), they had already passed to the east about one day's march ahead.[78] Pushing on with his cavalry and about fifty infantrymen,

Howard camped at Camas Meadows the night of August 19, 1877. Despite ordinary precautions, a few of the Nez Perces were able to creep into the camp and stampede most of the pack mules and some of the cavalry horses. The next day some of these were recovered following a skirmish between Howard's cavalry and the Indians.[79]

The raid was an understandable military maneuver but it proved to be extremely embarrassing to Howard who had already had his share of troubles. On August 19 he had again asked McDowell if he should continue the chase [80] (this was before he had received McDowell's reply to his first inquiry of August 14), and he also wrote to the governor of Montana Territory, knowing that General Sherman, then traveling through that region and at the moment in the company of the governor, would read the letter. To the governor, Howard said that he believed it impossible for him to overtake the Indians since every time he got near them they would flee on fresh horses stolen from the surrounding country. And he added that he would have to stop for his command to be refitted and supplied if they were to go on with the pursuit since the cavalry had had no rest for more than eleven hundred miles.[81]

Even after the Camas Meadows affair, Howard had hopes of catching the Nez Perce before they entered Yellowstone Park. For two more days they pushed on until on the night of August 22 they were within a short distance of the pass leading to the park. Howard so desperately wanted to end the campaign that he had the troops up at 2 A.M., but a few hours after sunrise the Indian scouts reported that the Nez Perces had already gone through the pass and had escaped.[82]

It seemed now as if it were completely useless to keep trying. The men and officers became despondent over this most recent failure. Not only did morale collapse but the physical condition of the troops was such that it would have been hazardous to have attempted a further advance without allowing time for recuperation.[83] A halt obviously was necessary. For four days most of Howard's command rested on the edge of Henry Lake which is in the northeast corner of Idaho, close to the Montana and Wyoming borders. Howard refused to take any rest himself. He with Guy and a quartermaster set out by wagon for Virginia City, Montana where they could obtain needed supplies of food, clothing, and horses. They traveled all night reaching their destination on August 24.[84]

Howard sent dispatches to both Sherman and McDowell. To Sherman he gave a brief summary of his operations since the Big Hole battle and his estimate of the Nez Perces' future movements. Toward the end he said, "My command is so much worn by overfatigue and jaded animals that I cannot push it much farther." He was convinced that if there were other troops ahead to take care of the Nez Perces, he could stop near Henry Lake and "in a few days work my way back to Fort Boise slowly, and distribute my troops before snow falls in the mountains." [85]

On receiving this report, Sherman concluded that Howard himself was weary and was thinking of giving up the chase. He immediately wired back that Howard's force "should pursue the Nez Percés to the death, lead where they may. . . . If you are tired, give the command to some young energetic officer. . . ." [86]

While at Virginia City, Howard received McDowell's caustic telegram of August 17. Howard, in reply, hastened to explain but the explanation does not sound too convincing. He did not depend on others, he said; he "Did not wish to complain of want of cooperation. . . . My duty shall be done fully and to the letter without complaint." [87] But McDowell was not impressed. Once again he sent to General Sherman a copy of Howard's telegram with his own sarcastic comments written in the margin.[88]

Back at Henry Lake, Sherman's reply to Howard's telegram of August 24 arrived and apparently touched the feelings not only of Howard but of his whole command. This, added to the thinly concealed reprimand of General McDowell, served as a goad and, according to Howard, had the effect of jacking up sagging morale.[89] He immediately replied to General Sherman: "You misunderstood me. I never flag. It was the command, including the most energetic young officers, that were worn out and weary by a most extraordinary march. You need not fear for the campaign. Neither you nor General McDowell can doubt my pluck and energy. . . . we move in the morning and will continue to the end." [90]

Apparently Sherman still wanted someone else to take Howard's place, for the day following his telegram to Howard he wrote him a letter stating that, since he was on his way to Howard's department, he would like to see him and discuss certain matters, and that he saw no particular reason why Howard should continue to command a detachment in another department. Tactfully, he said that Lieutenant

Colonel C. C. Gilbert was available for the job and that, though he did not order Howard to return to Oregon, he would nonetheless believe it to be quite in order if he should do so.[91]

Sherman gave the letter to Gilbert, who left Fort Ellis, Montana on the last day of August to try to overtake Howard and deliver the letter to him. But Gilbert was unable to find Howard, and after more than two weeks of vain pursuit gave up the chase.[92] Howard soon found out what was going on and confessed to be glad that he had kept out in front because of "the lying press [which] undertook to disgrace me. . . ."[93] Later Howard admitted to Sherman that "it would have been a great hardship to me personally to have stopped short of success."[94]

The troops to the north of Yellowstone Park had long since been alerted, and Colonel S. D. Sturgis of the 7th Cavalry was in a position to intercept the Indians when they headed north, as Howard believed they would, and as they subsequently did.[95] Sturgis was badly handicapped because he did not know where Howard was (several couriers had been killed by Indians), nor could he discover the whereabouts of the Indians. Consequently, the Nez Perces slipped by Sturgis, who finally joined Howard on September 11 as the latter was moving north along Clark's Fork (of the Yellowstone) just beyond the national park.[96] Once again a promising plan had come to nought.

Sturgis wanted to redeem himself. Taking his own command plus some of Howard's men, Sturgis caught the Nez Perces on September 13 just north of the Yellowstone River, had a running fight with them for about twenty miles, and captured some of their ponies. But he did not defeat them nor did he stop their northward retreat.[97] Meanwhile on September 12 Howard sent a dispatch to Colonel Nelson A. Miles, whose camp was quite a distance to the north and east at the mouth of the Tongue River (where the present Miles City is located). He told his old friend, a subordinate of General Terry in the Department of Dakota, that Sturgis was pursuing the Nez Perces and that he himself was following as rapidly as possible. He implied that the Indians might possibly get away and continue down Clark's Fork and then go directly north to the Musselshell River. Therefore he pleaded with Miles to make every effort to march rapidly "to prevent the escape of this hostile band, and at least hold them in check until I can overtake them."[98]

Howard and Sturgis now agreed that they would deliberately

shorten their marches in order to check the flight of the Nez Perces. Howard had long since discovered that the Indians allowed him to pace them. When he halted, they usually did the same; when he made a short march, so did they. Consequently, Howard hoped that Miles, who was a greater distance away, would have time to get in front of the Nez Perces if Howard and Sturgis so regulated their advance.[99]

Conflicting evidence makes it difficult to determine just exactly what Howard's plans were for the period between September 26, when he was in the Judith Basin (between the Musselshell and Missouri Rivers) and October 1 when he arrived at Carroll on the Missouri River near the mouth of the Little Rocky Creek. There is no doubt that after October 1 he was determined to join Miles at least in person, if not with his whole command. On September 26 Howard sent a dispatch to Miles telling him that he was detaching his own cavalry force and sending it back to the coast, but that he was retaining Sturgis' cavalry as part of his command. He also asked Miles to secure a steamer "that will take 400 foot men from Carroll to Omaha."[100] Did this mean that Howard had himself given up the pursuit and was now depending completely on Miles? Six days earlier he had written to his adjutant in Oregon that he expected "to give one more blow and then turn homeward, probably from Judith Basin."[101]

On the other hand, Howard reported on September 26 to his superior, General McDowell, that though he was sending his own cavalry home he would himself "continue to pursue [the] enemy along their trail."[102] The next day he wrote to Gibbon that news had arrived of the Indians' crossing at Cow Island directly north of where he then was, that Miles was supposed to be near Carroll, and that he with his command would "proceed directly to Carroll by long marches and support Miles in any movement he may make."[103] Yet on the same day he told McDowell that, although Miles was doing all he could do to intercept the Indians, they would "probably reach British Columbia to-night."[104]

If Howard believed on September 27 that the Indians were on the very point of reaching the Canadian border he could not have had any hope of catching them himself. Undoubtedly he was thinking in terms of returning to his own department, or at least of going to Carroll (somewhat to the east) for supplies instead of continuing due north in pursuit of the Indians. But when he reached Carroll he learned that the Nez Perces were still south of the line and that Miles was approaching them undetected. This meant that there was still some possibility that he could be of assistance. He now left the bulk of the troops under Sturgis' command at Carroll and proceeded up the river in a westerly direction accompanied by the artillery battalion (acting as infantry), some scouts, and several aides on board the steamer *Benton* which Miles had left for Howard's use.[105]

This small force went as far as Cow Island on the Missouri River where the Indians had crossed ten days before. Howard now was more determined than ever to find Miles. He set out from Cow Island on October 3 with an escort of less than twenty, including his son Guy, two friendly Nez Perces, and Chapman, a half-breed interpreter. It had become very cold and the ground was covered with a light fall of snow.[106] On the afternoon of October 4 this small band met two couriers who were returning from Sturgis to Miles and who gave Howard the first news he had of Miles' engagement with the Nez Perces.[107]

Miles had started from the mouth of the Tongue River on September 18 and was across the Missouri a week later. By marching in a northwesterly direction, with the Little Rocky Mountains on his left, he caught up with the Nez Perces on the morning of September 30. Immediately Miles attacked. His troops cut off a sizeable number of the Indians' horses but were unable to drive the hostiles from their camp. Both sides suffered heavy casualties and that night a cold wind and snow added to the misery of the wounded.[108]

Late that afternoon Miles scribbled a message to Howard, Sturgis, and to the officer commanding his supply train, stating the facts of the day's events. He appended a P.S.: "We captured the most of their herd but I may have trouble in moving on account of my wounded. Please move forward with caution and rapidly." [109]

Howard did not receive this message, but Sturgis did and on the evening of October 2 he proceeded to move to Miles' support. Miles was still besieging the hostiles' camp on October 3 but apparently did not feel very confident of complete success for he wrote to General Terry that he hesitated to assault the Indians' fortified position because that would be too costly.[110] Obviously Miles needed help.

When Howard and his escort arrived at Miles' camp on the evening of October 4 there was still some firing in progress. Howard's aide, Lieutenant C. E. S. Wood, has described the meeting between Miles and Howard. Miles, said Wood, was visibly cool to

Howard, his superior. When Howard, against Wood's advice, told Miles that he would not assume command, Miles immediately brightened. He became even more relieved when Howard told him that he would do all he could to get Miles a brigadier generalship and that if there were a surrender he (Miles) would receive it.[111]

The next morning Guy Howard wrote to Sturgis urging him to bring up the two howitzers he had with him because they were "in special demand here." [112] But there was no need of the howitzers or for Sturgis' troops, who were within about two hours' march of the battlefield when they heard that Joseph had surrendered.[113]

Two friendly Nez Perces whom Howard had brought along to act as emissaries went to the enemy camp on the morning of October 5. Each had a daughter there and after much discussion they finally persuaded Joseph and White Bird to surrender. Joseph apparently had become convinced of the hopelessness of continuing the fight now that Howard was on the scene and his force only a short distance away.[114]

Joseph's reply to the surrender demand is a classic of Indian prose. There is dispute as to who actually delivered the speech. Probably Joseph gave it to one of the friendly Nez Perces and Chapman the interpreter actually spoke the words.[115] Howard's aide, Lieutenant C. E. S. Wood, recorded the speech as it was made. "Tell General Howard I know his heart. What he told me before I have in my heart. I am tired of fighting. Our chiefs are killed. Looking Glass is dead. Too-hul-hul-sote is dead. The old men are all dead. It is the young men who say yes or no. He who led on the young men is dead. It is cold and we have no blankets. The little children are freezing to death. My people, some of them, have run away to the hills, and have no blankets, no food; no one knows where they are—perhaps freezing to death. I want to have time to look for my children and see how many of them I can find. Maybe I shall find them among the dead. Hear me, my chiefs. I am tired; my heart is sick and sad. From where the sun now stands I will fight no more forever." [116]

Late that afternoon in the gathering dusk on a snow-swept field Joseph came across the lines to surrender. He offered his rifle to General Howard who simply motioned in the direction of Colonel Miles. Within a short time most of the remaining Nez Perces, disheveled and hungry, came forward to surrender. That evening a few, including White Bird, escaped into Canada.[117]

Shortly after the surrender and after the prisoners had been cared for, both Miles and Howard prepared dispatches for their superiors. Miles, according to Wood's account, read to Howard the report he planned to send to General Terry. In this version Miles mentioned Howard's arrival the evening before the surrender and his presence at the surrender ceremony. Wood believed, as did Howard, that someone else removed this portion of the dispatch before it was made public, because when General Sheridan eventually gave it out to the press there was no mention of Howard. Miles' account began, "We have had our usual success," and then it continued with a brief description of his march across country, his battle with the Indians, and their surrender.[118] Miles' next dispatch, on October 6, contained a more detailed recital of events and at the end he stated briefly that Howard had arrived on the evening of the 4th with a small escort.[119] Miles also mentioned Howard in a generous way in both a congratulatory order to his troops and in his report to General Terry.[120] Yet the country learned of the Nez Perce surrender through Miles' first dispatch and the editorial comment naturally gave the credit to him.[121]

Howard and his troops boarded the steamer *Benton* on October 10 and moved down the Missouri River arriving at Bismarck in the Dakota Territory on October 22. Howard and his aide, Wood, left the steamer here to go by train to Sheridan's headquarters in Chicago. The troops would proceed to Omaha and entrain there for the coast. Before leaving the boat at Bismarck, Howard had a chance to see newspaper accounts of the last battle and the surrender. When he read Miles' dispatch, beginning "We have had our usual success," he was completely taken aback by this apparent betrayal. He was, in Wood's words, "absolutely brokenhearted." [122]

Howard and Miles had been friends since the early days of the Civil War. Miles for a time had served as Howard's aide; later he got his own regiment and by the close of the war he had risen to the rank of brevet major general. The two remained in touch during the years following. Miles had served on the 1874 Court of Inquiry which vindicated Howard. And just the previous March (1877) Howard had written a strong recommendation to Sherman urging him to grant Miles a brigadiership whenever where was a vacancy.[123]

Now at the close of the Nez Perce campaign friction arose between them over the question of Joseph's surrender. Unfortunately neither Howard nor Miles could let the matter drop and they carried on an unpleasant correspondence for a number of months which ended in a complete and final rupture of their long friendship. Miles believed that Howard, in his written report and congratulatory orders to his command, and also in public statements, distorted the truth and did not adequately acknowledge the part Miles' troops had played in the capture of the Nez Perce.[124]

Howard seems only to have wanted his own troops, who had marched so far and had undergone so much hardship, to have their just share of praise. His first obligation was to them and he had to be especially careful that feelings were not hurt on that side. No one reading his reports and congratulatory order, except a very sensitive and ambitious Colonel Miles, could possibly take exception to them. One might even say that Howard had gone out of his way to help Miles. He had not assumed command on his arrival in Miles' camp, he did not take from Miles the distinction of receiving Joseph's surrender, and his praise of Miles directly following the close of the campaign is all that any subordinate could ask of his superior.[125]

In response to one of Miles' letters the following spring he wrote that he was "astonished" at Miles' accusations. "My own report has," he wrote, "I think, done you and your officers no injustice. I claim nothing but simple truth, and would, as you know, rather have honored you than myself. You fought the battle and succeeded and if there is any language in which I can state it to the credit of yourself, your officers and your men I was willing, and remain willing to do so." [126]

Wood says that he wrote the first draft of Howard's official report containing all the details of the surrender as he understood them, but that Howard would not allow any adverse criticism of Miles to go in "saying we should do good to those who despitefully use us. . . ." [127] Neither did Howard display any bad feeling in the book he wrote of the campaign, *Nez Perce Joseph*.

The epilogue of the Nez Perce story is not a happy one. Instead of returning to their own country, the captive Nez Perces went instead to the Indian Territory. They desperately wanted to return, at least to the Lapwai reservation (to which they were supposed to have gone in the first place), but there was little chance of that. The Indian Bureau inspector, Colonel E. C. Watkins, had stated as early as July that he was against returning the hostiles to Lapwai and that he favored sending them to the Indian Territory. Generals Sherman and Sheridan concurred in this opinion.[128]

In 1878 the captured Nez Perces were taken to the Indian Territory where several died in the comparatively unhealthy climate. Miles believed that one of the terms of the surrender was the promise that the Indians would return to Howard's department, and in the spring of 1878 he started action to have this promise fulfilled. Before making his final decision, Sherman asked Howard's opinion. Howard wrote back (through General McDowell) that he did not approve of their return because their presence on the Lapwai reservation "would be an unending source of disaffection and turmoil between Indians and whites and among the loyal and disloyal Indians themselves." He also believed it unwise "to put such a premium upon disloyalty and crime [129] as would be done by sending these Indians back to enjoy the same privileges as those who have been all the time 'true.'" As for the promise made to the Nez Perces, Howard said that "Even if the orders to return to my Department should be deemed as one of the conditions for the surrender the terms were violated by the Indians conniving at White Bird's and followers' escape." [130] General Sherman finally decided that the captured Nez Perces were to stay in the Indian Territory. Later, in 1882, some of the widows and orphans returned to Lapwai; in 1885 others, including Joseph, went to another reservation in eastern Washington.[131]

The Nez Perce War provided an opportunity for Howard to conduct an entire campaign on his own. That he did not have complete success was probably the result of a combination of unfortunate circumstances, including bad luck. The handicaps were so great that it is surprising that the regular troops were able to do as well as they did. Problems of supply, particularly the problem of remounts; the tremendously difficult terrain over which the campaign was conducted; the virtual impossibility of keeping pace with the Indians who, although encumbered with their women and children, were able to outstrip the troops without much difficulty (primarily because they could secure fresh mounts from the countryside as they moved along)—all these factors combined to work against Howard and his men.

Howard's bad luck evinced itself at several points during the campaign. The first came when he was not able to trick the Indians before they started their epic retreat over the Lolo Trail. The failure of the volunteers to stick by Captain Rawn at the eastern end of the trail meant that the Indians gained the Bitterroot Valley sooner than they would have otherwise. The small size of Gibbon's force prevented him from winning a complete victory. Sturgis' failure to intercept the Nez Perces as they entered the region of Clark's Fork also contributed to Howard's misfortune. The best chance Howard had of gaining a complete victory was just before the Camas Meadows episode. Had he taken the short route he would have reached a pass into the Yellowstone National Park before the Indians arrived, and could conceivably have had a showdown battle there.

It is easy to criticize Howard's conduct of the campaign, yet it is doubtful whether he actually made any serious mistakes during the more than three months of the Nez Perce War. If he made any at all, it probably was his failure to follow up his victory at the Clearwater. The rout of the Indians seemed so complete that it is remarkable Howard did not take fuller advantage of his success. Then, too, perhaps he waited longer than necessary before starting the pursuit over the Lolo Trail. There were good reasons for the delay, and these have already been discussed, but once he started Howard was so far behind that he could hardly have brought any assistance in time to help Captain Rawn who was trying to block the eastern end of the Lolo Trail.

The halt at Henry Lake was essential, and there should be only praise for the way Howard pressed ahead to give aid to Gibbon and to keep on the trail of the Nez Perces down to the final surrender. True, he did complain to McDowell and Sherman, but he did not slacken the pace at any time while awaiting orders. All in all, it was a remarkable campaign. The end was unfortunate for Howard because another gained the distinction of actually capturing the hostile band. But Howard was there at the finish, his two Indian scouts were an important factor in arranging the surrender, and the near presence of his own command undoubtedly had a bearing on the Indians' decision to end the war.

The restoration of peace in the Department of the Columbia was only temporary and the next year saw a new Indian conflict break out. General Howard's last active campaign, against the Bannock and Paiute Indians, occurred in the summer of 1878. During the Nez Perce War the Bannocks had remained peaceful. Indeed, Buffalo Horn, chief of the Bannocks, had served as a scout under Howard in that campaign. Inevitably, however, they had cause for dissatisfaction. Especially was there discontent over white encroachments on a region of southern Idaho east of Boise called Camas Prairie, a favorite spot for these Indians.[132]

The Paiutes of eastern Oregon had been assigned to the Malheur reservation, but a change in agents in 1876 had created so much dissatisfaction that many of this tribe left the reservation. Close relationship existed between the Bannocks and Paiutes and there was considerable visiting back and forth in the period prior to the outbreak.[133] In the ensuing war the two tribes joined forces.

On May 30, 1878 Bannock Indians wounded two cattlemen on Camas Prairie. This was the immediate cause of the war.[134] General McDowell, the division commander, urged Howard to arrange a peaceful settlement of the outstanding difficulties, but when such a course appeared futile Howard promptly made preparations for a punitive campaign.[135] He first went to Walla Walla and conferred with Colonel Frank Wheaton of the 2d Infantry whose job it would be to hold in check the Indians north of the Columbia River. From Walla Walla Howard continued on to Boise arriving there on June 12.[136]

Meanwhile the Indians had swung around to the south of Boise, crossed the Snake River, and continued on into eastern Oregon rounding up stock, pillaging, and killing as they went. By the time Howard reached Boise, the Bannocks were in the vicinity of Steens (sometimes spelled Steins) Mountain in southeastern Oregon, uniting there with the Paiutes.[137]

On June 16, Howard issued a general field order giving instructions for the formation of three columns to proceed against the hostile Indians.[138] Howard accompanied the right column commanded by Major Joseph Stewart of the 4th Artillery, but it was four companies of the 1st Cavalry under the command of Captain Reuben F. Bernard, constituting the left column, which first struck the enemy. Bernard, an energetic and colorful officer, had a skirmish with the Indians at Silver Creek on June 23, but failed to inflict any serious loss on them.[139] After this the Indians turned north heading for the Columbia River via the John Day River valley.

Howard feared lest the hostiles cross the Columbia and stir up the Indians in that region. To prevent this he sent word to Colonel Wheaton to arm a river steamer to guard against any crossing in force.[140] With the route north effectively blocked, the Indians could now turn only to the south and east.[141] Meanwhile Howard and a force of several hundred men had been pursuing them through barren and mountainous country finding as they went evidence of continued depredations and of skirmishes between the Indians and settlers. Pursuit through a country described by Howard as "rugged in the extreme; filled with trees and underbrush in parts, with foot-hills and mountains, deep ravines and craggy rocks," [142] was necessarily slow and difficult. Still on July 8, near Pilot Rock, south of Pendleton in northeastern Oregon, Howard was able to concentrate his force, including some men from Wheaton's command, to assault the Indians in their chosen position. Three times the cavalry under Captain Bernard dislodged the Indians driving them back some five miles and forcing them to abandon quantities of supplies and used-up horses.[143]

Howard now expected the Indians to move eastward across the Snake River in the vicinity of Lewiston, Idaho. Consequently he gave orders for the continued pursuit of the Indians and, leaving Wheaton in immediate charge of the direct pursuit, himself went on to Walla Walla, and then up the Snake River to the mouth of Grand Ronde. But in the meantime he had learned that the Indians had turned back from their retreat.[144] Howard therefore was not on hand for the engagement between a portion of the 21st Infantry, under the command of Captain Evan Miles, and the Indians at the Umatilla Agency on July 13.[145] Miles succeeded in routing the enemy and a week later Lieutenant Colonel James W. Forsyth of the 1st Cavalry gained a victory over the Indian rear guard on the North Fork of the John Day River.[146] By July 28 Howard could report: "The crisis of the campaign has certainly passed." [147]

These successive engagements broke up the hostile force into small bands and brought about their ultimate surrender. Some of the Indians returned unnoticed to reservations but the majority became prisoners of war. Although the work of rounding up the scattered Indians went on through the month of August and even as late as October, Howard turned over this task to subordinates after August 12.[148] Howard had conducted a skillful campaign [149] and had brought to a successful conclusion the last major Indian uprising in the Northwest.

The Bannock War marked the last time that Howard had to take the field against Indians. In all his dealings with them he had shown understanding, justice, and resolution. His basic thesis that it was possible to maintain peace with the Indians was fundamentally sound, but even he knew that because of distrust and misunderstanding on both sides and because of the selfishness of some white men, there would continue to be trouble as long as the Indians could carry on a separate, semi-dependent existence. Hence he became an advocate of as rapid assimilation as possible, of allowing the Indians to own land individually, and of extending the authority of United States law to all Indians.[150]

Howard had no sympathy for whites who committed murder and other outrages on Indians. He saw no justice in punishing Indians who had committed misdeeds and at the same time commending "Anglo Saxon cut throats for the same crimes." [151] But he never went completely in the opposite direction, that is toward a sentimental view of the Indians. His remark that "savagery is savagery" and his observation that the moral tone of the American Indians was low came from one who spoke with authority on this subject. The restraint of law alone would not, he believed, be enough to raise them to the same degree of civilization with whites. The most effective means of achieving this goal would be through education.[152] In addition he favored putting an end to the reservation system which at best was a slow road to civilization for the Indians.[153]

Howard's views on Indian affairs, which embraced what was then known as the peace policy, were not any more popular in the Northwest than they had been in the Southwest. Still there were some who recognized the contribution to peace which he had made. Among these was the governor of Idaho Territory, Mason Brayman. Following the conclusion of the Bannock campaign, Brayman wrote Howard a letter of thanks noting the difficulties Howard had overcome, the unjust criticism directed against him, and expressing his admiration for Howard's "courage, patience . . . skill . . . patriotism and spotless Christian character." [154] Perhaps letters such as these compensated in part for the hostility of others who misunderstood Howard's motives, believing him to be too much in sympathy with the Indians.

Though the last two years of Howard's tour of duty in the Department of the Columbia saw no further Indian conflicts, there did occur some events of note in the Howard household. The most notable of these was the marriage of Grace, the second child, during the early fall of 1879.[155] Shortly after the wedding came a visit from former President and Mrs. Grant, returning from their round the world tour. Lizzie had to put on a reception for the guests who included General and Mrs. McDowell, and, as Howard wrote to Guy, "Momma did splendidly." [156] About a year later President and Mrs. Hayes visited Howard's department.[157]

Service in the Northwest

Garfield's victory over Hancock in the election of 1880 was a relief to Howard who feared lest the South be in power again, "completely enthroned." [158] But Hayes would remain in office until March 1881 and shortly after the election he summoned Howard to Washington. The President wanted to discuss with him the problem of the Military Academy at West Point. Out of this conference came Howard's appointment as superintendent of the Academy. Because of the peculiar conditions prevailing at that time at West Point, the position would be an especially challenging one. So Howard was to return to the East leaving behind a creditable record and some warm friends in the West. One of these, Henry A. Morrow, colonel of the 21st Infantry, from Vancouver wrote his former commander a farewell letter thanking him for his kindness and applauding him for his "kind, considerate, honest, faithful and able administration" which gave Morrow "an exalted idea" of Howard's "integrity & ability. You have," he said in conclusion, "my love, my respect & my admiration." [159] Not often did Howard have the satisfaction of receiving communications of this type from his brother officers.

Final Army Assignments

For some years after the Civil War the United States Military Academy at West Point rested under a cloud. Many of its graduates had deserted the United States and had fought for the Confederacy. The belief that it fostered snobbishness and a military aristocracy not in keeping with the democratic character of the country was widespread.[1] The events of the years just before Howard became superintendent had done little to dispel this impression. These events hinged around the presence at the Academy of a small number of Negro cadets. The first, J. W. Smith, appointed in 1870, turned out to be, in the words of a West Point professor, "malicious, vindictive, and untruthful."[2] Smith did not last; in fact of ten additional Negro appointees, only seven actually qualified and only one was graduated. That was in 1877.[3] The summer before there arrived at West Point a new superintendent and another colored cadet. Replacing Colonel T. H. Ruger was Major General John M. Schofield, onetime commander of the Army of the Ohio, and the first general officer to have the command of the newly created Department of West Point.[4]

The new colored cadet was J. C. Whittaker who was to be the principal reason why Howard was eventually sent to West Point. Whittaker was not a good student[5] yet had managed to stay in the Academy until the spring of his fourth year. As was the case with all the colored cadets, he had had only official association with the white boys; but he had experienced no serious academic trouble until he was found deficient in philosophy in the January 1879 examination.[6] Then on April 6, 1880 Whittaker was found in his room, bound up with rope and with his ears cut. A threatening note was close by.

Schofield immediately began an investigation but before long he and the investigating officers had doubts as to the authenticity of Whittaker's story that he had been molested.[7] They strongly suspected that the wounds had been self-inflicted and that Whittaker in his desperation to avoid dismissal had turned to these extreme measures. Schofield finally became convinced that this is what had happened and he even believed that outside interests had put Whittaker up to it to discredit the Academy and its superintendent.[8]

Whittaker's guilt, however, was not clearly demonstrated. Many believed he was innocent and naturally were indignant at Schofield's stand. The New York *Tribune*, for instance, asserted that Schofield's handling of the case had undermined confidence in him. It predicted that Schofield would receive some other duty and that the Department of West Point would be abolished.[9] With such a division of opinion a change in administration at West Point was almost a certainty. Schofield naturally believed he was being sacrificed [10] and in November applied for duty as commander of a military division, a command commensurate with his rank of major general.[11] He did not expect such rapid action on his application. The following month President Hayes ordered Howard to the command of the Department of West Point and created the Military Division of the South for Schofield, a solution which Sherman called a "grievous wrong." [12]

President Hayes undoubtedly selected Howard for the job because of his Freedmen's Bureau and Howard University experience. He may have wanted to still the criticism of West Point especially after the Whittaker case broke and after publication of Schofield's annual report which reiterated his (Schofield's) belief that Whittaker was guilty and his conviction that now was not the time to admit colored cadets to West Point.[13]

Early in December 1880 Howard had an interview with Hayes [14] and on December 6 discussed the West Point situation with General Sherman. Sherman was annoyed that the President had ordered Howard to Washington without his knowledge. He expressed sympathy for Schofield and made some remarks which Howard took to be a reflection on his work as commissioner of the Freedmen's Bureau. He hurt Howard's feelings and the next day Howard wrote Sherman saying that what took place during the interview "has affected me very much. . . ." He proceeded to defend his Bureau work. He could, he contended, give West Point "a quiet and orderly administration. . . ." [15]

Sherman replied, as one might expect, in a kindly yet honest way. If the President ordered Howard to West Point then he would give him his "earnest support," but he did not want to see Howard go there because the country would believe it to be on account of the

Whittaker case, and Sherman pointedly expressed his opinion that Whittaker had faked his wounds. West Point was not the place "to try the experiment of social equality. . . . I believe," he concluded, "the Army and the Country construe you to be extreme on this question" and therefore he preferred General George W. Getty for the West Point command.[16]

A few weeks later Sherman, in a letter to President-elect Garfield, explained his attitude toward General Howard. He admitted that Howard was brave and conscientious, but he also was credulous, "easily used and influenced." His war performance was entirely satisfactory and the Court of Inquiry over which Sherman had presided showed that Howard had not done anything wrong and that he had shown "due zeal" in his administration of the Bureau. "But," he went on, "as a business man I have not the faith in him our President has."[17] Despite Sherman's opposition, Howard got the assignment, but the race question proved an academic one for no Negro cadets were in attendance while he was at West Point.[18]

Howard began his brief tenure as superintendent of the Military Academy on January 21, 1881. He described the position as "the hardest office to fill that I had ever had."[19] While no revolutionary changes marked his administration, he did effect certain reforms designed to improve the state of discipline and the morale of the cadets.

His first concern was to relax what he believed to be a too rigid discipline weighted down with a complicated system of reporting and punishment. His policy was to encourage in the cadets a greater sense of honor and a desire "to keep the important regulations because it is right so to do." He took away the officer assigned to each cadet company, ended the all-night cadet guard in the barracks, and at the same time enforced existing regulations.[20] By the time he wrote his annual report in October he could state that he had had good results in his endeavor to introduce "a kindly and paternal execution" of the regulations.[21]

Probably there existed at West Point about as much hazing of the new cadets during Howard's regime as had always taken place or would go on after he left. He had the optimism, nonetheless, to state in his report for 1881 that there had been no hazing during the previous summer encampment, and "scarcely any attempt" the following year.[22] Evidently a mild case had broken out during the first summer Howard had assumed his position. He had occasion to make a formal appeal to the cadets to blot out "the last vestige of this unmanly custom," and to prove they were gentlemen by showing "kindness and courtesy to strangers." [23]

During the summer encampment of his second year, there occurred a most unfortunate incident involving two cadets one of whom was hospitalized as a result of injuries received during a fist fight. Such fights to settle arguments had become a sort of code which Howard deprecated as a "brutal practice." The incident, he said in orders, had brought shame not only on those immediately involved but on the whole Academy.[24]

In applying punishment for various offenses, Howard usually tried to impress upon the offender his moral obligation to himself and his fellow cadets.[25] Yet he was willing to reward good behavior. Because of the good conduct of the corps of cadets during the summer encampment of 1882 he cancelled all outstanding punishments on what were designated the weekly punishment lists.[26]

To try to make the relationship between the cadets and the superintendent a little more human he instituted, a few months after his arrival, the practice of being available to students for an hour every day except Sunday.[27] That this had a wholesome effect is indicated by a secondhand story told to Howard by a fellow officer, L. L. Langdon, who reported what a cadet sergeant was reputed to have said: " 'We don't have to go now to and [sic] ask permission of another officer, to see the Superintendent, and the consequence is we would be ashamed to go to him unnecessarily or about a trifle. Whereas with the late Superintendent it was our delight to bother *him* and stir him up.' " Another cadet officer, according to Langdon said: "We never think of deceiving General Howard. He *trusts* us." [28] Howard's letters of this period reveal that his administration must have been firm but benevolent, and his handling of parents showed not only ability but genuine kindness and thoughtfulness.[29]

The innovation which undoubtedly most pleased the cadets was the reorganization of the mess. When Howard arrived at West Point the cadet mess was under the control of a certain Major Beekman DuBarry, a contract caterer who had been serving up unpalatable fare for a number of years. His principal assistant was his father-in-law who at the time was over seventy.[30] Complaints were frequent and Howard ordered an investigation. On the basis of this he directed that DuBarry order the chief cook to "see to it that there is an improvement in the cooking of the hash; that if he is incapable of making these improvements another man, better able to prepare plain food, be selected for his place." [31]

The ultimate solution was to bring in one of the officers who had served under Howard in the Department of the Columbia, Captain William F. Spurgin, to take over the job of quartermaster and commissary of cadets.[32] In his report for 1882 Howard could state that not only had the mess hall been painted and repaired, but that Spurgin had "succeeded in cutting off all excrescences which had been the growth of years, and, substantially without increase of expenditure, wonderfully improved the table in the character of the food and the variety of kinds furnished." [33]

Howard also reinvigorated the religious life of the Academy by bringing in a new man as chaplain who, as Howard told a cousin, "is all alive with blood & youth and spiritual power." He arranged for the chaplain to have a room in the cadets' barracks, and he also revived Protestant services at the soldiers' chapel.[34]

Yet all was not routine at West Point. The Academy was easily accessible from New York and was a favorite attraction for visitors, native and foreign. In March 1881, Mark Twain paid a visit, and in the following October the French delegation, come to participate in the one hundredth anniversary of the British surrender at Yorktown, came en masse to West Point. This must have been quite an affair for Howard described to a friend the reception at the dock, the cannon salute, review by the cadets, the evening parade, and a formal dinner at the hotel followed by a reception. "We hardly allowed anybody to talk anything but the 'parlez-vous francais' for at least three days," Howard wrote his son-in-law.[35]

The highlight of the year was the graduation. Visiting dignitaries added to the glamor of the occasion which involved reviews, inspections, parades, receptions, parties, and hops. Howard described those of the 1882 graduation as "unsurpassed." There was, he wrote a friend, "no jar, no hitch, no flaw. . . ." When it was all over he admitted to being sad "at the parting with the young men." [36]

While at West Point Howard pursued his usual habit of improving his mind by reading extensively, working on his conversational French, and entering a story contest sponsored by the Youth's Companion.[37] There was time also for horseback rides in the surrounding region and time to enjoy the beauties of West Point in the spring.[38] There was sorrow too at West Point. Soon after arriving, news came of the death of Howard's old friend Edgar

Ketchum and early in the summer of 1881 occurred the shooting of President Garfield. Throughout the following weeks there is frequent reference in Howard's correspondence to Garfield's condition. Then on the day following the President's death which came on September 18, bewildered and depressed by the event, he wrote to his daughter, Grace: "How strange that God did not hear & answer the prayers of his people to restore our President, but without a miracle I suppose it was impossible & He thinks it better not to perform such miracles now. Perhaps there is too much sin for him to hear our prayers & grant us such great blessings." [39]

During that summer of 1881 Howard combined a week's vacation with a YMCA meeting at Ocean Grove, New Jersey. Lizzie and the children (those who were at home) went along too. Later Howard went alone to a Soldiers and Sailors Association meeting in Portland, Maine.

Daughter Grace gave birth to another girl in January 1882, Howard's second grandchild. It was a sign of advancing age, but despite gray hair Howard did not believe, as he wrote soon after arriving at West Point, that he looked "very old for fifty." [40] While he retained a good measure of his youthful vigor, such was not the case with Lizzie. In the spring of 1882 she was at that point in life when others found her a little hard to live with. Howard was aware of the change. "She shows her age a great deal," he told Charlie's wife. "Often comes to the table without crest or crown—her hair is getting sprinkled with whitish threads—She often has neuralgia head-aches and often treats her young husband as she shouldn't." [41]

This private matter had to be lived with. Inside the West Point family, however, there developed a difficulty which Howard had to meet head on. Throughout almost his whole tenure he had as Commandant of Cadets Colonel Henry M. Lazelle, a classmate of Howard's in his first year at the Academy, who was kept back a year for disciplinary reasons. Howard's first comment about Lazelle, in 1850, had been, "Lazelle I don't like over much. . . . He does not seem to me to be very good hearted & his habits & manners I don't like." [42] Lazelle had had trouble with Schofield and he most certainly went out of his way to make things difficult for Howard, or so Howard reported. There was one complaint of Lazelle's "hardness" from the aunt of a cadet,[43] and Howard's relations with him became so strained that during a part of 1882 the two had no contacts except those of an official nature. According to Howard, Lazelle for an unaccountable reason refused all peace overtures and, following Howard's return from a trip to Colorado during the summer of 1882, treated his superior "with marked and deliberate discourtesy without apparent cause. . . ." Howard therefore asked that Lazelle be relieved from duty as commandant.[44] The adjutant general complied by relieving Lazelle on August 4, less than a month before Howard himself departed from West Point.[45] The incident illustrates Howard's faculty for arousing hostility especially on the part of a certain class of his brother officers. It also illustrates that Howard would go so far in extending the hand of friendship and then when insubordination became unbearable he would act with decisiveness.

It was too bad that this sour note marred the last months of Howard's regime, for, generally speaking, his had been a successful one. He felt confident of this himself, telling his brother Charles that, despite the fact that "all negro haters" opposed him at first, most of these had gone. He wrote in April 1882, "The testimony just at present is that the Corps was never in better discipline. There are very few complaints from any quarter." [46] A father of a cadet, and himself a West Point graduate, writing to a Louisiana Congressman (who sent the letter on to Howard), had warm praise for Howard calling him " 'the right man in the right place.' " He was, according to this unsolicited testimonial, "Courteous, considerate & kind," moving about "like a father in charge of his family & one look in his face is sufficient to inspire confidence & respect." [47] The Board of Visitors for 1882, whose president was General Horace Porter, commended the fine state of discipline of the cadets.[48]

That Howard's regime at West Point would be short seemed evident from the beginning. He had received the appointment in the first place from President Hayes over the objections of Sherman, and Hayes left the White House in March 1881. Furthermore, for some time there had been agitation from Schofield, the Board of Visitors (on more than one occasion), and from others to discontinue the Department of West Point with a general officer in command, and to have the superintendency placed again in the hands of a colonel of engineers as had been customary for so long prior to Schofield's tenure.[49] Howard did not favor the change although this opinion, he said, did not stem from any personal desire to stay on.[50] Indeed, he admitted after leaving, that West Point "became irksome to me . . . for various reasons. . . ." [51] And just after learning of his transfer he confessed to a friend that by leaving he thereby got rid of "a thousand petty annoyances. . . ."[52] The change appears to have come solely because of the pressure to discontinue the department and not because of any desire to get rid of Howard. Howard jokingly referred to the possibility of the latter in a note to his old friend, E. B. Webb, saying: "Confidentially beneath all a cabinet lady says, 'Too much prayer & too little rum.'" In a more serious vein he made reference to the long-standing agitation against "having 4 square miles called a Department. . . ."[53]

The order came while Howard was away and after his return he had only about a month to prepare for another move.[54] Colonel Wesley Merritt became Howard's successor.[55] Howard gave up the command to Merritt on September 1, 1882,[56] and soon after departed with his family for Omaha, Nebraska and command of the Department of the Platte. So ended a tenure of less than two years, too brief to make more than a ripple in the broad stream of West Point history.[57]

Headquarters city for the Department of the Platte was Omaha on the eastern edge of Nebraska and on the Missouri River. In 1882 it was still something of a frontier town.[58] When the Howards arrived there on September 5 they put up temporarily at Fort Omaha some three miles outside of town but shortly after they were able to rent what Lizzie called an "old barn of a house" on the corner of 18th and Dodge Streets.[59] Guy, back from a trip to France, joined his father as aide. The Department of the Platte in the Military Division of the Missouri included the states of Iowa, Nebraska, Wyoming, Utah, and a part of Idaho. By this time the Indians of this department were fairly well pacified and so most of Howard's duties were routine. A riot at Rock Springs, Wyoming, between whites and Chinese was the only incident of any real consequence during the five and one half years Howard was in command of this department.[60] To keep the troops busy and to have them prepared for any contingency was a continuing problem. Howard made use of a part of the time by having his officers and men take the field under campaign conditions. These summer training camps were something of an innovation as well as an indication of the keen interest Howard showed in his profession.[61]

In June 1883 Howard combined a tour of inspection with a pleasure trip to the Yellowstone National Park for himself, Lizzie, and a visiting lady from England, Mrs. Samuel Bright, sister-in-law of the statesman, John Bright. Altogether it was a most fortunate trip for Howard. For several years he had labored under a heavy weight, the subscription of ten thousand dollars he had made to Howard University to endow a professorship in the law department. Financial reverses had made it impossible for him to do more than pay the interest on the bequest and he sometimes could not do even that. On coming to Omaha he had begged the trustees of Howard University to relieve him of his pledge but they would not allow it. Finally, during the Yellowstone trip he made the acquaintance of Henry M. Flagler, associate of John D. Rockefeller, who was visiting the park with his wife. The members of the two parties became friends and in the course of the six days spent in the park Howard had the opportunity of telling Flagler of his plight. On returning East, Flagler mailed Howard a check for $10,000 which he graciously referred to as one which Howard "so kindly agreed to use." [62] Howard could then discharge his obligation to the University.[63]

Howard was absent from his command for seven months in 1884 on a trip abroad. He visited, among other places, Egypt and Turkey and represented the United States Army at French army maneuvers.[64]

Howard kept up his writing and lecturing while in Omaha, contributing articles to the G. A. R. newspaper the *National Tribune,* the *Encyclopedia Britannica,* and to various periodicals. To his brother, Rowland, who was critical of some of Howard's articles in the *National Tribune,* he wrote that he was well aware of his literary shortcomings and for that reason did not allow Lizzie or Guy to see his efforts before they were sent to the publisher, "because they would in that case never see the light. I have endeavored to write & let the blemishes go, & so blush & feel badly over a just criticism." [65]

Life had other sources of anxiety and discouragement. Johnny, the fifth child, had a serious accident in the Yellowstone Park in the summer of 1885 and for a time was near death. Prior to this Howard had tried without success to get President Arthur to give him an appointment to the Naval Academy.[66] Chancey, besides having eye trouble, could not seem to get established in any permanent position. Furthermore, Lizzie was both ailing and despondent. Howard admitted to his brother Charles a few months after arrival in Omaha that she was not "really very happy." [67] Another source of worry to him was Guy's failure to make an open profession of his adherence to the cause of Christ. Instead Guy moved away from his father's brand of Christianity and did what the latter had done years before as a young officer, he attended the Episcopal Church.

Still there were moments of happiness as for instance when news arrived of the birth of Grace's third child, or when Guy married, on his parents' wedding anniversary, an Omaha girl, Jeanie Woolworth.

Near the end of 1885 Howard began to become concerned over the major generalship which would soon fall vacant with the forthcoming retirement of General John Pope. For twenty years Howard had been in the same rank and now that he was the senior brigadier general he could not bear to see another promoted over him. Yet there was a chance of that happening because Alfred H. Terry had his eye on the coming vacancy. Other brigadiers also were eager for promotion and Howard was deeply disturbed, so much so that he appealed once again to General Sherman to speak in his behalf to President Grover Cleveland. That another should be placed above him would be, as he told Sherman, "almost intolerable to my sensitive heart. I would rather stand before a hostile battery than receive such stabs." [68]

Terry argued that because he had accepted his appointment as brigadier general earlier than Howard had, that he in truth was senior. Since Howard's date of rank antedated Terry's by a couple of weeks Howard naturally could not see the justice of his rival's claim.[69] The death of W. S. Hancock on February 9, 1886 created still another vacancy. When Terry received the first of these early in March [70] and when the papers, according to Howard, showed "intense satisfaction" with the choice,[71] Howard began to worry over his chances for even the second vacancy. All anxiety ceased when on March 19 he heard through the adjutant general that his name would be presented to the Senate for confirmation. But the satisfaction of the promotion was largely nullified by the fact that another man had filled the first vacancy, and that he had, in that sense, been passed over.[72] The Senate confirmed the nomination and from the second day of April 1886 Howard could use "Major General, USA" after his signature.

With promotion came also a change of assignment for as a major general he would now command one of the three military divisions into which the country was then divided.[73] The remaining vacancy after Schofield and Terry had had their choice was the Military Division of the Pacific with headquarters at San Francisco.

The Howard family left Omaha in a special car on April 13, 1886 and arrived in San Francisco four days later. They were to be on the West Coast for two and a half years. During that rather brief interval Howard had no arduous duties to perform. The family lived at Fort Mason, or Black Point, and Howard maintained an office, first at the Presidio, and later in downtown San Francisco.

A few months after arriving he described to Jamie his daily routine. He would begin the day reading and studying between six and seven in the morning. He then conducted lessons with his sixth child and youngest son, Harry, until eight, had breakfast and attended to private correspondence until half past nine or ten. Next he would ride on horseback the two and a half miles to the Presidio, attend to public business, and return home for lunch at one. At the time he wrote this letter he was going to the dentist most every afternoon so it can be assumed that his military duties were slight indeed.[74] Later, when his office was in the city, he kept office hours from eleven to four.

Howard continued to write for current periodicals and to engage in religious activities. He had become so prominent in church circles that he frequently was called upon to find positions for clergymen, to preach sermons, and perform other essentially nonsecular duties. On more than one occasion he had to remind his fellow Christians that he was not an ordained minister.[75]

In his professional work he strongly urged in his annual reports a strengthening of defenses on the Pacific coast. Apparently these were in a pitiable condition but in that part of the nineteenth century Congress, reflecting the general attitude of the country, did not see fit to appropriate money for such non-essentials and Howard's recommendations were not accepted.[76]

As for active campaigning, the only important occurrence was the war against Geronimo in the Department of Arizona (a part of Howard's Military Division of the Pacific) commanded by none other than Brigadier General Nelson A. Miles. Howard did not have an active role in this campaign, indeed it seems that Miles and Lieutenant General Sheridan, in command of the Army, frequently bypassed Howard, Miles' immediate superior. Miles and Howard had some differences concerning Geronimo's surrender terms but Howard's total participation was negligible.[77]

Toward the end of Howard's tour of duty in San Francisco, one of his old associates in the Army of the Cumberland, Benjamin

Harrison, became the Republican presidential candidate. To his daughter Grace, he described Harrison as "a thoroughly upright man; firm & of high order of talent." [78] Later he remarked to his mother, "It would be a comfort to me to have a friend like Harrison in the Presidential chair." [79] Under previous administrations Howard had not been accorded many favors, and as he remarked to his aide, Sladen, in 1887, "my recommendation has not half the weight as it had when I was 2 Lt of Ordnance." [80] His hopes consequently picked up with the prospect of seeing an old friend and army associate established in the White House.

Howard moved up a couple of rungs on the army ladder in 1888 with Terry's retirement in April and Sheridan's death in August. This left only one man superior to Howard and of course since Schofield was the highest ranking officer in the army he would make his headquarters in Washington. Howard would have first choice of division assignments and since the number one position was generally conceded to be the Military Division of the Atlantic that is where he chose to go.

In November 1888, for the last time in his army career, Howard changed posts and moved his family across the continent to Governors Island in New York harbor. He assumed command there on December 12, 1888.

Twenty-three years had passed since the end of the war and by this time even the Indian fighting had all but completely died out. By the end of the eighties there was danger that with inactivity would come inefficiency, complacency, and unreadiness. Howard seemed to be aware of this and in his annual reports he urged the adoption of more modern weapons, the continuing need for training of officers in their profession, more intensive instruction in the use of small arms for the men, a wider employment of summer camps, and more adequate coast defenses. In one report he recommended that the army be doubled in size.[81] Yet adequate funds for the army were not forthcoming and not much could be accomplished in the face of Congressional and public apathy.

Howard's command was immense, covering Arkansas and all states east of the Mississippi, except Illinois. Howard had his command reduced slightly when in 1891 President Harrison ordered the discontinuance of divisions and reorganized the country into eight departments. Howard continued in command of the Department of the East (formerly included in the Division of the Atlantic) which covered almost as much territory as the division once did. Within this vast region were scattered a number of army posts many of which were situated along the coast as part of the harbor defenses.

During the years when Howard had this command (1888–1894), despite the outbreak of such major labor disturbances as the Homestead and Pullman strikes, he was not called upon to use the regular troops of his department in the suppression of any of them. The one exception was the sending of the 9th Infantry to Chicago (outside his department) during the Pullman strike.[82]

With official duties reduced to a minimum there remained ample time for other pursuits and Howard made full use of his opportunities. He made trips to Cuba and Mexico, the latter in connection with the writing of a biography of Zachary Taylor for Appleton's Great Commander series. In October 1892 he got leave to go abroad once again, this time to Spain to gather material for a life of Isabella of Castile. In the pursuit of his official duties he made extensive tours of inspection throughout his department sometimes taking along members of the family.

Once he went with Sherman to a meeting of the Society of the Army of the Tennessee in Cincinnati. That was in September 1889. In these years Sherman lived in New York as did General Slocum so the three old associates could get together from time to time, and when Sherman died in February 1891 Howard had charge of the funeral procession.

The previous autumn Howard had joined the principal surviving Union officers of the battle of Gettysburg for a reunion on the battlefield at the request of the Comte de Paris, historian of the American Civil War. This kind of reunion appealed to Howard. It was the opposite with reunions with Confederates. In 1889 he replied to an invitation to attend such a reunion with the remark that meetings of that kind were "not altogether wholesome in their tendency. It seems," he continued, "too much like brothers making up after a quarrel, where the two are equally at fault. The hard thing now is to secure the faithful carrying out [of] the measures secured by the war, namely, the positive equality of rights of every citizen before the law. How can I help it by what you propose?"[83]

In addition to his literary pursuits Howard also engaged in the usual church activities. The family joined the Broadway Tabernacle and Otis and his youngest son, Harry, devoted considerable time to the Camp Memorial Church and Mission in lower Manhattan.

It was while the Howards were in New York that John, the fourth son, received a second lieutenant's commission in the army. He thus joined his father and older brother Guy as a regular. Guy had done well and in 1893, as a captain in the quartermaster's department, was sent to Burlington, Vermont to take charge of the reconstruction of Fort Ethan Allen. Jamie had become a successful engineer, Grace and her husband were enjoying a growing family on the West Coast, and though Chancey had some difficulties in business he nonetheless had a happy family. The two youngest children, Harry and Bessie, lived at home.

Howard's name had been mentioned as a possible secretary of war in Benjamin Harrison's cabinet just before the new administration took office, but this turned out to be only rumor.[84] Then early in 1892 Frances Willard, president of the Women's Christian Temperance Union, asked Howard if he would consent to run for President of the United States on the Prohibition party ticket. He declined,[85] explaining to his daughter that by running as a third party candidate he would only be helping Cleveland get elected, and, he wrote, he was not that good a Democrat.[86]

Howard's retirement from the army after forty-four years service came quietly on his sixty-fourth birthday, November 8, 1894. On that day he bade farewell to the officers on the post at Governors Island and in the evening attended a banquet given in his honor by a Brooklyn G. A. R. post. Here he took leave of his three aides-de-camp and entered into that period long awaited by the army regular, the period of retirement. But as so many others found it, so too did Otis Howard; it came to him "like a shock," and it was some time before he could adjust to his new condition.[87]

When Howard left the army in 1894 he did so with a feeling of genuine regret, for the army had been his life for forty-four years. But he had never allowed the army to absorb him as was so often the case with other officers. These tended to exhibit a military outlook, a narrowness of view which was quite different from Howard's breadth of interest in much that was non-military.

Especially did Howard's concern with religious and church-related matters set him off from the average army officer. He attended church meetings, YMCA conferences, served on religious bodies, and generally made an effort to make his mark in the affairs of protestant Christianity. Not only that but he made a conscious and sincere effort to put into practice what he considered the principles of Christianity.

He once wrote that it was part of his general purpose to "try every day to make some body happier & better." He would set an example to his family and to society by holding family prayer and by faithful church attendance and would not concede that these were out of harmony with the life of a soldier.[88] Yet, despite a reputation for piety, Howard never believed that he deserved it. Once in writing to Sherman he took exception to some remarks Sherman had made at an Army of the Tennessee dinner to the effect that Howard was too pious. On hearing of this he replied to Sherman that he never liked too much "religiousness" in other men and though he would never want to be anything but "truly loyal to our Lord, I would not like to talk through my nose, or put on any airs whatever."[89] Nor, in all fairness, did he. He advised his oldest son, Guy, that "It is not necessary to be *religious,* that is abominable." But, he continued, "it is necessary to have a large, contented spirit, moving grandly to accomplish something in your heavenly Father's world."[90]

Other evidence exists that Howard was far from pious in the unpleasant sense of that word and also was not prudish or opposed to normal human pleasures. For instance, though he himself tried always to observe the Sabbath he did not insist that everyone else do the same. In answer to a request in 1890 from his brother Charles that he sign a petition objecting to the opening of the forthcoming Chicago World's Fair on Sunday, Howard replied that he would rather not sign. "I am not very stiff and rigid about the Sabbath," he wrote, and he went on to say that if some people could only get to the fair on Sunday then it might be wise to open it to them. "Somehow," he told his brother, "we churchmen must show a greater loving sympathy with overburdened people than we do."[91]

It is true that he openly objected to profanity[92] and that he took an active stand against drinking. He had had enough acquaintance with the evils of drink to convince him that the temperance cause was worthy of his support.[93] But he did not feel the same way about some other of man's petty vices. He once cautioned a correspondent against trying to exact a pledge from school children against the use of tobacco. "Too much pledging is apt to overreach itself," he warned.[94] Nor, did he take a stand against gambling and dancing. He considered card playing in general an innocent pastime even though he did not himself indulge. And he considered most forms of dancing "healthful & pleasant & not hurtful." He replied to an inquiry about his views on these two forms of recreation with a defense of the youth of his day saying that he regarded it "as criminal, as anti-Christian to be always putting upon young persons burdens altogether unnecessary, unscriptural & irritating." [95] Certainly Howard does not belong in that numerous body of nineteenth century American busybodies who believed it their special duty to look after the morals of the nation.

On current issues of the day he took a progressive attitude unusual for a high ranking army officer. While in San Francisco in 1888 he rhetorically asked his brother Charles what the nation was going to do with "the thoroughly unchristian principle of boycotting and strikes." Nothing very unorthodox about that! But in the very next sentence he expressed a most unorthodox opinion by suggesting that "perhaps the greed of capitalists provokes them." [96] When it came to Social Darwinism he found, he said, no objection to Darwin and "eternal development," but he did object to the doctrine of the survival of the fittest when "care for the weak & oppressed" was destroyed or when it interfered with the Holy Word.[97] He opposed the policy of Chinese exclusion first adopted by the Congress in 1882,[98] and even had the audacity to predict at a social gathering that some day woman suffrage would become a reality and that he, for one, would not oppose it! [99]

As a faithful reader of the Bible he was somewhat troubled by the current Darwinian doubts cast on the validity of the historical accounts in the Old Testament, particularly in Genesis. But the adjustment came with relative ease.[100] To his biographer, Mrs. Laura Holloway, he announced that he had "never trusted to the letter of the scriptures of the old and new Testaments for the letter killeth but the spirit maketh alive." [101] Howard's faith that the Messiah had come was unshakable. He believed that this faith, plus sacrifice and love were the proper basis of conduct rather than "everlasting, painful uncertainty & doubting." [102]

Howard's ideas on education were the kind which liberal educators of later generations could wholeheartedly endorse, but could not be classified as unorthodox in the second half of the nineteenth century. He urged his sons to gain a solid foundation in a general education before turning to a specialty. To Jamie, who had become an engineer, he wrote urging him to adopt a regular habit of daily reading and to take at least one good monthly magazine, spending as little time as possible on the newspapers. ". . . our business men," he wrote, "are apt to become absorbed in the business itself, and therefore at forty or fifty are very narrow and apt to be egotistical."[103]

Otis Howard had always found time for activities and recreation outside his profession; especially was he a wide reader. He had kept up his writing and had turned out several books which, while they have no lasting merit as literary works, nonetheless show that Howard had a certain flair for writing. Among his many works were several books for boys, biographies of Zachary Taylor and Queen Isabella, and accounts of his Indian experiences. The autobiography, written after retirement, is still an important work for students of the Civil War and Reconstruction.

Since the closing months of the Civil War, Howard had held progressive views on the race question but since leaving the Bureau had not had much opportunity for placing these views before the public. Back in 1867 he had said that Negroes had "just about as much sense as white men of the same education and advantages" which was certainly true enough though doubtless his correspondent, a Mississippian, could hardly have shared such a view.[104] Yet despite this favorable and, for that day, advanced view of the Negro's ability he could at the same time face reality. In an address delivered early in 1869 he noted that only a tenth of the freedmen were getting even a taste of education and that the job of educating the rest was one which could not be accomplished overnight. He even went out of his way to criticize ignorant Negro ministers who led "frenzied meetings" which he considered "very objectionable." He also deplored the sights he had seen in some of the Southern state legislatures of illiterate Negroes being subjected to ridicule for their poor English and he could not help but feel uneasy at the thought of these men sharing the law-making process.[105]

After leaving Washington for the West Coast, Howard could do very little in behalf of the freedmen although in his correspondence he frequently made reference to conditions in the South. He maintained a hopeful attitude but could not help but feel discouraged when it was obvious that the Negroes were still receiving harsh and unequal treatment. For example, in December 1874 he read reports of an occurrence at Vicksburg, Mississippi in which a group of seven hundred Negroes was involved in a riot with forty whites and the outcome was the death of one hundred and fifty blacks and only three whites. To Frederick Douglass he expressed incredulity that the

Negroes were the aggressors (as the newspaper report had stated) and he begged that the nation not go back on its pledges to the freedmen.[106]

As in the immediate post-war period he still relied on education as the best way for the Negro to pull himself up—education and the ballot. In 1884 he wrote an article for *The Advance* which was an overly optimistic report on the progress Negroes had made thus far. He believed that Southerners were coming to see that since the Negro had the ballot he would have to be treated fairly. He also stated that the Southern people were acting in good faith. It is insulting, he wrote, to impute bad motives to Southern whites; "Certainly if we never trust them or give them an opportunity they can make no demonstration."[107] A short time later in a private communication he showed that he was really not so sanguine.[108] By the time of the Democratic victory in the presidential election of 1884 the conservative reaction was well under way in all parts of the South and had triumphed in most. Since 1872 Howard had already seen a great part of his work undone and he would see an even stronger reaction after 1884. State after state of the South in the 1880's and 1890's enacted legislation putting social and political restrictions on the colored population so that before the end of the century not only had Negroes lost what civil rights they had gained during Reconstruction but had also been virtually disfranchised.

Yet the schools of higher education which Howard had assisted in founding continued to reaffirm the assertion that a Negro deserved the same opportunities for education as whites. This was done in the face of a growing acceptance of Social Darwinian racial views which assumed the inherent inferiority of colored people. Howard's continuing support of the cause of Negro education thus ran contrary to prevailing opinion and further put him in a unique position as an army officer.

Naturally Howard's greatest interest was in Howard Univesity. In 1877, just before the opening of the Nez Perce campaign, he confided to a friend that he thought daily of the University and tried to pray "that the promise of its beginnings may have a rich fulfillment in its growth and real worth."[109] He used his influence to try to keep it from becoming an all-Negro institution in keeping with his belief that the University should remain true to its charter, that is, open to all persons regardless of race.[110]

Any effort in behalf of the American Negro seemed almost futile by the time Howard had retired from the Army. Conditions got worse in the next few years until the nadir was reached in a disgraceful race riot at Springfield, Illinois in 1908. This event and the appearance of Howard's autobiography the previous year have been noted as turning points in the position of the Negro in American society.[111] The race riot produced an inevitable reaction, coming as it did in Lincoln's home town and within one year of the centennial of his birth, and Howard's autobiography once again affirmed the need for accepting the Negro as potentially an intellectual equal of the white and thus denied the current Social Darwinian racial theories. He stated unequivocally that there was no limit to the Negro's capacity to learn and what white men could learn so too could the Negro.[112] Surely he had maintained through the most discouraging years a faith and an optimism which have been gloriously vindicated in the years which have followed the appearance of the autobiography.

Howard had warm sympathy and understanding for Negroes; he had the right amount of dignity in his relationships with them coupled with a natural ease which won their confidence. But he also had the practical man's approach to the race problem in this country, and his words of advice on the subject are as applicable in the second half of the twentieth century as they were when he wrote them in 1869, "They [the freedmen] are among us, they are with us, they are of us, and they will no doubt continue with us to the end, so that the sooner we trample upon mere prejudice and folly the better." [113]

The anomaly of Howard's position as an advocate of racial equality and as a high ranking officer in the United States Army had proved so impossible of comprehension that more than one person, and often this meant a fellow officer, simply never understood him at all. Lincoln's Secretary of the Navy, Gideon Welles, had called him a "pious fraud." General Daniel Sickles once is reported to have referred to Howard as a "weak man and a hypocrite. . . ." [114] Sherman thought Howard was too pious. It is hard to characterize a man such as Howard, but surely such words simply do not fit. Where was he a fraud, where weak, a hypocrite, or pious in the worst sense of that word? There are other words which could be used which would better describe Howard's character. Such words might be sensitive, tolerant, loyal, Christian, brave, self-righteous, proud. The last two traits were, in the long run, detriments. Time and again Howard failed to hold his addiction for self-righteousness under control; too often did he automatically see himself as right and those in disagreement as wrong. He made mistakes (any man is entitled to some), but he hated to admit that he might be wrong, as at Chancellorsville, for instance, in his handling of the building block affair, or in his complaints to McDowell during the Nez Perce campaign. His incessant readiness to plunge into useless debate over what must in the last analysis be considered trivial matters, as for instance the unseemly argument with Miles over the surrender of Joseph, could not but brand him as overly-sensitive if not self-righteous. Pride also accounts for much of this willingness to contest every slight from whatever source. A more practical approach to the attacks of Fernando Wood, viewing them as politically inspired and nothing else, must have saved him from months of anxiety and needless public exposure of questionable acts. There is no doubt about it, he sought the applause of his countrymen, his ego thirsted for it and when it was not forthcoming, or when he received jeers instead, his soul was troubled. Yet he constantly was aware of this desire for praise and he could better take the jibes of his detractors because he was fundamentally a Christian who knew what humility was. Thus when we detect in Howard's character this unpleasant trait of desire for recognition we can at the same time be aware that all the time he had this fault in mind and was trying to control it.

These things aside, his was a noble character, and in reviewing a career of forty-four years in the army the trait which most stands out is his loyalty to his superiors and above all else to his country. The motto of his West Point class, "When our Country Calls," was a very part of his being. Devotion to duty, devotion to his superiors, and love of country characterize Howard's whole life. Too often we tend to slight the loyal men of 1861 who had no hesitancy about offering up their lives in the service of their country, who were loyal to the flag, and who put aside local sympathies for the good of the nation. Oliver Otis Howard never wavered in his loyalty to flag and country and without such as he, this nation might not have survived the terrible ordeal of civil war. At least, when he performed his final duties on that November day in 1894 he could look back on a life devoted to the service of his country, a life rich in productive accomplishments for all Americans. And more to his credit, that career was not yet over. Ahead lay additional years of constructive service to the nation.

The Closing Years

When retirement came, General Howard was not at any loss for something to do. Ever since the end of the Civil War he had devoted much of his spare time to lecturing and writing, and it was only natural that he should continue in these pursuits after leaving the army. Even before retirement, he had been in touch with Cyrus Kehr, patent lawyer and lecture agent of Chicago, making preliminary arrangements for a lecture tour to start officially in the fall of 1895.[1] Returning East in March 1895 from Portland, Oregon (where he and Lizzie had boarded for the winter near their daughter Grace), Howard delivered several lectures along the way. On May 5, 1895, they reached Burlington, Vermont which they intended making their permanent home.

From then until his death in 1909 Howard lectured up and down the country, often for G. A. R. posts, but also for churches, YMCA's, and Sunday schools and at holiday celebrations. He had a number of set lectures from which to choose. The most popular were "Gettysburg," "The March to the Sea," "Personal Recollections of Abraham Lincoln," and "Grant at Chattanooga." If he were asked to speak on Sunday he would take an appropriate subject, frequently drawing on his personal religious experiences.

His literary efforts continued to be extensive. He turned out countless articles for the popular periodicals and for church publications. Usually the subject matter concerned his war experiences, but frequently he wrote on contemporary or historical subjects. A major work was his autobiography, begun in the summer of 1896, but because of countless interruptions completion and publication were not until 1907.

Lecturing and writing could fill most of Howard's waking hours and keep him away from the lovely home he built in Burlington a good part of the time, but he was not content solely with these occupations. His restless energies soon had him involved in the presidential election of 1896. Although he had always been a

Republican in sympathy, his official position had made it impossible to engage actively in politics. Now that the restraints were off, he could plunge wholeheartedly into the excitement of a campaign. Howard made speeches in Vermont and his native state of Maine and then, in company with Generals Daniel E. Sickles, Russell A. Alger, and other veterans of the war, he went on an extensive speaking tour of the Middle West. The Democratic opposition referred to them as "the Wrecks of the Civil War," but they carried out a rigorous schedule of whistle stop campaigning.[2]

This was the famous "free silver" campaign between McKinley and Bryan and Howard had a hard time adjusting himself to the Eastern businessman's view that only a sound gold standard could be tolerated. In 1893 he had admitted to be leaning toward the silver side [3] and during the campaign he stuck by the Republican platform which deviously called for an international commission to discuss bimetalism when the party leaders had no faith in such a scheme.[4] Though not a strong gold man, Howard did stand forth against currency depreciation and "tendencies to anarchy and to centralization," while upholding the Republican position on the tariff.[5]

In other ways Howard was not a typical McKinley Republican in the generally accepted sense of that term. He squirmed a bit under the realization that men of enormous wealth played such a prominent part in the inner circles of the party. He refused to admit that money had anything to do with McKinley's election [6] but he feared that "The trusts, the monopolies, the narrow souled men, with their millions, accompanied with inordinate pretension and ostentatious display are but exponents of tendencies which our wise men must study to repress." [7]

Undoubtedly Howard believed that his national prominence, his services to the party, and his friendship with "Major" McKinley deserved some recognition from the new administration, although he was reluctant to further his own candidacy. Others, including brother Charles, were more forward. Some months before the election, Charles began to promote the idea of Otis becoming secretary of war.[8] Charles wrote to a mutual friend of McKinley and General Howard, General Wager Swayne, who had served under Howard in the Army of the Tennessee and also in the Freedmen's Bureau, hoping that Swayne would speak to McKinley. Swayne indignantly refused at that early date to have anything to do with such an idea believing it undignified as well as unfair to McKinley to pester him before the election. Howard immediately sent Swayne's letter on to Charles with the admonition not to allow any friend to do anything at all in the direction of securing for him the office of secretary of war.[9]

Following the election Swayne wrote Howard, gently implying that maybe he would have better success trying for the ambassadorship to Turkey.[10] Before trying for the position which was less desirable, Swayne went after the big prize, the cabinet post.[11] But McKinley had more pressing obligations and the position went to General Russell A. Alger. Howard unquestionably had half expected to be named [12] but, once turned down, he switched immediately to the ambassadorship to Turkey.[13] Once more Howard had to face the unpleasant choice of retaining his Christian humility or gaining public recognition. In a letter to his close friend, William E. Dodge, he first asked advice, then stated the disadvantages of the job. But he told Dodge of having forwarded a letter of recommendation from a clergyman to an influential person disclaiming all the while seeking office. "It is abhorrent to my soul to seek office," he concluded.[14] Two days later he wrote the Secretary of State, John Sherman, asking for the Turkey position but suggesting also Mexico and Germany as alternate possibilities.[15] Howard was in Washington for the inauguration, commanding the veteran contingent, and at that time talked briefly with the President. McKinley asked him if he would like to go to Constantinople "simply for duty," to which Howard replied, "certainly." [16] No wonder that he had his hopes up and no wonder there was disappointment when later in March he learned that another had been named for the post.[17]

By this time Howard ought to have been accustomed to this kind of treatment from the politicians. But he had difficulty in understanding that politicians hand out favors mostly for political reasons and not out of a sense of gratitude. While the President was making his appointments and the press had made mention of Howard as a possibility for a diplomatic post, the old charge that Howard had made money as president of Howard University was once again bandied about. This got his goat, and he poured out his feelings to Charles. "I don't want to write any more letters to McKinley or to the Secretaries, if I can help it," he wrote. "I have found this out, that from Maine to California, people seek to ride me as if I was a free horse, young, active and of elegant build; but the moment I appear to want anything . . . then somebody is ready to shoot at me from an ambush so dark and hedged in that you cannot tell whether that somebody is a democrat, a populist or a bush-whacker." [18]

The hurt continued and in May he wrote Alger complaining that he had been misunderstood on the silver question. The office and public praise were not what he sought. "What I really coveted was a feeling that I was esteemed, trusted and appreciated" by the President.[19] So ended Howard's only serious effort to enter actively into public service following retirement. His thirst for public recognition abated, and he soon found an interest which was more suited to his talents, that of fostering the growth of Lincoln Memorial University.

Howard's interest in this institution near Cumberland Gap, Tennessee stemmed from his association with his lecture agent, Cyrus Kehr of Chicago. Since about 1890 Kehr had toyed with the idea of founding an educational institution as a living memorial to Lincoln. In February or March 1896 he mentioned his idea to Howard.[20]

Early in June Howard left Burlington to visit the battlefields around Chattanooga where he was to assist in locating the site for a monument. At Cumberland Gap, a mountain missionary learned that Howard would be coming through that region and, hoping that Howard might become interested in his work for the mountain whites, he wrote Harry S. Howard, the General's son, seeking to arrange a visit.[21] The missionary was the Reverend A. A. Myers who, with his wife Ellen, had been working since 1890 amongst the poor mountain folk in the area around Cumberland Gap. The American Missionary Association had supported their efforts to establish schools for these people who hitherto had had no educational opportunities of any kind.

Though they had started about fifteen log cabin elementary schools and the Harrow School as an academy or high school, there was still no institution of higher learning to serve this mountain region touching eastern Tennessee and Kentucky and western Virginia and North Carolina. To establish a college was the dream of Brother Myers and especially of his wife Ellen. They had seen in the last five years a great industrial boom in the Cumberland Gap area. British and American investors had poured in vast sums to develop the coal and iron resources of the mountain country, and to establish a new industrial center, Middlesboro, Kentucky. They had also built the fabulous seven hundred room Four Seasons Hotel, a short distance from Cumberland Gap. Now, by 1896, the boom had ended, the great hotel had been torn down and the whole area languished in economic blight. Men of wealth who might have been counted upon to aid the Myers' missionary and educational efforts no longer would throng to the fashionable hotel. Ellen Myers was by now an invalid and her husband's health ruined by his intense efforts in a gruelling work. It seemed as if their hopes for a college to crown their life's work might never be realized.[22] Thus the desire to have General Howard visit the Harrow School. Perhaps he would come to their aid.

Howard, en route to Chattanooga, agreed to stop over at Cumberland Gap and give his lecture on "Grant at Chattanooga" and divide the proceeds with the Myers' school.[23] On the evening of June 18, 1896 four men sat on the veranda of the Harrow School building, the gap just to the west, massive, wooded mountains to the north, and more gently rolling hills to the south. Accompanying Howard on his trip to Chattanooga was the Brooklyn merchant and former Congressman, Darwin R. James. Also present were Myers and his friend, the Reverend Frederick B. Avery, an Episcopalian minister of Painesville, Ohio who for some years had taken an interest in educational work for the mountain people of Kentucky and Tennessee. Perhaps sensing that this was his great opportunity, Myers spoke at length of the work he and his wife were doing and the difficulties they faced. He also spoke of the great opportunity present in the former hotel property which could be had at an extremely low figure.

As Howard listened to the aging missionary there came to his mind the memory of his last meeting with President Lincoln many years before. It was in late September 1863 just before Howard left with his corps to join the Western armies near Chattanooga. For almost two hours Lincoln had talked with him. At one point the President had questioned Howard about advancing through Cumberland Gap and seizing Knoxville so as to relieve the Unionists of east Tennessee from Confederate control. He dwelt on this subject for some time urging Howard to understand and appreciate these people and said, "They are loyal, there, General, they are loyal." [24]

Now Myers was talking about schools for educating the sons and daughters of these same people so dear to Lincoln's heart. There also came to mind Cyrus Kehr's proposals for a living monument to Abraham Lincoln. Impulsively Howard was on his feet, pacing up and down the porch, mulling over these various thoughts. Suddenly he stopped and said, "Friends, if you will make this school a larger enterprise I will take hold and do what I can." [25] At Howard's suggestion they agreed to name the proposed institution Lincoln Memorial University and to secure the Four Seasons Hotel property, which included a sizable sanatorium suitable for a school building and dormitory.[26]

The details of obtaining the property and of establishing the University with Harrow School as a foundation Howard left to Myers and to Cyrus Kehr who was immediately brought into the scheme.[27] Howard at first had no intention of taking what he called "the laboring oar," for this was the time of the McKinley-Bryan campaign and he had no time to spare for Lincoln Memorial University.[28] Later he held off from becoming too involved because of the possibility of his obtaining a cabinet post.[29] Consequently when Myers, Kehr, and a group of local patrons, including Captain Robert F. Patterson, a Confederate veteran of Lee's army, obtained a charter (dated February 12, 1897) they elected Howard to the board of trustees, but not to any other more responsible position.[30] Myers was president of the board, and Kehr became the president of the University.[31]

During the remainder of 1897 Howard remained in the background writing occasional letters to men of wealth trying to help the university pay off the debt on the property.[32] Early in May 1898 Kehr asked Howard if he would consider becoming the managing director of Lincoln Memorial University with practically unlimited authority, and at the board meeting on May 25 Howard was elected to that position.[33]

Howard missed that particular meeting because at the time the United States was engaged in war with Spain and Howard, though the offer of his services (to return to active duty) to the President[34] was declined, took an active part nonetheless with the Army and Navy Christian Commission. He visited army camps in Virginia, Georgia, and Florida speaking to the troops and bringing to them his "Christian Message."[35] From Key West he sailed to Santiago, Cuba on July 22, 1898.[36]

As soon as he had finished his war service, General Howard plunged immediately into the work of raising money for Lincoln Memorial University. First he sent out about a hundred letters to numerous friends and men of prominence, placing before them the urgent needs of the university.³⁷ Next he arranged an extension of the mortgage.³⁸ During 1899, Howard not only got a further extension and raised several thousand dollars to meet immediate needs, but he practically ran the whole enterprise.³⁹ The directors minutes show that the board agreed to abide by any recommendation he might make.⁴⁰ At the annual meeting in May 1899 Howard was elected president of the board, and to the board's executive committee, while retaining his position of managing director.⁴¹ It was he who appointed the Reverend John Hale Larry of Providence, Rhode Island to the position of assistant managing director,⁴² which really meant that Howard wanted someone on the spot to direct affairs. Kehr had not lived up to expectations⁴³ and Myers was obviously not the man to take the lead in this larger enterprise.

Just when Howard was making definite progress towards paying off the University's debt, the family received word that Guy, the oldest son, had been killed in the Philippines. He died a hero's death in action against the insurgents; both Otis and Lizzie felt the loss deeply. A few months later Howard spoke of his son as "my strong helper . . . the critic I could trust . . . my hope for the future." Now "crowds & crowds of hopes are baffled & dashed to the ground in his death." ⁴⁴

In part to compensate for the blow of Guy's death, Howard immersed himself even more in the work of Lincoln Memorial University.⁴⁵ By the end of the year he had succeeded in raising enough money to pay off the principal mortgage of over $11,000, and a smaller second mortgage was paid by the end of March 1900.⁴⁶

It was not only financial worries with which Howard had to deal; there were the petty and major bickerings which seemed to be going on constantly at the University. Eventually these were dumped in Howard's lap. It appears that after the death of Myer's wife in 1897 his mind was not entirely sound. As early as October 1898 ⁴⁷ there was a hint of trouble, but the greatest difficulty arose after Larry's appointment in the summer of 1899. Though he apparently was Myers' choice,⁴⁸ Larry met with underhanded opposition even before he arrived at Cumberland Gap. He tried to get on with Myers and admitted that "but for his restless, erratic, scheming spirit" the school would never have existed.⁴⁹ But Myers made no effort to cooperate. From a distance, Howard heard from all parties, mostly from Larry who had Myers in his hair much of the time. Finally in January 1901 Myers resigned from the board of trustees.[50]

Despite Larry's hard work and devoted efforts he could not get on with the local people, nor was he at all successful in raising money.[51] Consequently at the annual meeting in May 1901 Howard brought in Frederick B. Avery, the Episcopalian minister who had been with Howard on his first visit to Cumberland Gap in 1896, to become managing director and a possible choice for president.[52]

Howard was trying to straighten things out so that he could step down from his active role. He had been unwell in March and the cares of the University which were mostly on his shoulders were more than he should have had to carry at his age. His friends were concerned for him and wanted to relieve him of the burden of active command.[53]

He was still lecturing extensively, and his constitution must have been indeed strong to stand the constant travel. Avery told how after one of the board meetings he had accompanied Howard on their return trip North by train. During the night they changed trains three times and Howard had to sleep, when he could, curled up in his seat. This drew from Avery the comment, "He certainly is wonderfully brave, generous and self sacrificing. . . . more and more I feel honored in the privilege of being a yoke fellow with such a man as Gen. Howard. . . ."[54]

By January 1902 the University again was in desperate need of money. Avery, his health failing, had not been a successful fund raiser and the University's secretary and assistant treasurer, Charles F. Eager, turned to Howard to bail them out.[55] Once again Howard had to take over the duties of managing director, a position he held until 1907.[56] Larry continued as president of the University, but he stayed only until 1903 when Dr. William L. Stooksbury became the acting president.[57]

At the annual meeting of the board of trustees in May 1908, Howard proposed the formation of a committee to prepare a program and campaign for the centennial of Lincoln's birth, which would be coming the following year.[58] Needless to say he was on the committee. Howard worked tirelessly on this special campaign to raise an endowment of $500,000, speaking, writing, urging, in behalf of this his last great work.[59] Though many other hands shared in the building of this memorial institution, Howard's help given over a period of thirteen years was indispensable to the success of the undertaking. It was truly a labor of love, remarkable for a man who could with justification have shifted the burden to younger shoulders. The college for the mountain folk is not only a memorial to Lincoln; it is also a living monument to the one-armed soldier.

Laboring for the University was only a part of Howard's activity during these last years of his life. He kept up his writing and lecturing and also his political interests, campaigning vigorously for McKinley in 1900 and for Theodore Roosevelt in 1904.[60] He commanded the veterans division at both inaugural ceremonies and was in the saddle seven hours at McKinley's inaugural parade in 1901.[61] This at the age of seventy! In the final stages of the Taft-Bryan campaign in 1908 he took part in a big Republican rally at Madison Square Garden.[62]

Right to the end he was on the go. In the summer of 1909 he filled speaking engagements in Wisconsin, Kansas, Nebraska, and Iowa.[63] Early in October of that year he attended the Hudson-Fulton celebration in New York. A reporter on one of the city papers thought he saw Howard being helped to the reviewing stand and commented the next day that the general was feeble. Howard immediately wrote the editor that, on the contrary, he had gone on from there to give several addresses in Philadelphia immediately after, and had returned "feeling as vigorous and strenuous as I did at forty years of age. . . . I do not know whether it is of any consequence whether I am feeble or strong," he concluded, "but we have a wonderful work yet to do to get our great monument of Abraham Lincoln thoroughly completed in this his centennial year. It is my last work, I have no doubt, and I need all the vigor the newspapers can give me." [64]

On Friday, October 22, 1909 he left for London, Ontario, and on Saturday evening delivered his address on the battle of Gettysburg. Sunday he spoke at a YMCA gathering, then returned to Burlington on Monday.

Tuesday after breakfast he felt a pain in his chest, and a feeling of nausea came over him briefly. But he soon felt better and together with Harry walked to his office in the center of town. One thing he did that morning was to write to Dr. W. L. Stooksbury, president of Lincoln Memorial, about money for the medical school in Knoxville which the University had recently taken over.[65] Then he started work on an article about changes in warfare in the past fifty years. As he was dictating, shortly after noon, he felt another sharp pain in his chest, and he knew then that he should see a doctor. He and Harry walked out through the park and took a cab to the doctor's office. The doctor's face turned grave after his examination and he told Harry to get the general to bed as quickly as possible. Howard insisted on going to the third floor spare room, apparently because Lizzie was ill under the care of a nurse on the second floor. Harry helped him undress and he went to bed, but his rest was interrupted from time to time by attacks of nausea.

About five the doctor returned bringing some nitroglycerine tablets to bring down Howard's blood pressure. The doctor did not appear worried, and Howard was not suffering any great amount of pain. After the family supper, Harry's wife, Sue, took up some broth and found Howard sitting on the edge of the bed. She sat next to him, her right arm around him. He tried a spoonful of broth, but it brought on vomiting, and just after she had placed the cup on the bureau he suddenly fell back on her pinning her so she could hardly move. Calling for help, she managed to find his wrist but could feel no pulse. By that time Harry was in the room. He laid his father on the bed, and after realizing that he could do no more, closed the general's eyes and kissed him. Soon the doctor arrived and pronounced him dead. His heart had stopped beating just as he had predicted. "Someday it will just stop," he had told Harry, "and I will be on the other shore." Harry ran to get his mother. She stood silently looking at the now lifeless body and turned and left the room without a word. Death had come at 7:20.

That evening General Leonard Wood, on a visit to Fort Ethan Allen, came to pay his respects, and a guard of honor from the 10th Cavalry, a Negro regiment, stood outside the house. The funeral was on Friday, October 29. There were the full military honors. After the simple, dignified service at the Congregational church, the procession moved on to the cemetery overlooking the waters of Lake Champlain. Behind the flag-draped casket walked a cavalry horse with black pall and reversed stirrups. Three volleys, and then taps by a Negro bugler—and the casket was lowered into the grave in the center of a large circular plot, the donation of the city of Burlington.[66] Only five days before he had spoken in Ontario; three days earlier he had written a last letter in behalf of Lincoln Memorial University. With a minimum of suffering he had closed his rich useful life and had crossed over to "the other shore."

Notes

TABLE OF ABBREVIATIONS

LR	— Letters Received
LS	— Letters Sent
USMA	— United States Military Academy
HU	— Howard University
LMU	— Lincoln Memorial University
LC	— Library of Congress
NA	— National Archives
BR	— Records of the Bureau of Refugees, Freedmen and Abandoned Lands
MOOLL	— Military Order of the Loyal Legion
AAG	— Assistant Adjutant General
AGO	— Adjutant General's Office
MDP	— Military Division of the Pacific
D. of C.	— Department of the Columbia

Early Life [1–11]

1. Howard to F. J. Woodward, Nov. 6, 1869, Howard Papers, Bowdoin College Library. Hereafter all references will be to these papers unless otherwise noted.

2. Heman Howard, *The Howard Genealogy: Descendents of John Howard of Bridgewater, Mass. from 1643 to 1903* (Brockton, Mass., 1903), 1.

3. Harry S. Howard to F. Couch, Feb. 8, 1895.

4. William A. Otis, *A Genealogical and Historical Memoir of the Otis Family of America* (Chicago, 1924), 55, 145.

5. Oliver Otis Howard, *Autobiography of Oliver Otis Howard: Major General United States Army* (New York, Baker & Taylor, 1907), I, 12–13. Though Howard refers to this association in his autobiography, he significantly makes no mention of it in two lengthy autobiographical letters written at the age of twenty to a sick cousin while Howard was a cadet at West Point, even though these letters contain much detail of his childhood. Howard to Augustus Howard, Aug. 14, Oct. 4, 1851.

6. Howard, *Autobiography*, I, 9–11.

7. *Ibid.*, 16.

8. Howard to Augustus Howard, Oct. 4, 1851.

9. Howard to his mother, Aug. 4, 1846; Howard to Augustus Howard, Oct. 4, 1851.

10. Howard to his mother, Feb. 27, 1847.
11. Howard to his mother, April 17, 1847.
12. ". . . I have a great desire to be a good writer. . . ." Howard to his mother, March 30, 1848.
13. O. O. Howard, MS Diary, Feb. 26, 1847.
14. Howard to his mother, July [26], 1849.
15. Howard to Rowland B. Howard, March 25 [1847].
16. Rowland Howard referred to his older brother as "your temperate self." Rowland B. Howard to Howard, Oct. 8, 1848. See also Howard to his mother, Oct. 29, 1848.
17. Howard to his mother, Aug. 16, 1848, March 26, 1849; Eliza Gilmore to Howard, April 7, 1849.
18. Eliza Gilmore to Howard, April 8, 24, 1847.
19. Howard to his mother, July 30, 1848.
20. Howard to his mother, Nov. 8, 1848.
21. Howard, *Autobiography*, I, 35–36; Howard to Augustus Howard, Dec. 5, 1851.
22. Eliza Gilmore to Howard, March 5, 1848.
23. Eliza Gilmore to Howard, April 20, 1849.
24. Howard to his mother, April 21, 1849.
25. Howard to his mother, May 10, 1849.
26. His pay was fourteen dollars a month at Leeds, eighteen at East Livermore. Howard, *Autobiography*, I, 36.
27. John Otis to Howard, June 20, 1850.
28. Howard to his mother, Dec. 8, 1850.
29. Howard, *Autobiography*, I, 41–42.
30. Howard to his mother, Aug. 24, 28, 1850.
31. Post Orders No. 3, Orders No. 51, Aug. 31, 1850, 439, United States Military Academy (hereafter referred to as USMA).
32. Howard to his mother, Aug. 28, 1850.
33. Howard to his mother, Sept. 22, 1850.
34. Howard to his mother, Oct. 10, 1850.
35. Howard to his mother, Aug. 28, Sept. 8, Oct. 10, Nov. 6, Dec. 20, 1850.
36. Howard to his mother, Dec. 20, 1850, April 19, May 9, 1851.
37. Howard to his mother, Sept. 27, 1851, April 11, 1852.
38. Howard to his mother, Sept. 27, 1851.
39. Howard to Rowland B. Howard, May [9], 1851.
40. He wrote a letter to his father, never sent, requesting his permission to resign, thus showing to what a state of despair he had come. July 27, 1851.
41. Howard to his mother, Aug. 23, 1851.
42. Howard to his mother, Sept. 27, 1851.
43. Howard, *Autobiography*, I, 53.
44. Howard to his mother, Aug. 31, 1852. The three were Cadets Abbot, Turnbull, and Wood.
45. Howard to his mother, Jan. 15, 1854.
46. Howard to his mother, Oct. 31, 1852.
47. J. E. B. Stuart to Howard, June 17, 1859. See also, Howard, *Autobiography*, I, 53.
48. Howard to his mother, Aug. 31, Nov. 13, 1853, Howard University (hereafter referred to as HU).
49. Howard to Rowland B. Howard, Oct. 17, 1852.

50. Howard's views are revealed in a letter written by his brother Rowland who was replying to Howard's arguments. Rowland B. Howard to Howard, April 10, 1854.
51. Howard to his mother, April 26, 1853.
52. Howard to his mother, June 19, 1853.
53. Orders, U. S. Corps of Cadets, Jan. 25, 1849—Dec. 28, 1859. Special Orders No. 4, Feb. 25, 1854, USMA.
54. Official Register of Officers and Cadets of the U. S. Military Academy 1834–1856.
55. Rowland B. Howard to Howard, Oct. 16, Nov. 6, 1853, Jan. 1, 1854.
56. Howard to his mother, Jan. 1, 1854, HU.
57. Howard to his mother, Feb. 12 [1854], HU.
58. Howard to his mother, April 30, 1854.
59. Howard to his mother, June 15, 1854.

Prewar Service in the Regular Army [12–22]

1. Howard at this time held the rank of brevet second lieutenant in the Ordnance Department. The notification from the War Department was signed by the secretary, Jefferson Davis. Davis to Howard, Aug. 7, 1854.
2. Howard to his mother, Oct. 3, 1854, HU.
3. Howard to his mother, Jan. 5, 1854 [1855], HU.
4. Rowland B. Howard to Howard, March 4, 1880; Howard, *Autobiography*, I, 66–67.
5. Howard to his mother, March 6, 1855, HU.
6. Mrs. Howard to Mrs. Gilmore, Sept. 9, 1855.
7. Howard to Charles H. Howard, Sept. 25, 1855.
8. Howard to his mother, July 1, 1855, HU.
9. Howard to his mother, April 8, 1855, HU.
10. Howard to his mother, Dec. 18, 1855.
11. Howard, *Autobiography*, I, 68–69.
12. S. Cooper to Howard, May 8, 1856.
13. J. Gorgas to Howard, July 30, 1856.
14. Howard to Rowland B. Howard, Aug. 4, 1856, HU.
15. Howard to Mrs. Howard, Aug. 20, 1856.
16. Howard to Mrs. Howard, Aug. 13, 20, Sept. 1, 1856.
17. Howard to his mother, Dec. 15, 1856.
18. Howard to his mother, Nov. 16, 1856.
19. Howard to his mother, Dec. 22, 1856.
20. Howard to his mother, Jan. 4, 1857.
21. Howard to Mrs. Howard, March 29, 1857.
22. See e.g. Howard to Mrs. Howard, Feb. 18, 1857.
23. Howard to Mrs. Howard, Jan. 23, 1857, HU; Howard to Mrs. Howard, March 15, 1857.
24. Howard to Mrs. Howard, Feb. 25, 1857.
25. Howard to Mrs. Howard, March 18, 29, April 12, 1857.
26. Howard to Mrs. Howard, March 15, 1857.
27. Howard to Mrs. Howard, April 12, 1857. Howard's pay in March 1857 was $120 a month. Howard to Mrs. Howard, March 8, 1857.
28. Howard to Mrs. Howard, April 26, 1857.
29. Howard to Mrs. Howard, May 15, 1857.
30. Howard to Mrs. Howard, April 15, 1857.

31. Howard to his mother, Nov. 26, 1854.
32. Howard to his mother, Nov. 16, 1856.
33. Howard to Mrs. Howard, Feb. 11, 1857.
34. Howard to Mrs. Howard, March 25, 1857.
35. Howard to his mother, Oct. 22, 1853, HU.
36. Rowland B. Howard to Howard, April 23, 1857; Mrs. Howard to Howard, May 3, 1857.
37. Howard to Mrs. Howard, May 24, 1857.
38. Howard to Mrs. Howard, May 26, 1857.
39. I John, 1:7.
40. Howard to Mrs. Howard, May 31, 1857.
41. Howard to Mrs. Howard, June 7, 9, July 26, 1857; Howard to his mother, June 15, 1857.
42. Rowland B. Howard to Howard, July 4, 1857.
43. Howard to Mrs. Howard, July 12, 18, 1857.
44. Mrs. Howard to Howard, Aug. 4, 1857. When Lizzie announced that she planned to name the baby Grace, Otis replied that he had only one objection and that was that many Negroes had that name and "our child might not like the association." It was a name, however, which would be satisfactory to him. Howard to Mrs. Howard, July 18, 1857.
45. S. Cooper to Howard, July 25, 1857; John Flynn to Howard, Aug. 30, 1857.
46. Howard to his mother, Sept. 22, 1857.
47. Howard to his mother, Dec. 6, 1857.
48. Peter Michie, "Reminiscences of Cadet and Army Service," *Personal Recollections of the War of the Rebellion* (N. Y., 1897), Military Order of the Loyal Legion (hereafter referred to as MOOLL), New York Commandery, 2d series, 196; Morris Schaff, *The Spirit of Old West Point, 1858-1862* (Boston and N. Y., 1907), 70.
49. Howard to his mother, Nov. 22, 1860.
50. Howard, MS Diary, April 21, 1858, HU.
51. Howard to his mother, Oct. 16, 1860.
52. Among the officers of the court was Major Robert Anderson soon to be the center of the nation's attention as commander of Fort Sumter in Charleston harbor. Howard, MS Diary, Dec. 20, 1858, HU.
53. Charles H. Howard to Howard, July 6, 1858; Howard to his mother, May 23, 1859; Howard, *Autobiography*, I, 96-97; Rowland B. Howard to Howard, July 3, 1860.
54. Howard to his mother, Dec. 1, 1860.
55. Hardee later commanded Confederate forces against Howard in Georgia and the Carolinas.
56. Howard, MS Diary, Feb. 25, 1858, HU. This was his permanent rank at the start of the Civil War when he resigned his commission in the regular army. His next regular army commission would be that of brigadier general!
57. Howard to his mother, Sept. 2, 1859, Feb. 28, 1860.
58. Howard to his mother, Sept. 29, 1857, HU.
59. Howard to Charles H. Howard, Oct. 24, 1857, HU; Howard to his mother, Dec. 6, 1857.
60. Howard to his mother, Nov. 6, 1857; Howard to Charles H. Howard, Jan. 7, 1858, HU.
61. Howard, MS Diary, Jan. 16, 1858, HU.
62. *Ibid.*, Dec. 28, 1858, HU.

63. *Ibid.*, Dec. 28, 1858, Jan. 9, 1859, HU.
64. Howard to his mother, Nov. 2, 1860.
65. Howard MS Diary, April 9, 1859, HU. Other entries of a similar nature: Nov. 21, 1857, Jan. 9, 1858, April 11, 1859.
66. Howard to his mother, Nov. 11, 1860.
67. Howard to his mother, Dec. 31, 1860.
68. Charles H. Howard to Howard, Jan. 17, 1861.
69. Howard to his mother, March 21, 1852. Howard expressed essentially the same views in 1870. Howard to A. H. Love, March 31, 1870.
70. [Capt.] J. S. Benton to Howard, May 9, 1861.
71. The War Department did permit many regular officers to resign their commissions to take positions in volunteer regiments. See Fred A. Shannon, *The Organization and Administration of the Union Army, 1861–1865* (Cleveland, 1928), I, 164. Lincoln on Aug. 28, 1861 directed the adjutant general to furnish officers of the grade of captain and below to the volunteers, and to permit those already with the volunteers to the extent of 100 to remain. Adjutant General's Office, Letters Received, P-343, National Archives (hereafter referred to as: AGO, LR, and NA).
72. Howard to his mother, May 15, 1861.
73. Howard, *Autobiography*, I, 112.

Brigade Command [23–35]

1. Howard to Mrs. Howard, May 29, 1861.
2. Blaine to Howard, May 29, 1861.
3. By resigning, Howard unknowingly forestalled his transfer to active duty with the Ordnance Department. Special Orders, No. 147, AGO, May 30, 1861, relieved Howard from duty at West Point and ordered him to report immediately by letter to the Colonel of Ordnance. This was in response to an appeal from Lt. Col. J. W. Ripley, Ordnance Department, to the Secretary of War dated May 30, 1861. AGO, LR, 0-52, NA.
4. H. L. Abbot and T. H. Ruger.
5. San Francisco *Chronicle*, May 23, 1872, quoted in N. Y. *Herald*, June 3, 1872.
6. Abner R. Small, *The Road to Richmond: The Civil War Memoirs of Major Abner R. Small of the Sixteenth Maine Volunteers*, Harold A. Small, ed. (Berkeley, University of California Press, 1939), 9.
7. Howard to Mrs. Howard, June 3, 1861.
8. Small, *Road to Richmond*, 10; William E. S. Whitman and Charles H. True, *Maine in the War for the Union* (Lewiston, Me., 1865), 60.
9. Howard, *Autobiography*, 131–34.
10. Lincoln attended a review of the Third Maine at Meridian Hill. Howard here met the President for the first time. O. O. Howard, "Personal Recollections of Abraham Lincoln," *Century*, LXXV (1908), 873.
11. Howard to Mrs. Howard, July 7, 1861.
12. The order was from McDowell's adjutant, July 6, 1861. Howard's reply stating that he was selecting the Fourth and Fifth Maine, and the Second Vermont in addition to his own regiment, is in the volume of letters sent of the Third Maine (Howard to Capt. J. W. Fry, July 8, 1861, NA). At the battle of Bull Run all four division commanders and eight of the eleven brigade commanders were West Point graduates. A ninth brigade commander, Andrew Porter, belonged to the regular army though he was not

an Academy man. On the other hand, of the forty regimental commanders only four were graduates of the Military Academy.
13. Howard to Mrs. Howard, July 15, 18, 20, 24, 1861; K. P. Williams, *Lincoln Finds a General* (N. Y., 1949–1959), I, 88–97; G. W. Bicknell, *History of the Fifth Regiment Maine Volunteers* (Portland, Me., 1871), 27–38; Howard, *Autobiography*, I, 152–62.
14. Howard to his mother, July 29, 1861.
15. Mrs. Howard to Howard, July 22, 1861.
16. Howard to Mrs. Howard, Aug. 25, 1861.
17. Howard to his mother, July 29, 1861.
18. Howard to Mrs. Howard, Aug. 8, 1861.
19. Washburn to Howard, Aug. 23, 1861.
20. Howard to his mother, Aug. 21, 1861.
21. Howard to Mrs. Howard, Sept. 4, 1861.
22. Regimental Order No. 53, Sept. 17, 1861, Regimental Letter and Order Book, Third Maine Infantry, 27, NA.
23. Howard to Charles H. Howard, Oct. 27, 1861.
24. Howard to Mrs. Howard, Oct. 31, 1861, May 23, 1862.
25. Howard to Mrs. Howard, Nov. 2, 10, 1861.
26. Howard to Mrs. Howard, Dec. 26, 1861.
27. Howard to Mrs. L. C. Holloway, Nov. 29, 1884.
28. Howard to Mrs. Howard, March 30, April 2, 1862; Thomas L. Livermore, *Days and Events: 1860–1866* (Boston and N. Y., 1920), 49–51. *The War of the Rebellion: A compilation of the Official Records of the Union and Confederate Armies* (Washington, 1880–1901), Series I, vol. 11, pt, 3, 44, 45, 47, 48; Series I, vol. 12, pt. 1, 412–14; cited hereafter as O. R. Since all references are to Series I, the series number hereafter will be omitted; O. R. to be followed by the volume number, part number (if any) and page, as O. R., 12; 1; 412–14.
29. Howard to Mrs. Howard, April 4, 1862.
30. Howard to Mrs. Howard, April 18, 1862.
31. Howard to Mrs. Howard, May 4, 1862.
32. Howard to Mrs. Howard, May 7, 1862.
33. Howard to Mrs. Howard, May 12, 1862.
34. David Hunter, commander of the Department of the South, on May 9, 1862 emancipated all slaves in this department by proclamation. Lincoln immediately repudiated the proclamation.
35. Howard to Mrs. Howard, May 17, 1862.
36. Hal Bridges, *Lee's Maverick General: Daniel Harvey Hill* (N. Y., 1961), 49.
37. Howard, *Autobiography*, I, 242–48; Howard's Report, June 1862, O. R., 11; 1; 769. Years later, Howard received the Medal of Honor for his gallantry at Fair Oaks.
38. Howard to Charles Harrop, March 26, 1883.
39. Howard to Mrs. Susan W. Scefridge, Dec. 19, 1892; Howard, *Autobiography*, I, 251.
40. Howard to Mrs. Howard, June 3, 1862. Howard soon learned to write legibly with his left hand. At the close of the previous summer Mrs. Howard and the children had moved from West Point to Auburn, Maine.
41. Charles H. Howard to Howard, June 29, July 2, 4, 1862; Rowland B. Howard to Mrs. Howard, July 16, 1862; H. Hamlin to Maj. Gen. Hiram G. Berry, July 18, 1862, in Edward K. Gould, *Major-General Hiram G.*

Berry (Rockland, Me., 1899), 191; Portland *Daily Advertiser*, July 4, 1862; Howard, *Autobiography*, I, 255; Howard to Mrs. Howard, Aug. 23, 1862.
  42. O. R., 12; 3; 702.
  43. Howard to Mrs. Howard, Aug. 28, 1862.
  44. O. R., 12; 3; 692.
  45. *Ibid.*, 722.
  46. Howard to Mrs. Howard, Sept. 4, 1862.
  47. Howard to Mrs. Howard, Sept. 8, 1862.
  48. Officers of Howard's Brigade to Maj. Gen. G. W. McClellan [Sept. 10, 1862], Appointments, Commissions, Promotions Branch of the Adjutant General's Office, NA (hereafter referred to as ACP, NA).
  49. On Sept. 13, 1862, Sedgwick was placed in temporary command of the 12th (Banks') Corps, and Howard was given command of the First Division. (O. R., 19; 2; 283.) The old arrangement was restored when General Joseph K. F. Mansfield took command of the 12th Corps (*Ibid.*, 297.).
  50. Howard to Mrs. Howard, Sept. 8, 1862.

Division and Corps Command [36–43]

  1. Howard to Guy Howard, Sept. 7, 1862.
  2. Howard to Mrs. Howard, Sept. 10, 1862.
  3. Howard to Mrs. Howard, Sept. 26, 1862.
  4. *Ibid.*
  5. The details of this portion of the battle are from Howard's Report, O. R., 19; 1; 306. See also, George A. Bruce, *The Twentieth Regiment of Massachusetts Volunteer Infantry, 1861–1865* (Boston, 1906), 166–71.
  6. Howard to Mrs. Howard, Oct. 14, 1862.
  7. Howard to Charles H. Howard, Nov. 8, 1862.
  8. Howard to Mrs. Howard, Nov. 9, 1862.
  9. O. R., 19; 2; 583.
  10. Howard to Mrs. Howard, Dec. 2, 1862.
  11. Howard to Mrs. Howard, Nov. 14, 1862.
  12. Washburn to Howard, Nov. 20, 1862.
  13. H. Hamlin and others to Lincoln, Dec. 22, 1862, ACP, NA.
  14. McClellan to the Adjutant General, Oct. 27, 1862, Army of the Potomac, Letters Sent (hereafter referred to as LS), NA.
  15. Howard to his mother, Dec. 7, 1862.
  16. Howard to Mrs. Howard, Dec. 13, 1862.
  17. O. R., 21; 90, 94.
  18. "I did hope for success in the last battle, I prayed for it when Hooker's men were giving way, but it was not the will of God." Howard to Mrs. Howard, Dec. 26, 1862.
  19. O. R., 21; 219.
  20. *Ibid.*, 224.
  21. Howard to Mrs. Howard, Jan. 1, 1863.
  22. New York *Times*, Jan. 16, 1863.
  23. Journal of the Executive Proceedings of the Senate, XIII, 89, 90, 128, 211, 212, 261.
  24. Howard to Mrs. Howard, Jan. 27, 1863.
  25. Howard to Mrs. Howard, Jan. 30, 1863.

26. Howard to Mrs. Howard, Feb. 10, March 5, 8, 22, 1863.
27. O. R., 25; 2; 51.
28. Howard to Gen. S. Williams, Assistant Adjutant General (hereafter referred to as AAG), March 23, 1863, Generals' Papers and Books, NA; Howard to Mrs. Howard, March 18, 1863.
29. Howard to Mrs. Howard, March 31, 1863; O. R., 25; 2; 176.
30. Augustus C. Hamlin, *The Battle of Chancellorsville* (Bangor, Me., 1896), 26–33; ". . . somewhat more than half . . . were German or of foreign lineage." Ella Lonn, *Foreigners in the Union Army and Navy* (Baton Rouge, 1951), 513.
31. Edward C. Culp, *The 25th Ohio Vet. Vol. Infantry in the War for the Union* (Topeka, Kan., 1885), 59.
32. Walter H. Hebert, *Fighting Joe Hooker* (Indianapolis, 1944), 178.
33. Howard to Mrs. Howard, April 3, 12, 1863.

Chancellorsville and Gettysburg [44–58]

1. Howard to Mrs. Howard, May 1, 1863.
2. O. R., 25; 2; 324.
3. *Ibid.*, 328.
4. See Douglas S. Freeman, *R. E. Lee: A Biography* (N. Y., 1934–1935), II, 520; also Freeman's *Lee's Lieutenants: A Study in Command* (N. Y., 1942–1944), II, 539–40.
5. John Bigelow, Jr., *The Campaign of Chancellorsville: A Strategic and Tactical Study* (New Haven, Yale U. Press, 1910), 276.
6. O. R., 25; 2; 360–61.
7. The separate order to Howard as quoted in Bigelow (276–77) is somewhat shorter.
8. Oliver O. Howard, "The Eleventh Corps at Chancellorsville," *Battles and Leaders of the Civil War* (N. Y., 1884, 1888), III, 196; Carl Schurz, *The Reminiscences of Carl Schurz* (N. Y., 1907–1908), II, 417.
9. Bigelow, *Chancellorsville*, 279.
10. *Ibid.*, 336–37.
11. Army of the Potomac, LS, III, 307, NA.
12. O. R., 25; 1; 630; Bigelow, *Chancellorsville*, 283–85; Hartwell Osborn, "On the Right at Chancellorsville," *Military Essays and Recollections* (Chicago, 1907), MOOLL, Illinois Commandery, IV, 182–83; Adin B. Underwood, *The Three Years' Service of the Thirty-Third Mass. Infantry Regiment 1862-1865* (Boston, 1881), 36.
13. "I . . . did believe, with all the other officers that he [Jackson] was making for Orange Court House." Howard to Rev. J. E. Rankin, Aug. 5, 1869.
14. Hamlin, *Chancellorsville*, 55–62.
15. "My scouts reports were instantly and constantly reported to Genl Hooker." Howard to Rev. J. E. Rankin, Aug. 5, 1869.
16. Owen Rice, "Afield with the Eleventh Corps at Chancellorsville," *Sketches of War History* (Cincinnati, 1888), MOOLL, Ohio Commandery, I, 379. See also, William Simmers and Paul Bachschmid, *The Volunteer's Manual: or Ten Months with the 153 Penn'a Volunteers* (Easton, Pa., 1863), 22.
17. O. R., 25; 1; 628.
18. Bigelow, *Chancellorsville*, 292, 295, 296.

19. Howard to John A. Owens, Aug. 5, 1881; Bigelow, *Chancellorsville*, 296–97; Howard to Mrs. Howard, May 12, 1863; Osborn, "On the Right at Chancellorsville," 188.
20. Bigelow, *Chancellorsville*, 300–01.
21. *Ibid.*, 303–04; Howard to Mrs. Howard, May 7, 1863.
22. Bigelow, *Chancellorsville*, 322–23, 337; R. E. Colston, commanding the second Confederate line, wrote in 1886: "The halt at that time was not a mistake, but a necessity." "Lee's Knowledge of Hooker's Movements," *Century*, XXXII, n.s., X (1886), 782; William R. Livermore, *The Story of the Civil War* (N. Y., 1933), Part III, Book I, 174–77.
23. The corps took no active part in the severe fighting on May 3, nor in the rest of the campaign.
24. Meade said that the vote was 4–2. Meade to Mrs. Meade, May 10, 1863, George G. Meade, *The Life and Letters of George Gordon Meade*, George G. Meade, ed. (N. Y., 1913), I, 374. Bigelow, *Chancellorsville*, 420.
25. *Report of the Joint Committee on the Conduct of the War*, 38th Congress, 2d Session, I, 78, 135.
26. "[The troops] should not be discouraged or depressed, for it is no fault of theirs (if I may except one corps) that our last efforts were not crowned with glorious victory." O. R., 25; 2; 438.
27. Bigelow, *Chancellorsville*, 480. Most writers adhere to this conclusion, e.g. William Swinton, *Campaigns of the Army of the Potomac* (N. Y., 1882), 306; Livermore, *The Story of the Civil War*, Part III, Book I, 183.
28. See, J. G. Nicolay to Therena Bates, May 10, 1863, Nicolay Papers, Library of Congress (hereafter referred to as LC); Heintzelman MS Journal, May 13, 1863, LC; James Gillette to his mother, May 9, 1863, Gillette Papers, LC.
29. Many years later Howard admitted that Chancellorsville was the only battle, after he had become a corps commander, that he did not extensively reconnoitre the position in person or by thoroughly trusted officers. Howard to J. T. Lockman, Jan. 1, 1897.
30. *Report of the Joint Committee on the Conduct of the War*, 38th Congress, 2d Session, I, xlix; Hebert, *Fighting Joe Hooker*, 223.
31. Howard to J. A. Owens, Aug. 5, 1881.
32. Army of the Potomac, LS, III, 319–20, NA. See also Hooker's order relieving Averell, May 3, 1863, O. R., 25; 2; 383.
33. Howard to F. W. Haskell, Dec. 31, 1884.
34. For a more detailed account of Howard's part in this battle, see the author's "O. O. Howard: General at Chancellorsville," *Civil War History*, III (March, 1957), 47–63.
35. N. Y. *Herald*, May 6, 1863; N. Y. *Tribune*, May 6, 1863.
36. N. Y. *Herald*, May 12, 1863.
37. Howard to Mrs. Howard, May 12, 1863.
38. *Report of the Joint Committee on the Conduct of the War*, 38th Congress, 2d Session, I, 151.
39. Howard to Mrs. Howard, May 22, 1863. In an article entitled "Personal Recollections of Abraham Lincoln" written in 1908, Howard stated: "I was made to realize very soon, especially after the defeat of Chancellorsville, that Mr. Lincoln had become very strongly my friend. He would not suffer me to be removed from the head of the corps until it had had another trial. He closed his answer to my opposers and critics with the

words, 'Give him time, and he will bring things straight.'" *Century*, LXXV (1908), 876.

40. In J. W. Schuckers, *The Life and Public Services of Salmon Portland Chase* (N. Y., D. Appleton & Co., 1874), 467. W. C. Bryant, editor of the N. Y. *Evening Post*, wrote Lincoln asking for the reinstatement of Sigel. May 11, 1863, Robert Todd Lincoln Collection of Papers of Abraham Lincoln, LC.

41. O. R., 27; 3; 69.

42. Louis C. Hatch, ed., *Maine: A History* (N. Y., 1919), II, 451-53.

43. N. A. Farwell to Howard, June 12, 1863; F. B. Gilman to Howard, April 24, 1863.

44. Howard to Mrs. Howard, June 24, 1863.

45. Hatch, ed., *Maine: A History*, II, 454.

46. O. R., 27; 3; 375.

47. Howard to Rowland B. Howard, May 16, 1863.

48. O. R. 27; 3; 419-20.

49. Howard to Prof. M. Jacobs, March 23, 1864.

50. Howard to Prof. S. P. Bates, Dec. 14, 1875.

51. Howard to Prof. H. Coppée, March 4, 1864.

52. O. R., 27; 1; 702.

53. Howard to Prof. H. Coppée, March 4, 1864.

54. O. R., 27; 1; 703.

55. Charles H. Howard to E. Whittlesey, July 9, 1863.

56. R. L. Ashhurst, *Remarks on Certain Questions Relating to the First Day's Fight at Gettysburg* (Philadelphia, 1897), 25; O. R., 27; 3; 465.

57. O. R., 27; 1; 704, 751. Jubal A. Early wrote in 1877: "The enemy had begun firing with artillery from Cemetery Hill as soon as my line was formed, and still continued it." "Causes of Lee's Defeat at Gettysburg," *Southern Historical Society Papers*, IV (1877), 254.

58. Howard to S. P. Bates, Sept. 14, 1875; E. P. Halsted, "Incidents of the First Day at Gettysburg," *Battles and Leaders*, III, 285.

59. There are numerous sources which support this view including the reports of various Confederate commanders. O. R., 27; 2; 317-18, 445, 555, 607. See also, Schurz, *Reminiscences*, III, 18-19; Early, "Causes of Lee's Defeat at Gettysburg," 66-67; A. J. Fremantle, *Three Months in the Southern States: April, June, 1863* (Mobile, Ala., 1864), 128; Freeman, *Lee's Lieutenants*, III, 97-98; R. E. Lee, III, 69; and especially Williams, *Lincoln Finds a General*, II, 689-91.

60. Butterfield to Hancock, O. R., 27; 3; 461; Winfield S. Hancock, "Gettysburg: Reply to General Howard," *Galaxy*, XXII (1876), 822.

61. This view is effectively stated in Jesse B. Young, *The Battle of Gettysburg: A Comprehensive Narrative* (N. Y., 1913), 209. The diary of Colonel Charles S. Wainwright seems to imply that Hancock was on the field issuing orders while the 1st Corps, to which Wainwright was attached as an artillery officer, was still fighting to the west of Gettysburg. This must, however, be an error because even Hancock makes no such claim. Also, Wainwright in the same diary entry states that after he had reached Cemetery Hill he "neither saw nor heard anything of him [Hancock]. . . ." Charles S. Wainwright, *A Diary of Battle: The Personal Journals of Colonel Charles S. Wainwright 1861-1865*, edited by Allan Nevins (N. Y., Harcourt, Brace, & World, 1962), 236-37.

62. See e.g. Warren's testimony in the *Report of the Joint Committee on the Conduct of the War* (1865), I, 377; Swinton, *Campaigns of the Army of the Potomac*, 335; Comte de Paris, *History of the Civil War in America* (Philadelphia, 1883), III, 572–73. But see also Henry E. Tremain, *Two Days of War: A Gettysburg Narrative and Other Excursions* (N. Y., 1905), 27.
63. O. R., 27; 1; 696.
64. *Ibid.*, 366. In this dispatch Hancock indicated that his arrival time was 4:25 and not 3:00 as he wrote later in his report. *Ibid.*, 368.
65. O. R., 27; 3; 466. Confusion over the command existed well into evening. At 9:30 Sickles stated in a dispatch to Meade's chief of staff: "General Hancock is not in command—General Howard commands." *Ibid.*, 468.
66. O. R., 27; 1; 696–97.
67. *Ibid.*, 73.
68. Howard to Meade, 2:15 P.M., July 3, 1863, *ibid.*, 697.
69. Howard to Mrs. Howard, July 5, 9, 1863.
70. For a time during these operations Howard had command of the Center, comprising the 5th and 11th Corps. O. R., 27; 3; 533.
71. Meade to Halleck, July 13, 1863, O. R., 27; 1; 91; Stephen M. Weld, *War Diary and Letters of Stephen Minot Weld, 1861–1865* ([Cambridge, Mass.], 1912), 241–42; *Report of the Joint Committee on the Conduct of the War* (1865), I, 336, 381; Howard, *Autobiography*, I, 444–45. But see, John Hay, *Lincoln and the Civil War in the Diaries and Letters of John Hay*, Tyler Dennett, ed. (N. Y., 1939), 68.
72. N. Y. *Tribune*, July 16, 1863.
73. O. R., 27; 1; 700. The original is in the Robert Todd Lincoln Collection of Papers of Abraham Lincoln, LC.
74. July 21, 1863; Meade, *Life and Letters of George Gordon Meade*, II, 138.
75. Howard to Halleck, July 29, 1863, O. R., 27; 3; 778.
76. Steinwehr to Howard, July 29, 1863, *ibid.*, 779–80.
77. Buschbeck to Steinwehr, Smith to Steinwehr, July 30, 1863, *ibid.*, 785–86.
78. Howard to Mrs. Howard, July 31, 1863.
79. Howard to Mrs. Howard, Aug. 29, 1863.
80. Howard to Mrs. Howard, Aug. 30, 1863. The First Division (Gordon's) was detached from the Army of the Potomac, August 5, 1863. O. R., 29; 2; 7. Meade's returns for August, 1863 showed the 11th Corps having about 6500 officers and men present for duty. *Ibid.*, 118.
81. Howard to Mrs. Howard, Sept. 23, 1863.
82. O. R., 29; 1; 148.
83. *Ibid.*, 158.
84. Howard to Mrs. Howard, Oct. 13, 1863.
85. "I met Mr Lincoln several times during the war and always entertained for him feelings of confidence and esteem, and finally of great personal affection. The last time I saw him was in the fall after Gettysburg at the White House. It was just prior to my leaving the Army of the Potomac for the West with a part of the 11th Corps. He gave me his map, which being 'mounted,' was in his judgment better than mine for field service. This was after we had conversed for some time upon the military situation in the vicinity of Knoxville & of Chattanooga and just as I was about leaving his room. I used the

map thereafter & have it still." Howard to O. H. Oldroyd, Jan. 13, 1882. See also Howard, "Personal Recollections of Abraham Lincoln," 877.
86. Howard to Mrs. Howard, Oct. 1, 1863.

Western Victories [59–72]

1. Howard to Mrs. Howard, Oct. 5, 10, 1863.
2. O. R., 30; 4; 404.
3. Howard to Mrs. Howard, Oct. 24, 1863. See also O. O. Howard, "Grant at Chattanooga," *Personal Recollections of the War of the Rebellion* (N. Y., 1891), MOOLL, N. Y. Commandery, 246–47.
4. Howard to Mrs. Howard, Oct. 30, 1863.
5. O. R., 31; 1; 72.
6. Howard to Mrs. Howard, Oct. 30, 1863.
7. Howard to Mrs. Howard, Nov. 25, 1863.
8. Thomas to Howard, 8:45 A.M., Nov. 25, 1863, O. R., 31; 2; 113–14. Buschbeck's Report, *ibid.,* 360–61.
9. *Ibid.,* 49–50.
10. Burnside to Howard, 2 A.M., Dec. 6 [1863]; also, O. R., 52; 1; 500.
11. O. R., 31; 2; 581.
12. Sherman to Howard, Dec. 18, 1863; also, O. R., 31; 3; 439–40.
13. Schurz, *Reminiscences,* III, 79–80.
14. One of Sherman's staff officers, George W. Nichols, late in the war wrote: "General Sherman may not be a religious man in the sense that Howard is, but he valued and respected Howard all the more for his Christian faith and practice. In the direction of a march, in the accomplishment of an arduous or dangerous duty, when speed and certainty were required, he knew that Howard would never fail him." George W. Nichols, *The Story of the Great March: From the Diary of a Staff Officer* (N. Y., 1865), Feb. 5, 1865, 142.
15. Howard to Mrs. Howard, Dec. 20. 1863.
16. Blaine to Howard, Jan. 28, 1864.
17. *Congressional Globe,* Jan. 18, 1864, 38th Congress, 1st Session, pt. 1, 257.
18. *Ibid.,* 421.
19. Philadelphia *Evening Bulletin,* Feb. 8, 1864.
20. *Army and Navy Journal,* Feb. 20, 1864, I, 403.
21. Howard to Blaine, Feb. 23, 1864.
22. Howard to Hancock, Feb. 25, 1864.
23. Hancock to Howard, March 14, 1864.
24. Howard to G. H. Stuart, March 8, 1864, G. H. Stuart Papers, LC.
25. E. B. Webb to Howard, March 15, 1864.
26. Howard to Mrs. Howard, April 4, 1864.
27. *Ibid.*
28. O. R., 32; 3; 258; also, Sherman to Howard, April 5, 1864.
29. In February, when Schofield's confirmation by the Senate as commander of the Department and Army of the Ohio was in doubt, Halleck wired Grant asking him to name some alternates in the event Schofield was rejected. In his reply Grant named in order: J. B. McPherson, P. H. Sheridan, and O. O. Howard. Halleck to Grant, Feb. 14, 1864, O. R., 32; 2; 389; Grant to Halleck, Feb. 15, 1864, *ibid.,* 394.

30. O. R., 38; 4; 113, 114, 126.
31. Sherman to Howard, May 13, 1864, *ibid.,* 162.
32. Journal of Lt. Col. Joseph S. Fullerton, May 14, 1864, O. R., 38; 1; 854. See also Howard to Thomas, May 14, 1864, O. R., 38; 4; 178; Howard to Col. F. A. Seely, March 29, 1882; Charles F. Morse, *Letters Written During the Civil War* ([n. p.], 1898), 165.
33. O. R., 38; 1; 66.
34. "I . . . am now turning the enemy's right flank, I think." Howard to Thomas, 4:35 P.M., May 27, 1864, O. R., 38; 4; 324.
35. Two regimental histories criticized Howard for failure to co-ordinate the attacks, and to send up adequate reinforcements. Alexis Cope, *The Fifteenth Ohio Volunteers and Its Campaigns* (Columbus, Ohio, 1916), 450–73; Robert L. Kimberly and Ephraim S. Holloway, *The Forty-First Ohio Veteran Volunteer Infantry in the War of the Rebellion* (Cleveland, 1897), 83–88. William B. Hazen, in command of a brigade, called this engagement, "the most fierce, bloody, and persistent assault by our troops in the Atlanta Campaign." *A Narrative of Military Service* (Boston, 1885), 256.
36. O. R., 38; 1; 68.
37. O. R., 38; 4; 602.
38. See Howard to Thomas, June 27, 1864, *ibid.,* 612; Howard to Mrs. Howard, June 28, 1864.
39. Howard to Thomas, July 4, 1864, O. R., 38; 5; 43; Howard to Mrs. Howard, July 7, 1864.
40. O. R., 38; 5; 96; Howard's Report, O. R., 38: 1; 200–01. O. M. Poe, Sherman's engineer officer, wrote his wife: "We did expect some trouble at Pace's Ferry, in laying the Pontoon Bridges, but Genl. Howard's (4th) Corps having crossed at Powers' Ferry, three miles above, the Division of T. J. Wood, swept down the river bank, and secured the ground where we wanted the bridge to rest, taking the rebels somewhat by surprise." July 18, 1864, Poe Papers, LC.
41. Howard to Schofield, July 21, 1864, O. R., 38; 5; 218.
42. Lloyd Lewis, *Sherman, Fighting Prophet* (N. Y., 1932), 388–89; Manning F. Force, *General Sherman* (N. Y., 1899), 332; John A. Logan, *The Volunteer Soldier of America* (Chicago & N. Y., 1887), 48–50; William T. Sherman, *Personal Memoirs of Gen. W. T. Sherman* (N. Y., 1890), II, 85; Sherman to Halleck, July 27, Aug. 16, 1864, O. R., 38; 5; 271–72, 522–23. For a complete discussion of this subject see James P. Jones, "The Battle of Atlanta and McPherson's Successor," *Civil War History,* VII (Dec., 1961), 399–405.
43. Force, *General Sherman,* 229; John G. Nicolay and John Hay, *Abraham Lincoln: A History* (N. Y., 1917), IX, 277; O. R., 38; 5; 240, 261.
44. *Ibid.,* 277.
45. O. R., 38; 3; 40.
46. *Ibid.,* 41.
47. Alfred H. Burne, *Lee, Grant, and Sherman: A Study in Leadership in the 1864–65 Campaign* (Aldershot [U. K.], Gale & Polden, 1938), 110.
48. "At Ezra Church the prescience of General Howard and the speed with which his troops entrenched themselves saved the day." *Ibid.,* 112.
49. Howard to Mrs. Howard, July 29, 1864.
50. O. R., 38; 3; 43.
51. *Ibid.;* Blair to Col. W. G. Clark, AAG, Aug. 29, 1864.
52. O. R., 38; 3; 44.

53. *Ibid.,* 88.
54. Howard to Sherman, Aug. 31, 1864, O. R., 38; 5; 725.
55. Sherman to Howard, Aug. 31, 1864, *ibid.,* 726.
56. Aug. 31, 1864, *ibid.*
57. 2 P.M. Aug. 31, 1864, O. R., 52; 1; 612–13.
58. Howard to Sherman, Aug. 31, 1864, O. R., 38; 5; 727.
59. Sherman to Halleck, Sept. 4, 1864, *ibid.,* 792.
60. Sherman to Halleck, Sept. 3, 1864, *ibid.,* 777.

The End of the War [73–86]

1. Howard to Mrs. Howard, Sept. 15, 1864.
2. Howard to Mrs. Howard, Sept. 22, 1864.
3. Howard to Mrs. Howard, Nov. 11, 1864.
4. O. R., 39; 1; 734; Sherman to Howard, Nov. 12, 1864, O. R., 39; 3; 750.
5. Charles A. Willison, *Reminiscences of a Boy's Service with the 76th Ohio* (Menasha, Wisc. [1908]), 101; D. Leib Ambrose, *History of the Seventh Regiment Illinois Volunteer Infantry* (Springfield, Ill., 1868), 281. See also, Charles W. Wills, *Army Life of an Illinois Soldier* (Washington, 1906), 327–28; Joseph A. Saunier, ed., *A History of the Forty-Seventh Regiment Ohio Veteran Volunteer Infantry* (Hillsboro, Ohio [1903]), 357–58; Charles F. Hubert, *History of the Fiftieth Regiment Illinois Volunteer Infantry in the War of the Union* (Kansas City, 1894), 325–26.
6. O. R., 44; 13.
7. Howard to Sherman, Nov. 23, 1864, O. R., 44; 67. See also O. R., 44; 521, and Howard to Kilpatrick, Nov. 21, 1864, *ibid.,* 508–09.
8. William Duncan, "The Army of the Tennessee under Major-General O. O. Howard," *Glimpses of the Nation's Struggle* (St. Paul, 1898), 4th Series, MOOLL, Minnesota Commandery, 170.
9. O. R., 44; 658.
10. Maj. Gen. J. C. Foster to Halleck, Dec. 12, 1864, *ibid.,* 699. Duncan, "The Army of the Tennessee under Major-General O. O. Howard," 170–74.
11. O. R., 44; 677; Howard, *Autobiography,* II, 87.
12. O. R., 44; 683–84.
13. *Ibid.,* 72, 366.
14. *Ibid.,* 692. See also, Hazen, *A Narrative of Military Service,* 330.
15. For an account of the capture of the fort see T. W. Connelly, *History of the Seventieth Ohio Regiment* (Cincinnati [1902]), 136–38.
16. Howard to Mrs. Howard, Dec. 26, 1864.
17. Some of the incidents of Stanton's trip are related in, E. D. Townsend, *Anecdotes of the Civil War in the United States* (N. Y., 1884), 115–17.
18. Howard to Mrs. Howard, Jan. 13, 1865.
19. Howard to F. A. Flower, April 18, 1887. See also Howard to his mother, April 17, 1865.
20. John G. Barrett in *Sherman's March Through the Carolinas* (Chapel Hill, 1956) minimizes the military importance of this campaign and contends that Thomas at Nashville made a greater contribution by destroying Hood's army. He does recognize the psychological importance of Sherman's campaign. See especially 280–81.
21. Sherman to Grant, Jan. 2, 1865, O. R., 47; 2; 6–7.
22. O. R. 47; 2; 50–51.

23. Howard to Sherman, Feb. 3, 1865, *ibid.,* 286.
24. "Rained all day. . . . Worst marching for troops I ever saw; had to wade much of the time. . . ." March 8, 1865; Manning F. Force, "Marching Across Carolina," *Sketches of War History* (Cincinnati, 1888), MOOLL, Ohio Commandery, I, 7–8. "Marched 8 miles, 4 miles through knee deep mud and water. Then made corduroy bridges and lifted wagons out of the mire till daylight." March 16, 1865, James L. Matthews, "Civil War Diary of Sergeant James Louis Matthews," *Indiana Magazine of History,* XXIV (1928), 311.
25. Two judicious accounts of the burning of Columbia are: James F. Rhodes, "Who Burned Columbia?" *American Historical Review,* VII (1902), 485–93, and James D. Hill, "The Burning of Columbia Reconsidered," *South Atlantic Quarterly,* XXV (1926), 269–82.
26. E.g., William G. Simms, *Sack and Destruction of the City of Columbia, S. C.* ([Atlanta], 1937), and Harriette C. Keatinge, *Narrative of the Burning of Columbia, S. C., Feb. 17, 1865, and Journey to Fayetteville, N. C. with Sherman's Army, Feb.–Mar. 1865,* Typescript, Manuscripts Division, LC.
27. O. R., 47; 1; 198–99, 227–28, 243, 252, 265.
28. *Ibid.,* 199.
29. See, Michael C. Garber, Jr., "Reminiscences of the Burning of Columbia, South Carolina," *Indiana Magazine of History,* XI (1915), 291.
30. O. R., 47; 2; 475. A division commander in the 15th Corps issued an order Feb. 18 that regimental commanders should send in names of officers "who last night were conducting themselves in any way ungentlemanly or unbecoming officers. It is reported that some of the officers of this command *even* participated with their men in the outrageous conduct that last night characterized portions of our army." 15th Army Corps, vol. 22, Book 55, 161, NA.
31. Howard to Doctor Goodwyn, Mayor of Columbia, Feb. 19, 1865, O. R., 47; 2; 485. The cattle were reported to be old and tough, but the city fed on them for several weeks. James G. Gibbs, *The Burning of Columbia* (Typescript [1908]), Manuscripts Division, LC.
32. Connelly, *History of the Seventieth Ohio Regiment,* 149.
33. McCarter Journal, 83, Manuscripts Division, LC.
34. Sherman to Howard, March 14, 1865, O. R., 47; 2; 822.
35. O. R., 47; 1; 423; Sherman to Howard March 18, 1865, O. R., 47; 2; 886.
36. *Ibid.,* 908–09.
37. Hazen to Maj. Max Woodhull, AAG, March 20, 1865, *ibid.,* 915.
38. Howard to Sherman, March 22, 1865, *ibid.,* 952.
39. The appointment was to date from the fall of Savannah, ACP, NA. See also, N. Y. *Tribune,* March 1, 1865.
40. Journal of the Executive Proceedings of the Senate, XIV, 208, 218.
41. Lt. Col. W. E. Strong, AAG, to Howard, April 6, 1865; Sherman to Howard, April 7, 1865, O. R., 47; 3; 119.
42. *Ibid.,* 180.
43. Howard to his mother, April 17, 1865.
44. Howard to Mrs. Howard, April 29, 1865.
45. Grant to Howard, May 7, 1865, O. R., 47; 3; 421.
46. Howard to F. A. Flower, April 18, 1887.
47. Howard to Mrs. Howard, Jan. 6, 1865.
48. Howard, *Autobiography,* II, 208.
49. Howard to Mrs. Howard, April 29, 1865.

50. Sherman to Howard, May 17, 1865; also found in O. R., 47; 3; 515–16. See also, Sherman to J. E. Yeatman, May 21, 1865, Sherman's Letter Book, LS, April 14—May 27, 1865, 159–61, NA.
51. Henry Hitchcock, *Marching with Sherman: Passages from the Letters and Campaign Diaries of Henry Hitchcock*, M. A. DeWolfe Howe, ed. (New Haven, Yale University Press, 1927), 321; *National Intelligencer*, May 25, 1865; O. O. Howard, "Remarks in Commemoration of General William Tecumseh Sherman," *Personal Recollections of the War of Rebellion* (N. Y. 1897), MOOLL, N. Y. Commandery, 2d Series, 59–60.
52. William F. G. Shanks, *Personal Recollections of Distinguished Generals* (N. Y., 1866), 302–03.
53. Nichols, *The Story of the Great March*, 142.
54. MS Diary, Feb. 3, 1865, Bowdoin College Library; David P. Conyngham, *Sherman's March Through the South* (N. Y., 1865), 54.
55. See Howard's report of the Atlanta campaign, O. R., 38; 1; 199.
56. Osborn wrote of Howard's "persistent fighting when engaged, and determination to win; [and] the reckless disregard of his own person." MS Diary, Feb. 3, 1865.
57. After Fredericksburg, Howard wrote: "I believe I always have good commanding officers [reference to Couch and Sedgwick] at least I have the good fortune to get along well with them." Howard to Mrs. Howard, Dec. 26, 1862. See also Sherman's remarks in O. R., 38; 1; 84.
58. O. R., 38; 3; 55.
59. Howard to Sherman, Jan. 17, 1865, O. R., 47; 2; 70.
60. *Ibid.*, 429.
61. T. A. Meysenburg to Howard, June 9, 1865.

Early Months of Freedmen's Bureau [87–102]

1. U. S. Statutes at Large, XIII, 507.
2. Sherman to J. E. Yeatman, May 21, 1865, Sherman Letter Book, LS, April 14—May 27, '65, 159–61, NA; Thomas L. Fletcher to the President, March 21, 1865, Records of the Bureau of Refugees, Freedmen, and Abandoned Lands, LR, F-42, NA (hereafter Bureau records will be referred to as BR); Clara Barton to Sen. Henry Wilson, March 9, 1865, Clara Barton Papers, LC; S. P. Chase to Stanton, May 20, 1865, Stanton Papers, LC.
3. *Dictionary of American Biography*, XX, 607.
4. The *National Freedman*, stated, "we have cause to rejoice at the wisdom which has selected so good and so capable a man as Maj. Gen. O. O. Howard. Gen. Howard's connection with our armies has made him acquainted with the condition of the negro population and the measures needed for their relief. His known character as a Christian soldier, greatly increases our confidence and esteem." This view the *Freedmen's Record* seconded: "All agree that a better appointment could not have been made." *National Freedman*, June 1865, vol. 1, no. 5, 164; *Freedmen's Record*, July 1865, vol. 1, no. 7, 107.
5. O. O. Howard "Address at Augusta, Maine," *National Freedman*, August 15, 1865, vol. 1, no. 7, 233.
6. Howard, *Autobiography*, II, 163–93. The most comprehensive history of the Bureau is that by George R. Bentley, *A History of the Freedmen's Bureau* (Philadelphia, 1955). It supplants an older work by Paul S. Peirce, *The Freedmen's Bureau* (Iowa City, 1904). Both have extensive material on

government activities on behalf of the freedmen during the war years, before the founding of the Bureau. See e.g. Bentley, *Freedmen's Bureau*, 16–29.

7. *Ibid.*, 26, 89–91.
8. Howard to Mrs. Howard, Sept. 22, 1864.
9. Howard, "Address at Augusta, Maine," 233–39.
10. BR, Circulars and Circular Letters, 1, May 15, 1865, NA.
11. *Ibid.*, 2, May 19, 1865, NA.
12. *Ibid.*, 3, May 22, 1865, NA.
13. Howard to Halleck, May 27, 1865, BR, LS, I, 11, NA; John Eaton, *Grant, Lincoln and the Freedmen* (N. Y., 1907), 237–38.
14. BR, Circulars and Circular Letters, 5, May 30, 1865, NA.
15. Howard to Stanton, May 30, 1865, BR, LS, I, 21, NA.
16. Howard to the Officers of the various Associations for Freedmen & Refugees, June 17, 1865, BR, LS, I, 65, NA.
17. Howard, *Autobiography*, II, 218–19.
18. Howard, "Address at Augusta, Maine," 233–34.
19. Howard to Stanton, Sept. 13, 1865, BR, LS, I, 276, NA.
20. Fullerton sent back very critical reports stating that nothing was being done and that Saxton should have Georgia taken from him. Fullerton to Howard, July 23, 1865, BR, LR, F-122, NA.
21. Howard to Kiddoo, Nov. 27, 1866.
22. Griffin to Howard, May 4, 1867, BR, LR, T-150, NA.
23. Howard to Stanton, Oct. 30, 1865, BR, LS, I, 419, NA.
24. Howard to E. B. Ward, Oct. 7, 1868.
25. Wright to Sheridan, Dec. 18, 1865, BR, LR, G-11, NA.
26. Sprague to Howard, June 30, 1865, BR, LR, S-252, NA.
27. Brown to Howard, Aug. 16, 1865, BR, LR, B-58, NA.
28. Saxton to Howard, Sept. 9, 1865, BR, S-171, NA.
29. Kiddoo to Howard, May 14, 1866, BR, LR, T-145, NA.
30. E.g. Thomas M. Vincent, AAG, to Commanding General, Dep't. of Virginia, Jan. 11, 1866, BR, LR, A-20, NA.
31. Howard to a Gentleman in Virginia, March 27, 1868.
32. Tillson to Gov. James Johnson, Oct. 25, 1865, BR, LR, G-15, NA.
33. Max Woodhull, AAG, to Tillson, Nov. 1, 1865, BR, LS, I, 362, NA.
34. Woodhull to Tillson, Nov. 21, 1865, LS, I, 378, NA.
35. Sewall's Report on N. C., S. C., and Georgia, Dec. 15, 1865, BR, LR, S-610, NA.
36. Woodhull to Sprague, Oct. 9, 1865, BR, LS, I, 327, NA.
37. Howard's Report, Nov. 1, 1867, BR, LS, IV, 122–23, NA.
38. Carlin to Howard, March 14, 1867, BR, LR, T-95, NA.
39. Howard to T. D. Eliot, April 8, 1866, BR, LS, II, 138, NA; Howard to Gen. U. S. Grant, Nov. 30, 1867, BR, LS, IV, 176, NA.
40. Howard to Sherman, Oct. 20, 1869, BR, LS, VI, 2, NA.
41. BR, Roster of Officers and Agents, State of Florida, July 1, 1868, NA.
42. Woodhull to William H. Day, Sept. 20, 1865, BR, LS, I, 288, NA.
43. Howard to Guy Howard, June 21, 1865.
44. Howard to Mrs. Howard, July 22, 1865.

Relief Work and Land Policy [103–121]

1. Whittlesey to Howard, July 12, 1865, BR, LR, B-2, NA.
2. Fisk to Howard, July 31, 1865, BR, LR, F-102, NA.

3. Swayne to Howard, May 4, 1866, BR, LR, A-255, NA.
4. Samuel Thomas, AAG to Eldridge, June 20, 1866, BR, LS, II, 234, NA.
5. Peirce, *Freedmen's Bureau*, 98; Bentley, *Freedmen's Bureau*, 141–42. One ration consisted of a bushel of corn and eight pounds of pork. John W. De Forest, *A Union Officer in the Reconstruction*, J. H. Croushore and David M. Potter, eds. (New Haven, Yale U. Press, 1948), 88, note 10.
6. Woodhull to Sprague, Jan. 15, 1866, BR, LS, II, 26, NA.
7. Howard to Stanton, Sept. 28, 1866, BR, LS, II, 349, NA.
8. Howard to Scott, March 2, 1867, BR, LS, III, 89, NA.
9. Peirce, *Freedmen's Bureau*, 93–94.
10. Howard, *Autobiography*, II, 260–62.
11. See, e.g., J. G. de Roulhac Hamilton, *Reconstruction in North Carolina* (N. Y., 1914), 301–03.
12. John W. De Forest, novelist and, for a time, Bureau agent, tells amusing stories of ration issues in South Carolina. See chapters 3 and 4 of *A Union Officer in the Reconstruction*.
13. U. S. Statutes at Large, XIII, 508.
14. Howard to Assistant Commissioners, June 26, 1865, BR, LS, I, 96, NA.
15. Howard to Stanton, July 19, 1865, BR, LS, I, 165, NA.
16. Howard to T. W. Conway, July 21, 1865, BR, LS, I, 181, NA.
17. Howard to Col. O. Brown, July 24, 1865, BR, LS, I, 187, NA.
18. BR, Circulars and Circular Letters, Circular No. 13, July 28, 1865.
19. Fullerton to Col. O. Brown, Aug. 22, 1865, BR, LS, I, 240, NA; see also Jonathan T. Dorris, *Pardon and Amnesty under Lincoln and Johnson* (Chapel Hill, 1953), 229–30.
20. Fisk to Howard, Aug. 27, 1865, BR, LR, F-105, NA.
21. Howard to Stanton, Sept. 4, 1865, BR, LS, I, 259, NA.
22. Howard to Mrs. Howard, Sept. 9, 1865.
23. Howard to Mrs. Howard, Sept. 13, 1865.
24. Lt. Stuart Eldridge to Lt. Col. R. S. Donaldson, Sept. 11, 1865, Johnson Papers, LC.
25. Saxton to Howard, Sept. 5, 9, 1865, BR, LR, S-83, S-171, NA.
26. Howard to Saxton, Sept. 12, 1865, BR, LS, I, 274, NA.
27. Bentley, *Freedmen's Bureau*, 98; Howard, *Autobiography*, II, 238–40.
28. Howard to Committee of Colored People of Edisto Island, Oct. 22, 1865, BR, LS, I, 415, NA.
29. Davis Tillson to Howard, March 5, 1866, BR, LR, G-115, NA; William E. Strong to Howard, March 25, 1866, BR, LR, S-178, NA.
30. Howard, *Autobiography*, II, 229–44. The quotation appears on p. 244.
31. Howard to Assistant Commissioners, Nov. 11, 1865, BR, LS, I, 424, NA.
32. Howard to W. B. Cadbury, March 26, 1866.
33. Howard to Rachel W. M. Townsend, June 12, 1869, BR, LS, V, 418, NA.
34. Howard to L. H. Putnam, March 16, 1870, BR, LS, VI, 176, NA.
35. Howard, *Autobiography*, II, 416–22; Howard's Report for 1867, LS, IV, 104–05, NA; also 40th Congress, 2d Session, House Ex. Doc. 1, Serial 1324, 662–63. For a more extensive account of the Barry Farm project see pp. 185–188.
36. J. A. Sladen to Rev. James B. Simmons, Aug. 16, 1870, BR, LS, VI,

322, NA; G. W. Balloch to Howard, Dec. 10, 1885; Howard to Mrs. Guy Howard, Dec. 16, 1885; John A. Cole to Howard, June 10, 1870.

37. Howard, *Autobiography*, II, 420.
38. Howard to Major G. W. Nichols, Dec. 29, 1865.
39. Circular No. 7, July 2, 1866, BR, Circulars and Circular Letters, 30, NA; Samuel Thomas, AAG, to Assistant Commissioners, July 9, 1866, BR, LS, II, 250, NA.
40. Howard to W. D. Kelley, Sept. 11, 1866; Howard's Report, BR, Nov. 1, 1866, BR, LS, II, 423, NA; 39th Congress, 2d Session, House Ex. Doc. 1, Serial 1285, 741, 743; Howard to Brig. Gen. O. L. Shepherd, May 29, 1868, BR, LR, A-237, NA; Bentley, *Freedmen's Bureau*, 144–46.
41. Johnson to Steedman, Aug. 23, 1865, Johnson Papers, LC.
42. O. Brown to Howard, Sept. 9, 1865, BR, LR, B-170, NA; E. M. Gregory to Howard, Oct. 31, 1865, BR, LR, T-31, NA.
43. Thomas to Howard, Nov. 2, 1865, BR, LR, M-65, NA.
44. See, e.g., W. L. Fleming, *Civil War and Reconstruction in Alabama* (N. Y., 1905), 469–70.
45. See, e.g., Howard to Rev. George Whipple, Nov. 27, 1865, BR, LS, I, 403, NA.
46. Eric L. McKitrick, *Andrew Johnson and Reconstruction* (Chicago, 1960), 278–84.
47. Howard to Henry Wilson, Nov. 25, 1865; Howard's Report, 1865, BR, LS, I, 526–28, NA; also 39th Congress, 1st Session, House Ex. Doc. 11, Serial 1255, 32–34.
48. *Ibid.*; Howard to Charles H. Howard, Dec. 5, 1865.
49. Howard to J. H. Chapin, Jan. 10, 1866, BR, LS, II, 21, NA.
50. Lyman Trumbull to Howard, Jan. 4, 1866; Howard to Thaddeus Stevens, Jan. 6, 1866.
51. McKitrick, *Andrew Johnson and Reconstruction*, 282–84. The New York *Tribune* asserted that Johnson had approved the bill unofficially before it had been presented to Congress. Feb. 22, March 6, 1866.
52. McKitrick, *Andrew Johnson and Reconstruction*, 284–87.
53. Fullerton to Johnson, Feb. 9, 1866, Johnson Papers, LC. The twenty-page letter begins: "In reply to your verbal request I have the honor to submit the following objections. . . ." See also John H. and LaWanda Cox, "Andrew Johnson and His Ghost Writers," *Mississippi Valley Historical Review*, XLVIII (Dec., 1961), 463–68.
54. Howard to Col. T. S. Bowers, June 21, 1865, BR, LS, I, 77, NA.
55. Fullerton to Howard, July 20, 1865; Fullerton to Saxton, Aug. 28, 1865, BR, LS, I, 248, NA.
56. Trumbull to Howard, Feb. 19, 1866.
57. On Feb. 11, from Boston, Howard had written his adjutant, Max Woodhull: "There is great faith in Mr. Stanton, but much fear & trembling about Mr Johnson." BR, LR, H-37, NA.
58. Trumbull to Howard, Feb. 21, 1866.
59. Howard to the Assistant Commissioners, Feb. 23, 1866, BR, LS, II, 82, NA.
60. Howard to Tillson, Feb. 28, 1866.
61. Steedman to Johnson, April 15, 1865, Johnson Papers, LC.
62. Blair to Johnson, April 4, 1866, Johnson Papers, LC.
63. See, e.g., New York *Herald*, May 23, 29, 1866. Bentley, *Freedmen's Bureau* (125–35) contains an account of the Steedman-Fullerton investigation.

64. Steedman to Johnson, June 26, 1866, Johnson Papers, LC.
65. Howard to Stanton, May 22, 1866, BR, LS, II, 199, NA.
66. Bentley, *Freedmen's Bureau*, 131.
67. Howard to Johnson, Aug. 23, 1866, BR, LS, II, 287–95, NA.
68. Bentley, *Freedmen's Bureau*, 127, 132.
69. *Ibid.*, 126–28.
70. Howard to Johnson, Aug. 23, 1866, BR, LS, II, 287–95, NA; Howard to E. D. Townsend, Sept. 3, 1866, BR, LS, II, 311.
71. Bentley, *Freedmen's Bureau*, 133–35.

Labor and Legal Matters [122–135]

1. See, e.g. Fisk to Howard, July 6, 1865, BR, LR, F-9, NA; Samuel Thomas to Howard, July 29, 1865, BR, LR, T-95, NA; Sprague to Howard Sept. 21, 1865, BR, LR, S-94, NA; Fisk to Howard, Jan. 6, 1866, BR, LR, K-27, NA.
2. Wells to Johnson, July 29, 1865, Johnson Papers, LC.
3. U. S. Statutes at Large, XIV, 28; J. G. Randall and David Donald, *Civil War and Reconstruction* (Boston, 1961), 571–74.
4. McKitrick, *Andrew Johnson and Reconstruction*, 10.
5. Circular No. 11, July 12, 1865, BR, Circulars and Circular Letters, 12, NA.
6. Howard to R. W. Habersham, Dec. 19, 1865, BR, LS, I, 456, NA.
7. Howard to O. Brown and the other assistant commissioners, June 20, 1865, BR, LS, I, 75, NA.
8. Howard to Assistant Commissioners, June 29, 1865, BR, LS, I, 109, NA. The practice of charging a fee was discontinued in Jan. 1867. Howard to Assistant Commissioners, Jan. 24, 1867, BR, LS, III, 37, NA.
9. Bentley, *Freedmen's Bureau*, 148–51.
10. Howard to J. B. Yeatman, July 10, 1865, BR, LS, I, 136, NA.
11. Osborn, in Florida, blamed members of Gen. E. McCook's Union cavalry for first spreading the rumor. Osborn to Howard, Nov. 1, 1865, BR, LR, F-39, NA.
12. Howard [to Bureau officers], Oct. 4, 1865, BR, LS, I, 315, NA.
13. Howard to Osborn, Jan. 12, 1866, LS, II, 23, NA. The historian, J. G. de Roulhac Hamilton, no partisan of the Bureau, admits that Bureau interference in behalf of orphaned colored children "checked a disposition on the part of many to hold colored children in a state of subjection." *Reconstruction in North Carolina*, 313.
14. Bentley, *Freedmen's Bureau*, 149.
15. See, e.g. Howard to Gen. Jno. E. Smith, July 13, 1865, BR, LS, I, 147, NA; Howard to R. K. Scott, Sept. 17, 1867, BR, LS, III, 535, NA.
16. Howard to Charles Nordhoff, March 19, 1866, BR, LS, II, 114, NA.
17. Howard to Stanton, Dec. 21, 1866, BR, LS, II, 492–93, NA.
18. Bentley, *Freedmen's Bureau*, 151.
19. Otis A. Singletary, *Negro Militia and Reconstruction* (Austin, Texas, 1957), 3–6.
20. McKitrick, *Andrew Johnson and Reconstruction*, 456–60, 475–76.
21. Bentley, *Freedmen's Bureau*, 165.
22. Bentley, while conceding that there was much truth in the reports of violence and cruelty, tends to minimize them and implies that most were groundless or exaggerated. *Ibid.*, 110–15.
23. Fullerton to Brown, June 15, 1865, BR, LS, I, 55, NA.

24. G. Pillsbury [to Howard], Aug. 8, 1865, BR, LR, P-86, NA.
25. Tillson to Howard, Nov. 28, 1865, BR, LR, G-37, NA.
26. Fisk to Howard, May 10, 1866, BR, LR, K-128, NA.
27. Gilbreth to Howard, May 13, 1866, BR, LR, G-177, NA.
28. Gen. Absalom Baird to Howard, July 31, 1866, BR, LR, L-154, NA.
29. Baird to Howard, Aug. 27, 1866.
30. Kiddoo to Howard, Aug. 8, 1866, BR, LR, T-190, NA.
31. Ketchum to Assistant Commissioners, Sept. 24, 1866, BR, LS, II, 341, NA.
32. Grant to Howard, Jan. 18, 1867, BR, LR, A-110, NA.
33. Howard to Stanton, Feb. 14, 1867, BR, LS, III, 67, NA.
34. Bentley, *Freedmen's Bureau*, 165.
35. Gideon Welles, *Diary of Gideon Welles* (Boston, Houghton, Mifflin, 1911), III, 42–43; Orville H. Browning, *The Diary of Orville Hickman Browning*, J. G. Randall, ed. (Springfield, Ill., 1933), II, 130; Benjamin P. Thomas and Harold M. Hyman, *Stanton: The Life and Times of Lincoln's Secretary of War* (N. Y., 1962), 522.
36. Howard to Rev. G. F. Morgan, Sept. 14, 1866.
37. Sprague to Howard, Oct. 1, 1866, BR, LR, M-469, NA.
38. Kiddoo to Howard, Oct. 25, 1866, BR, LR, T-270, NA.
39. Mower to Samuel Thomas, AAG, March 9, 1867, BR, LR, L-48, NA.
40. Davis to Howard, Nov. 27, 1866, BR, LR, K-251, NA. Other such examples are: J. R. Lewis to Howard, Oct. 3, 1866, BR, LR, T-244, NA; P. H. Sheridan to Howard, Oct. 17, 1866, BR, LR, L-202, NA; J. B. Kiddoo to Howard, Jan. 25, 1867, BR, LR, T-38, NA.
41. Osborn to Howard, Nov. 1, 1865, BR, LR, F-39, NA.
42. BR, Register of Letters Received, H. A. Wicker to Howard, Aug. 11, 1866, VII, 361, W-218, NA.
43. Sewall to Howard, Sept. 17, 1866, BR, LR, S-494, NA.
44. Whittlesey to Howard, Feb. 25, 1867, BR, LR, W-54, NA.
45. Howard's Report, Oct. 20, 1869, LS, VI, 17, NA; also in 41st Congress, 2d Session, House Ex. Doc. 1, pt. 2, Serial 1412, 509.
46. Howard to Capt. Charles C. Soule, June 21, 1865, BR, LS, I, 79, NA.
47. "We are mortally averse to conceding the Freedmen the right to testify in our courts. . . ." So wrote a Southern lawyer to a former Union army officer in November 1865. V. C. Barringer to S. D. Atkins, Nov. 14, 1865, BR, LR, A-105, NA.
48. Howard, *Autobiography*, II, 253.
49. *Ibid.*, 251–52.
50. For a discussion of Bureau courts see Bentley, *Freedmen's Bureau*, 152–68.
51. *Ibid.*, 159–62.
52. Howard to Fisk, Sept. 9, 1865, BR, LS, I, 271, NA.
53. Howard to Whittlesey, Oct. 5, 1865, BR, LS, I, 317, NA.
54. Sharkey to Thomas, Sept. 18, 1865, BR, LR, M-18, NA.
55. Woodhull to Thomas, Nov. 24, 1865, BR, LS, I, 400, NA.
56. Woodhull to Thomas, Dec. 27, 1865, BR, LS, I, 477–78, NA.
57. Osborn to Howard, Dec. 8, 1865, BR, LR, F-57, NA.
58. Tillson to Howard, Feb. 24, 1866.
59. Howard to Absalom Baird, April 9, 1866, BR, LS, II, 143, NA.
60. U. S. Statutes at Large, XIV, 28.
61. Kiddoo to Howard, June 26, 1866, BR, LR, T-167, NA.

62. Scott to Howard, Dec. 18, 1866, BR, LR, S-612, NA.
63. Howard to Stanton, Jan. 19, 1867, BR, LS, III, 24–31, NA. James W. Patton, historian of Reconstruction in Tennessee, states that the state courts did not extend equal treatment to freedmen. *Unionism and Reconstruction in Tennessee* (Chapel Hill, 1934), 157–58.
64. Howard to Scott, July 26, 1867, BR, LS, III, 398, NA.

The Controversial Bureau [136–156]

1. Bentley, *Freedmen's Bureau*, 123, 133, 196.
2. The charge that the Bureau became enmeshed in politics can be found e.g in, *ibid.*, 214; E. Merton Coulter, *The South During Reconstruction, 1865–1877* ([Baton Rouge], 1947), 89–91; Robert S. Henry, *The Story of Reconstruction* (N. Y., 1938), 386; J. G. Randall, *The Civil War and Reconstruction* (Boston, 1953), 733; Samuel E. Morison and Henry S. Commager, *The Growth of the American Republic*, 5th edition (N. Y., 1962), II, 82.
3. Bentley, *Freedmen's Bureau*, 137; De Forest, *A Union Officer in the Reconstruction*, xvi.
4. Bentley, *Freedmen's Bureau*, 136–37. Walter L. Fleming, a Southern historian who had little use for the Freedmen's Bureau, stated, "The Freedmen's Bureau, which had much influence over the negroes for demoralization, was too weak in numbers to control effectively the negroes in politics." "The Formation of the Union League in Alabama," *Gulf States Historical Magazine*, II (Sept., 1903), 89.
5. J. A. Sladen to Hopkins, March 15, 1867.
6. Oct. 25, 1867, BR, Endorsement Volume IV, 55–56, NA.
7. Whittlesey to Scott, Nov. 19, 1867, BR, LS, IV, 167.
8. Swayne to Howard, Dec. 26, 1867, BR, Register of Letters Received, XI, 39, NA; Howard to Swayne, Dec. 28, 1867, BR, LS, IV, 215, NA; Whittlesey to Gen. Julius Hayden, Jan. 15, 1868, BR, LS, IV, 249, NA.
9. Howard to Scott, Dec. 11, 1867, BR, LS, IV, 195, NA.
10. Howard to Brown, April 29, 1868.
11. Scott to Howard, May 2, 1868.
12. Later, Scott served for a brief period as a special agent for the Bureau in collecting debts owed the government by planters at a time of a crop shortage. Howard to Scott, Oct. 19, 1868, BR, LS, V, 74, NA; Whittlesey to Col. James P. Low, Dec. 11, 1868, BR, LS, V, 228, NA.
13. F. D. Sewall to Col. C. C. Sibley, June 10, 1867, BR, LS, III, 267, NA.
14. Scott to Howard, Dec. 23, 1867, BR, LR, S-722, NA.
15. T. Harry Williams, "An Analysis of Some Reconstruction Attitudes," *Journal of Southern History*, XII (1946), 483–84.
16. Mower to A. Ketchum, May 6, 1867, BR, LR, L-86, NA.
17. Howard to Mower, May 24, 1867.
18. Mower to Howard, May 30, 1867.
19. E. Whittlesey to Hayden, March 2, 1868, BR, LS, IV, 328, NA.
20. Howard to Weirman, Sept. 16, 1868, BR, LS, V, 31, NA.
21. Gillem to Howard, July 25, 1867, BR, LS, M-217, NA.
22. Howard to Gillem, Aug. 8, 1867, BR, LS, III, 430, NA.
23. Swayne to Howard, June 8, 1867.
24. Brown to Howard, June 13, 1867.
25. Howard to T. L. Tullock, June 6, 1867, BR, LS, III, 261, NA; Howard

to O. Brown, June 13, 1867; A. Ketchum to Langston, Aug. 26, 1867, BR, LS, III, 482, NA.

26. R. D. Parsons to H. D. Cooke, Sept. 18, 1867; H. D. Cooke to Howard, Sept. 21, 1867; Howard to Langston, Sept. 24, 1867.
27. John M. Langston, *From the Virginia Plantation to the National Capitol* (Hartford, American Publishing Co., 1894), 263.
28. Bentley, *Freedmen's Bureau*, 186–87.
29. Conway to Howard, April 26, May 1, 1867.
30. Scott to Howard, Dec. 23, 1867, BR, LR, S-722, NA.
31. See John H. and LaWanda Cox, "General O. O. Howard and the 'Misrepresented Bureau,'" *Journal of Southern History*, XIX (1953), 437–50.
32. F. D. Sewall to Gen. S. Burbank, June 18, 1867, BR, LS, III, 285, NA.
33. Circular Letter, Dec. 11, 1867, BR, LS, IV, 194, NA.
34. Howard to assistant commissioners and to heads of divisions, Sept. 13, 1867, BR, LS, III, 525, NA.
35. 40th Congress, 2d Session, House Ex. Doc. 1, pt. 1, Serial 1324, 692.
36. Howard to B. F. Wade, Jan. 27, 1868, BR, LS, IV, 266, NA.
37. Howard to T. D. Eliot, Feb. 8, 1868.
38. Howard to Wilson, March 26, 1868.
39. Howard to Gen. S. Burbank, July 7, 1868, BR, LS, IV, 472, NA.
40. Howard to Scott, July 6, 1868, BR, LS, IV, 469, NA.
41. Howard to Smith, July 11, 1868, BR, LS, IV, 481, NA.
42. Bentley, *Freedmen's Bureau*, 201–02; Circular No. 6, July 17, 1868, Circular No. 7, Aug. 3, 1868, BR, Circulars and Circular Letters, 72–73, NA.
43. E.g. Gen. C. H. Smith to Howard, July 21, 1868, BR, LR, A-334, NA; Gen. O. L. Shepherd to Howard, July 27, 1868, BR, LR, A-338, NA; R. K. Scott to Howard, Aug. 2, 1868; Howard to John M. Schofield, Oct. 5, 1868, BR, LS, V, 45, NA.
44. Howard to George Whipple, May 25, 1867; Howard to J. M. McKim, Jan. 4, 1868.
45. Bentley, *Freedmen's Bureau*, 104–06.
46. Johnson to Thomas, Aug. 14, 1865, Johnson Papers, LC.
47. Bentley, *Freedmen's Bureau*, 68–69.
48. Grant to Stanton, Aug. 30, 1865, Stanton Papers, LC.
49. Patton to Johnson, Sept. 13, 1865, BR, LR, A-430, NA.
50. Dr. Shakspeare Allen to Howard, Feb. 8, 1866.
51. New York *Tribune*, Nov. 10, 15, 1865; A. Baird to Max Woodhull, Dec. 9, 1865, BR, LR, L-81, NA.
52. Thomas to Howard, March 26, 1866.
53. New York *Tribune*, Aug. 6, 1866; Howard to Baird, Aug. 8, 1866, BR, LS, II, 274, NA.
54. Tillson to Howard, May 7, 1866.
55. *Congressional Globe*, Jan. 10, 1866, 39th Congress, 1st Session, pt. 1, 171.
56. Howard to Eliot, Jan. 16, 1866, BR, LS, II, 29, NA.
57. Wilson to Howard, July 12, 1867, BR, LR, W-193, NA.
58. Ward to Howard, Oct. 2, 1868.
59. Howard to Ward, Oct. 7, 1868.
60. McKim to Howard, Feb. 28, 1866.
61. Shipherd to Whipple, Nov. 7, 1866, BR, LR, A-515, NA.
62. Conway to Howard, July 10, 1868, BR, LR, L-208, NA.

NOTES 323

63. Hatch to Howard, Oct. 24, 1868.
64. Howard to O. Brown, July 21, 1868, BR, LS, IV, 501, NA.
65. Hatch to Howard, Feb. 5, 1869.
66. Howard to the Assistant Commissioners, June 14, 1865, BR, LS, I, 62–63, NA.
67. Woodhull to Sprague, Nov. 24, 1865, BR, LS, I, 399, NA.
68. Howard to Brown, March 23, 1866, BR, LS, II, 125, NA.
69. Ketchum to Baird, June 8, 1866, BR, LS, II, 218, NA.
70. Howard to Mower, July 1, 1867, BR, LS, III, 308, NA.
71. Howard to Ward, Oct. 7, 1868.
72. O. H. Crandall to Sen. E. B. Washburne, Jan. 20, 1868, E. B. Washburne Papers, LC.
73. Capt. A. S. Flagg to O. Brown, March 3, 1866, BR, LR, V-215, NA.
74. O. Brown to Howard, March 7, 1866, BR, Register of Letters Received, V, 269, NA.
75. Howard to Kiddoo, Aug. 21, 1866.
76. Howard to Saxton, June 20, 1865, BR, LS, I, 72, NA.
77. Howard to Thomas, July 22, 1865, BR, LS, I, 186, NA.
78. Howard to Sheridan, Dec. 2, 1865, BR, LS, I, 425, NA.
79. Howard to Saxton, Dec. 27, 1865, BR, LS, I, 480, NA.
80. Howard to Carlin, March 4, 1867.
81. Howard to Swayne, May 22, 1867, BR, LS, III, 230, NA.
82. Sewall's Report, Oct. 30, 1866, BR, LR, S-539, NA; Sewall to Howard, May 9, 1867, BR, LR, S-296, NA.
83. Circular No. 22, Dec. 22, 1865, BR, Circulars and Circular Letters, 23, NA.
84. Proceedings of a Board of Officers Convened at Charlotte, N. C., March 21, 1867, BR, LR, N-63, NA; General Court Martial Orders, No. 5, Vicksburg, Miss., Feb. 9, 1868, BR, LR, M-78, NA.
85. Woodhull to O. Brown, Feb. 24, 1866, BR, LS, II, 84, NA.
86. Howard to Adjutant General, March 1, 1866, BR, LS, II, 91, NA.
87. Howard to Swayne, Sept. 6, 1866, BR, LS, II, 317, NA.
88. Howard to Tillson, Oct. 9, 1866, BR, LS, II, 364, NA.
89. Howard to Kiddoo, Jan. 16, 1867, BR, LS, III, 18, NA.
90. Howard to Sibley, June 6, 1868, BR, LS, IV, 437, NA.
91. Carlin to Howard, Dec. 16, 1867. Superintendent of Schools, J. W. Alvord, believed that the law did not prohibit this action. The policy adopted by the Bureau was that the device ought to be used sparingly and only when the freedmen were unable themselves to pay the teacher; also that care should be taken to guarantee that the money actually went to the teachers. Endorsement on communication from William P. Carlin, assistant commissioner for Tennessee, Sept. 27, 1867, BR, Endorsement Volume III, 575–76, NA.
92. Howard to Hon. J. W. Smith, Aug. 21, 1867, BR, LS, III, 472, NA.
93. E.g. Howard to Hon. Joseph Holt, Oct. 9, 1869, BR, LS, V, 534, NA.
94. Howard to Carpenter, Oct. 1, 1868, BR, LS, V, 37–38, NA.
95. Sewall to Rev. J. G. Fee, May 24, 1867, BR, LS, III, 234, NA.

Education [157–168]

1. Circular No. 2, May 19, 1865, BR, Circulars and Circular Letters, 2, NA.
2. Howard, "Address Before the New England Society," 29–30, HU.

3. Howard to S. S. Greene, July 14, 1865, BR, LS, I, 153, NA.
4. Howard to Fessenden, May 4, 1866, BR, LS, II, 181, NA.
5. Howard to Rev. C. F. McRae, Oct. 27, 1865; Howard to J. B. Smith, Dec. 30, 1865, BR, LS, I, 489, NA.
6. Howard to T. J. Wood, Dec. 8, 1866, BR, LS, II, 476, NA.
7. Howard to John M. Schofield, Nov. 5, 1868, BR, LS, V, 161, NA. The Negro leader, John M. Langston, in a letter to Howard in 1870 wrote, "This system [of segregated schools] however must eventually fail; for it is abnormal, doubly expensive, thus making a double tax necessary, and fails utterly to educate the colored or the white class in such manner and with regard to each other, so as to fit them to live together harmoniously, as fellow citizens & neighbors, cultivating toward each other a good social as well as a good political understanding." Langston to Howard, Sept. 17, 1870, BR, LR, L-88, NA.
8. In 1865, the American Freedmen's Aid Commission had been formed. Bentley, *Freedmen's Bureau*, 64; H. L. Swint, *The Northern Teacher in the South* (Nashville, 1941), 18; Howard to the Officers of the Various Associations for Freedmen and Refugees, June 17, 1865, BR, LS, I, 65, NA; Howard to E. M. Stanton, Aug. 16, 1865, BR, LS, I, 254, NA.
9. Howard to Shipherd, July 17, BR, LS, I, 160, NA.
10. Bentley, *Freedmen's Bureau*, 257, n. 101.
11. Henry, *Story of Reconstruction*, 244.
12. Howard to James E. Rhoades, Oct. 9, 1865.
13. Howard to Dr. H. Mariel, Dec. 4, 1865, BR, LS, I, 445, NA.
14. See S. C. Armstrong to Howard, June 24, 1869.
15. Peirce, *Freedmen's Bureau*, 78. Howard listed twenty-five institutions of higher learning which the Bureau assisted in founding. By the early 1870's there were seventy schools involved in the training of Negro teachers. Presumably all of these received Bureau aid. Howard, *Autobiography*, II, 402–15.
16. Howard to Rt. Rev. Charles B. McIlvaine, March 4, 1867, BR, LS, III, 92, NA; Howard to C. T. Chase, May 4, 1867, BR, LS, III, 198, NA; Howard to B. Sears, May 7, 1867.
17. Howard to R. B. Foster, June 9, 1871.
18. Howard to T. B. Merrick, Feb. 27, 1874.
19. D. O. W. Holmes, *The Evolution of the Negro College* (N. Y., 1934), 99–109.
20. W. E. B. DuBois, *The Souls of the Black Folk* (London, 1905), 101–02.
21. See Holmes, *The Evolution of the Negro College* for more information on the institutions which the Bureau helped.
22. S. C. Armstrong to Howard, June 24, 1869.
23. The present Saint Augustine's College.
24. Howard to Abbott, July 19, 1867.
25. Howard to McKim, March 11, 1867.
26. Shipherd to Howard, May 6, 1867, BR, LR, A-246, NA.
27. Griffin to Howard, May 4, 1867, BR, LR, T-150, NA.
28. Shipherd to Howard, June 6, 1867, BR, LR, A-286, NA; Howard to G. Whipple, Aug. 20, 1867, BR, LS, III, 470, NA.
29. Simmons to Howard, June 27, 1870, BR, LR, S-62, NA.
30. Howard to Smith, Dec. 10, 1868, BR, LS, V, 225, NA.
31. Howard to J. T. Sprague, Sept. 25, 1868, BR, LS, V, 28, NA.
32. Howard to Alvord, July 31, 1869, BR, LS, V, 456, NA.

33. Howard to Wilson, Nov. 25, 1865.
34. Howard to Rev. Lemuel Moss, April 28, 1866.
35. See H. M. Bond, *Negro Education in Alabama* (Washington, 1939), 111–19, and Henry, *Story of Reconstruction,* 128–29.
36. Tillson to Howard, April 29, 1866.
37. Howard to Colton, March 14, 1867.
38. Alvord to Howard, Dec. 11, 1865; Ketchum to Langston, Aug. 26, 1867, BR, LS, III, 482, NA.
39. Howard to Smith, Dec. 30, 1865, BR, LS, I, 489, NA.
40. "Education of the Colored Man" (pamphlet), 30, HU.
41. Howard to the Secretary of War, Nov. 19, 1869, BR, LS, VI, 59, NA. Howard had anticipated the continuation of the Bureau's educational work by the Department of Education as early as 1867. Howard to J. M. McKim, Oct. 1, 1867; Howard's Report, Nov. 1, 1867, 40th Congress, 2d Session, House Ex. Doc. 1, pt. 1, Serial 1324, 691.
42. 41st Congress, 3d Session, House Ex. Doc. 1, pt. 1, Serial 1446, 317–18.
43. Howard to Alvord, Oct. 15, 1870, BR, LS, VI, 395, NA.
44. 41st Congress, 2d Session, House Ex. Doc. 1, pt. 2, Serial 1412, 507.
45. Howard to W. P. Fessenden, May 4, 1866, BR, LS, II, 181, NA.
46. Howard to Col. George W. Williams, Nov. 25, 1886.

Howard University [169–184]

1. Some of Howard's other activities, especially his connection with the Freedmen's Savings and Trust Company, will be discussed in a later chapter.
2. Howard University, Board of Trustees, *Minutes,* June 17, 1873, 186 (hereafter referred to as HU, Trustees *Minutes*); John L. Ewell, *The History of the Theological Department of Howard University* ([Washington], 1906), 7. Howard was not present at this first meeting. House Reports, 41st Congress, 2d Session, no. 121, Serial 1438, 136 (hereafter cited as Howard Investigation).
3. HU, Trustees *Minutes,* Nov. 20, 1866, 3–4.
4. Daniel S. Lamb, *Howard University Medical Department* (Washington, R. Beresford, 1900), 3; Walter Dyson, "The Founding of Howard University," *Howard University Studies in History* (June, 1921), 1, 9–11.
5. HU, Trustees *Minutes,* Jan. 8, 1867, 7; James M. Nabrit, "From Prayer Meeting to University"*Christian Education,* XXVI (Sept., 1942), 29. The name in the charter is "The Howard University." Dyson, "Founding of Howard University," 17.
6. HU, Trustees *Minutes,* Dec. 18, 1866, 5.
7. Dyson, "Founding of Howard University," 18–19.
8. *Ibid.,* 17.
9. Howard to Balloch, Dec. 21, 1866, BR, LS, II, 491, NA; Howard Investigation, 59.
10. HU, Trustees *Minutes,* Jan. 29, 1867, 10; E. M. Cushman to Howard, Jan. 30, 1867.
11. Dyson, "Founding of Howard University," 12; Dyson, *Howard University, The Capstone of Negro Education, A History: 1867–1940* (Washington, The Graduate School, Howard University, 1941), 51.
12. Howard to G. F. Shaw, March 23, 1867.

13. HU, Trustees *Minutes,* March 19, 1867, 21–22; Dyson, *Howard University,* 402; Lamb, *Howard University Medical Department,* 82.
14. Washington *Chronicle,* May 2, 1867.
15. Howard's Report, BR, LS, IV, 103, NA; Lamb, *Howard University Medical Department,* 4; Dyson, *Howard University,* 156.
16. Lamb, *Howard University Medical Department,* 1.
17. *Ibid.,* 1–2; Howard, *Autobiography,* II, 398–400.
18. Special Orders No. 57, April 15, 1867, BR, Special Orders and Special Field Orders, 188, NA.
19. Howard, *Autobiography,* II, 400–01; Peirce, *Freedmen's Bureau,* 114.
20. Howard's Report, Nov. 1, 1867, BR, LS, IV, 103, NA.
21. HU, Trustees *Minutes,* June 25, 1867, 37.
22. In 1885 a part of the original tract was sold to the government for a reservoir for a little over $100,000. Dyson, "Founding of Howard University," 13.
23. HU, Trustees *Minutes,* April 8, 1867, 23–24; Howard Investigation, 192.
24. *Ibid.,* 154.
25. *Ibid.,* 159.
26. *Ibid.,* 154–56.
27. *Ibid.,* 192; HU, Trustees *Minutes,* Aug. 14, 20, Dec. 2, 1867, 42, 43, 51. The executive committee of the trustees voted on August 19, 1867 to sell an acre lot to General Howard for a thousand dollars, payable in five years, with interest, in consideration of his building a house on the acre lot of at least $10,000 value. Howard University, Board of Trustees, Executive Committee, *Minutes,* Aug. 19, 1867; E. W. Robinson to R. M. Hall, Aug. 20, 1867.
28. HU, Trustees *Minutes,* April 8, 1867, 24; Howard University to Howard, April 11, 1867, BR, Register of Letters Received, IX, 40, NA.
29. Howard Investigation, 102, 108, 113; Dyson, *Howard University,* 110.
30. Lamb, *Howard University Medical Department,* 277.
31. Howard to James McClintock, Feb. 4, 1868.
32. Howard Investigation, 111–13.
33. Searle to Howard, April 22, 1867.
34. Howard to Searle, April 22, 1867.
35. Howard to Whittlesey, April 23, 1867.
36. Howard Investigation, 154.
37. *Ibid.,* 384, 385, 390, 391.
38. Eaton testified that Howard made his decision to withdraw from the company before the company had sold any block. *Ibid.,* 384.
39. *Ibid.,* 72.
40. *Ibid.,* 114.
41. Loomis to Howard, June 19, 1867; Howard to Loomis, June 21, 1867.
42. Howard to Searle, Nov. 8, 1867.
43. Howard to James McClintock, Feb. 4, 1868.
44. Howard to William R. Boggs, June 11, 1868.
45. Howard Investigation, 76.
46. E. Whittlesey to Howard, Aug. 20, 1868.
47. T. Harvey to Howard, Sept. 30, 1868.
48. The University Building was torn down in 1937 to make way for the Founders' Library. Dyson, *Howard Universtiy,* 98, 110; Dwight Holmes,

The Passing of the Old: Some Reflections On the Demolition of the Main Building at Howard University (Washington, 1937), 1.
49. Lamb, *Howard University Medical Department*, 14.
50. *National Intelligencer*, Dec. 22, 1868; Lamb, *Howard University Medical Department*, 14.
51. Howard to Schofield, Dec. 22, 1868.
52. Howard to Van Derburgh, Dec. 28, 1868.
53. James A. Hardie to Howard, Dec. 30, 1868.
54. Mullett to Howard, Jan. 4, 1869.
55. New York *Tribune*, Jan. 5, 1869.
56. Washington *Chronicle*, Jan. 11, 1869.
57. Alvord to Howard, Jan. 26, 1869.
58. Charles H. Howard to Howard, Feb. 22, 1869.
59. HU, Trustees *Minutes*, Feb. 15, March 1, 1869, 74, 75; Howard Investigation, 164–65.
60. HU, Trustees *Minutes*, Feb. 15, 1869, 74; Howard Investigation, 166.
61. Charles H. Howard to Howard, Feb. 22, 1869.
62. HU, Trustees *Minutes*, April 5, 1869, 77; Howard Investigation, 166–67; Washington *Chronicle*, March 27, 1869.
63. *Ibid.*
64. The report is printed in, Howard Investigation, 87–102.
65. *Ibid.*, 69, 82, 83.
66. *Ibid.*, 226, 323, 395.
67. E. D. Townsend to Howard, March 16, 1869.
68. E. N. Kirk and others to Howard, March 24, 1869, BR, LR, K-35, NA.
69. Whittlesey to Howard, March 17, 1869; Whittlesey to E. N. Kirk and others, March 29, 1869, BR, LS, V, 334, NA.
70. HU, Trustees *Minutes*, April 5, 1869, 77; W. F. Bascom to Howard, April 6, 1869.
71. HU, Trustees *Minutes*, Aug. 27, 1867, 45.
72. Dyson, *Howard University*, 380–81.
73. Howard to George Whipple, Jan. 16, 1868, BR, LS, IV, 253, NA.
74. Armstrong to Howard, May 29, 1870.
75. HU, Trustees *Minutes*, Sept. 21, 1868, 66; Committee of Howard University Trustees to Howard, April 1, 1869.
76. Howard to J. S. Travelli, April 8, 1869.
77. Howard to David Clark, April 7, 1869; Howard to W. F. Bascom, April 6, 1869, Howard Investigation, 513.
78. Howard to Secretary of War, Sept. 25, 1869, BR, LS, V, 517, NA.
79. Dyson, *Howard University*, 100–01.
80. John A. Rawlins to Howard, Sept. 1, 1869, BR, LR, W-201, NA.
81. Dyson, *Howard University*, 101.
82. HU, Trustees *Minutes*, March 19, 1867, 22.
83. *Ibid.*, Dec. 7, 1868, 70.
84. Howard to C. Lowe, June 9, 1869.
85. Howard, *Third Annual Report*, in *Howard University Annual Reports of the President: 1867–1910*, 13.
86. *Ibid.*
87. The College of Liberal Arts opened in September 1868 with one student. Dyson, *Howard University*, 156.
88. Howard, *Annual Report, 1869*, in *Howard University Annual Reports*

of the President: 1867–1910, 6. Howard University retained the preparatory department until 1919 and it was 1910 before the college had as many as one hundred students. Dyson, *Howard University*, 163, 165.
89. Howard to Forney, June 12, 1869.
90. Howard, MS Diary, Jan. 19, 1871, HU.
91. Dyson, *Howard University*, 110–11.
92. Howard Investigation, 239.
93. E. Whittlesey to D. Egan, Nov. 18, 1870, BR, LS, VI, 449, NA; H. R. Searle to Howard, Nov. 10, 1869; Dyson, *Howard University*, 111.
94. Howard, *Fifth Annual Report*, in *Howard University Annual Reports of the President: 1867–1910*, 3–4.
95. Howard to Mrs. Howard, July 12, 1869.
96. Howard to Charles H. Howard, Aug. 7, 1869, HU; Howard, *Third Annual Report*, 15.
97. *Annual Report of Howard University* (Washington, 1874), 13. The cancelled note is in the Howard Papers, Bowdoin College.
98. Howard to Hooker, Dec. 31, 1870.
99. Hooker to Howard, Jan. 9, 1871.
100. Howard to Queen Victoria, July 13, 1868.
101. See, e.g. J. A. Cook to Howard, April 12, 1872.
102. Howard, *Third Annual Report*, 11.
103. Dyson, *Howard University*, 53–54.
104. *Ibid.*, 53.
105. Howard, *Third Annual Report*, 11–12; Dyson, *Howard University*, 119.
106. Howard to Ensign Otis, Jan. 30, 1871.
107. Howard to Rowland B. Howard, Jan. 18, 1870.
108. Howard to Trustees of Howard University, Dec. 1, 1873.
109. HU, Trustees *Minutes*, Dec. 1, 27, 1873, 201–03; Langston, *From the Virginia Plantation to the National Capitol*, 310–12. The trustees accepted Howard's resignation Dec. 25, 1874; Langston's as vice-president, June 30, 1875. HU, Trustees *Minutes*, Dec. 25, 1874, 231. Dyson, *Howard University*, 383.
110. *Ibid.*, 59–62.
111. Except for the years 1883–1889, and 1906–1909 during which Howard was an honorary trustee. *Ibid.*, 415, 420.
112. Howard, an appeal to the public, May 13, 1891; J. Barnard to Howard, Nov. 9, 1907.
113. Howard, *Autobiography*, II, 402–16. See also Howard to Mrs. H. B. Stowe, Dec. 4, 1878.

Bureau-Related Activities: The Barry Farm and the Freedmen's Bank [185–190]

1. Howard Investigation, 481.
2. The Bureau constructed some low-rent tenements in Washington for destitute freedmen. One project furnishing three-room apartments for 228 families was on Capitol Hill. *Ibid.*, 210.
3. *Ibid.*, 520.
4. *Ibid.*, 481.
5. Special Order No. 61, April 23, 1867, BR, Special Orders, 1867, NA.
6. Howard Investigation, 485.

7. *Ibid.*, 184, 520.
8. Pomeroy to Howard, May 8, 1867. Sample contract in Howard Investigation, 328–29.
9. *Ibid.*, 321.
10. *Ibid.*, 482.
11. *Ibid.*, 321.
12. *Ibid.*, 210.
13. *Ibid.*, 482; Whittlesey to Major D. G. Swain, May 24, 1869, BR, LS, V, 405, NA.
14. Charles H. Howard to Howard, July 1, 1867.
15. Howard Investigation, 330.
16. Excerpt from the minutes of the Barry Farm trustees, *ibid.*, 344.
17. It might have been in October since the Barry Farm trustees voted the allotment on the first of that month.
18. Howard Investigation, 242–45.
19. McKim to Howard, Oct. 4, 1866, *ibid.*, 254.
20. Howard to McKim, July 8, 1867, *ibid.*, 254–55.
21. *Ibid.*, 249–50.
22. *Ibid.*, 477.
23. This is the explanation of J. Harry Thompson, the original owner, of Joseph A. Sladen, Howard's aide, and of Howard himself. *Ibid.*, 250, 254, 519.
24. *Ibid.*, 256.
25. *Ibid.*, 259, 344, 477.
26. Howard to J. A. Peters, Feb. 24, 1871.
27. Balloch to Howard, Dec. 10, 1885.
28. Howard to Balloch, Nov. 19, 1885.
29. See Report of Select Committee, 46th Congress, 2d Session, Senate Report No. 440, Serial 1895, i-ii.
30. W. L. Fleming, *The Freedmen's Savings Bank* (Chapel Hill, University of North Carolina Press, 1927), 146.
31. Circular Letter, May 7, 1867, BR, LS, III, 202, NA.
32. Howard to W. A. Booth, Feb. 4, 1867.
33. F. D. Sewall to O. Brown, Jan. 2, 1869, BR, LS, V, 251, NA.
34. Howard to A. E. Buck, July 7, 1871, BR, LS, VII, 145, NA.
35. M. T. Hewitt to Howard, Sept. 16, 1865.
36. 46th Congress, 2d Session, Senate Report No. 440, Serial 1895, 263–64.
37. Howard to R. M. Manly, March 14, 1873.
38. Howard to J. D. Brady, Dec. 27, 1886; see also 46th Congress, 2d Session, Senate Report No. 440, Serial 1895, 264–68.
39. See Fleming, *Freedmen's Savings Bank*, chs. 5–6.
40. *Ibid.*, 124.
41. The Bureau agents who paid bounties to colored veterans tried to get them to deposit their money in the Freedmen's Bank, but, according to the word of one agent, Edward C. Beman, in his experience only three out of 4321 persons paid by him ever did so. *Proceedings, Findings and Opinion of Court of Inquiry . . . in the Case of Oliver Otis Howard* (Washington, 1874), 149.
42. See Howard to Frederick Douglass, Jan. 15, 1875, and Howard to Editor, Chicago *Tribune*, Jan. 18, 1875.
43. Fleming, surely no strong friend of either the Bureau or the Bank, wrote that "The bank . . . had a promising future, and the friends of the

Negroes were justified in relying upon it to assist the former slaves to economic freedom." *Freedmen's Savings Bank,* 50.

44. In March 1880 Howard appeared before a committee of the Senate to give testimony concerning his connection with the Freedmen's Bank, but there were no charges against him. 46th Congress, 2d Session, Senate Report No. 440, Serial 1895, 263–78.

Church Dispute and House Investigation [191–208]

1. *Manual of the First Congregational Church, Washington, D. C.* (Washington, 1870), 8–9.
2. *Dictionary of American Biography,* II, 536.
3. First Congregational Society, *Minutes,* 50. The Society was the business organization whereas the church was the religious body.
4. *Ibid.,* 67.
5. I. Kimball to Howard, Feb. 15, 1866.
6. Walter L. Clift, "History of the First Congregational Church," in *Fiftieth Anniversary of the Founding of the First Congregational Church* (Washington [1915]), 44–45; Howard to Rev. Joshua Leavitt, June 23, 1866.
7. First Congregational Church, *Record,* 49–50.
8. O. O. Howard, *Address at the Laying of the Corner-Stone of the First Congregational Church* (Boston, 1867), 6.
9. *Manual of the First Congregational Church,* 8.
10. Howard to J. A. Sladen, Oct. 20, 1866; Clift, "History of the First Congregational Church," 46.
11. Howard to C. B. Boynton, May 22, 1866.
12. First Congregational Society, *Minutes,* Feb. 19, 1867, 109.
13. Howard, *Autobiography,* II, 427.
14. Howard to H. H. Boody, May 27, 1867.
15. Howard to Rev. J. E. Rankin, Nov. 19, 1890; Howard, *Autobiography,* II, 428–30.
16. Howard to Rev. Ray Palmer, May 8, 1867.
17. R. P. Buck to Howard, June 5, 1867; Howard to H. H. Boody, June 22, 1867.
18. Howard to Rev. Ray Palmer, July 1, 1867.
19. Howard to the Congregational Churches, June 10, 1867.
20. Clift, "History of the First Congregational Church," 47.
21. Howard to Theodore Tilton, May 16, 1867.
22. Howard Investigation, 104, 131.
23. Howard to R. P. Buck, July 6, 1867; First Congregational Society, *Minutes,* Sept. 24, 1867, 176.
24. Howard to Greble, Oct. 4, 1867.
25. Clift, "History of the First Congregational Church," 29.
26. Washington *Chronicle,* March 13, 1868; *Advance* (Chicago), Feb. 20, 1868.
27. C. B. Boynton, *A Duty Which the Colored People Owe to Themselves* (Washington, 1867), 8.
28. Clift, "History of the First Congregational Church," 29.
29. First Congregational Church, *Record,* Nov. 25, 1867, 70–71.
30. *Ibid.,* 71.

NOTES

31. E. H. Fairchild to Howard, Jan. 24, 1868; S. Hine to Howard, Jan. 27, 1868.
32. First Congregational Church, *Record*, 75–76; C. B. Boynton to Howard, Feb. 3, 1868.
33. First Congregational Church, *Record*, 76–78.
34. Washington, *Chronicle*, March 13, 1868.
35. J. E. Ekin to Howard, Feb. 19, 1868; Washington, *Chronicle*, March 13, 1868.
36. Cincinnati *Gazette*, Jan. 31, 1868.
37. Howard to H. V. N. Boynton, Feb. 1, 1868.
38. *National Intelligencer*, Nov. 20, 1868; Howard, *Autobiography*, II, 433.
39. *Ibid.*, 433–34; Howard to J. A. Ekin, Feb. 20, 1868.
40. Cincinnati *Gazette*, Feb. 13, June 30, 1868.
41. Howard to Whipple, Feb. 12, 1868.
42. Cincinnati *Gazette*, Feb. 13, 1868.
43. Eliot to Howard, Feb. 17, 1868.
44. Howard to Eliot, Feb. 18, 1868.
45. Cincinnati *Gazette*, Feb. 24, 1868.
46. First Congregational Church, *Record*, 82–83, 85–88.
47. E.g. Howard to H. W. Beecher, May 22, 1868.
48. Cincinnati *Gazette*, June 30, 1868.
49. Howard to Editor, Cincinnati *Gazette*, June 30, 1868.
50. Howard Investigation, 132.
51. First Congregational Church, *Record*, Nov. 8, 1868.
52. *Proceedings of an Ex Parte Council, Held at the First Congregational Church, Washington, D. C. November 18th to 20th, 1868* (Philadelphia, 1868); *National Intelligencer*, Nov. 18–21, 1868.
53. Howard Investigation, 428–29; N. Y. *Tribune*, Dec. 4, Nov. 27, 1868.
54. Howard Investigation, 157; J. Hurlburt to Howard, Jan. 12, 1869.
55. Howard Investigation, 104.
56. Washington *Chronicle*, Jan. 19, 1869; *Independent*, Jan. 21, 1869.
57. *National Intelligencer*, Jan. 16, 1869.
58. Washington *Chronicle*, Jan. 19, 1869; *Independent*, Jan. 21, 1869.
59. Washington *Chronicle*, Jan. 19, 1869.
60. Howard to Mrs. Howard, Feb. 8, 1869.
61. *Independent*, April 29, 1869; First Congregational Society, *Minutes*, 187–88.
62. *Ibid.*, 189–90.
63. First Congregational Church, *Record*, 112–14; *National Intelligencer*, April 24, 1869.
64. *Ibid.*, April 26, 1869.
65. Howard to J. E. Rankin, Aug. 27, 1870 [1869]; A. D. Kingsbury to Howard, Sept. 2, 1869.
66. Clift, "History of the First Congregational Church," 31–32; *Manual of the First Congregational Church*, 10.
67. He became president of Howard University in 1889. *Dictionary of American Biography*, XV, 374.
68. Howard to J. T. Drew, Oct. 6, 1870.
69. Clift, "History of the First Congregational Church," 46.
70. Samuel A. Pleasants, *Fernando Wood of New York* (N. Y., 1948), chs. 6–10.

71. *Congressional Globe,* April 6, 1870, 41st Congress, 2d Session, pt. 3, 2462.
72. *Ibid.,* March 30, 1870, 2295.
73. Washington *Chronicle,* April 1, 1870.
74. Howard to Wood, April 1, 1870.
75. Howard Investigation, 429.
76. *Congressional Globe,* April 8, 1870, 41st Congress, 2d Session, pt. 3, 2461–63.
77. During the investigation, Sherman wrote to Howard expressing his sympathy and his absolute trust in Howard's "truth and honor" but at the same time he expressed again his dissatisfaction with Howard's continued connection with the Bureau. "You cannot serve two masters: you cannot be purely a military man, and conduct such a machine as the Freedmen's Bureau—with colleges, schools and churches" was Sherman's admonition. Sherman to Howard, May 2, 1870.
78. Howard Investigation, 59.
79. J. E. Rankin to Howard, April 13, 1870; A. F. Boyle to Howard, April 11, 1870.
80. E.g., E. B. Webb to Howard, April 13, 1870.
81. Howard Investigation, 516–21.
82. *Ibid.,* 426–28.
83. *Ibid.,* 465.
84. *Ibid.,* 480–82.
85. Howard to S. P. Lee, June 14, 1870.
86. Howard to E. S. Tobey, June 27, 1870.
87. *Congressional Globe,* July 13, 1870, 41st Congress, 2d Session, pt. 6, 5526.
88. Howard Investigation, 13.
89. *Ibid.,* 20–21.
90. *Ibid.,* 48, 54.
91. Howard to Editor, Philadelphia *Evening Bulletin,* July 16, 1870.
92. *Congressional Globe,* Feb. 22, 1871, 41st Congress, 3rd Session, pt. 2, 1525–34; Howard, MS Diary, Feb. 22, 1871, HU.
93. Arnell to Howard, March 2, 1871; *Congressional Globe,* March 2, 1871, 41st Congress, 3d Session, pt. 3, 1850–51; W. Townsend to Howard, March 2, 1871.

Peace with the Apaches [209–219]

1. Delano to Howard, Feb. 28, 1872.
2. Frank C. Lockwood, *The Apache Indians* (N. Y., 1938), chs. VIII and IX; Hubert H. Bancroft, *History of Arizona and New Mexico* (San Francisco, 1889), 552–59.
3. Ralph H. Ogle, *Federal Control of the Western Apaches, 1848–1886* (Albuquerque, 1940), 79–81.
4. *Ibid.,* 86–90.
5. Lockwood, *Apache Indians,* 186–87.
6. *Ibid.,* 101–02.
7. Maj. Gen. J. M. Schofield to Lt. Gen. P. Sheridan, Dec., 29, 1871, AGO, 1872, 274, NA. Schofield commanded the Military Division of the Pacific and Sheridan the Military Division of the Missouri. This communication

deals with Indian depredations of 1871 especially those by Cochise and his band of Chiricahua Apaches.
8. *Alta California,* Nov. 22, 1871, AGO, 1871, 4216, NA.
9. General Orders No. 10, Nov. 21, 1871, AGO, 1871, 2465, NA.
10. Ogle, *Federal Control of the Apaches,* 102.
11. Delano to Secretary of War, Feb. 29, 1872, AGO, 1872, 717, NA.
12. O. O. Howard, *My Life and Experiences Among Our Hostile Indians* (Hartford, 1907), 123.
13. Report of Brigadier General O. O. Howard, U. S. A., June, 1872, 42d Congress, 3d Session, House Ex. Doc. 1, pt. 5, Serial 1560, 544 (hereafter referred to as Howard, Apache Report).
14. Howard to Indian Commissioner, General F. A. Walker, March 18, 1872, Indian Office, Arizona, H-1249, NA; E. P. Smith to Mrs. Howard, March 18, 1872.
15. Howard to Mrs. Howard, March 21, 27, 30, April 3, 1872.
16. Howard to Delano, April 7, 1872, Indian Office, Arizona, H-1314, NA.
17. Howard to Mrs. Howard, April 15, 1872.
18. Howard to Grant, April 15, 1872, Indian Office, Arizona, I-1392, NA; Howard to Schofield, April 18, 1872, Indian Office, Arizona, H-1352, NA.
19. George Crook, *General Crook, His Autobiography,* edited and annotated by Martin F. Schmitt (Norman, Okla., University of Oklahoma Press, 1946), 169.
20. Howard to Crook, May 9, 1872, AGO, 1872, 2100, NA.
21. Howard to Delano, May 24, 1872, Indian Office, Arizona, H-1422, NA.
22. Howard, Apache Report, 541.
23. Howard to Benjamin Tatham [June 26–29?, 1872].
24. Grant to Adjutant General, July 3, 1872, AGO, 1872, 2663, NA.
25. Howard to Dr. H. Bendell, Aug. 29, 1872, Indian Office, Letters of General Howard, NA; Howard to Mrs. Howard, Sept. 5, 1872.
26. Thomas E. Farish, *History of Arizona* (Phoenix, 1915), II, 230.
27. *Ibid.,* 228, 231.
28. Howard, *Hostile Indians,* 188–89.
29. Howard to Commanding Officer, Fort Craig and Fort McRea, Sept. 19, 1872, Indian Office, Letters of General Howard, NA.
30. O. O. Howard, *The Indians: Account of Gen'l Howard's Mission to the Apaches and Navajos,* Re-printed from the Washington *Daily Morning Chronicle,* Nov. 10, 1872, 6.
31. Howard, *Hostile Indians,* 207.
32. Howard to Crook, Oct. 11, 1872, Indian Office, Letters of General Howard, NA.
33. *Ibid.*
34. Howard, *Hostile Indians,* 224.
35. In 1891 Howard wrote to Sladen, ". . . every promise you and I made those Apaches, through Jeffords, was afterwards broken by the agents of our Government. The Indians were bad enough, but considering our light and knowledge, I think we have been a little worse than Indians." Howard to J. A. Sladen, March 4, 1891.
36. Howard to F. A. Walker, Oct. 23, 1872, Indian Office, Arizona, H-1329, NA.
37. Safford to Howard, Nov. 16, 1872.
38. Howard, *Hostile Indians,* 224.

39. Crook to AAG, Military Division of the Pacific (hereafter referred to as MDP), Dec. 13, 1872, AGO, 1872, 5312, NA.
40. Crook to AAG, MDP, Jan. 24, 1873, AGO, 1873, 783, NA; Report of Thomas J. Jeffords, Aug. 31, 1873, in *Annual Report of the Commissioner of Indian Affairs for the Year 1873* (Washington, 1874), 292.
41. Howard's endorsement on letter from Crook to AAG, MDP, Jan. 24, 1873, AGO, 1873, 783, NA.
42. Crook to AAG, MDP, Feb. 11, 1873, AGO, 1873, 831, NA.
43. Correspondence of Major William R. Price, to Headquarters, District of New Mexico, Aug. 1, 1873, War Department, LR, 7497, NA.
44. Major William R. Price to AAG, Dist. of New Mexico, Aug. 1, 1873, War Department, LR, 7497, NA.
45. Howard to Indian Commissioner, Sept. 23, 1873, War Department, LR, 1873, 7497, NA.
46. Crook to Adjutant General, Dec. 8, 1873, War Department, LR, 7497, NA.
47. H. R. Clum, Acting Indian Commissioner, to Secretary of Interior, Sept. 26, 1873, Indian Office, Correspondence, Land Division, vol. 12, no. 331, NA; William Vanderer, Inspector, to Indian Commissioner, Jan. 23, 1874, War Department, LR, 7497, NA; L. E. Dudley, Superintendent of Indian Affairs, Santa Fe, to Indian Commissioner, June 30, 1874, in *Report of the Commissioner of Indian Affairs for 1874*, 43d Congress, 2d Session, House Ex. Doc. 1, pt. 5, 608; Farish, *History of Arizona*, II, 235.
48. Report of T. J. Jeffords, in *Annual Report of the Commissioner of Indian Affairs for the Year 1873*, 292.
49. E. C. Watkins to Howard, April 18, 1878.

Bounty Paying Court of Inquiry [220–235]

1. C. W. Foster to Howard, Feb. 24, 1866, BR, LR, A-137, NA.
2. Bentley, *Freedmen's Bureau*, 87.
3. Howard to Gen. R. Schenck, Feb. 27, 1867, BR, LS, III, 84, NA; *Proceedings, Findings and Opinion of Court of Inquiry . . . in the Case of Oliver Otis Howard* (Washington, 1874), 35, 43–44 (hereafter cited as *Court of Inquiry*).
4. *Ibid.*, 238–39.
5. See Circular No. 16, April 17, 1867, and Circular No. 19, May 27, 1867 which contain instructions for paying bounties. BR, Circulars and Circular Letters, 52, 53, 56, NA.
6. Balloch to Howard, June 8, 1868, BR, LS, IV, 438, NA.
7. Whittlesey to T. D. Eliot, June 26, 1868, BR, LS, IV, 463, NA.
8. 41st Congress, 2d Session, House Ex. Doc. 241, Serial 1425, 38–39.
9. H. M. Whittlesey to Balloch and Drew, Sept. 13, 1869, BR, LS, V, 503, NA.
10. Howard to E. B. French, Dec. 18, 1869, BR, LS, VI, 87, NA.
11. Howard to D. S. Mays, Aug. 15, 1871, BR, LS, VII, 170, NA. For two other instances in which Howard pursued defrauders in the Freedmen's Bureau, see Howard to Secretary of War, Jan. 4, 9, 1872, BR, LS, VII, 295, 302, NA.
12. See, e.g. Lt. Col. C. E. Compton to Howard, July 12, 1870, BR, LR, T-96, NA.
13. Sewall to Howard, March 10, 1869, BR, LR, S-108, NA.

14. Whittlesey to Seely, Feb. 21, 1872, BR, LS, VII, 334, NA.
15. Bentley, *Freedmen's Bureau,* 148; Howard to Rowland B. Howard, Feb. 16, 1874.
16. *Court of Inquiry,* 104, 597–98; Balloch's Report for 1867, BR, LS, IV, 93, NA.
17. Howard to Brodhead, Jan. 27, 1870.
18. Brodhead to Howard, Jan. 27, 1870; Brodhead to Howard, Feb. 9, 1874, BR, LR, VI, 100; Brodhead to Secretary of the Treasury, March 10, 1874 (4th Indorsement on letter of W. W. Belknap to Secretary of the Treasury, Feb. 27, 1874), *Court of Inquiry,* 317.
19. C. F. Herring to Boutwell, Sept. 30, 1871, *Court of Inquiry,* 439.
20. *Ibid.;* Howard to Secretary of War, Dec. 30, 1871, BR, LS, VII, 287–88, NA.
21. Howard to Balloch, Oct. 7, 1871, BR, LS, VII, 195, NA.
22. Howard to Boutwell, Oct. 7, 1871, BR, LS, VII, 196, NA; Boutwell to Howard, Oct. 13, 1871, BR, LR, 913, NA.
23. Howard to Whittlesey, Oct. 19, 1871, BR, LS, VII, 209, NA.
24. New York *Sun,* Oct. 18, 1871; see also, New York *Herald,* Oct. 21, 1871.
25. Howard to Ketchum, Oct. 20, 1871. Ketchum in a letter signed "M," retold the story, as he had it from Howard, to the New York *Evening Mail.* Oct. 23, 1871.
26. Howard to Balloch, Oct. 31, 1871, BR, LS, VII, 230, NA.
27. 42d Congress, 2d Session, House Journal, Serial 1501, 89; BR, LR, 1223, NA.
28. Howard to Secretary of War, Dec. 30, 1871, BR, LS, VII, 287–88, NA; 42d Congress, 2d Session, House Ex. Doc. 51, Serial 1510, 3–4.
29. New York *Tribune,* Jan. 11, 13, 1872; Howard to Reid, Jan. 16, 1872.
30. Howard to Secretary of War, March 4, 1871, BR, LS, VII, 54, NA.
31. See e.g. Whittlesey to E. R. Belcher, May 13, 1871, BR, LS, VII, 115, NA; Whittlesey to Charles H. Howard, June 5, 1871, BR, LS, VII, 129, NA.
32. Howard to Whittlesey, Aug. 30, 1871, BR, LS, VII, 180, NA; Howard to A. E. Buck, July 7, 1871, BR, LS, VII, 145, NA.
33. Howard to Secretary of War, Oct. 20, 1871, BR, LS, VII, 210–21, NA.
34. Howard to Cobb, Feb. 28, 1872, BR, LS, VII, 338, NA.
35. Whittlesey to Secretary of War, March 14, 1872, BR, LS, VII, 351, NA; Whittlesey to Bureau Agents, March 15, 1872, BR, LS, VII, 353, NA; Whittlesey to E. B. French, March 16, 1872, BR, LS, VII, 355, NA.
36. 43d Congress, 1st Session, House Ex. Doc. 10, Serial 1606, 22–23 (hereafter referred to as House Ex. Doc. 10). This document also appears in War Department, Adjutant General's Office, *Annual Report 1873–1878,* and in *Court of Inquiry,* Exhibit B.
37. *Ibid.,* 216; see also Belknap to J. A. Garfield, May 22, 1872, *ibid.,* 427–28.
38. Howard, *Autobiography,* II, 448–49; Howard to Chairman of Mil. Com. of House of Representatives, Feb. 7, 1873, House Ex. Doc. 10, 42–43. See also, *Court of Inquiry,* 454; John H. Cook to Howard, Jan. 31, 1873, House Ex. Doc. 10, 51. But see also T. M. Vincent to Adj. Gen., Feb. 20, 1873, *ibid.,* 52–56.
39. McMillan to Adj. Gen., July 13, 1872, *ibid.,* 28–29; Vincent to Adj. Gen., Oct. 7, 1872, *ibid.,* 21–22.

40. Howard to Mrs. Howard, Sept. 5, 1872.
41. See the printed correspondence in House Ex. Doc. 10, 28 ff.
42. *Ibid.*, 35.
43. *Court of Inquiry*, 410; also 42d Congress, 3d Session, House Journal, Serial 1551, Dec. 3, 1872, 30.
44. Howard to Charles H. Howard, Jan. 2, 1873.
45. Howard to W. H. Ward, July 21, 1873.
46. Howard to S. P. Lee, Dec. 29, 1873.
47. Harry S. Howard to Author, July 19, 1957; Howard, *Autobiography*, II, 65.
48. Howard to S. P. Lee, Dec. 29, 1873.
49. Howard to R. P. Buck, May 5, 1874.
50. Shaw to Vincent, March 19, 1873, *Court of Inquiry*, 409.
51. Howard to R. P. Buck, May 5, 1874.
52. See, e.g. Belknap to Howard, Dec. 23, 1872.
53. See, e.g. Howard to J. M. Brown, Jan. 29, 1873.
54. See, e.g. J. H. Cook to Howard, Jan. 31, 1873, BR, LR, VIII, 106½; this letter also in House Ex. Doc. 10, 50–51.
55. Howard to Whittlesey, July 23, 1873.
56. See, e.g. Belknap to Howard, Dec. 24, 1873.
57. Howard to Balloch, March 12, 1873.
58. Howard to E. B. French, March 25, 1873.
59. House Ex. Doc. 10, 1–3; Belknap sent a second communication Jan. 5, 1874, House Ex. Doc. 10, pt. 2, 1–6.
60. 43d Congress, 1st Session, House Journal, Serial 1593, Dec. 12, 1873, 100, 102.
61. Howard to John Coburn, Dec. 17, 1873.
62. Howard to Charles H. Howard, Feb. 10, 1874.
63. Howard to Rowland B. Howard, Feb. 19, 1874.
64. Howard to Rowland B. Howard, Feb. 16, 1874.
65. Howard to Balloch, Feb. 17, 1874.
66. Howard to Rowland B. Howard, Feb. 19, 1874. In Dec. 1875 a grand jury refused to indict Balloch on this question of financial irregularity, since they believed there was no criminal intent. H. H. Wells, U. S. Attorney, to E. Pierrepont, Attorney General, Dec. 22, 1875, in Annual Report of the Adjutant General on the Operations of the Freedmen's Branch of His Office, 1876, 10, in War Department, Adjutant General's Office, *Annual Report, 1873–78*. Balloch remained for many years an active figure in community circles, in the Congregational Church, and in the affairs of Howard University. He served as a trustee of the latter until after 1900.
67. *National Cyclopedia of American Biography*, XIV, 332–33.
68. Howard to Col. G. N. Lieber, April 8, 1885.
69. Schofield to Gen. A. H. Terry, Dec. 27, 1880, LS, Nov. 1880—Oct. 1883, 65–68, Schofield Papers, LC.
70. Special Orders No. 35, War Department, Adjutant General's Office, Feb. 16, 1874; also, *Court of Inquiry*, 1.
71. Special Orders No. 51, War Department, Adjutant General's Office, March 9, 1874, *Court of Inquiry*, 2.
72. Howard to G. A. Rollins, Feb. 20, 1874.
73. "Court seems strongly in sympathy." Howard to Charles H. Howard, April 6, 1874. The Court of Inquiry transcript is contained in over six hundred pages of printed record, already cited above.

74. *Court of Inquiry*, 3.
75. House Ex. Doc. 10, 2-3.
76. See e.g. *Court of Inquiry*, 40-48.
77. *Ibid.*, 515-28.
78. *Ibid.*, 529-45.
79. *Ibid.*, 546-92.
80. *Ibid.*, 601-02. The vote was unanimous except on the matter of investment of bounty money. Here the vote was 4-3 in Howard's favor. McDowell, Pope, and Getty believed the investment illegal. Washington *Chronicle*, May 15, July 7, 1874.
81. *Court of Inquiry*, 31-32.
82. *Ibid.*, 602.
83. Orville E. Babcock, Grant's private secretary.
84. General Edmund Schriver, Inspector General of the army.
85. Howard to Charles H. Howard, July 11, 1874.
86. 43d Congress, 2d Session, House Ex. Doc. 59, Serial 1645, 3-4; 44th Congress, 1st Session, House Ex. Doc. 144, Serial 1689, 2-9. These same documents also appear in War Department, Adjutant General's Office, *Annual Report, 1873-1878*.
87. Howard to E. P. Smith, Nov. 7 [1874].
88. Howard to Sherman, Nov. 15 [1875].
89. Sherman to Howard, Nov. 30, 1875. A Democratic Congress had been elected in 1874. Max Woodhull, Howard's former adjutant with the Bureau, believed that the motive for the attack on Howard was political. Woodhull to Howard, April 3, 1877.
90. Howard to Grant, Feb. 21 [1876].
91. Allan Nevins, *Hamilton Fish: The Inner History of the Grant Administration* (N. Y., 1936), 804-10.
92. Howard to Whittlesey, March 23 [1876].
93. Howard to Meigs, April 10 [1876].
94. Howard to Sherman, Jan. 18, 1877.
95. Sherman to Howard, Feb. 1, 1877.
96. Howard to Sherman, Jan. 5 [1878].
97. Sherman to Raynor, Jan. 20, 1878, LS, 1866-1878, 500-01, Sherman Papers, LC; Sherman to Howard, Jan. 26, 1878, 506-07, Sherman Papers, LC; Raynor to Sherman, Jan. 22, 1878; Raynor to Howard, Jan. 23, 1878.
98. New York *Tribune*, March 12, 13, 1878.
99. See G. W. Dyer to Howard, April 30, 1878.
100. Howard to J. H. Cook, Dec. 12 [1874]; G. W. Dyer to Howard, March 9, 1875.

Washington D. C. [236-243]

1. Howard to E. Whittlesey, July 16, 1866.
2. Howard to Oakes Ames, Oct. 19, 1871. Two years later Lizzie lost a baby which was born prematurely. Howard to Charles H. Howard, Nov. 29, 1873.
3. Washington *Chronicle*, Jan. 13, 1868.
4. Howard to E. Greble, July 28, 1868.
5. Howard to Rev. Jarvis Buxton, July 15, 1871.
6. Mrs. Howard to Howard, April 11, 1872.
7. Howard, *Autobiography*, II, 459-61.

8. Ketchum to Howard, Aug. 14, 1869.
9. Washington *Chronicle,* May 25, 1867; J. A. Cox to Howard, Sept. 30, 1869.
10. Howard to Scott, Aug. 19, 1887, Sept. 5, 1888; Howard to Allen Rutherford, Jan. 18, 1889; Howard to A. S. Pratt, Jan. 19, 1889.
11. Circular Letter, May 15, 1867, BR, LS, III, 221, NA; Howard to Rev. George Whipple, May 21, 1867, BR, LS, III, 227, NA.
12. De Forest, *A Union Officer in the Reconstruction,* 102–03.
13. Howard to J. R. Sypher, Aug, 30, 1866.
14. Howard to his mother, Dec. 31, 1867, Feb. 28, 1868. Later, he wrote of Johnson as "a special providence" sent by God just as were Pharaoh and Herod "whose wicked purposes were over ruled to the good of God's people." Howard to Frederick Douglass, July 10, 1870.
15. Howard to Mrs. Howard, Feb. 18, 1869.
16. Howard to T. W. Conway, Jan. 10, 1868.
17. Howard, MS Diary, Jan. 12, 1871, HU.
18. Howard to John B. Thacher, March 16, 1873.
19. Howard to Mrs. Howard, Oct. 16, 1873.
20. Howard, "Account of Tour Through the Southern States," MS, HU; Howard to J. T. McCleary, Dec. 5, 1903. The story reached the newspapers and the attention of J. G. Whittier who used it as the subject of a poem, "Howard at Atlanta."
21. Howard to W. W. Belknap, Jan. 29, 1872.
22. Howard to Mrs. Howard, April 18, 1872.
23. Howard, MS Diary, Feb. 9, 1871, HU; Sherman to [C. C.] Augur, Feb. 10, 1871, LS, 1866–1871, 230–31, Sherman Papers, LC.
24. Howard to W. W. Belknap, June 26, 1872.
25. Howard to Sherman, Nov. 11, 1872.
26. Sherman to Howard, Nov. 12, 1872.
27. E. D. Townsend to Howard, Nov. 13, 1872.
28. Sherman to P. H. Sheridan, Nov. 16, 1872, LS, 1866–1878, 223, Sherman Papers, LC.
29. Howard to D. O'Dell, April 29, 1873.
30. Howard to Barney, Nov. 14, 1873; Barney to Howard, Nov. 24, 1873.
31. Howard to Grant, Nov. 27, 1873. See also Howard's personal letter to Grant expanding these same reasons, Nov. 27, 1873.
32. Howard to Sherman, Nov. 27, 1873.
33. Sherman to Howard, Nov. 29, 1873.
34. Washington *Chronicle,* July 7, 1874.

Service in the Northwest [244–269]

1. Howard to E. P. Smith, March 26 [1875].
2. Their home was in Portland until 1878, when they moved to Vancouver Barracks six miles from the city. Howard, *Autobiography,* II, 479.
3. *Ibid.,* II, 476–77. At Howard's recommendation, the military force in Alaska was withdrawn and a civilian government instituted. Howard's Report, 44th Congress, 2d Session, House Ex. Doc. 1, pt. 2, Serial 1742, 89–90.
4. Howard to Rowland B. Howard, Sept. 30 [1874].
5. Howard, *Autobiography,* II, 468; Howard to E. Whittlesey, Dec. 15, 1874.
6. Howard to Rev. H. W. Stratton, May 24 [1876].

NOTES

7. Howard to W. D. Howells, Aug. 10 [1875]; Howard to Charles H. Howard, Jan. 25, 1877; Howard, *Autobiography*, II, 474.
8. Howard to his mother, Nov. 27, 1879.
9. Howard to Sherman, July 11, 1876; Sherman to Howard, July 12, 1876.
10. Howard to John Taylor, Oct. 25 [1878].
11. Howard to E. P. Smith, Nov. 7 [1874].
12. Howard to Charles H., or Rowland B. Howard, Dec. 18, 1874.
13. Howard to Hayes, June 19 [1876].
14. The "z" is sounded and the final "e" of Perce should not be accented. Francis Haines, *The Nez Perces* (Norman, Okla., 1955), 15.
15. *Ibid.*, 139, 147-49.
16. *Ibid.*, 193-94; Howard to W. B. Cudlipp, July 12, 1876.
17. Report of the Commissioner of Indian Affairs, in Report of the Secretary of the Interior, 1876, 44th Congress, 2d Session, Serial 1749, 384.
18. See e.g. Helen A. Howard, *War Chief Joseph* (Caldwell, Idaho, 1941), 90. This contains an excerpt from a letter of Governor Grover giving reasons for making Joseph's band go onto a reservation.
19. O. O. Howard, *Nez Perce Joseph* (Boston, 1881), 32.
20. Helen A. Howard, *War Chief Joseph*, 101.
21. Report of Civil and Military Commission to Nez Percé Indians, in Report of the Secretary of the Interior, 1877, 45th Congress, 2d Session, Serial 1800, 607.
22. *Ibid.*, 609-10; Helen A. Howard, *War Chief Joseph*, 71.
23. Howard, *Nez Perce Joseph*, 35; Supplementary Report of Gen. O. O. Howard, Dec. 26, 1877, in Report of the Secretary of War, 1877, 45th Congress, 2d Session, Serial 1794, 586 (hereafter referred to as Howard, Supplementary Report).
24. Monteith to J. Q. Smith, Feb. 9, 1877, Nez Perce War, AGO, 1364, NA.
25. Helen A. Howard, *War Chief Joseph*, 106.
26. W. T. Sherman, endorsement on letter of acting Secretary of the Interior to the Secretary of War, March 13, 1877, Nez Perce War, AGO, 1364, NA: Report of General of the Army, in Report of the Secretary of War, 1877, 45th Congress, 2d Session, Serial 1794, 9 (hereafter referred to as RSW, 1877).
27. Monteith to Howard, March 19, 1877.
28. Howard, Supplementary Report, 593-95. For information about this council and the ensuing Nez Perce war see *An Army Doctor's Wife on the Frontier: Letters from Alaska and the Far West, 1874-1878*, Abe Laufe, ed. (University of Pittsburgh Press, 1962), 246-312. Emily McCorkle Fitz-Gerald, the doctor's wife, was at Lapwai during much of this time. Her letters contain numerous comments on General Howard.
29. Howard, *Nez Perce Joseph*, 70.
30. Howard to Charles H. Howard, May 22, 1877; Monteith to Howard, May 30, 1877, Department of the Columbia (hereafter referred to as D. of C.), LR, 1877, 958, NA.
31. Helen A. Howard, *War Chief Joseph*, 124-25.
32. *Ibid.*, 125.
33. Joseph, "An Indian's View of Indian Affairs," *North American Review*, CXXVIII (April, 1879), 424.
34. Helen A. Howard, *War Chief Joseph*, 126-30.
35. *Ibid.*, 130.

36. Howard, Supplementary Report, 599.
37. Howard, *Nez Perce Joseph*, 92.
38. Howard, Supplementary Report, 600–01.
39. Howard to [L. P.] Brown, June 15, 1877, D. of C., LS, 1877, V, 108, NA; Howard to AAG, D. of C., June 15, 1877, D. of C., LR, 1877, NA.
40. Howard, Supplementary Report, 602.
41. Howard to AAG, MDP, June 16, 1877, Claims of Nez Perce Indians, 56th Congress, 1st Session, Senate Document 257, Serial 3867, 10 (hereafter referred to as Nez Perce Claims.)
42. Howard, Supplementary Report, 602.
43. See e.g. Howard to Captain David Perry, June 20, 1877, D. of C., LS, 1877, IV, 36, NA.
44. Howard to Green, June 23, 1877, D. of C., LS, 1877, IV, 40, NA; Howard, Supplementary Report, 602.
45. McDowell to Sherman, July 3, 4, 1877, Nez Perce Claims, 28.
46. Howard, Supplementary Report, 602–03.
47. *Ibid.*, 603; L. V. McWhorter, *Hear Me, My Chiefs!* (Caldwell, Idaho, Caxton Printers, 1952), 304; Howard, *Nez Perce Joseph*, 166.
48. [H. C.] Wood to AAG, MDP, July 14, 1877, Nez Perce Claims, 37; McDowell to Howard, July 17, 1877, *ibid.*, 40.
49. H. C. Wood to the President, July 14, 1877, D. of C., LS, 1877, II, 196, 197, NA; Keeler to McDowell, July 12, 1877, Nez Perce Claims, 37.
50. Hubert H. Bancroft, *History of Washington, Idaho, Montana, 1845–1889* (San Francisco, 1890), 508.
51. Haines, *The Nez Percés*, 238–39.
52. Howard to AAG, D. of C., July 15, 1877, Nez Perce Claims, 41; Helen A. Howard, *War Chief Joseph*, 186–87.
53. Howard, Supplementary Report, 606.
54. McDowell's written comment on a copy of Howard's letter to AAG, MDP, July 15, 1877, the letter stating that he (Howard) would await Green's arrival from Ft. Boise and that of the 2d Infantry from Georgia. The Nez Perce War, AGO, 6724, NA. McDowell had all of Howard's correspondence to the end of August copied and sent to General Sherman. In the margins McDowell made comments, almost always critically sarcastic. Other copied letters in addition to the one cited above in Nez Perce War, AGO, box no. 1181, NA.
55. Howard, Supplementary Report, 607; Howard to S. S. Fenn, July 21, 1877, D. of C., LS, 1877, IV, 94, NA.
56. Howard to Wilkinson, Aug. 5, 1877, D. of C., LS, IV, 263, NA.
57. Howard to Col. Alfred Sully, Aug. 1, 1877, D. of C., LS, 1877, IV, 256, NA; Howard to Commanding Officer, Post of Missoula, July 25, 1877, *ibid.*, 240, NA.
58. Howard to Green, July 31, 1877, *ibid.*, 256, NA.
59. Keeler to McDowell, July 30, 1877, Nez Perce Claims, 53–54.
60. Howard, Supplementary Report, 607–08.
61. *Ibid.*, 608; J. F. Mills to McDowell, July 27, 1877, Nez Perce Claims, 51.
62. Report of Capt. C. C. Rawn, Sept. 30, 1877, in RSW, 1877, 500–01.
63. See Howard to AAG, MDP, July 27, 28, 29, 1877, Nez Perce Claims, 55–56.
64. Howard, Supplementary Report, 609.
65. R. C. Drum, AAG, Military Division of the Missouri, to McDowell,

July 24, 1877, Nez Perce Claims, 47; Report of Brigadier General Alfred H. Terry in RSW, 1877, 500.
  66. Report of Colonel John Gibbon, *ibid.*, 502.
  67. *Ibid.*, 503–04. McWhorter says that there was no fighting on the 10th. *Hear Me, My Chiefs!* 397; see Howard to AAG, MDP, Aug. 14, 1877, Nez Perce Claims, 60. This indirectly states the time of the Indians' departure from Gibbon's front.
  68. Howard to [AAG, D. of C.], Aug. 5, 1877, *ibid.*, 58–59; Howard, Supplementary Report, 608–09.
  69. *Ibid.*, 609.
  70. *Ibid.*, 609–10; McWhorter, *Hear Me, My Chiefs!* 397; G. O. Shields, *The Battle of the Big Hole* (Chicago and N. Y., 1889), 78.
  71. Howard, Supplementary Report, 610.
  72. Terry commanded the Department of Dakota; General George Crook, the Department of the Platte.
  73. Howard to AAG, MDP, Aug. 14, 1877, Nez Perce Claims, 60–61.
  74. Sherman to McDowell, June 25, 1877 (telegraphed to Commanding Officer, D. of C., June 26, 1877), *ibid.*, 20–21.
  75. *Ibid.*, 53, 56.
  76. [J. C.] Kelton to Howard, Aug. 17, 1877, *ibid.*, 61.
  77. *Ibid.*
  78. Howard, *Nez Perce Joseph*, 217–22.
  79. Howard to AAG, MDP, Aug. 20, 1877, Nez Perce Claims, 65; Howard, Supplementary Report, 611–12.
  80. Howard to AAG, MDP, Aug. 19, 1877, Nez Perce Claims, 64.
  81. Howard to Gov. of Montana Territory [Aug. 19, 1877], D. of C. LS, 1877, V, 29, NA.
  82. Howard, Supplementary Report, 612.
  83. E. Miles to AAG, D. of C., Aug. 23, 1877, D. of C., LR, 1877, 3066, NA; Howard, Supplementary Report, 617.
  84. Howard, *Nez Perce Joseph*, 235.
  85. Howard to Sherman, Aug. 24, 1877, Sherman's Report in RSW, 1877, 12–13.
  86. Sherman to Howard, Aug. 24, 1877, *ibid.*, 13.
  87. Howard to AAG, MDP, Aug. 24, 1877, Nez Perce Claims, 66.
  88. Nez Perce War, AGO, box no. 1181, NA.
  89. Howard, *Nez Perce Joseph*, 237; Howard to Sherman, Nov. 27 [1877].
  90. Howard to Sherman, Aug. 27, 1877, Sherman's Report in RSW, 1877, 13. Sherman's reply to this was such as to reassure Howard. Among other things, he wrote: "Have every possible faith in your intense energy, but thought it probable you were worn out. . . ." Sherman to Howard, Aug. 28, 1877 (Helena, Mont.), *ibid.*
  91. Sherman to Howard, Aug. 29, 1877, Nez Perce War, AGO, 6436, NA.
  92. Gilbert to Howard, Sept. 16, 1877, D. of C., LR, 1877, 2916, NA.
  93. Howard to AAG, MDP, Sept. 16, 1877, Nez Perce Claims, 73; Howard to Gilbert, Sept. 21, 1877, D. of C., LS, 1877, V, 75, NA.
  94. Howard to Sherman, Nov. 27 [1877].
  95. Gibbon to Howard, Aug. 18, 1877, D. of C., LR, 1877, 2872, NA.
  96. Sturgis' Report in RSW, 1877, 510; Howard, Supplementary Report, 622.
  97. Sturgis' Report in RSW, 1877, 511–12.

98. Howard to Miles, Sept. 12, 1877, Howard, Supplementary Report, 623.
99. Howard to Miles, Sept. 20, 1877, D. of C., LS, 1877, V, 74, NA; Sturgis' Report in RSW, 1877, 512; Howard, Supplementary Report, 628.
100. Howard to Miles, Sept. 26, 1877, D. of C., LS, 1877, V, 82, NA.
101. Howard to AAG, D. of C., Sept. 21, 1877, D. of C., LS, 1877, V, 76, NA.
102. Howard to AAG, MDP, Sept. 26, 1877, Nez Perce Claims, 73.
103. Howard to Gibbon, Sept. 27, 1877, D. of C., LS, 1877, V, 85, NA.
104. Howard to [AAG, MDP], Sept. 27, 1877, Nez Perce Claims, 73.
105. Howard, *Nez Perce Joseph*, 264–65; Howard, Supplementary Report, 629.
106. Howard, *Nez Perce Joseph*, 265; C. E. S. Wood, "The Pursuit and Capture of Chief Joseph," in C. A. Fee, *Chief Joseph* (N. Y., 1936), 322.
107. Howard, Supplementary Report, 629.
108. Report of Colonel N. A. Miles in RSW, 1877, 527–28.
109. Miles to General Howard, General Sturgis, or Major Brotherton, Sept. 30, 1877, D. of C., LR, 1877, 2939, NA.
110. Miles to Terry, Oct. 3, 1877, Terry's Report in RSW, 1877, 514–15.
111. C. E. S. Wood, "Pursuit and Capture," 325–26.
112. Guy Howard to Sturgis, Oct. 5, 1877, D. of C., LS, 1877, V, 91, NA.
113. Sturgis Report in RSW, 1877, 513.
114. Howard, Supplementary Report, 630; C. E. S. Wood, "Chief Joseph, the Nez Percé," *Century*, XXVIII (May, 1884), 141. McWhorter is most emphatic on this point. "The importance of Howard's arrival on the ultimate decision of the battle should not be underestimated. To the Nez Perces it meant another army was within striking distance. The charge on their fortified position which Miles dared not attempt alone could be undertaken when the two forces were joined." McWhorter, *Hear Me, My Chiefs!* 492.
115. Howard, Supplementary Report, 630; Haines, *The Nez Percés*, 279–80; C. E. S. Wood, "Pursuit and Capture," 330. There have been various versions of this story, both as to who actually said the words (several accounts have Joseph making this speech to Howard) and the words themselves.
116. Howard, Supplementary Report, 630.
117. C. E. S. Wood, "Chief Joseph, the Nez Percé," 142. On Joseph's surrender of his rifle see McWhorter, *Hear Me, My Chiefs!* 497, note 10 for a detailed discussion of various conflicting accounts.
118. C. E. S. Wood, "Pursuit and Capture," 330; Howard to Miles, Dec. 26, 1877, D. of C., LS, 1877, IV, 223, NA; Howard to Gen. D. S. Stanley, Sept. 28, 1895; Miles to Terry, Oct. 5, 1877, Nez Perce Claims, 74–75; Chicago *Tribune*, Oct. 10, 1877.
119. Miles to AAG, Dept. of Dakota, Oct. 6, 1877, Terry's Report in RSW, 1877, 516.
120. General Miles' congratulatory order, Oct. 7, 1877, Nez Perce Claims, 76–77; Miles' Report in RSW, 1877, 528–29.
121. See e.g. Chicago *Tribune*, Oct. 11, 1877; *Army and Navy Journal*, Oct. 13, 1877. Sherman wired to Sheridan on October 10, 1877. His message began: "Genl Miles & his command again carry off honors to which they are fairly entitled." Nez Perce War, AGO, 6286, NA.
122. C. E. S. Wood, "Pursuit and Capture," 333.
123. Howard to Sherman, March 14, 1877.
124. Miles to Howard, Jan. 8, 31, June 8, 1878.

125. Howard to Miles, Oct. 7, 1877, Howard, Supplementary Report, 631–32.
126. Howard to Miles, March 29, 1878.
127. C. E. S. Wood, "Pursuit and Capture," 335.
128. Watkins to J. S. Smith, July 20, 1877, Nez Perce War, AGO, 5219, NA; Sherman to Sheridan, Aug. 31, 1877, Nez Perce War, AGO, 5558, NA; Sheridan to Gen. E. D. Townsend, Oct. 10, 1877, Nez Perce War, AGO, 6286, NA.
129. Howard was not one to grant an excessive amount of praise to the Nez Perces for their manner of conducting the campaign as has been true of other writers. Two years after the war he wrote: ". . . more horrid outrages than those they committed near the Mount Idaho country cannot be found in any annals of Indian massacres. . . . The details concerning the dead, concerning what preceded the final acts that ended life are sickening in their horrors. . . . these savages were not saints. . . ." Howard to Editor, *Army and Navy Journal*, April 13, 1879. See also, Howard, "The True Story of the Wallowa Campaign," *North American Review*, CXXIX (July, 1879), 63.
130. Howard to McDowell [May 20, 1878], Nez Perce War, AGO, 3570, NA. McDowell concurred in Howard's opinion.
131. Haines, *The Nez Percés*, 295–96.
132. C. F. Brimlow, *The Bannock Indian War of 1878* (Caldwell, Idaho, 1938), 43–44.
133. *Ibid.*, 48–49, 73–74.
134. Howard to AAG, MDP, May 30, 1878, Appendix to Report of General McDowell, in Report of the Secretary of War, 45th Congress, 3d Session, House Ex. Doc. 1, pt. 2, Serial 1843, 127 (hereafter referred to as McDowell Report, 1878).
135. Howard's Report for 1878, in Report of the Secretary of War, 45th Congress, 3d Session, House Ex. Doc. 1, pt. 2, Serial 1843, 209–11 (hereafter referred to as Howard Report, 1878).
136. *Ibid.*, 213.
137. Howard to AAG, MDP, June 15, 1878, McDowell Report, 1878, 152; Brimlow, *Bannock Indian War*, 109–10.
138. General Field Orders No. 1, June 16, 1878, Howard Report, 1878, 215–16.
139. Howard to [AAG, MDP], June 24, 1878, McDowell Report, 1878, 159.
140. Howard Report, 1878, 221.
141. Brimlow, *Bannock Indian War*, 136–39.
142. Howard Report, 1878, 220.
143. Howard to AAG, MDP, July 9, 1878, McDowell Report, 1878, 170.
144. Howard Report, 1878, 222–24.
145. Extract from Miles' Report in Howard Report, 1878, 224–26.
146. Howard Report, 1878, 227–28.
147. Howard to AAG, MDP, July 28, 1878, McDowell Report, 1878, 179.
148. Brimlow, *Bannock Indian War*, 162–65, 177.
149. General John Pope congratulated Howard on his "extraordinary success" and remarked on what a "fine impression" it had made throughout the country. Pope to Howard, Oct. 3, 1878.
150. Howard to G. H. Atkinson, Oct. 23, 1878.
151. Howard to Mr. Scott, Nov. 21, 1878.

152. Howard to Fords, Howard and Hurlbut, April 19, 1881.
153. Howard to General I. McDowell, Dec. 20, 1878; Howard to W. Stickney, June 15 [1880].
154. Brayman to Howard, March 19, 1879.
155. Howard to Frank [Smith], July 8, 1879.
156. Howard to Guy Howard, Oct. 20, 1879.
157. Howard to his mother, Nov. 5, 1880.
158. *Ibid.*
159. Morrow to Howard, Jan. 1, 1881. See also Col. E. L. Mason to Howard, Dec. 25, 1880.

Final Army Assignments [270-289]

1. Senator John A. Logan, formerly of the Army of the Tennessee, was especially bitter against West Point. To Howard he wrote in February 1881, after Howard had become superintendent, that he hoped that the Academy would become "so thoroughly patriotic in its feelings that we should have no record in future of an Officer of the Army disgracing his name, and the service by joining in a rebellion as they did in 1861, and as Cadets have said since the war, they would have no hesitancy in doing." Logan to Howard, Feb. 2, 1881.
2. George L. Andrews, "West Point and the Colored Cadets," *International Review,* IX (Nov., 1880), 479.
3. *Ibid.*
4. Report of the General of the Army, 1876, 44th Congress, 2d Session, House Ex. Doc. 1, pt. 2, Serial 1742, 23.
5. Peter S. Michie, "Caste at West Point," *North American Review,* CXXX (1880), 612.
6. Andrews, "West Point and the Colored Cadets," 478-84.
7. Schofield to Adjutant General, April 6, 7, 1880, Schofield Papers, LC; John M. Schofield, *Forty-Six Years in the Army* (N. Y., 1897), 445.
8. Schofield to Sherman, July 31, 1880, Schofield Papers, LC.
9. N. Y. *Tribune,* April 26, 1880.
10. Schofield, *Forty-Six Years in the Army,* 446.
11. Schofield to Adjutant General, Nov. 12, 1880, Schofield Papers, LC.
12. Schofield, *Forty-Six Years in the Army,* 447; Sherman to Howard, May 14, 1882.
13. Schofield's Report, 1880, 46th Congress, 3d Session, House Ex. Doc. 1, pt. 2, Serial 1952, 228-30. The N. Y. *Tribune's* reaction to the report was hostile. Nov. 17, 1880.
14. Howard, *Autobiography,* II, 486.
15. Howard to Sherman, Dec. 7, 1880, Sherman Papers, LC.
16. Sherman to Howard, Dec. 7, 1880.
17. Sherman to Garfield, Dec. 30, 1880, quoted in Dyson, *History of Howard University,* 495-96.
18. Whittaker was given a court-martial and found guilty. President Garfield disapproved the court's sentence on technical grounds, but ordered Whittaker dismissed from the Academy for academic reasons. N. Y. *Tribune,* Jan. 4, March 22, 1882.
19. Howard, *Autobiography,* II, 487.

20. Howard to Rowland B. Howard, March 9, 1881.
21. Howard's Report, 1881, Report of the Secretary of War, 47th Congress, 1st Session, House Ex. Doc. 1, pt. 2, Serial 2010, 158.
22. *Ibid.;* 47th Congress, 2d Session, House Ex. Doc. 1, pt. 2. Serial 2091, 158.
23. Post Orders No. 10, Special Orders No. 54, July 11, 1881, 74, USMA.
24. Post Orders No. 10, Special Orders No. 55, Aug. 10, 1882, 134, USMA.
25. See e.g. Post Orders No. 10, Special Orders No. 17, Feb. 7, 1881, 45, USMA, and Special Orders No. 18, Feb. 18, 1881, 45–46, USMA.
26. Post Orders No. 10, Special Orders No. 58, Aug. 26, 1882, 135, USMA.
27. Post Orders No. 10, Special Orders No. 48, June 11, 1881, 69, USMA.
28. Langdon to Howard, Sept. 24, 1881.
29. See e.g. Howard to T. Looker, March 19, 1881. To his son-in-law Howard wrote, "We are just completing the January Examination. The deficients appeal strongly to ones heart." Howard to J. T. Gray, Jan. 17, 1882.
30. Howard to Adjutant General, July 8, 1881.
31. Howard to DuBarry, July 11, 1881, Letters of the Superintendent, 258, USMA.
32. Howard's Report, 1881, Report of the Secretary of War, 47th Congress, 1st Session, House Ex. Doc. 1, pt. 2, Serial 2010, 170.
33. Howard's Report, 1882, 47th Congress, 2d Session, House Ex. Doc. 1, pt. 2, Serial 2091, 163.
34. Howard to Addison Martin, Jan. 24, 1882; Howard, *Autobiography,* II, 488.
35. Howard to J. T. Gray, March 1, 1881; Howard to Lizzie Van Blarcom, Oct. 12, 1881.
36. Howard to Lizzie Van Blarcom, June 14, 1882.
37. Howard to Mary W. L. Van Blarcom, March 19, 1881; Howard to Charles H. Howard, Nov. 26, 1881; Library Circulation Records 1879–1885, Officers, Civilians, Soldiers, 88, 115, 129, 160, USMA.
38. Howard to Dora Martin, Sept. 8 [1881]; Howard to James W. Howard, May 22, 1882.
39. Sherman to Howard, July 4, 1881; Howard to Sherman, July 6, 1881, Letters of the Superintendent, 235, USMA; Howard to Mrs. James T. Gray, Sept. 20, 1881.
40. Howard to C. H. Milliken, Feb. 28, 1881. He gave his weight as 160 pounds. He had his fiftieth birthday November 8, 1880.
41. Howard to Mrs. Charles H. Howard, May 13, 1882.
42. Howard to his mother, Nov. 23, 1850.
43. Miss J. S. Jennings to Howard, June 22, 1882.
44. Howard to Gen. R. C. Drum, July 2, 31, 1882.
45. Howard to Miss J. S. Jennings [Aug. 4, 1882].
46. Howard to Charles H. Howard, April 25, 1882.
47. E. H. Stevens to Hon. R. L. Gibson, June 23, 1882.
48. Report of the Board of Visitors to the United States Military Academy . . . 1882, 47th Congress, 2d Session, House Ex. Doc. 1, pt. 2. Serial 2091, 531.
49. Schofield to Adjutant General, Nov. 12, 1880, Schofield Papers, LC; Sherman's Report, in Report of Secretary of War, 1881, 47th Congress, 1st

Session, House Ex. Doc. 1, pt. 2, Serial 2010, 37. Sherman wanted to keep a general officer in command. *Ibid.*, 38; Gen. M. C. Meigs to Howard, Feb. 15, 1881.

50. Howard to Hon. C. A. Boutelle, Oct. 10, 1881.
51. Howard to Miss Susan P. Delafield, Nov. 30, 1883.
52. Howard to R. P. Buck, Aug. 1, 1882.
53. Howard to Webb, Aug. 1, 1882.
54. J. A. Sladen to Howard, July 14, 1882.
55. See Report of Secretary of War, 47th Congress, 2d Session, House Ex. Doc. 1, pt. 2, Serial 2091, 5; N. Y. *Tribune,* Sept. 1, 1882.
56. Post Orders No. 10, General Orders No. 13, Sept. 1, 1882, 137, USMA.
57. Two cadets who were at West Point during Howard's administration rose to prominence in later years. They were : Enoch H. Crowder of the class of 1881, and John J. Pershing who entered in July 1882. Official Register, USMA, 1881–1890.
58. Howard to R. P. Buck, Oct. 4, 1882.
59. Howard to Rowland B. Howard, Dec. 7, 1882. A year later Howard bought a house on the corner of Chicago and 22d Streets.
60. Gen. S. Breck to Howard, Sept. 5, 1885.
61. Col. E. L. Mason to Howard, Oct. 26, 1885, Howard's Report, Report of the Secretary of War, 49th Congress, 1st Session, House Ex. Doc. 1, pt. 2, Serial 2369, 146–48.
62. Flagler to Howard, July 8, 1883.
63. Howard to W. W. Patton, July 13, 1883.
64. See Howard, *Autobiography,* II, 494–545 for details of the trip.
65. Howard to Rowland B. Howard, Dec. 4, 1883.
66. His efforts to get Chancey into West Point had also failed.
67. Howard to Charles H. Howard, Dec. 8, 1882.
68. Howard to Sherman, Feb. [March] 6, 1886. A short time before this Howard had discussed all this with his brother Rowland and had said, "I hope no friend will worry the President in my behalf." Howard to Rowland B. Howard, Feb. 16, 1886.
69. See Howard to Mrs. L. S. Holloway, Jan. 18, 1886.
70. Howard to Terry, March 4, 1886.
71. Howard to Schofield, March 4, 1886.
72. He wrote to R. G. Drum, the adjutant general: "Many thanks for your kind & timely dispatch. It relieved me & my family from the pain of longer suspense. I am disappointed to drop down on the Register, but thankful for this expression of remaining confidence." Howard to Drum, March 19, 1886.
73. At this time the lieutenant general in command of the army was Sheridan. Schofield and Terry were the other major generals.
74. Howard to James W. Howard, Aug. 28, 1886.
75. Howard to M. S. A. Looney, Dec. 29, 1887.
76. Howard's Report, Report of the Secretary of War, House Ex. Docs., 49th Congress, 2d Session, Serial 2461, 137.
77. 49th Congress, 2d Session, Senate Ex. Doc. 117, Serial 2449, 6–34, 37; Howard's Report, Report of the Secretary of War, 49th Congress, 2d Session, House Ex. Doc. 1, pt. 2, Serial 2461, 145–46.
78. Howard to Grace H. Gray, June 25, 1888.
79. Howard to his mother, Sept. 23, 1888.
80. Howard to Sladen, Nov. 2, 1887.

81. Howard's Report, Report of the Secretary of War, 51st Congress, 1st Session, House Ex. Doc. 1, pt. 2, Serial 2715, 143–49; 53d Congress, 3d Session, House Ex. Doc. 1, pt. 2, Serial 3295, 102–03.
82. *Ibid.,* 102; Howard's Report, Report of the Secretary of War, 52d Congress, 2d Session, House Ex. Doc. 1, pt. 2, Serial 3077, 100.
83. Howard to J. H. Tourgee, Feb. 19, 1889.
84. Howard to G. W. Balloch, Feb. 7, 1889.
85. Howard to Frances Willard, Feb. 1, 1892.
86. Howard to Bessie Howard, Jan. 29, 1892, Lincoln Memorial University (hereafter referred to as LMU).
87. Howard, *Autobiography,* II, 565.
88. Howard to Mrs. L. C. Holloway, Nov. 28, 1884.
89. Howard to Sherman, Jan. 3, 1888.
90. Howard to Guy Howard, March 14 [1877].
91. Howard to Charles H. Howard, Dec. 5, 1890.
92. E.g. Howard to Capt. H. R. Pease, July 29, 1869.
93. E.g. Howard to E. B. Carley, Sept. 28, 1881.
94. Howard to A. Watson, Oct. 13, 1868.
95. Howard to Rev. J. H. Dixon, March 5, 1883.
96. Howard to Charles H. Howard, Oct. 27, 1888.
97. Howard to Mrs. Charles H. Howard, Oct. 24, 1893.
98. Howard to Prof. T. Raftery [March 24, 1882?].
99. Howard, MS Diary, Feb. 11, 1871, HU.
100. Howard to Prof. Thomas Condon, Nov. 26, Dec. 2, 1879.
101. Howard to Mrs. Holloway, Nov. 28, 1884.
102. Howard to J. Oppenheimer, March 2, 1877.
103. Howard to James W. Howard, July 10, 1888; see also Howard to James W. Howard, Nov. 4, 1878.
104. Howard to Y. E. Tate, April 9, 1867.
105. Howard, "Education of the Colored Man," MS copy of an address, HU.
106. Howard to Douglass, Dec. 12, 1874.
107. Howard to *The Advance,* Dec. [n.d.], 1884.
108. Howard to his mother, Jan. 31, 1885.
109. Howard to L. P. Olds, March 27, 1877.
110. Howard to the Board of Trustees of Howard University, Jan. 9, 1895.
111. Ulysses G. Lee, "Springfield and the Restoration of Conscience," paper read before the American Historical Association, Dec. 30, 1955, Washington, D. C.
112. Howard, *Autobiography,* II, 391.
113. Howard, "Education of the Colored Man," MS, HU.
114. Welles, *Diary,* III, 323; Browning, *Diary,* II, 126.

The Closing Years [290–299]

1. Howard to Kehr, Sept. 28, 1894.
2. Howard, *Autobiography,* II, 569.
3. Howard to Gen. O. Smith, Aug. 4, 1893.
4. Howard to Gen. G. A. Malden, Nov. 9, 1896.
5. Howard to Lt. Col. L. E. Dudley, Aug. 4, 1896.
6. Howard to Cyrus Kehr, Nov. 4, 1896.
7. Howard to J. Greusel, Nov. 6, 1896.

8. Charles H. Howard to Howard, June 19, 1896.
9. Swayne to Howard, Aug. 7, 1896.
10. Swayne to Howard, Nov. 9, 1896.
11. Swayne to McKinley, Dec. 9, 1896.
12. Howard to Col. Thomas M. Anderson, Feb. 9, 1897.
13. Howard to Swayne, Feb. 9, 1897.
14. Howard to Dodge, Feb. 17, 1897.
15. Howard to J. Sherman, Feb. 15, 1897.
16. Howard to R. A. Alger, March 8, 1897.
17. Howard to R. A. Alger, March 25, 1897.
18. Howard to Charles H. Howard, April 5, 1897.
19. Howard to Alger, May 6, 1897.
20. Howard to W. E. Barton, April 6, 1897; Kehr to Howard, Jan. 23, 1898, June 6, 1900.
21. A. A. Myers to Harry S. Howard, June 9, 1896.
22. R. L. Kincaid, *The Wilderness Road* (Harrogate, Tenn., 1955), 316–39; F. B. Avery, Address at Lincoln Memorial University, June 1930, LMU.
23. Harry S. Howard to Myers, June 16, 1896; Myers to Harry S. Howard, June 13, 1896.
24. Howard, "Personal Recollections of Abraham Lincoln," 877; see also O. O. Howard, "The Folk of The Cumberland Gap," *Munsey's Magazine*, XXVII (July, 1902), 506, and *Globe and Commercial Advertiser* (New York), Oct. 27, 1909.
25. Howard, *Autobiography*, II, 568; Kincaid, *Wilderness Road*, 341–42.
26. Avery, Address at Lincoln Memorial University, LMU.
27. Kehr to Howard, July 15, 30, 1896.
28. Howard to Kehr, Sept. 18, 1896.
29. Howard to Kehr, Jan. 4, 1897. In this letter Howard wrote that there were reasons which he did not care to put in writing why he must not take the presidency.
30. Lincoln Memorial University, *Directors Record*, Feb. 18, 1897, 15, LMU.
31. *Ibid.*, 9, 17. Like Howard University, Lincoln Memorial University began without any college students. The idea was to build on the foundation of the Harrow School but as soon as possible to start normal, industrial, and collegiate departments at the Four Seasons property. Kehr to Howard, Feb. 25, 1897.
32. E.g. Howard to John Wanamaker, Oct. 1, 1897.
33. Kehr to Howard, May 7, 1898; Lincoln Memorial University, *Directors Record*, May 25, 1898, 21, LMU.
34. Howard to McKinley, April 21, 1898.
35. Howard, *Autoboigraphy*, II, 570.
36. Howard to Bessie Howard, July 22, 1898, LMU. He wrote of these experiences in a book entitled, *Fighting for Humanity, or Camp and Quarter-Deck* (N. Y., 1898).
37. Howard to Myers, Aug. 22, 1898; Howard to Kehr, Aug. 25, 1898.
38. Howard to A. Cox, Sept. 15, 1898; E. P. Fairchild to Howard, Nov. 30, 1898.
39. Howard to D. K. Pearsons, Feb. 9, 1899; C. F. Eager to Howard, Feb. 13, 14, 1899.
40. Lincoln Memorial University, *Directors Record*, Feb. 4, May 17, 1899, 28–30, LMU.

41. *Ibid.*, 31, LMU.
42. Larry to Howard, May 25, 1899.
43. Howard to C. F. Eager, June 19, 1900.
44. Howard to Mr. Clement, Feb. 5, 1900.
45. Howard to Whitelaw Reid, Nov. 22, 1899.
46. Partial Statement of Managing Director of Receipts and Disbursements (Lincoln Memorial University), Bowdoin College Library.
47. C. F. Eager to Howard, Nov. 29, 1898.
48. Kehr to Howard, Oct. 23, 1899.
49. Larry to Howard, Nov. 2, 1899.
50. Myers to Howard, Jan. 30, 1901.
51. Howard to E. O. Achorn, April 26, 1901; Howard to J. H. Larry, June 8, 1901.
52. Avery to Howard, May 29, 1901.
53. D. R. James to Howard, June 7, 1901.
54. Avery to H. Y. Hughes, May 29, 1901.
55. Eager to Howard, Jan. 18, 1902.
56. Howard to E. S. Converse, March 5, 1902; Lincoln Memorial University, *Directors Record*, May 17, 1904, May 7, 1907, 61, 88, LMU.
57. Lincoln Memorial University, *Catalogue*, 1903–1904.
58. Lincoln Memorial University, *Directors Record*, May 2, 1908, 89, LMU.
59. Howard to T. A. Lord, Oct. 10, 1908, LMU.
60. Howard to C. E. Lobdell, Nov. 13, 1900; Howard to T. Roosevelt, Nov. 14 [1904].
61. Howard, *Autobiography*, II, 574; G. B. Cortelyou to Howard, Oct. 11, 1904.
62. B. E. Hall to Howard, Oct. 13, 1908.
63. O. O. Howard, Engagements Book, LMU.
64. Oct. 5, 1909, quoted in the *Globe and Commercial Advertiser* (New York), Oct. 27, 1909.
65. Howard to Stooksbury, Oct. 26, 1909, LMU.
66. Harry S. Howard to Bessie H. Bancroft, Oct. 30, 1909, LMU; Harry S. Howard to R. L. Kincaid, Oct. 13, 1950, LMU; Mrs. Harry S. Howard to R. L. Kincaid, Oct. 14, 1950, LMU.

Bibliography

Howard Papers

The O. O. Howard collection at the Bowdoin College Library, Brunswick, Maine contains a great wealth of material. Howard liked to preserve records, and in this one collection there are thousands of original letters and copies of letters, copies of Howard's speeches and articles, and scrapbooks of newspaper clippings. In more detail the collection may be described thus:

ORIGINAL LETTERS. The letters have been pasted into scrapbooks and the volumes numbered consecutively from one through eighty. The first four volumes contain principally letters from Howard and the immediate members of his family and embrace the years from his boyhood until a few years after the Civil War. The remaining volumes of letters received cover the years from the postwar period to the time of Howard's death in 1909.

While Howard was commissioner of the Freedmen's Bureau he received a great many letters of a private or semi-official nature. These he retained and they have been pasted into scrapbooks in chronological order. These letters fall into the period 1865–1871.

There are several miscellaneous volumes: an unnumbered volume containing personal letters of the Howard family, one labelled "Important Communications, USA," one volume of letters relating to the First Congregational Church, Washington, D. C., two volumes concerning Lincoln Memorial University, and a volume of telegrams received.

COPIES OF LETTERS SENT. Howard's letters, other than to his family, for the years 1864 to 1873 were copied into ledgers by clerks. In 1867 there begins a series which lasts until Howard's retirement from the army in 1894 of letterpress copies of the original letters sent. These include personal letters to members of Howard's family as well as official letters. There is duplication, in the years 1867 to 1873, of the letters copied into the ledgers already mentioned.

MANUSCRIPT DIARY. Howard kept a diary during part of the time he was a student at Bowdoin College. He was not a faithful recorder and there are numerous gaps in the daily entries.

OSBORN DIARY. This is evidently a copy which Major Thomas W. Osborn, an artillery officer who accompanied Howard on the Carolina campaign, made from his original notes taken during that campaign. The copy is dated April 4, 1865 at Goldsboro, N. C. Osborn explains that no appreciable changes have been made yet, since this is not the original, it has been used guardedly.

The Library of Howard University, Washington, D. C. has a number of important Howard items. In addition to several Howard letters, written in the period before the Civil War, there are two manuscript diaries, one which Howard kept at West Point during a part of the time he was an instructor there in the years just before the outbreak of the Civil War; the other contains isolated entries between the dates January 1, 1871, and March 27, 1871.

At the Lincoln Memorial University, Harrogate, Tennessee, both in the Library and in the Lincoln Room, are Howard letters and related documents. The letters are from the period following his retirement from the army. There is also Howard's lecture engagement book for the same period.

Other Unpublished Primary Sources

In the office of the Secretary of Howard University are the Minutes of the Board of Trustees and of the Executive Committee of the Board of Trustees.

The First Congregational Church *Record,* and the First Congregational Society *Minutes* provided important source material for the section dealing with the early history of the First Congregational Church, Washington, D. C.

The West Point Library has much material relating to Howard for each of the three periods that he was at the Academy, 1850–1854, 1857–1861, 1881–1882. Used in the preparation of this work were: Orders, U. S. Corps of Cadets, 1850; Post Orders for 1850 and 1881; Letters of the Superintendent, 1881–1882; and Library Circulation Records, 1879–1885.

The *Directors Record* of Lincoln Memorial University containing the Directors Minutes, Record of Officers, and Record of Professors and Teachers provided important information for the chapter on the early history of Lincoln Memorial University.

Various manuscript collections at the Library of Congress have been consulted. Among these are the following: Clara Barton Papers, James Gillette Papers, Benjamin Harrison Papers, Andrew Johnson Papers, Robert Todd Lincoln Collection of the Papers of Abraham Lincoln, John A. Logan Papers, Rufus Mead, Jr. Papers, John Nicolay Papers, O. M. Poe Papers, John M. Schofield Papers, Carl Schurz Papers, W. T. Sherman Papers, Edwin M. Stanton Papers, George H. Stuart Papers, Elihu B. Washburne Papers, and the Samuel P. Heintzelman Journal.

In the National Archives are the records of the Freedmen's Bureau. With a very few exceptions, only the materials relating to the commissioner's office have been used. They are: the originals of letters received, arranged according to sender and date and now placed in numbered boxes; and copies of letters sent written chronologically into numbered volumes of letters sent, ordinarily one volume for each year of the Bureau's life. There are other records which have been used such as the volumes of Circulars and Circular Letters, and the registers of letters received. For a more detailed description of Freedmen's Bureau records consult the *Preliminary Checklist of the Records of the Bureau of Refugees, Freedmen, and Abandoned Lands 1865–1872* compiled by Elizabeth Bethel, Sara Dunlap, and Lucille Pendell, War Records Office, National Archives (Washington, 1946). Also valuable is the description given in the bibliography of George R. Bentley's, *A History of the Freedmen's Bureau* (Philadelphia, 1955), 266–67.

The Army Section of the National Archives also contains the records of the various units of the Union Army during the Civil War and in the postwar period. Thus can be found, for instance, the letters sent and the Regimental Letter and Order Book of the Third Maine Regiment, the letters sent of the Army of the Potomac, of the 15th Army Corps, and the like. Interesting data can be had from a group of papers entitled Generals' Papers and Books, and there are additional records of individual officers under a section denominated ACP (appointments, commissions, promotions). The Army Section records in the National Archives also provided primary sources for the chapters on the Apache and Nez Perce Indians: for instance, the letters sent of the Departments of Arizona and of the Columbia, and letters in the Adjutant General's Office pertaining to the Nez Perce War.

The Interior Department Section, in another part of the National Archives, has documents which gave up valuable information on the Apache and Nez Perce Indians. In the Indian Office is a separate group of letters from General Howard to that office during Howard's trip to Arizona and New Mexico in 1872.

BIBLIOGRAPHY 353

Published Primary Sources and Secondary Works

Although manuscript source materials have formed the basis for this biography, numerous printed primary and secondary sources have proved useful. Howard's autobiography (*Autobiography of Oliver Otis Howard: Major General United States Army*, 2 vols., N. Y., 1907) of course is a most valuable source of information as are, to a smaller degree, Howard's other writings to be noted below.

A personal friend of General Howard, Mrs. Laura C. Holloway, wrote a biography entitled, *Howard: the Christian Hero* (N. Y., 1885) but this falls short of present day standards for critical biography nor does it, of course, cover the last twenty-four years of Howard's life.

The account of Howard's early life is based primarily on the original letters in the Howard collection. Two published works were helpful in sketching in Howard's ancestry: William A. Otis, *A Genealogical and Historical Memoir of the Otis Family in America* (Chicago, 1924), and Heman Howard, *The Howard Genealogy: Descendants of John Howard of Bridgewater, Massachusetts from 1643 to 1903* (Brockton, Mass., 1903).

Excellent descriptions of pre-war West Point can be found in Morris Schaff, *The Spirit of Old West Point, 1858–1862* (Boston, 1907), and Peter Michie, "Reminiscences of Cadet and Army Service," *Personal Recollections of the War of the Rebellion*, Addresses Delivered before the Commandery of the State of New York, Military Order of the Loyal Legion of the United States, 2d Series, edited by A. N. Blakeman (N. Y., 1897). An excellent modern history of West Point is Sidney Forman, *West Point: A History of the United States Military Academy* (N.Y., 1950).

For the Civil War period the one indispensable work is, of course, *The War of the Rebellion: A Compilation of the Official Records of the Union and Confederate Armies* (128 vols., Washington, 1880–1901) more commonly known as the Official Records. Less valuable is the *Report of the Joint Committee on the Conduct of the War* (3 vols., Thirty-Eighth Congress, 2d Session, Washington, 1865).

Howard contributed to the literature of the Civil War with a number of magazine articles and published addresses. Among these are the following: "Personal Recollections of Abraham Lincoln" (*Century Magazine*, LXXV, 1908, 873–77); "Remarks in Commemoration of General William Tecumseh Sherman" (*Personal Recollections of the War of the Rebellion*, Addresses Delivered before the Commandery of the State of New York, Military Order of the Loyal Legion of the United States, 2d series, edited by A. N. Blakeman, N. Y. and

London, 1897); "Ulysses S. Grant: Recollections of Distinguished Men" (*Century Magazine*, LXXIV, 1907, 956–60); "The Eleventh Corps at Chancellorsville" (*Battles and Leaders of the Civil War*, III, 1884, 1888, 189–202); "Jackson's Attack upon the Eleventh Corps" (*Century Magazine*, XXXII, n.s., X, 1886, 761–70); "Campaign and Battle of Gettysburg, June and July, 1863" (*Atlantic Monthly*, XXXVIII, 1876, 48–71); "Grant at Chattanooga" (*Personal Recollections of the War of the Rebellion*, Addresses Delivered Before the New York Commandery of the Loyal Legion of the United States, 1883–1891, J. G. Wilson and T. M. Coan, editors, N. Y., 1891).

Any bibliography concerned with the Civil War must necessarily be selective. There is no intention, even, of including here mention of all secondary works used in the writing of this work. This means that much of the standard Civil War literature, many excellent monographs, biographies, and general works are omitted. Only those works of particular significance to this biography have been included. One of the general histories deserving special mention because of its unique approach is Kenneth P. Williams, *Lincoln Finds a General: A Military Study of the Civil War* (5 vols., N. Y., 1949–1959). The works of Douglas S. Freeman, *R. E. Lee: A Biography* (4 vols., N. Y., 1934, 1935) and *Lee's Lieutenants: A Study in Command* (3 vols., N. Y., 1942–1944) are indispensable for any account of the Eastern battles. Older works of continuing value are William R. Livermore, *The Story of the Civil War: A Concise Account of the War in the United States . . . in Continuation of the Story by John Codman Ropes* (2 vols., N. Y, 1933), and the Comte de Paris, *History of the Civil War in America* (4 vols., translated by L. F. Tasistro, Philadelphia, 1883). Ella Lonn's *Foreigners in the Union Army and Navy* (Baton Rouge, 1951) explains the role of foreign-born soldiers in the 11th Corps. Two works of special interest because of Howard's Maine background are: Louis C. Hatch, ed., *Maine: A History* (5 vols., N. Y., 1919), and William E. S. Whitman and Charles H. True, *Maine in the War for the Union* (Lewiston, 1865). Pertinent to Howard's service in the Western theatre is a military critique by an English writer, Alfred E. Burne, *Lee, Grant and Sherman: A Study in Leadership in the 1864–65 Campaign* (Aldershot, [U. K.] 1939). A standard work on army administration is Fred A. Shannon, *The Organization and Administration of the Union Army, 1861–1865* (2 vols., Cleveland, 1928).

Among the numerous published diaries and memoirs of the Civil War period which are of particular relevance to a life of Howard are: Abner R. Small, *The Road to Richmond: The Civil War Memoirs of Major Abner R. Small of the Sixteenth Maine Volunteers*, Harold A. Small, ed. (Berkeley, Cal., 1939), Carl Schurz, *The Reminiscences of*

BIBLIOGRAPHY   355

Carl Schurz (3 vols., N. Y., 1907, 1908), Charles S. Wainwright, *A Diary of Battle: the Personal Journals of Colonel Charles S. Wainwright 1861–1865,* Allan Nevins, ed. (N. Y., 1962), William T. Sherman, *Personal Memoirs of Gen. W. T. Sherman* (2 vols., N. Y., 1890), and William F. G. Shanks, *Personal Recollections of Distinguished Generals* (N. Y., 1866). George W. Nichols, *The Story of the Great March, from the Diary of a Staff Officer* (N. Y., 1865), Henry Hitchcock, *Marching with Sherman: Passages from the Letters and Campaign Diaries of Henry Hitchcock,* M. A. DeWolfe Howe, ed. (New Haven, 1927), and W. B. Hazen, *A Narrative of Military Service* (Boston, 1885) provide useful first-hand information on the Atlanta, Savannah, and Carolina campaigns.

In the field of biography, in addition to Freeman's life of Lee, already cited, special mention should be made of Walter H. Hebert, *Fighting Joe Hooker* (Indianapolis, 1944), and Lloyd Lewis, *Sherman, Fighting Prophet* (N. Y., 1932). Samuel R. Kamm, *The Civil War Career of Thomas A. Scott* (Philadelphia, 1940) tells of the transfer to the West by rail of the 11th and 12th Corps.

For secondary works concerning the various battles and campaigns in which Howard participated only a few can be given special mention. John Bigelow, Jr., *The Campaign of Chancellorsville: A Strategic and Tactical Study* (New Haven, 1910) is an exhaustive account of that engagement. Augustus C. Hamlin, *The Battle of Chancellorsville: The Attack of Stonewall Jackson and His Army upon the Right Flank of the Army of the Potomac* (Bangor, Me., 1896) contains important detail but is marred by its bias. General Howard's participation in the battles of Chancellorsville and Gettysburg is treated in considerable detail in two articles by the author, "O. O. Howard: General at Chancellorsville" (*Civil War History,* III, March, 1957, 47–63), and "General O. O. Howard at Gettysburg" (*Civil War History,* IX, Sept., 1963, 261–76). Two works pertinent to the battle of Gettysburg are E. P. Halstead's, "Incidents of the First Day at Gettysburg" (*Battles and Leaders of the Civil War,* N. Y., 1884, 1888, III, 284–85), Winfield S. Hancock, "Gettysburg: Reply to General Howard" (*The Galaxy,* XXII, 1876, 821–31), and Jesse B. Young, *The Battle of Gettysburg: A Comprehensive Narrative* (N. Y. and London, 1913). James P. Jones, "The Battle of Atlanta and McPherson's Successor" (*Civil War History,* VII, Dec., 1961, 393–405) contains a full discussion of Howard's appointment to the command of the Army of the Tennessee; and John G. Barrett, *Sherman's March through the Carolinas* (Chapel Hill, 1956) is a comprehensive account of that campaign.

Of the many regimental histories used in the preparation of this work that of an 11th Corps unit, *The Three Years' Service of the Thirty-*

Third Mass. Infantry Regiment, 1862–1865 by Adin B. Underwood (Boston, 1881) is one of the best. The two most satisfactory accounts of the burning of Columbia are James Ford Rhodes, "Who Burned Columbia?" (*American Historical Review*, VII, 1902, 485–93) and James D. Hill, "The Burning of Columbia Reconsidered" (*South Atlantic Quarterly*, XXV, 1926, 269–82).

Finally, not only is the second edition of *The Civil War and Reconstruction* by James G. Randall and David Donald (Boston, 1961) a fine overall account of the Civil War but it contains a superb bibliography. This same work is also satisfactory for the Reconstruction period. Two additional standard works on Reconstruction are Robert S. Henry, *The Story of Reconstruction* (Indianapolis, 1938), and E. Merton Coulter, *The South During Reconstruction, 1865–1877* ([Baton Rouge], 1947). Eric L. McKitrick's *Andrew Johnson and Reconstruction* (Chicago, 1960) takes a strong anti-Johnson stand, whereas Benjamin P. Thomas and Harold M. Hyman in *Stanton: the Life and Times of Lincoln's Secretary of War* (N. Y., 1962) are sympathetic toward their subject. *The Diary of Gideon Welles*, edited by John T. Morse, Jr. (3 vols., Boston, 1911), and *The Diary of Orville Hickman Browning*, edited by James G. Randall (Springfield, Ill., 1933), contain significant references to General Howard, while *Negro Militia and Reconstruction* by Otis A. Singletary (Austin, Texas, 1957) was useful for its information on violence during the Reconstruction period.

There are many government documents relating to the Freedmen's Bureau, among these are the Report of the Committee on Education and Labor which investigated Howard's administration of the Bureau (41st Congress, 2d Session, House Report 121, Serial 1438) and the document titled *Proceedings, Findings and Opinion of Court of Inquiry . . . in the Case of Oliver Otis Howard* (War Department, Judge-Advocate-General's Department, Records of Courts-Martial, Washington, 1874). For a complete list of government documents pertinent to an account of the Freedmen's Bureau, including the annual reports of the commissioner, see George R. Bentley, *A History of the Freedmen's Bureau* (Philadelphia, 1955, 268–71).

Howard has chapters in his autobiography dealing with the Freedmen's Bureau in addition to three unpublished addresses in the library of Howard University and two published articles. These are: "Account of Tour Through the Southern States," "Addresses before the New England Society" (c. 1867), "Education of the Colored Man" (c. 1868), "Address at Augusta, Maine" (*National Freedman*, Aug. 15, 1865, vol. I, no. 7, 233), and "The Freedman during the War" (*New Princeton Review*, I, 1866, 373–85).

The most important work on the Freedmen's Bureau is George R.

Bentley, *A History of the Freedmen's Bureau* (Philadelphia, 1955) which now takes the place of the older work by Paul S. Peirce, *The Freedmen's Bureau: A Chapter in the History of Reconstruction* (State University of Iowa Studies in Sociology, Economics, Politics and History, vol. III, no. 1, Iowa City, 1904). Both informative and amusing is the work by the writer and Bureau agent, John W. De Forest, *A Union Officer in the Reconstruction*, edited, with an introduction and notes by James H. Croushore and David M. Potter (New Haven, 1948). John H. and LaWanda Cox have contributed two articles which concern Bureau affairs: "Andrew Johnson and His Ghost Writers" (*Mississippi Valley Historical Review*, XLVIII, Dec., 1961, 460–79), and "General O. O. Howard and the 'Misrepresented Bureau'" (*Journal of Southern History*, XIX, 1953, 427–56). See also the author's "Atrocities in the Reconstruction Period" (*Journal of Negro History*, XLVII, Oct., 1962, 234–47). One of the most significant, though biased, writers on the Reconstruction period and on topics relating to the Freedmen's Bureau is Walter L. Fleming. Particularly useful were the following works by this writer: *Civil War and Reconstruction in Alabama* (N. Y., 1905); *The Freedmen's Savings Bank: A Chapter in the Economic History of the Negro Race* (Chapel Hill, 1927); and "The Formation of the Union League in Alabama" (*Gulf States Historical Magazine*, II, September, 1903, 73–89).

Two of the several histories of Reconstruction in the various states used in this work were: J. G. de Roulhac Hamilton, *Reconstruction in North Carolina* (N. Y., 1914), and James W. Patton, *Unionism and Reconstruction in Tennessee* (Chapel Hill, 1934).

For works relating to the establishment of educational institutions for freedmen see, Horace M. Bond, *Negro Education in Alabama: A Study in Cotton and Steel* (Washington, 1939); Dwight O. W. Holmes, *The Evolution of the Negro College* (N. Y., 1934); and Henry L. Swint, *The Northern Teacher in the South, 1862–1870* (Nashville, 1941).

The only comprehensive history of Howard University is that by Walter Dyson, *Howard University: The Capstone of Negro Education, A History: 1867–1940* (Washington, 1941). Another work by Dyson is his "The Founding of Howard University" (*Howard University Studies in History*, Washington, 1921, no. 1, I, 1–24). Useful also were the *Annual Reports of the President: 1867–1910*, and the following works: John L. Ewell, *The History of the Theological Department of Howard University* ([Washington], 1906); Dwight O. W. Holmes, *The Passing of the Old: Some Reflections on the Demolition of the Main Building at Howard University* (Washington, 1937); Daniel S. Lamb, *Howard University Medical Department Washington, D. C.: A*

Historical, Biographical and Statistical Souvenir (Washington, 1900); Beulah H. Melchor, *The Land Possessions of Howard University: A Study of the Original Ownership and Extent of the Holdings of Howard University in the District of Columbia* (Washington, 1945); and James M. Nabrit, "From Prayer Meeting to University" (*Christian Education*, XXVI, September, 1942, 29–34).

Among the other works which have some bearing on the Freedmen's Bureau and its work are: Jonathan T. Dorris, *Pardon and Amnesty under Lincoln and Johnson: The Restoration of the Confederates to their Rights and Privileges, 1861–1898* (Chapel Hill, 1953); W. E. Burghardt DuBois, *The Souls of the Black Folk: Essays and Sketches* (London, 1905); John Eaton, *Grant, Lincoln, and the Freedmen: Reminiscences of the Civil War with Special Reference to the Work for the Contrabands and Freedmen of the Mississippi Valley* (N. Y., 1907): John M. Langston, *From the Virginia Plantation to the National Capitol: or the First and Only Negro Representative in Congress from the Old Dominion* (Hartford, 1894); *The Other Phase of Reconstruction, Speech . . . Delivered at Congregational Tabernacle, Jersey City, New Jersey, April 17, 1877* (Washington, 1877); and Paul Lewinson, *Race, Class & Party: A History of Negro Suffrage and White Politics in the South* (N. Y., 1932).

Howard's *Address at the Laying of the Corner-stone of the First Congregational Church, Washington, D. C.* (Boston, 1867), and *Manual of the First Congregational Church, Washington, D. C.* (Washington, 1870) supply interesting facts concerning the early history of the First Congregational Church as does Walter L. Clift, "History of the First Congregational Church" in *Fiftieth Anniversary of the Founding of the First Congregational Church* (Washington [1915]). Two documents dealing with the church dispute are Charles B. Boynton, *A Duty Which the Colored People Owe to Themselves* (Washington, 1867), and *Proceedings of an Ex Parte Council, Held at the First Congregational Church, Washington, D. C. November 18th to 20th, 1868* (Philadelphia, 1868).

Howard was involved with three different groups of Indians during his career: Cochise's band of Apaches, the Nez Perces, and the Bannocks. Here, again, the government documents are most important. Particularly useful were the following: Howard's report of his trip to Arizona and New Mexico in 1872, 42d Congress, 3d Session, House Executive Document 1, part 5, Serial 1560; Commissioner of Indian Affairs, Annual Report to the Secretary of the Interior for the years 1872 and 1873 (Washington, 1872, 1873); Report of the Commissioner of Indian Affairs in Report of the Secretary of the Interior, 1876, 44th Congress, 2d Session, House Executive Document

1, part 5, Serial 1749; Report of Civil and Military Commission to Nez Percé Indians Washington Territory and the Northwest, in Report of the Secretary of the Interior, 1877, 45th Congress, 2d Session, House Executive Document 1, part 5, Serial 1800. There are two documents especially valuable for the operations of the Nez Perce War: Report of the Secretary of War, 45th Congress, 2d Session, House Executive Document 1, part 2, Serial 1794; and Claims of Nez Perce Indians, 56th Congress, 1st Session, Senate Document 257, Serial 3867. The events of the Bannock War of 1878 are covered in Report of the Secretary of War, 1878, 45th Congress, 3d Session, House Executive Document 1, part 2, Serial 1843.

Howard wrote a general account of his Indian experiences, *My Life and Experiences Among Our Hostile Indians* (Hartford, 1907), a newspaper account of his visit to the Southwest in 1872, *The Indians: Account of Gen'l Howard's Mission to the Apaches and Navajos*, Reprinted from the Washington *Daily Morning Chronicle* of November 10, 1872, and two works on the Nez Perce campaign: *Nez Perce Joseph: An Account of His Ancestors, His Lands, His Confederates, His Enemies, His Murders, His War, His Pursuit and Capture* (Boston, 1881), and "The True Story of the Wallowa Campaign" (*North American Review*, CXXIX, July, 1879, 53–64).

Two of the volumes in the works of Hubert H. Bancroft bear on Howard's Indian experiences. These are: *History of Arizona and New Mexico* and *History of Washington, Idaho, Montana, 1845–1889*, vols. 17 and 31 of the works of Hubert Howe Bancroft (San Francisco, 1889, 1890).

For the Apache episode the following works were of particular value: Sidney R. DeLong, *The History of Arizona: From the Earliest Times Known to the People of Europe to 1903* (San Francisco, 1905); Thomas E. Farish, *History of Arizona* (2 vols., Phoenix, 1915); Woodworth Clum, *Apache Agent: the Story of John P. Clum* (Boston, 1936); George Crook, *General Crook His Autobiography*, edited and annotated by Martin F. Schmitt (Norman, Oklahoma, 1946); Frank C. Lockwood, *The Apache Indians* (N. Y., 1938); and Ralph H. Ogle, *Federal Control of the Western Apaches, 1848–1886* (Albuquerque, 1940).

Before the outbreak of the Nez Perce War, Howard's adjutant in the Department of the Columbia, H. Clay Wood, wrote a pamphlet called, *The Treaty Status of Young Joseph and His Band of Nez Percé Indians under the Treaties between the United States and the Nez Percé Tribe of Indians, and the Indian Title to the Land* (Portland, Oregon, 1876).

Most of the histories of the Nez Perce Indians and biographies of Chief Joseph are biased on the side of the Indians. This is true, for instance, of the two works by Francis Haines, *Red Eagles of the Northwest: The Story of Chief Joseph and His People* (Portland, Oregon, 1939) and *The Nez Percés: Tribesmen of the Columbia Plateau* (Norman, Oklahoma, 1955), and of that by L. V. McWhorter, *Hear Me, My Chiefs! Nez Perce History and Legend,* edited by Ruth Bordin (Caldwell, Idaho, 1952). More objective is Helen A. Howard [no relation to General O. O. Howard] *War Chief Joseph* (Caldwell, Idaho, 1941). Another biography of Joseph is that by Chester A. Fee, *Chief Joseph: the Biography of a Great Indian* (N. Y., 1936). An appendix to this work is "The Pursuit and Capture of Chief Joseph," written by an aide to General Howard during the campaign, Charles E. S. Wood. Wood also wrote an article for the *Century Magazine* (XXVIII, May, 1884, 135–42): "Chief Joseph, The Nez-Percé." Chief Joseph contributed an article, "An Indian's View of Indian Affairs," to the *North American Review* (CXXVIII, April, 1879, 412–33, which is Joseph's account of the Nez Perce War. A detailed account of the campaign can be found in the author's "General Howard and the Nez Perce War of 1877" (*Pacific Northwest Quarterly,* XLIX, Oct., 1958, 129–45). General John Gibbon's action against the Nez Perces is related in G. O. Shields, *The Battle of the Big Hole* (Chicago and N. Y., 1889). Interesting personal commentary on events connected with the Nez Perce war is provided in Abe Laufe, ed., *An Army Doctor's Wife on the Frontier: Letters from Alaska and the Far West, 1874–1878* (Pittsburgh, 1962). George F. Brimlow's *The Bannock Indian War of 1878* (Caldwell, Idaho, 1938) is adequate for that campaign.

Peter S. Michie in an article, "Caste at West Point" (*North American Review,* CXXX, 1880, 604–13), discusses the race situation at the Academy prior to Howard's becoming superintendent. George L. Andrews in "West Point and the Colored Cadets" (*International Review,* IX, November, 1880, 477–98) discusses the Whittaker case, which is also covered in the newspapers of that period. More on the same subject is to be round in John M. Schofield, *Forty-Six Years in the Army* (N. Y., 1897), and Schofield's Report in Report of the Secretary of War, 1880, 46th Congress, 3d Session, House Executive Document 1, part 2, Serial 1952.

Howard's regime as superintendent of the Military Academy is treated in his reports for the years 1881 and 1882, in Report of the Secretary of War, 1881 and 1882, 47th Congress, 1st Session, House Executive Document 1, part 2, Serial 2010, and 47th Congress, 2d Session, House Executive Document 1, part 2, Serial 2091.

Among the government documents which contain useful information concerning Howard's army career during the years 1855 through 1894 are the following: (each in the Report of the Secretary of War and each from House Executive Document 1, part 2) 49th Congress, 1st Session, Serial 2369; 49th Congress, 2d Session, Serial 2461; 51st Congress, 1st Session, Serial 2715; 52nd Congress, 2d Session, Serial 3077; and 53d Congress, 3d Session, Serial 3295.

Howard's autobiography and an article, "The Folk of the Cumberland Gap," (*Munsey's Magazine*, XXVII, July, 1902, 506–08), provide material for the account of the founding of Lincoln Memorial University, as does an excellent book by a former president of Lincoln Memorial, Robert L. Kincaid, *The Wilderness Road* (Harrogate, Tennessee, 1955). An address by F. B. Avery, "Address at Lincoln Memorial University, June 1930" supplements the above named works. See also the author's "Architects and Builders of a Living Memorial" (*Lincoln Herald*, LIX, Spring, 1957, 6–13).

Index

Abbot, Henry L., 8, 9
Abbott, Lyman, 163
Abolitionists, 123. *See also* Radical Republicans, slavery.
Acworth, Ga., action at, 67
Advance, 196, 287
Alabama, Bureau activity in, 96, 104, 105, 114, 133, 138, 141, 142, 148, 152, 153, 221; freedmen in during war, 92
Alaska, 244, 338
Alden, B. R., 9
Alger, Russell A., 291–293
Allatoona, Ga., 67
Alta California, 211
Alvord, John W., 164, 175, 176; supervises Bureau educational activities, 159; leaves Bureau, 168; and building block co., 173; president of Freedmen's Bank, 189; and evasion of Bureau law, 323
American Baptist Home Mission Society, 159
American Building Block. *See* Building block.
American Freedmen's Aid Commission, 116, 324
American Freedmen's and Union Commission, 149
American Freedmen's Union Commission, 163, 188
American Missionary Association, 149, 161, 163, 164, 209; aids schools for freedmen, 95, 159; aids Howard U., 181; aids A. A. Myers in E. Tenn., 293
Anderson, Robert, 303; at Fort Sumter, 20
Antietam, battle of, 36–38
Apache Indians, 209–219, 225
Appleton's Great Commander series, 282

Arivaipa Indians, 210
Arizona Territory, 209–219
Arkansas, Bureau activity in, 96, 99, 101, 105, 114, 119, 132, 137, 145, 148, 150; atrocities in, 130
Armstrong, Samuel C., 179; quoted, 162
Army and Navy Journal, 63, 217
Army of the Cumberland, 61, 65, 66
Army of Northern Virginia, 66
Army of the Ohio, 65, 72, 311
Army of the Potomac, 31, 33, 34, 38, 41–44, 50, 57, 58, 66, 83, 310
Army of Tennessee, 68
Army of the Tennessee, 60, 65, 66, 68, 74, 78, 83, 226, 234, 240; at Atlanta, 69; Sherman chooses commander for, 69–70; at battle of Ezra Church, 70–71
Army of Virginia, 33, 34
Arnell, Samuel M., 203, 205, 207, 208
Arthur, Chester A., 278
Atlanta, Ga., fall of, 72
Atlanta, battle of, 69–70
Atlanta campaign, 66–73, 312
Atlanta University, 162, 168
Atrocities. *See* Freedmen's Bureau, atrocity reports of.
Avarasborough, battle of, 80
Averell, William, 49
Avery, Frederick B., 294, 297

Babcock, Orville E., 233
Baird, Absalom, 97, 148, 150; reports on New Orleans riot, 128
Balloch, George W., 175, 177, 224; Bureau disbursing officer, 95–96; enjoys free hand in administering Bureau finances, 154; and origins of Howard U., 170; quoted, 188; handles bounty paying, 209, 220;

dismissed from Bureau, 223; irregularities in accounts of, 226; gives inadequate explanations, 227–228; Howard's concern for, 229–230; and Court of Inquiry, 231; and lax administration, 233; not indicted, 336
Bangor Theological Seminary, 20
Bannock Indians, 265–267
Bannock War, 265–267; action at Silver Creek, 266
Baptist Home Mission Society, 164
Barber, Hiram, 199–200
Barlow, Francis T., 35; at Chancellorsville, 45
Barney, Hiram, 242
Barry Farm project, 113, 169, 185–187, 191, 204–206
Bascom, William F., 195–196, 202
Beam, Henry D., 231
Beauregard, P. G. T., 27
Beecher, Henry W., 13, 192
Belknap, William W., 224, 225, 227, 230, 235, 240; consults with Howard, 211, requests Balloch's dismissal, 223; motives of, 226; believes Howard responsible for losses, 228; and charges against Howard, 231–233; Howard's view of, 233; scandal involving, 234
Beman, Edward C., 329
Bentonville, battle of, 80–81
Berea College, 155
Bernard, Ruben F., in Bannock War, 266–267
Berry, Hiram G., 39, 47
Big Hole, battle of the, 253–254
Bitterroot Valley, 252–254, 264
Black Codes, 122, 125–126, 146; in South Carolina, 149
Black Point, Cal., 280
Blaine, James G., 21; editor of Kennebec *Journal*, 13; recommends Howard for command, 23, 77; forwards Thanks of Congress to Howard, 62, 63; works for Howard's appointment as brigadier general, 64
Blaine, Mrs. James G., 236
Blair, Francis P., Jr., as commander of 17th Corps, 70, 78, 80, 81
Blair, Montgomery, 118
Boggs, W. R. and Mrs. W. R., 13

Bounty paying. *See* Freedmen's Bureau, and bounty paying.
Boutwell, George S., 223–224
Bowdoin College, 3–6, 236
Boynton, Charles B., 194; and founding of Howard U., 170; becomes president of Howard U., 171, 179; and donation of lot to Howard, 172; testimony in House investigation, 174; as pastor of First Congregational Church, 191; and Plymouth Church episode, 192–193; delivers sermon on racial question, 195–196; and church dispute, 200–201; resigns from First Congregational Church, 202
Boynton, Henry V. N., 235; and church dispute, 196–200; joins F. Wood in attack on Howard, 202–204; and House investigation, 206–207; believed by Howard to be member of cabal, 226; mentioned by Sherman, 234
Bradley, Joseph H., 206
Bragg, Braxton, 60, 61, 65
Brayman, Mason, 268
Brewster, Henry A., 170
Bridgeport, Ala., 59–60
Bright, Mrs. Samuel, 277
Broadway Tabernacle, 282
Brodhead, Joseph M., consulted by Howard, 186; testifies in House investigation, 206; and investment of bounty funds, 222–223, 232
Brown, Orlando, 108, 138, 150; and freedmen during war, 92; assistant commissioner for Virginia, 96; quoted, 99, 142; requests dismissal of agent, 151
Brown, Thomas P., 108
Browning, Orville, on Howard's atrocity report, 129
Bryan, William J., 291
Bryant, W. C., 309
Buchanan, Robert C., 98, 150
Buffalo Horn (Bannock Indian), 265
Buford, John, in Gettysburg campaign, 50–54
Building block (American Building Block), used at Howard U., 173–178, 204, 236, 240, 289
Building block company (D. L.

INDEX 365

Eaton and Co.), 173–176, 178, 179, 182, 199, 204–206, 236
Bull Run, first battle of, 27–28
Bull Run, second battle of, 33–34
Bureau of Refugees, Freedmen, and Abandoned Lands. *See* Freedmen's Bureau.
Burlington, Vt., 290, 298, 299
Burnside, Ambrose E., at battle of Antietam, 37; takes command of Army of the Potomac, 38; at Fredericksburg, 40; at Knoxville, 61
Buschbeck, Adolph, 46–47, 57, 61
Butler, Benjamin F., 91, 222
Butterfield, Daniel, 54, 56

Callis, John B., 138
Camas Meadows, action at, 255–256, 265
Camas Prairie, Idaho, 265–266
Camp Apache, 214
Camp Grant, 210, 213
Camp Memorial Church and Mission, 282
Carlin, Willam P., complains of civilian agents, 101; reprimanded by Howard, 152; quoted, 155
Carolina campaign, 73, 77, 84, 313
Carpenter, C. C., 155
Casey, Silas, 29
Cass, Lewis, 4
Cemetery Hill, 52–55
Chancellorsville, battle of, 43–49, 58, 67, 69, 73, 84, 85, 289
Chancellorsville, campaign of, 43–49
Chapin, J. A., 116
Chapman, cadet at West Point, 9
Chapman (half-breed interpreter), 260–261
Chase, Salmon P., Howard visits, 49; heads Washington YMCA, 238
Chattahoochee River, 68
Chattanooga, battle of, 60–61, 69; relief of, 59–60
Chickamauga, battle of, 58
Chie (Indian), 215
Chiricahua Apaches. *See* Apaches, Cochise.
Chiracahua reservation, 217–218
Church dispute, 192–202. *See also* First Congregational Church.
Cincinnati *Commercial*, 148

Cincinnati *Gazette*, 196–199
Civil Rights Act, 129, 133–135
Claflin, William, 178
Clark, David, 180, 182
Clearwater, battle of the, 250–252, 265
Cleveland, Grover, 279, 283
Closson, Henry W., 9
Cobb, C. L., 224
Coburn, Abner, 50
Cochise, 219, 333; refuses to attend conference 210; Howard's efforts to find, 214–215; description of, 215; meets with Howard, 215–216; and disagreement over terms, 217–218
Cole, John A., 182
Colston, R. E., 308
Colton, Erastus, 166
Columbia, capture and burning of, 78–80
Colyer, Vincent, 210–211
Committee on Education and Labor, 205
Congregational Church (Washington, D. C.). *See* First Congregational Church.
Congregational Union, 192–193
Congregationalist and Recorder, 196
Continental Divide, 253–254
Conway, Thomas, 108; work with freedmen during war, 92; assistant commissioner for Louisiana, 96; proves unsatisfactory, 97–98; criticizes A. C. Gillem, 141–142; agent for Union League, 143; criticizes Bureau, 149–150
Conyngham, D. P., 84
Cook, Burton C., 170
Cook, John A., 194
Cooke, Henry D., 238
Cooke, Jay, 238
Cooke, Jay and Co., 174
Corvallis, Montana, 254
Costar, Charles R., 52
Couch, Darius N., 41, 315
Court of Inquiry, 209, 227, 229–233, 235, 236, 243, 262, 272
Crook, George, 210, 219, 255; favors war against Apaches, 211; opinion of Howard, 212; cooperates with Howard, 212–213; fails to arrange meeting with Cochise, 214; criti-

cizes Howard's peace terms, 216–218
Cross, Edwin C., 35
Crowder, Enoch H., 346
Culps Hill, 54, 55
Cumberland Gap, 293–294
Cushman, E. M., 172

Dallas, Ga., 67
Dalton, Ga., 66, 69
Davis, Jefferson, 68, 302
Davis, Jefferson C. (Union officer), 62; not friendly to Bureau policies, 98; reports atrocities, 131
De Forest, John W., 137, 238
Delano, Columbus, offers Howard assignment to Arizona, 209, 211; Howard reports to, 213
Delano, James S., 199
Department of Arizona, 210–212, 280
Department of the Columbia, 243–245, 247, 265, 268
Department of Dakota, 252, 258
Department of the East, 281–283
Department of the Platte, 277–279
Department of the Tennessee. *See* Army of the Tennessee.
Department of West Point, 270–271, 276–277
Dialectic Society, at West Point, 9
District of Columbia, Bureau activity in, 96, 113, 185–187, 224
District of Montana, 252
Division of the Atlantic, the Missouri, the Pacific, the South. *See* Military Division of.
Dodge, William E., 292
Donald's School Days, 244–245
Doubleday, Abner, 55
Douglass, Frederick, 286
Dragoon Mountains, 215
Dragoon Springs, Ariz., 216
Drew, W. P., 221
DuBarry, Beekman, 273
DuBois, W. E. B., 162
Duncan, William, 75
Dyer, George W., 231–232

Eager, Charles F., 297
Early, Jubal A., at Gettysburg, 52, 55; quoted, 309
Eaton, D. L., 175

Eaton, D. L. and Co. *See* Building block co.
Eaton, John, 92, 96
Edie, John R., 139
Edisto Island, 110
Education, Negro, 159–162; opposition to, 165–166
Edward, Prince of Wales, visits West Point, 18
Eldridge, Stuart, 104; quoted, 109
Elections, of 1856, 13; of 1860, 20; of 1866, 129; of 1868, 137, 145, 167; of 1874, 245; of 1876, 245; of 1880, 269; of 1884, 287; of 1896, 290–291, 295; of 1900, 298; of 1904, 298; of 1908, 298
Eleventh Corps, 62, 73, 310; Howard takes command of, 43; in Chancellorsville campaign, 43–49; in Gettysburg campaign, 50–56; criticism of, 57; ordered West, 58; in relief of Chattanooga, 59–60; in battle of Wauhatchie, 60; at Chattanooga, 61; and relief of Knoxville, 61; consolidated with 12th Corps, 65
Eliot, Thomas D., supports Bureau Bill, 116; forwards House resolution to Howard, 149; asks Howard to deny he favors amalgamation, 198
Elvans, John R., 186; and Barry Farm project, 113
Emancipation Proclamation, 38, 39, 122
Encyclopedia Britannica, 278
Ewell, Richard S., 52, 53, 55
Ezra Church, battle of, 70, 71, 73, 312

Fair Oaks, battle of, 32, 102
Farwell, Nathan A., 50
Fenn, S. S., 252
Fessenden, William P., 158
Fifteenth Corps, 70, 74, 76, 80, 85
Fifth Corps, 310
First (U. S.) Cavalry, 249, 266, 267
First Congregational Church, Washington, D. C., 169, 172, 179, 183, 187, 220, 240; aided by Bureau, 155; founding of, 191–192; Sunday school episode, 193, 194; Negroes apply for membership, 194;

INDEX   367

Boynton-Howard dispute, 194–202; financial problems, 202; in House investigation, 204–206; Howard's interest in, 237. See also First Congregational Society.
First Congregational Society, 193, 330; purchases church lot, 192; issues bonds, 194; annual meeting of, 1869, 201; determines pastor's salary, 202
First Corps, 50–54, 309
Fisk, Clinton B., 133; recommended as commissioner, 91; appointed assistant commissioner, 97; urges stricter relief policy, 104; and land distribution plans, 108; reports on Memphis riot, 128
Fisk University, 162
Fitzgerald, Emily M., 339
Flagler, Henry M., 278
Florida, Bureau activity in, 96, 97, 101, 114, 118, 126, 134, 164; report on atrocities, 131
Forney, John W., 181
Forsyth, James W., 267
Fort Boise, 250, 257
Fort Brooke, 14
Fort Ethan Allen, 283, 299
Fort Lapwai, 248–250
Fort McAllister, 84; capture of, 75–76
Fort McDowell, 212, 214
Fort Mason, 280
Fort Omaha, 277
Fort Sumter, 20, 303
Fort Yuma, 212
Foster, J. B., 187
Four Seasons Hotel, 293, 295
Fourteenth Corps, 74
Fourth (U. S.) Artillery, 266
Fourth Corps, 69, 72; Howard takes command of, 65–66; in Atlanta campaign, 66–68; and crossing of Chattahoochee, 312
Franklin, William B., 31; commands grand division, 38; at Fredericksburg, 40
Fredericksburg, battle of, 40–41
Freedmen, 87, 91, 97; assistance for provided by Bureau, 88; condition of during war, 92; and Bureau land program, 106–111; on Sea Islands, 110–111; fail to obtain land, 112; and Barry Farm project, 113, 185–187; and Homestead Act, 114; rumors of insurrection of, 115; atrocities against, 116, 118; and Black Codes, 122; and Bureau labor policy, 124–126; condition of in South, 129–130; treatment of in courts, 132–135; Howard's concern for, 145; and Freedmen's Bank, 189–190; condition of following election of 1876, 245. See also Negroes, slavery.
Freedmen's Aid Society, 161
Freedmen's aid societies, 88, 155, 168, 196; commissioner needs support of, 91; approve Howard as commissioner, 92; and cooperation with Bureau, 94–95; and establishment of orphanages, 105; educational activities of coordinated by Bureau, 115, 159; pay teachers, 154; no segregation in schools of, 158; educational efforts of, 159–164; Howard praises teachers of, 166; want Howard to remain as commissioner, 178
Freedmen's Bank, 188–191, 224, 329
Freedmen's Bureau, 86, 205, 212, 239–243, 271; position of commissioner offered Howard, 82; early history, 87–102; judicial policy and activities of, 88, 93, 94, 115, 116, 120, 126, 132–135; labor policy of, 88, 110, 114–116, 121, 124–126; land policy of, 88, 92, 94, 96, 106–114, 116, 120, 186–187; legislation affecting, 88, 116, 119, 120, 133, 145; and Negro education, 88, 93–95, 115, 116, 144, 145, 154–155, 157–168, 209, 220, 240–241; relief activities of, 88, 94, 103–105, 120; responsibilities of, 88; role of in Reconstruction history, 90; Howard the central figure of, 90; commissioner, qualifications for, 91; commissioner, selection of, 91–92; policies of, 92–95, 106–114; matters relating to the personnel of, 94–102, 118, 137–153, 157, 224–225; records of, 94, 153, 154, 222, 225–227, 235; financial affairs of,

95–96, 116, 120, 154–155, 157–159, 186, 203, 208, 224–225; military character of, 95, 96, 153; organization of, 95–96; commissary division of, 96; medical activities of, 96, 105–106, 144, 224; quartermaster division, 96; and Barry Farm project, 113, 185–187; reputation of in South, 115; provides transportation, 115, 155; criticism of from Northern groups, 116; atrocity reports of, 116, 118, 126–135, 145, 152; attacked by Steedman and Fullerton, 118–120; becomes a political football, 119, 136; and Black Codes, 122–123; attitude of Southerners to, 124, 147; political activity of, 136–147; and Reconstruction Act of 1867, 139; and bounty paying, 145, 150, 157, 189, 203, 220–226, 231; effects of partisan activity on, 147; criticism of, 147–150; carries out inspections, 152–153; and Howard U., 155, 170–173; Howard remains as commissioner of, 179; offices of moved to Howard U., 180; and Freedmen's Bank, 188–190; attacked by Gen. Boynton, 199, 203–204; Howard's administration of attacked, 230

Freedmen's Bureau Bill (1865), 106, 109, 111, 112; provisions of, 106, 107; (1866, 1st), 116, 134, 136; vetoed by Johnson, 111; (1866, 2d), 119, 120, 133, 134

Freedmen's Record, 315

Freedmen's Savings and Trust Co. *See* Freedmen's Bank.

Freedmen's Union Commission, 159, 166

Frémont, John C., 13

Frémont-Buchanan campaign. *See* Election of 1856.

French, William H., 41

Fullerton, Joseph S., 97; and veto message, 117; and tour with Steedman, 118–120; administration in Louisiana attacked, 148; criticizes Saxton, 316

Gardner, Asa Bird, 230–232
Garfield, James A., 269, 272; death of, 275; and Whittaker case, 344
Geary, J. W., 60
Georgia, Bureau activity in, 96, 97, 100, 101, 103, 104, 111, 115, 117, 118, 127–128, 134, 138, 148, 154, 155, 166, 241
Georgia State Industrial College, 241
Geronimo, 280
Getty, George W., 272; on Court of Inquiry, 231, 337
Gettysburg, battle of, 51–56, 58, 73, 84, 85
Gettysburg, campaign of, 50–57, 63
Gibbon, John, in Nez Perce War, 252, 254, 255, 259, 264, 265; and battle of the Big Hole, 253–254
Gilbert, C. C., 258
Gilbreth, F. W., 128
Gillem, Alvan C., 141–142
Gilman, F. B., 50
Gilmore, Eliza, visits Howard at West Point, 8. *See also* Howard, Eliza, and Otis, Eliza.
Gilmore, John, marries O. O. Howard's mother, 2
Goldsboro, N. C., capture of, 81
Governors Island, 281, 283
Grangeville, Idaho, 250, 253
Grant, Ulysses S., 58, 77, 85, 153, 167, 193, 226, 234, 239, 242; commands Western armies, 59; at Chattanooga, 60–61; and campaign against Lee, 65–66; orders Howard to Washington, 82; asks Howard for atrocity report, 129; asks removal of Bureau officer, 148; Howard submits resignation to, 178; requests Howard to remain as Bureau commissioner, 179; and Howard's mission to Arizona, 210–212, 214; appoints Court of Inquiry, 229, 231; approves finding of Court, 233, 243; attends meeting of Society of Army of the Tennessee, 240; grants commission to Guy Howard, 245; visits Howard in Oregon, 268; suggests names for commander of Army of the Ohio, 311
Grant, Mrs. U. S., 268
Gray, Grace H., 275, 279, 283, 290. *See also* Howard, Grace.
Greble, Edwin, 194

INDEX 369

Greble, John T., 9
Green, John, in Nez Perce War, 250, 252, 253, 255
Gregory, Edgar M., 98, 152
Griffin, Charles, 163
Grimes, James W., 63
Grover, L. F., 246

Hale, Eugene, 204
Halleck, Henry W., 311; and second battle of Bull Run, 33; Howard visits, 49; orders 11th and 12th Corps West, 58
Hamlin, Hannibal, 27, 77; urges Howard's promotion, 39; supports Howard for regular army commission, 64
Hampton Institute, 160, 162, 168, 179, 238
Hancock, Winfield S., at Fredericksburg, 41; at Gettysburg, 53–56, 309, 310; controversy with Howard, 63, 65; in election of 1880, 269; death, 279
Hardee, William J., at West Point, 19; at Jonesboro, 71–72; in Savannah and Carolina campaigns, 75–77
Hardie, James A., 178
Harker, C. G., 67
Harney, William, 14
Harrison, Benjamin, 283; as candidate, 280; Howard's opinion of, 281; reorganizes army commands, 281
Harrow School, 293–294
Hatch, Edward, 150
Hayden, Julius, 141
Hayes, Rutherford B., 240, 251; congratulated by Howard, 245; visits Howard in Oregon, 268; appoints Howard superintendent of West Point, 269, 271, 276
Hayes, Mrs. R. B., 268
Hayes-Tilden election. See Election of 1876.
Hazen, William B., and capture of Ft. McAllister, 76; at Bentonville, 81; quoted, 312
Heintzelman, Samuel P., 31, 32
Henry Lake, Idaho, 254–257, 265
Henry in the War, 245
Hill, A. P., 51

Holloway, Mrs. Laura, 285
Holt, Joseph, 230, 233
Homestead Act for freedmen, 114
Homestead strike, 282
Hood, John B., and Atlanta campaign, 68–71, 73–74; operations of in Georgia and Alabama, 74
Hooker, Joseph, 73; quoted, 24–25, 182; at Antietam, 37; commands grand division, 38; commands Army of the Potomac, 42; in Chancellorsville campaign, 44–49; sends Howard to Washington, 49; commands 11th and 12th Corps, 58; and relief of Chattanooga, 59; at Lookout Mountain, 61; receives Thanks of Congress, 63; at Peach Tree Creek, 68
Hopkins, M. S., 138
House investigation, 174, 177, 199–200, 205–209
House of Representatives, investigation of Howard. See House investigation.
Howard, Bessie, 236, 283
Howard, Chancey, 57, 236, 278, 283, 346
Howard, Charles H., 19, 171, 229; birth, 2; conversion, 16; attends seminary, 20; aide to Howard, 23; wounded at Fair Oaks, 32; accompanies Howard to Washington, 49; quoted, 52; and building block co., 173–174; and collapse of hospital, 177; and Barry Farm, 187; and Chicago fair petition, 284; tries to obtain cabinet post for Howard, 291–292
Howard, Eliza O., 1; marries Colonel John Gilmore, 2. See also Otis, Eliza and Gilmore, Eliza.
Howard, Grace E., 18, 236, 303; birth, 17; baptism, 19; marriage, 268. See also Gray, Grace H.
Howard, Guy, 236, 268, 278, 284; birth, 13; baptism, 19; obtains commission, 245; in Nez Perce campaign, 256, 260–261; aide to Gen. Howard, 277; marriage, 279; assigned to Ft. Ethan Allen, 283; death, 296
Howard, Harry S., 283; explains Belknap's motivation, 226; birth,

236; at San Francisco, 280; religious activity of, 282; arranges Howard's visit to Cumberland Gap, 293; and Howard's death, 299

Howard, James W., 18, 236, 283, 285

Howard, John (ancestor of O. O. Howard), 1

Howard, John (son of O. O. Howard), 236, 278; obtains commission, 283

Howard, O. O., birth and early life, 1–2; physical appearance, 2, 18, 275; schooling, 2–3; ambition, 3, 4, 29, 39, 43, 63–64, 84; college career, 3–6; views on drinking, 4, 25, 29–30, 284; views on smoking, 4, 5; as West Point cadet, 6–11; service at Watervliet and Kennebec arsenals, 12–13; marriage, 12; service in Florida, 14–17; financial condition, 15, 237; conversion, 15–17; religious activities of, 17, 19, 30, 244, 280, 282–284; at West Point as instructor, 17–22; service with Third Maine, 21–29; enjoys political support, 23, 39; character of, 23, 24, 27, 69–70, 85–86, 226–227, 237, 240, 276, 284–289; manner of waging war, 25, 75; views on religion, 24, 25, 85–86, 191, 285; at first Bull Run, 27; election duty in Maryland, 30; and McClellan, 31, 33, 35, 36, 38; at Fair Oaks, 32, 305; loses right arm, 32; at second Bull Run, 34; opinion of Pope, 35, 36; at Antietam, 37–38; takes stronger antislavery position, 39; at Fredericksburg, 40–41; promotion to major general, 42; opinion of Hooker, 42, 50–51; commands 11th Corps, 43; at Chancellorsville, 44–49; suggested as candidate for governor, 50; in Gettysburg campaign, 51–57; writes Lincoln, 57; ordered West, 58; visits Lincoln, 58, 310; opinion of Grant, 59; at Chattanooga, 59–61; and relief of Knoxville, 61; relationship with Sherman, 61–62; receives Thanks of Congress, 62–63; in Atlanta campaign, 66–72; commands Army of the Tennessee, 69; military ability of, 73–74, 78, 84–86, 264–265, 311, 312; in March to the Sea, 74–77; in Carolina campaign, 77–81; and capture and burning of Columbia, 78–79; appointed brigadier general in regular army, 81; reaction to Lincoln's assassination, 81; and Johnston's surrender, 82; offered Freedmen's Bureau post, 82, 91–92, 315; and early days of Freedmen's Bureau, 87–102; and personnel policies of Bureau, 96–102, 150–153; relief policy, 104–105; land policy, 106–114; and Johnson's amnesty policy, 107–111; relationship with Johnson, 109, 136, 239; and Barry Farm project, 113, 185–187; supports legislation to extend Bureau, 116; and Steedman-Fullerton tour, 117, 119–120; and administration of Bureau, 120, 136, 153–156, 205; on treatment of freedmen, 124, 129, 145; promotes free labor system, 124–126; and atrocities, 129, 132; and Bureau judicial affairs, 132–133; and charges of political partisanship, 137–147; urges reduction of Bureau activities, 144–145; favors franchise for freedmen, 146; troubled by critics in North, 147–150; interprets law loosely, 154–156; and Negro education, 157–168 (*see also* Howard U.); views on segregation, 158, 193–196; helps found Howard U., 171; investigation by House committee, 172; and building block, 173–178; as president of Howard U., 180–184; pledge to Howard U., 182, 237, 278; and Freedmen's Bank, 188–190; and First Congregational Church, 191–202; charged with political ambition, 194, 198, 200–201; views on amalgamation, 197–198; and Fernando Wood, 203; and mission to the Apaches, 209–219; and bounty paying, 220–223; F. Wood renews attack on, 226–228; and Court of Inquiry, 230–233; life in Washington, 236–

INDEX 371

243; ordered to Department of the Columbia, 243; and Nez Perce War, 247–265; and Bannock War, 265–267; views on Indians, 267–268, 343; superintendent of West Point, 270–277; Sherman's opinion of, 271–272; commands Department of the Platte, 277–279; visits Near East and Europe, 278; promotion to major general, 279; commands Division of the Pacific, 279–280; commands Division of the Atlantic and Department of the East, 281–283; retires from army, 283; autobiography, 286, 288, 290; views on current issues, 284–288; lecturing and writing activities, 290–291; political activities, 290–291, 298; seeks cabinet post, 291–292; seeks ambassadorship, 292–293; and Lincoln Memorial U., 293–297; and Spanish War, 295; last illness and death, 298–299; as possible commander of the Army of the Ohio, 311

Howard, Mrs. O. O., 22, 62, 65, 109, 290, 305; at Watervliet and Augusta, 12–13; interest of in religion, 16; disapproves Howard's entering ministry, 17, 19; at West Point, 18–19; quoted, 28; visits Howard in Philadelphia, 102; church affiliation of, 191–192; entertains students, 209; life in Washington, 236–237; entertains Gen. and Mrs. Grant, 268; health declines, 275; in Omaha, 277–278; and Guy Howard's death, 296; and Howard's death, 299. *See also* Waite, Lizzie.

Howard, Rowland Bailey (father of O. O. Howard), 1; death, 2

Howard, Rowland Bailey (brother of O. O. Howard), 2, 8, 10, 229, 278; conversion, 16; urges Howard to enter ministry, 17

Howard, Seth, 1

Howard, Sue (Mrs. Harry S.), 299

Howard, Ward, 1

Howard University, 155, 161–162, 168, 191, 197, 204–206, 220, 225, 227, 236, 240, 245, 271, 292; not segregated, 158; founding of, 169–170; law establishing, 170; charter, 170; finances, 170–172, 182, 184; early history, 171–172; collegiate department, 171, 181, 328; land, 171, 206; law department, 171, 209, 237, 278; medical department, 171, 209; normal department, 171, 181; preparatory department, 171, 181; presidency, 171, 177, 179, 183–184, 191, 194; theological department, 171, 181, 209; and building block, 173–178; buildings, 175, 180; and collapse of hospital, 175–178, 201, 204, 206; and Barry Farm, 186–187; Howard's interest in, 287

Hudson-Fulton exposition, 298

Hunter, David, 31, 305

Impeachment of Andrew Johnson, 199, 239

Indian Bureau, 246

Isabella of Castile, Howard's life of, 282, 286

Jackson, Thomas J. (Stonewall), 45; in second Bull Run campaign, 33; at Antietam, 37; in Chancellorsville campaign, 44–48; attacks 11th Corps, 46–48; fatally wounded, 47

James, Darwin R., 294

Jameson, Charles D., 29

Jeffords, Thomas J., aids Howard in finding Cochise, 214–216; and peace terms with Cochise, 217–218; 333; opinion of Howard, 214

Jennings, Orville, 5

Jerome, D. H., 247

Johnson, Andrew, 94, 98, 122, 141, 149, 338; repudiates Sherman's surrender terms, 82; frustrates Bureau land program, 107–112; restores Sea Island lands, 110; vetoes Freedmen's Bureau Bill, 111, 117, 134, 318; fears insurrection by freedmen, 115; and Steedman-Fullerton tour, 118–120; plan of Reconstruction, 88, 127–128; considers dismissing Howard, 136, 145; as critic of Bureau, 147–148; impeachment, 199, 239

Johnson, Edward, 55

Johnston, Joseph E., in Atlanta campaign, 65–68; in Carolina campaign, 80–82; surrender of, 81–82
Joint Committee on the Conduct of the War, 48
Jonesboro, battle of, 71–72
Joseph (Nez Perce chief), 246, 250–252; rejects reservation plan, 247; and outbreak of Nez Perce War, 248–249; surrender of, 261

Kamiah, Idaho, 251, 253
Kansas-Nebraska Bill, Howard gives his support to, 9
Kearny, Phil, 32–33
Keeler, B. B., 251–252
Kehr, Cyrus, 290; and founding of Lincoln Memorial U., 293–296
Kenesaw Mountain, Ga., battle of, 67–69
Kennebec Arsenal, 12–13
Kennebec Regiment. See Maine volunteer regiments, Third.
Kentucky, Bureau activity in, 97, 98, 120, 144, 145; atrocities in, 131
Ketchum, A. P., 110, 128–129, 150, 231, 237
Ketchum, Edgar, 205, 206, 223, 231, 274–275
Keyes, Erasmus, 31, 32
Kiddoo, Joseph B., 151, 155; and drinking problem, 98; quoted, 99, 135; reports on atrocities, 128, 130
Kilpatrick, Judson, 80; in Atlanta campaign, 71; and March to the Sea, 74, 76
King's Bridge, Ga., 76
Knoxville, 61; relief of, 69

Labor. See Freedman's Bureau, labor policy of.
Langdon, L. L., 273
Langston, John L., in campaign of 1868, 142–143; at Howard U., 180, 183–184; on school segregation, 324
Lapwai reservation, 246–248, 263–264
Larry, John Hale, 296–297
Lawyer (Nez Perce chief), 246
Lazelle, Henry M., 275–276
Lee, G. W. C. (Custis), 8, 10
Lee, Robert E., 65, 66; at West Point, 9, 18; at Antietam, 36–38; at Fredericksburg, 39; at Chancellorsville, 44–45, 48, 73; at Gettysburg, 50, 56–57; surrender of, 81
Lee, Mrs. Robert E., 11
Leeds, Me., 1
Lincoln, Abraham, 47, 77, 122, 305; election of, 20; restores McClellan to command, 36; issues Emancipation Proclamation, 38; urged to promote Howard, 39; recommends Howard for promotion, 42; reviews army, 43; Howard's visit to: after Chancellorsville, 49; after Gettysburg, 57; before going West, 58, 310; names Grant to command in West, 59; and vote of thanks to Howard, 63; and Howard's appointment to regular army, 64, 81; assassination of, 81; selects Howard as commissioner, 82, 86, 92; inspiration for Lincoln Memorial U., 294; visits Howard at Meridian Hill, 304; befriends Howard, 308–309
Lincoln Memorial University; 296–299; origins, 293–295; name and charter of, 295
Lincoln Temperance Society, 238
Lincoln University, 162
Logan, John A., 74; commands Army of the Tennessee, 69; in Atlanta campaign, 69–70; in Carolina campaign, 79–81; at grand review, 83; snubs Howard, 240; and disloyalty at West Point, 344
Lolo Trail, 251–254, 264, 265
Longstreet, James, 61
Looking Glass (Nez Perce Indian), 248
Lookout Mountain Institute, 155
Loomis, L. L., 16
Loomis, S. L., 175, 177
Lothrop, Warren, 7
Louisiana, Bureau activity in, 96, 97, 98, 108, 114, 117, 128, 132, 140, 148–150; freedmen in during war, 92; atrocities in, 130; New Orleans riot, 148

McClellan, George B., 33, 85; succeeds McDowell, 28; and Peninsular campaign, 30–31; Howard's

INDEX 373

opinion of, 31, 33, 35, 36, 38; resumes command of army, 34–36; at Antietam, 36, 38; relieved of command, 38; recommends Howard for promotion, 39
McCook, E. M., 319
McDowell, Irvin, commands army at Washington, 26; at first Bull Run, 27; on Court of Inquiry, 231, 337; advises Howard on Nez Perces, 247; and Nez Perce War, 250–257, 259, 265, 289, 340; and Bannock War, 266; entertained by Howard, 268
McDowell, Mrs. Irvin, 268
McKim, J. M., 149, 163, 188
McKinley, William, and election of 1896, 291; fails to name Howard to cabinet post, 292; Howard campaigns for in 1900, 298
McMillan, James, 225
McNeely, Thompson W., 203–205, 208, 224
McPherson, James B., 311; in Atlanta campaign, 65–66, 68–69; death of, 69–71
Maine volunteer regiments, Third, 21, 23, 26, 28, 29, 85, 304; Fourth, 28, 304; Fifth, 28, 304
Malheur reservation, 266
Manly, Ralza M., 187
Mansfield, Joseph K. F., 306
March to the Sea, 73–77. *See also* Savannah campaign.
Maryland, Bureau activity in, 96, 120, 144, 145
Mason, Edwin L., 252
Meade, George G., 58; commands Army of the Potomac, 50, 66; in Gettysburg campaign, 51–57; defended by Howard, 57, 85; receives Thanks of Congress, 63; death of, 242
Meigs, M. C., on Court of Inquiry, 231; Howard appeals to, 234–235
Memphis, race riot in, 128
Merritt, Wesley, 277
Mexican War, 4
Meysenburg, T. A., 85; quoted, 86
Middlesboro, Ky., 293
Miles, Evan, 267
Miles, Nelson A., on Court of Inquiry, 231; and Nez Perce War,

258–263, 342; controversy with Howard, 262–263, 289; and Geronimo's surrender, 280
Military Division of the Atlantic, 281–282
Military Division of the Mississippi, 65
Military Division of the Missouri, 255, 277
Military Division of the Pacific, 247, 279–280
Military Division of the South, 271
Missionary Ridge, battle of, 60–61
Mississippi, Bureau activity in, 114, 115, 134, 141–142, 148, 149, 152, 153; freedmen in during war, 92
Missoula, Montana, 253, 254
Missouri, Bureau activity in, 96, 99
Monteith, John B., 246–248
Moody (War Department clerk), 225, 233
Moore, John, quoted, 85
Morrill, Anson P., 21, 24
Morrill, Lot, M., 24, 29, 39
Morris, Benjamin F., 169
Morrow, Henry A., 269
Mount Idaho, Idaho, 249, 250, 253
Mower, Joseph A., 140; reports atrocities, 130
Mullett, Alfred B., 176–177
Myers, A. A., 293–297
Myers, Ellen, 293, 294, 296

National Freedman, 315
National Tribune, 278
Negroes, follow army from Columbia, 80; status at end of war, 87–88; need protection, 89–90; as Bureau agents, 101–102; receive Bureau relief, 103–105; and Bureau Land program, 106–114; status following emancipation, 122–123; as voters, 137–147; political affiliations of, 139–140; denied equality in South, 146; alleged forced removal of from Georgia, 148; education of, 157–168 (*See also* Howard U.); as teachers, 160; desire for land, 185; disillusioned by failure of Freedmen's Bank, 190; and Congregational Church, 194–198; receive bounties, 220; and temperance

374 SWORD AND OLIVE BRANCH

movement, 238; unfavorable treatment of, 245; as cadets at West Point, 270–272; condition of, 286–288. See also freedmen, slavery.
New Hampshire volunteer regiments, Fifth, 32, 35
New Mexico, 210, 213–215
New Orleans, race riot in, 128, 148
New York *Herald*, 49, 118, 119, 148
New York *Times*, 41
New York *Tribune*, 148, 176, 224, 271, 318
New York volunteer regiments, Sixty-first, 35
Newton, John, 67, 68
Nez Perce Joseph, 245, 263
Nez Perces, 343; early history of, 246; and Nez Perce War, 249–261; at White Bird Canyon, 250; and battle of the Clearwater, 250–252; retreat over Lolo Trail, 251–253; and battle of the Big Hole, 253–254; and Camas Meadows affair, 256; retreat north of Yellowstone Park, 258–259; attacked by Miles, 260; surrender of, 261; sent to Indian Territory, 263–264
Nez Perce War, 244–245, 289, 343; origins, 246; outbreak, 248–249; action at White Bird Canyon, 250; battle of the Clearwater, 250–252; battle of the Big Hole, 253–254; Camas Meadows affair, 255–256; Sturgis' action with Nez Perces, 258; Miles' action with Nez Perces, 260–261; surrender of Nez Perces, 261; reports of surrender, 262; Howard-Miles controversy, 262–263; Howard's conduct of, 264–265
Nichols, Danforth B., 171
Nichols, George W., 311; quoted, 84
Ninth (U. S.) Infantry, 282
Nontreaty Nez Perces. See Nez Perces.
North Carolina, Bureau activity in, 96, 97, 104, 118–120, 153, 186–188

Ogeechee River, 75–76
Omaha, Nebraska, 277
Osborn, Thomas W., 126; on Howard, 84, 315; appointed assistant commissioner, 96–97; reports few atrocities, 131; quoted, 134
Osterhaus, Peter J., 74
Otis, Eliza, 1. See also Howard, Eliza, and Gilmore, Eliza.
Otis, John, 2, 6
Otis, Oliver, 1, 2
Otis, William, 6
Outrages. See Freedmen's Bureau, atrocity reports of

Paiute Indians, in Bannock War, 265–267
Panic of 1873, 190, 237, 238, 242
Papago Indians, 213
Patterson, Robert F., 295
Patton, R. M., 148
Peabody fund, 160
Peach Tree Creek, battle of, 68
Peninsular campaign, 30–33
Perley, Peleg, 5, 10
Perry, David, 249, 250
Pershing, John J., 346
Peters, John A., 208
Philadelphia *Evening Bulletin*, 63, 208
Philips Andover Academy, 236
Pickett's charge, 56
Pima Indians, 213
Pinal Indians, 210
Plymouth Church, Brooklyn, 192
Pocotaligo, S. C., action at, 78
Poe, O. M., 312
Pomeroy, Samuel C., and Barry Farm, 113, 185–186, 206; and founding of Howard U., 170; on committee to select president of Howard U., 170, 179; scandal, 239–240
Ponce (Indian), 215
Pope, John, and second Bull Run campaign, 33–35; relieved by McClellan, 35; Howard's opinion of, 35, 36; on Court of Inquiry, 231, 337; retirement, 279; congratulates Howard, 343
Porter, Andrew, 304
Porter, Fitz-John, 31
Porter, Horace, 276
Portland, Oregon, 244
Presidio, Cal., 280
Prince, Henry, 29

Prohibition party, 283
Pullman strike, 282
Race riots. *See* Memphis, New Orleans, Springfield, Ill., Vicksburg.
Radical Republicans, 39; Howard's relations with during war, 24, 31; Howard defends McClellan against, 33; and Reconstruction policy, 88, 124, 127; motives of, 89; concern for freedmen, 89–90; criticize Howard, 148
Rankin, Jeremiah E., 202
Rawlins, John A., 179
Rawn, Charles C., 253–254, 264, 265
Raynor, Kenneth, 235
Reconstruction, 287; Johnson's plan of, 88, 89; complexity of, 88–90; and Bureau land policy, 107; differing views on, 108; effect on of Southern actions, 123; and Freedmen's Bureau, 136
Reconstruction Acts of 1867, 90, 127, 129, 135–137, 139, 158
Refugees, 103, 105
Refugees and Freedmen's Fund, 171–172, 186
Reid, Whitelaw, 224
Resaca, Ga., action at, 66–67, 69, 73
Retained Bounty Fund, 170, 222, 232, 235
Reynolds, John, 55; in Gettysburg campaign, 50–54; death of, 51
Reynolds, Joseph J., on Court of Inquiry, 231
Richardson, Israel, 30–32
Richmond, Va., fall of, 81
Richmond Normal School, 186–187
Ripley, James W., 21, 304
Robinson, Ebenezer, W., 171
Rock Springs, Wyoming, 277
Rodes, Robert E., 52
Rogers, Anthony A. C., 205
Roosevelt, Theodore, 298
Rosecrans, William S., 58, 59
Ruger, T. H., 270

Safford, A. P. K., 211, 216
St. Augustine Normal School, 186–188
Savannah, capture of, 75–77
Savannah campaign, 84. *See also* March to the Sea.

Saxton, Rufus, considered as Bureau commissioner, 91; work with freedmen during war, 92; appointed assistant commissioner, 96; proves unsatisfactory, 97, 100, 316; on personnel problem, 99; on land policy, 109; and Sea Islands question, 110; reprimanded by Howard, 152
Schimmelfennig, Alexander, 46
Schofield, John M., 279, 311, 346; in Atlanta campaign, 65, 68, 72; and operations in N. C., 80; Howard reports hospital collapse to, 176; and Howard's mission to Apaches, 211–212, 217; on A. B. Gardner, 230; superintendent of West Point, 270–271; and command of Department of West Point, 276; commands army, 281
Schriver, Edmund, 233
Schurz, Carl, at Chancellorsville, 45, 49; at Gettysburg, 52; and anecdote about Howard, 62
Scott, Robert K., and Bureau relief policy, 105; on treatment of freedmen, 135; candidate for governor of S. C., 138; on Negro voting, 140; denies Bureau agents belong to Union League, 143; plan to reduce Bureau force, 145; and YMCA stock, 238; serves as special Bureau agent, 321
Sea Islands, 92, 97, 103, 191–192; disposal of lands on, 110–111; and Bureau Bill of 1866 (1st), 116; provision for omitted from Bureau Bill of 1866 (2d), 120
Searle, Henry R., 173–174, 192
Second Corps, 30, 37, 38, 41, 56, 57
Second (U. S.) Infantry, 250, 253, 266
Sedgwick, John, 306; commands brigade, 29; in Peninsular campaign, 31; Howard serves under, 33; wounded at Antietam, 37; in Chancellorsville campaign, 44; Howard's comment on, 315
Seely, G. A., 222
Segregation, Howard's views on, 158; J. L. Langston's views on, 324

Seminole Indians, 14
Seven Days battle, 33
Seventeenth Corps, 70, 71, 74, 78
Seventh (U. S.) Cavalry, 258
Seventh (U. S.) Infantry, 253
Sewall, Frederick D., accompanies Howard from Fair Oaks, 32; as inspector for Bureau, 101, 152–153; comments on atrocity reports, 131; criticizes bounty paying records, 221–222
Sharkey, William L., 134
Shaw, J. W., 227
Sheridan, Philip H., 85, 98, 152, 311, 346; attends meeting of Society of Army of the Tennessee, 240; and Nez Perce War, 255, 262–263; and Geronimo's surrender, 280; death, 281
Sherman, John, 292
Sherman, William T., 58, 84–86, 193; at Chattanooga, 60–61; on Howard, 62, 311, 332; in Atlanta campaign, 65–72; and March to the Sea, 74–76; in Carolina campaign, 77–81; and Johnston's surrender, 82; advises Howard, 83; and his Special Field Order no. 15, 110; orders Howard to active command, 178; heads Court of Inquiry, 231–233; Howard comments on, 233; Howard appeals to, 234–235, 279; attends meeting of Society of Army of the Tennessee, 240; disapproves of Howard's Bureau duty, 241–242; helps Guy Howard obtain commission, 245; and Nez Perce War, 247, 255, 257, 265, 341, 342; and disposition of Nez Perces, 263–264; disapproves Howard's appointment to West Point, 271–272, 276; death of, 282; considers Howard too pious, 284
Shipherd, J. R. 149, 159, 163
Sibley, Caleb C., 101, 155
Sickles, Daniel E., commands 3d Corps, 42–43; at Chancellorsville, 45–47; at Gettysburg, 52, 310; comments on Howard, 288; in 1896 election campaign, 291
Sigel, Franz, 43, 49, 309

Silver Creek, Oregon, action at, 266
Simmons, James B., 164
Sixteenth Corps, 70
Sixth Corps, 44
Sladen, J. A., 215
Slavery, 87; Howard's views on, 8–10, 13, 14, 31, 40, 41; abolished by Thirteenth Amendment, 122. *See also* Freedmen, Negroes.
Slocum, Henry W., 282; at Chancellorsville, 45; at Gettysburg, 52–55; in Atlanta campaign, 72; and March to the Sea, 74; in Carolina campaign, 80–81
Small, Abner, 26
Smith, C. H., 145
Smith, E. P., 164
Smith, J. Brinton, 166, 188
Smith, J. W., 270
Smith, Orland, 53, 57
Smyrna Camp Ground, Ga., action at, 68
Social Darwinism, 285, 287, 288
Society of the Army of the Tennessee, 282
Sons of Temperance, 238
South Carolina, Bureau activity in, 96, 99, 103, 105, 109, 110, 117, 127, 135, 137–140, 143, 145, 149, 152
South Mountain, battle of, 36
Sprague, John W., 99, 105; appointed assistant commissioner, 96–97; uses civilian agents, 101; reports atrocities, 130; ordered to investigate fraud, 150
Springfield, Ill., race riot in, 288
Spurgin, William F., 274
Stanley, David S., 68, 72
Stanton, Edwin M., 92, 94, 135, 148, 318; supports Howard, 24; and Howard's promotion to major general, 42; Howard's visit to: after Chancellorsville, 49, after Gettysburg, 57; meets Howard at Savannah, 77; and Howard's appointment to regular army, 81; repudiates Sherman's surrender terms, 82; provides facilities for Bureau, 87; asked to relieve Conway, 97; and Bureau's relief program, 105; and Bureau land pol-

INDEX

icy, 108; Howard reports to, 116, 126; orders Howard to report violations of Civil Rights Act, 129
Steedman, James, 115; and tour with Fullerton, 118–120
Steedman-Fullerton tour, 118–120, 136, 176, 203, 205, 239
Steinwehr, Adolph von, 52, 53, 57
Stevens, Thaddeus, 107
Stevenson, Ala., 59
Stewart, Joseph, 266
Stinchfield, Betsy, 1
Stinchfield, Roger, 1
Stinson, Harry, 236
Stone, George A., 78–79
Stoneman, George, 44, 45, 66
Stooksbury, William L., 297–298
Storrs School, 241
Strong, William E., 96, 111, 152
Stuart, George H., 64
Stuart, J. E. B., 9
Sturgis, S. D., 258–261, 265
Sumner, Edwin V., 30–33; at Antietam, 37; commands grand division, 38; at Fredericksburg, 40–41
Sunderland, Byron, 177, 179
Swayne, Wager, appointed assistant commissioner, 96–97; relief policy of, 104; and Bureau courts, 133; and political activity of Bureau agents, 138; attends state constitutional convention, 142; performs double duty, 152; charged with keeping poor records, 153; and cabinet post for Howard, 291–292

Taft, Alonzo, 234
Taft-Bryan campaign. *See* Election of 1908.
Talladega College, 161
Taylor, Zachary, 4; Howard's life of, 282, 286
Temperance movement, 238
Tennessee, Bureau activity in, 97, 101, 104, 108, 119, 128, 131, 133, 144, 145, 148, 152, 155, 221
Tenth (U. S.) Cavalry, 299
Terry, Alfred H., 346; and Nez Perce War, 252, 255, 258, 260; promoted to major general, 279; retirement, 281
Texas, Bureau activity in, 98, 99,

119, 128, 135, 151, 152, 155, 163–164; atrocities in, 130
Thanks of Congress, voted to Howard, 62–63, 65
Third Corps, 42, 45, 47, 50, 52, 54
Thirteenth Amendment, 122
Thomas, George H., 58; succeeds Rosecrans, 59; at Chattanooga, 61; in Atlanta campaign, 65–68, 72; opinion of Logan, 69; and operations against Hood, 74, 313; asked to investigate charges against Bureau, 148
Thomas, Samuel, on Southern attitude toward Bureau, 115; and equal rights legislation in Mississippi, 134; attacked in press, 148; criticized by Howard, 152
Tillson, Davis, 118, 154–155; uses civilian agents, 100; on Negroes as land owners, 111; reports on atrocities, 127–128; on Johnson's possible interference with Bureau courts, 134; attacked in press, 148; criticizes school teachers, 166
Too-hul-hul-sote (Nez Perce Indian), 248–249, 261
Tougaloo University, 160
Townsend, E. D., 120
Townsend, Washington, 208
Trumbull, Lyman, 117; supports Bureau Bill, 116
Tucson, Ariz., 216
Tulerosa reservation, 214–215
Twain, Mark, 274
Twelfth Corps, 37, 45, 47, 52, 54, 55, 58, 60, 65
Twentieth Corps, 65, 67, 68, 72, 74
Twenty-first (U. S.) Infantry, 267, 269

Umatilla Agency, 267
Union Aid Commission, 95
Union College, 241
Union League, 143
United States Military Academy. *See* West Point.

Van Buren, Martin, 4
Van Derburgh, George E., 173, 176, 178
Vassar College, 236

Vermont volunteer regiments, Second, 28, 304
Veterans Reserve Corps, 99
Veteran Retained Bounty Fund. *See* Retained Bounty Fund.
Vicars, Hedley, 16, 17
Vicksburg, Miss., race riot in, 286
Victoria, Queen of England, 183
Vincent; Thomas M., and transfer of Bureau records, 225; charges irregularities in Bureau records, 226–228; Howard believes to be part of conspiracy, 233; continues charges against Howard, 234–235
Virginia, Bureau activity in, 96, 99, 108, 133, 138, 142, 150, 151, 186–187; freedmen in during war, 92

Wadsworth, James S., 54
Wainwright, Charles S., 309
Waite, Lizzie (Elizabeth Ann), 11; meets Howard, 5; accompanies Howard to Boston, 6; visits Howard at West Point, 8, 10; marriage, 12. *See also* Howard, Mrs. O. O.
Wallowa Valley, 246, 247, 251
War Department, and resignations to enter volunteer service, 21; and beginnings of Bureau, 87; assists Bureau, 99; and closing of Bureau, 224–226; holds Howard responsible for missing funds, 234
Ward, E. B., 149, 151
Washburn, Israel, assures Howard of colonelcy, 21; recommends Howard for command, 23; friendship with Howard, 24; visits Howard, 28, 29; recommends Howard for promotion, 39; terminates governorship, 50
Washington *Chronicle*, 176, 177
Watervliet Arsenal, 12
Watkins, E. C., 249, 263
Wauhatchie, battle of, 60
Webb, E. B., 64, 277
Weirman, E. H., 141
Welles, Gideon, and Johnson's veto of Freedmen's Bureau Bill, 117; on Howard's atrocity report, 129; comment on Howard, 288
Wells, J. Madison, quoted, 122
West Point, 18–20, 305, 344; life at in 1850, 6; Howard arrives at, 6; social life at, 10; Howard appointed superintendent of, 269; Howard's tenure as superintendent, 270–277; visit of French delegation, 274; rank of superintendent, 276–277
West Point, Ga. railroad, 71
West Virginia, Bureau activities in, 144
Western Sanitary Commission, 91, 125
Wheaton, Frank, 253, 266–267
Wheelock, Edwin M., 163–164
Whipple, George, 149, 197
White Bird (Nez Perce Indian), 248, 249, 261, 264
White Bird Canyon, action at, 250
Whittaker, J. C., 270–272, 344
Whittier, J. G., writes poem about Howard, 338
Whittlesey, Eliphalet, 133, 138, 234; appointed assistant commissioner, 96–97; charged with mismanagement in N. C., 97, 118, 120; on Bureau relief policy, 104; comments on atrocity reports, 131–132; and selection of site for Howard U., 171; and building block co., 173–174; in temporary charge of Bureau, 212; on bounty paying system, 221–222; and final days of Bureau, 224–225
Wiedrich, Michael, 53
Wild, Edward A., 148
Willard, Frances, 283
Williams, A. S., 67
Williamsport, Md., 56–57, 85
Wilson, Henry, 145, 165; suggests Bureau might be anti-Negro, 149; and founding of Howard U., 170; wants Howard to remain as Bureau commissioner, 179
Wood, C. E. S., 260–263; account of Nez Perce surrender, 261
Wood, F., 235, 289; attacks Howard, 202–208; renews attack, 226, 228
Wood, H. Clay, 247, 251
Wood, Leonard, 299
Wood, Samuel, 149, 153
Wood, Thomas J., 67
Woodhull, Max, 101–102, 105, 134, 337

Woods, Charles R., 79
Woods, William B., 79
Woolworth, Jeanie (Mrs. Guy Howard), 279
Wright, H. G., 98
Wright, R. R., 241
Yakima Indian agency, 249
Yale University, 236, 245
Yavapai Indians, 210
Yeatman, James E., 91, 125
Yellowstone Park, 254, 256, 258, 277–278
YMCA. *See* Young Men's Christian Association.
Young Men's Christian Association, Washington, D. C., 204, 207, 237–238; aided by Bureau, 155
Yuma Indians, 212

THE NORTH'S CIVIL WAR
Paul A. Cimbala, series editor

1. Anita Palladino, ed., *Diary of a Yankee Engineer: The Civil War Diary of John Westervelt.*
2. Herman Belz, *Abraham Lincoln, Constitutionalism, and Equal Rights in the Civil War Era.*
3. Earl J. Hess, *Liberty, Virtue, and Progress: Northerners and Their War for the Union,* second revised edition with new introduction.
4. William L. Burton, *Melting Pot Soldiers: The Union's Ethnic Regiments.*
5. Hans L. Trefousse, *Carl Schurz: A Biography.*
6. Stephen W. Sears, ed., *Mr. Dunn Browne's Experiences in the Army: The Civil War Letters of Samuel W. Fiske.*
7. Jean H. Baker, *Affairs of Party: The Political Culture of Northern Democrats in the Mid-Nineteenth Century.*
8. Frank L. Klement, *The Limits of Dissent: Clement L. Vallandigham and the Civil War,* with a new introduction by Steven K. Rogstad.

www.ingramcontent.com/pod-product-compliance
Lightning Source LLC
Chambersburg PA
CBHW031229290426
44109CB00012B/215